THE MEDIEVAL DEVIL

READINGS IN MEDIEVAL CIVILIZATIONS AND CULTURES: XXIV
series editor: Paul Edward Dutton

THE MEDIEVAL DEVIL

A READER

edited by

RICHARD RAISWELL AND DAVID R. WINTER

UNIVERSITY OF TORONTO PRESS
Toronto Buffalo London

© University of Toronto Press 2022
Toronto Buffalo London
utorontopress.com

ISBN 978-1-4426-3417-6 (cloth)   ISBN 978-1-4426-3418-3 (EPUB)
ISBN 978-1-4426-3416-9 (paper)   ISBN 978-1-4426-3419-0 (PDF)

All rights reserved. The use of any part of this publication reproduced, transmitted in any form or by any means, electronic, mechanical, photocopying, recording, or otherwise, or stored in a retrieval system, without prior written consent of the publisher—or in the case of photocopying, a license from Access Copyright, the Canadian Copyright Licensing Agency—is an infringement of the copyright law.

LIBRARY AND ARCHIVES CANADA CATALOGUING IN PUBLICATION

Title: The medieval devil : a reader / edited by Richard Raiswell and David R. Winter.
Names: Raiswell, Richard, 1966–, editor. | Winter, David R., editor.
Series: Readings in medieval civilizations and cultures ; 24.
Description: Series statement: Readings in medieval civilizations and cultures ; XXIV | Includes bibliographical references and index.
Identifiers: Canadiana (print) 20220143293 | Canadiana (ebook) 20220143358 |
  ISBN 9781442634176 (cloth) | ISBN 9781442634169 (paper) |
  ISBN 9781442634183 (EPUB) | ISBN 9781442634190 (PDF)
Subjects: LCSH: Devil—History of doctrines—Middle Ages, 600–1500—Sources. |
  LCSH: Devil—Social aspects—Europe—History—To 1500—Sources. |
  LCSH: Demonology—History of doctrines—Middle Ages, 600–1500—Sources. |
  LCSH: Europe—Church history—600–1500—Sources.
Classification: LCC BF1521 .M43 2022 | DDC 235/.40902—dc23

We welcome comments and suggestions regarding any aspect of our publications – please feel free to contact us at news@utorontopress.com or visit us at utorontopress.com.

Every effort has been made to contact copyright holders; in the event of an error or omission, please notify the publisher.

We wish to acknowledge the land on which the University of Toronto Press operates. This land is the traditional territory of the Wendat, the Anishnaabeg, the Haudenosaunee, the Métis, and the Mississaugas of the Credit First Nation.

University of Toronto Press acknowledges the financial support of the Government of Canada and the Ontario Arts Council, an agency of the Government of Ontario, for its publishing activities.

CONTENTS

LIST OF FIGURES • ix

ACKNOWLEDGMENTS • xi

INTRODUCTION • xiii

ABBREVIATIONS • xvii

CHAPTER ONE: SOURCES FOR THE MEDIEVAL DEVIL • 1
1. The Serpent and the Fall of Humanity • 4
2. The Sons of God and the Giants • 7
3. Satans as God's Agents • 9
4. The Fall of Lucifer? • 11
5. God as the Creator of Evil? • 13
6. Satan as Spy and Tester • 15
7. The Demons of Ancient Greece • 17
8. Rabbinical Teachings on the Devil • 19
9. Satan Reappears • 22
10. The Homicidal Liar • 23
11. Fall of Lucifer Revisited • 26

CHAPTER TWO: DEVELOPMENT OF A NARRATIVE • 31
12. The Subversion of Humanity • 34
13. *Mastêmâ* the Devil? • 37
14. Interrogating Genesis • 40
15. Eve's Perspective of Humanity's Fall • 43
16. Gnostic Dualism • 46
17. Did God Create Evil? • 48
18. A Worldly Prince as the Devil? • 50
19. Devil as Kidnapper • 53
20. Sympathy for the Devil • 56
21. A Perverse Power, Hostile to Truth • 59
22. A Proto-Demonology? • 62

CHAPTER THREE: FORGING A COMMUNITY • 67
23. The Problem of Idols • 70
24. The Betrayal and Trial of Jesus • 72

25. The Susceptibility of Women to the Devil • 74
26. The Death of the Old Religion • 77
27. The Problem of Magic • 80
28. Survival of the Old Religion • 84
29. Alexander Encounters Gog and Magog • 88
30. Dealing with Unorthodox Views • 92
31. Policing Practice • 96
32. The Possibility of Demonic Night Flight? • 99
33. A Sorceress and Her Demons • 100

CHAPTER FOUR: THE EARLY MONASTIC DEVIL • 103
34. A "Proto-Monk" Is Assaulted by Demons in the Wilderness • 106
35. Saint Martin of Tours Fights the Devil • 110
36. Why Can Demons Do Such Great Things? • 113
37. Bishop Narcissus Sees a Horrible Demon • 117
38. Stable Hands Pray to the Devil • 120
39. Demonic Stratagems in the Carolingian World • 121
40. The Monastery as a Fortress against the Devil • 124
41. Besieged by Demons • 127

CHAPTER FIVE: THE DEVIL AND FEUDAL SOCIETY • 133
42. The Demonic Pact of Saint Cyprian • 135
43. The Pope Makes a Pact with the Devil • 138
44. The Man of Sin • 141
45. Demonic Vassalage • 143
46. The Devil as Feudal Lord • 146
47. The Life of Antichrist • 149
48. The Devil's Churchmen • 153
49. Trial by Landscape • 159

CHAPTER SIX: THE DEVIL'S DOMAIN • 161
50. The Development of Hell • 163
51. The Harrowing of Hell • 167
52. The Geography of Hell • 170
53. An Anglo-Saxon Monk Recounts a Vision of Hell • 175
54. Hell at Sea • 179
55. A Maiden Views Hell • 182
56. An Urban Hell • 184
57. Dante's Vision of the Structure of Hell • 192

CHAPTER SEVEN: VARIETIES OF POSSESSION AND EXORCISM • 197

58. Biblical Possessions • 200
59. Exorcisms by the Disciples • 202
60. Two Early Forms of Exorcism • 203
61. Dispossession by Person • 206
62. Dispossession by Objects • 210
63. Baptism • 213
64. Formalizing Dispossession • 216
65. Protection and Charms against Demonic Incursions • 223
66. Breaking the Devil's Hold • 226
67. Divine Possession, Gender, and Politics • 229

CHAPTER EIGHT: DEMONIZATIONS • 235

68. The Origins of Islam • 238
69. A Scholar Explains Islam • 239
70. Clerical Sodomy • 243
71. The Blood Libel • 248
72. Diabolized History • 250
73. Devil-Worshipping Heretics? • 255
74. Rooting Out Heresy • 258
75. Hordes from the East • 261
76. Satan's Knights? • 263
77. A Panorama of Pain • 264

CHAPTER NINE: THEORIZING THE DEVIL AND SOCIETY IN THE HIGH MIDDLE AGES • 269

78. The Devil as Nullity • 271
79. A Scholastic Theologian Wrestles with Demonic Bodies • 276
80. The Devil Makes His Case • 282
81. Contemplating the Devil's Place in Nature • 287
82. A Preacher's Stories about the Devil • 289
83. Demons in Monastic Training Manuals • 293
84. Various *Exempla* Demons from the British Isles • 297
85. An Anonymous Preacher Allegorizes Hell • 299

CHAPTER TEN: EXPERIENCING THE DEVIL IN WORD AND IMAGE • 301

86. The Miracle of Theophilus • 303
87. An Alternative Creation Story • 318

88. Demonic Horseplay • 320
89. Antichrist Takes the Stage • 328
90. Images of the Devil • 343

CHAPTER ELEVEN: TOWARD THE EARLY MODERN AGE • 345
91. Working with Demons • 348
92. Magic, Demons, and Heresy • 352
93. The Church of Antichrist • 353
94. The Problem of Satan as an "Angel of Light" • 358
95. Interrogators' View of Joan of Arc • 363
96. The Synagogue of Satan • 369
97. Merging Traditions • 373
98. Toward the Witch Hunts • 378

SELECT BIBLIOGRAPHY OF MODERN WORKS ON THE DEVIL • 385

SOURCES • 387

INDEX OF TOPICS • 393

FIGURES

1.1 Job on the Dunghill • 1
2.1 Archangel Michael Fighting the Dragon • 31
3.1 Witch of Berkeley • 67
4.1 Antony Attacked by Demons • 103
5.1 Knight, Death, and the Devil • 133
6.1 Overview of Hell • 161
7.1 Exorcism of the Gerasene Demoniac • 197
8.1 On Nocturnal Dance of Elves • 235
8.2 The Seven-Headed Dragon • 251
9.1 Temptation through Pride • 269
10.1 *Codex Gigas* • 301
11.1 Hell with Satan • 345

ACKNOWLEDGMENTS

This project has been far too long in the works. As it has evolved, we have incurred debts of gratitude to a number of people and institutions. In particular, we would like to thank Dr. Robert Buranello for his help with thirteenth-century Veronese. Dr. Michelle Brock has test-driven some of these selections in her "History of the Devil" course over the years, as has Gary Waite in his "Witchcraft and the Devil." Megan Lane MacDonald, Luke Baird, and Maggie MacEwen, along with students in Raiswell's "Science, Magic, Witchcraft, and the Occult" and Winter's "History of the Devil" courses, have been subjected to iterations of many of these sources and have offered helpful comments.

As always, the staff and resources of the Centre for Reformation and Renaissance Studies at Victoria University in the University of Toronto have been exceptionally helpful. Richard would like to thank in particular Natalie Oeltjen, Matt Kavaler, and Konrad Eisenbichler for their continuing support. The staff at the Robertson Library at the University of Prince Edward Island have been invaluable. Christine MacLauchlan has been tireless in tracking down copies of more obscure sources from across the globe. We would also like to thank the staff in the Arts Office at Brandon University for their assistance. Over the life of the project, this has included Janice Mahoney, Shari Maguire, and Sally Mott.

This project would have been impossible without the constant support of our partners, Elizabeth Schoales and Allison McCulloch. David would also like to thank his son, Xavier; Richard would like to thank also B. W. Bipps.

Finally, we'd like to thank the dapper gentleman we met at noon one day at the intersection of Yonge and Bloor streets who suggested this project to us.

INTRODUCTION

The last forty years have seen a burgeoning interest in the historical study of witchcraft among scholars and students alike. Courses examining the history of witchcraft are now a common and popular feature of history curricula across Europe and North America, supported by a growing number of primary-source anthologies. Indeed, Martha Rampton has recently published a very fine collection entitled *European Magic and Witchcraft* as part of the Readings in Medieval Civilizations and Cultures series. But while scholars have rightly pointed to how shifting attitudes toward elite and popular magic in the context of an increasingly centralized Church fed into what would become the witch panics of the early modern world, the subject of the devil has largely been treated as ancillary. Yet from his first appearances in scripture preventing Balaam from disobeying God's will to his role presiding over the cannibalistic orgies described by confessed participants in the middle of the fifteenth century, Satan has played a dynamic role in society, critiquing and policing its boundaries, fostering social cohesion as communities closed ranks against what they perceived to be demonic incursions.

The Medieval Devil, then, challenges students to take a new look at the development of medieval society by analyzing how the men and women of the period constructed its antithesis. By looking at how particular groups thought about the devil, discerned his presence, detected his machinations as underlying contemporary events, and sought to counter his actions over the span of the period, readers will be afforded a new point of entry into European history.

The medieval devil is a decidedly slippery character. Over this formative period, he is made and remade in response to new social and political pressures and shifting cultural priorities, occupying different explanatory niches according to the various communities detecting the stench of his presence. As students working through *The Medieval Devil* will quickly discover, there was no single medieval devil or any inevitable trajectory of devil belief. Rather, his identity and potency at any particular historical instance were as much a function of the projection of communal tensions and anxieties as it was of the musings of theologians and canonists.

In part, this flexibility stems from the fact that the biblical source texts upon which intellectuals relied to discern his nature and relationship to creation are imprecise, inconsistent, and even contradictory. Thus, from the earliest periods, those seeking to understand not just the existence but also the place and function of malevolence in the world—a world that the Bible described as created perfectly good—supplemented biblical assertions with ancillary texts in any attempt to forge a coherent figure with a defined role in sacred history.

But with churchmen principally concerned with divine matters, the medieval devil was often a creature better known through the observable evidence of his action in the world. As Christ said during the Sermon on the Mount, "By their fruits you shall know them" (Matt. 7.16). Thus the devil was often found underlying the lived experience of personal or communal misfortune and suffering, or detected in social difference, disorder, or deviance. He was never particularly well tethered to any formal theological position, and it was often this apparent *evidence* of his machinations that helped define his nature and powers, causing his presence to be found lurking in new places in the biblical text—in allusion and allegory, through typology and inference.

The result was not so much a hermeneutic circle as a hermeneutic spiral. Certainly, the sacred text conditioned experience, and experience conditioned how the text was understood. But this use of experiential evidence also served to expand the devil's reach in new and profound ways. It finds him inhabiting new spaces and endowed with new powers, tempting and perverting new groups of people and engaging in hitherto uncontemplated outrages.

While he gave meaning to misfortune and sense to senselessness, the devil was also a critical but versatile cultural resource, for he offered a handy means of accounting for social, political, and religious difference. Any deviation from the dominant community's understanding of the proper and natural order of things could easily be explained by attributing it to the master of disorder. This process proved definitive as the new religion expanded into regions with differing faith traditions, for it gave Christians a ready means for interpreting the inherent peculiarities of the indigenous systems it encountered, effectively allowing them to demonize those they perceived as enemies or rivals. In the cosmological contest between good and evil, the gods who resided with the peoples at the edges of Christendom could be nothing other than fallen angels. An analogous process operated within the bounds of the faith, for the activities of those who departed from gender or sexual norms, deviated from received intellectual orthodoxies, or diverged from accepted standards of thought or behavior in other ways could be explained by pointing to their apparent fidelity to the will of their dark lord.

To be sure, the effect of such demonizations was to strip their subjects of agency and to assimilate all difference and variation into a homogenizing category. However, doing so also situated deviance within an explanatory framework that endowed it with meaning and significance, thereby translating it into meaningful cultural information. The consequences of this dynamic were enormous, shaping personal and cultural relations between individuals and nations, informing the ways in which Europeans viewed history, economics, psychology, biology, and dozens of other disciplines, and conditioning, at a fundamental level, the epistemological lens through which they understood creation. It made the world and its contents a contest; it gave history a direction and endowed future events with purpose and direction.

The Medieval Devil, then, offers students an opportunity to engage with this figure of malevolence, examining his role as a cultural and explanatory resource who gave meaning to experience and whose presence justified—even necessitated—the development of particular institutions of protection, whether those be the walls of the monastery or the excesses of persecution. Our emphasis in compiling this collection has been squarely on the history of the medieval devil, offering students the resources they need to piece together the equivalent of a biography of the prince of malice as his field of operation expanded hand in hand with that of society in general. It invites them to consider how anxieties about broader changes in medieval society caused the devil to be found occupying new niches, praying on new malcontents—and those cast off as its casualties.

With that said, it is difficult when dealing with a biblically grounded figure whose presence is detected based upon an emerging discourse articulated principally by churchmen to separate history from theology. Inevitably, then, many sections include selections from the Bible. Our point is not to suggest that these texts were directly accessible to readers or even auditors. Rather, they are included to give students a sense of the trajectory of interpretation that led to the creation of the divine opposite. However, when they are approaching biblical texts, it is important that students read them for what they actually say. Students should not approach them looking for the origins of any particular devil with whom they are familiar, either from their own faith tradition or from their favorite horror film. Rather, we urge students to read these texts as historical artifacts, guided by the questions we have provided at the end of each selection, and to think about the texts in terms of the intellectual environments in which they were created and in which they were later consumed. Later selections will address the interpretation of these texts and their assimilation into the expanding legend of the medieval devil.

Still, the nature of the extant source material means that the devil who emerges in the pages that follow is very much the product of churchmen and churchwomen. While we have made every effort to include material that was produced outside an ecclesiastical context, such sources necessarily tend to come from later in the period, when literacy was more widespread. This means that it is very difficult for modern scholars to discern popular or dissenting views about the devil. Where such ideas were taken up by ecclesiastics, they were generally presented in a hostile light. Thus, it is unlikely that where such critiques of popular or heterodox demonism exist, these authors are accurately reflecting what their subjects actually thought. Alas, we find no vestiges in the following pages of a popular skeptical tradition, one that saw in the church's preaching of the devil a cynical means of social control. To a significant degree, then, the medieval devil—particularly the early medieval devil—is a prisoner of the archival record.

We make no attempt in *The Medieval Devil* to differentiate *the* devil from *devils* or *demons*. Historically, this is because a host of preternatural spirits linked to notions of chaos and disorder were assimilated into the demonic from an early point in the devil's history. But within the context of the period covered by this collection, people were not entirely sure how to differentiate Satan, the devil, and demons. Some sources use the terms interchangeably; other authors distinguish between them. The issue is how people understood such texts and the ideas they contained, and what they meant to them.

Moreover, with the exception of Antichrist, we have made no effort to deal with the profusion of other preternatural and monstrous figures believed to lurk across the landscape. Some of these are demonized, but often they do not function in quite the same way as the demonic, perform different roles in defining and policing society's boundaries, and are rarely anchored to any theological tradition.

Finally, it is worth stressing that this is a book about the devil. Some of the material is strong stuff. Much of it is racist, misogynistic, and otherwise bigoted. It contains descriptions of appalling violence. Parts are sexually explicit and exceptionally vulgar, and we have deliberately translated some phrases in such a way as to maintain the rhetorical force they were originally intended to have. It would be impossible to provide students with the resources they need to understand how and why the devil was used to such effect without such graphic material. This is what gave medieval people nightmares and impelled them to take drastic measures to protect themselves and those of their community. Both instructors and students should be aware of what is to come.

Unless otherwise indicated, all revisions and modernizations to texts have been made by us. These, along with the new translations we offer, are intended primarily to be accessible to undergraduate readers. We have made a conscious choice not to capitalize divine pronouns, attributes, and sacraments even when the source texts from which we are working have done so. Particularly for sources from earlier periods, the relationship between many rituals and attributes on one hand and the divine on the other had yet to be formally made clear. Thus, in capitalizing them, as historians, we believe we might be imposing anachronistic readings on texts. For the sake of consistency, we have maintained this practice throughout the book. Within the documents themselves, material in square brackets are editorial additions or comments; parentheses contain material that is authorial and part of the source itself.

ABBREVIATIONS

Given that the Christian Bible was the first point of reference for many of the authors represented in this collection, many of the following documents are often peppered with references to scripture. Where authors quote scripture directly, we have supplied a reference to the Vulgate in square brackets. Where it has been necessary to abbreviate the titles of longer biblical books, we have used the conventions below.

Note that the sequence and names of some of these texts are different in non-Catholic Bibles.

OLD TESTAMENT

Gen.	Genesis
Exod.	Exodus
Deut.	Deuteronomy
Num.	Numbers
Tob.	Tobit
Ps.	Psalms
Prov.	Proverbs
Eccles.	Ecclesiastes
Wisd. of Sol.	Wisdom of Solomon
Isa.	Isaiah
Jer.	Jeremiah
Lam.	Lamentations
Ezek.	Ezekiel
Dan.	Daniel
Zeph.	Zephaniah [also known as Sophonias]
1 Macc.	1 Maccabees

NEW TESTAMENT

Matt.	Matthew
Rom.	Romans
1 Cor.	1 Corinthians
2 Cor.	2 Corinthians
Eph.	Ephesians
1 Thess.	1 Thessalonians
2 Thess.	2 Thessalonians

1 Tim.	1 Timothy
2 Tim.	2 Timothy
Heb.	Hebrews
1 Pet.	1 Peter
2 Pet.	2 Peter
Rev.	Revelation

CHAPTER ONE

SOURCES FOR THE MEDIEVAL DEVIL

Figure 1.1 School of Albrecht Dürer, "Job on the Dunghill" (1509). Albrecht Dürer (1471–1528) was one of the great artists of the Late Middle Ages. He spent much of his career in his home city of Nuremberg, where he produced many woodcuts and engravings that were used to illustrate printed books. This illustration depicts Satan scourging Job (doc. 6) being watched over by a woman—presumably, Job's wife.

ONE: SOURCES FOR THE MEDIEVAL DEVIL

While the devil of medieval Christianity was constructed from a wide range of European, African, and Near Eastern cultural materials, the fundamental components of his identity and personality were taken from Christian scripture, that is, the Bible. This was the primary source from which Satan was built and the filter through which his apparent involvement in human affairs was typically measured and judged.

But while the devil is ultimately a creature of scripture, fabricated from the building blocks of the Old and New Testaments, the Bible does not present a coherent narrative about the devil. In part, at least, this is because the literary product that we know as the Bible is a collection of dozens of separate texts produced by a range of authors in three ancient languages (Hebrew, Aramaic, and Greek) over a span of almost a millennium—that is, between roughly 800 BCE and 120 CE. From a strictly historical perspective, this means that the texts were written under very different historical conditions, with writers responding to lived misfortune through the lens of a conception of evil that was itself evolving and developing.

Moreover, textually, the Bible has comparatively little to say about the devil's duties or functions, or even about his fundamental nature. The focus of the Bible is on the history of the chosen people and the message of salvation. As a result, what can be gleaned from the sacred text about evil and its personification in the figure of Satan or the devil has to be pieced together from isolated comments, many of which are in fact intended to amplify rhetorically a point the writer is endeavoring to make about the divine or about sin and redemption in response to a particular set of historical circumstances. In practice, then, the devil is an exceptionally elusive and contingent creature: one about whom much must be inferred or deduced from the sparse clues provided in the Bible.

Complicating the situation even further, however, is the fact that there exist a number of "quasi-diabolical" presences in both the Old and New Testaments, that is, figures who were not explicitly demonic but who seemed to strive to bring disorder into God's perfectly ordered cosmos. While these rival gods and preternatural beings that inhabited ancient Near Eastern lore would have been recognizable and familiar to contemporary Israelites, they tend to be assimilated into scripture as figures of malevolence, later to be woven into the narrative of Satan that would emerge in the Christian era.

Thus, early medieval scholars looking to understand the devil's roles and powers are faced with a diverse set of sources, drawn from a variety of traditions, composed under very different circumstances, and written in a variety of languages. All of this means that, while the devil's origins lie deeply embedded in the linguistic and cultural strata of the Bible's many constituent texts, his story is neither stable, "unfolding," nor uncontroversial. Reconciling competing, even contradictory claims about the personification of evil from a range of chronologically disparate accounts lifted from different linguistic and cultural traditions means that the devil of these early sources is generally a product of the concerns of the interpreter and of the circumstances in which he and the Church found themselves: the devil always fulfils the role required of him.

This is a challenging chapter, both for those familiar with the Bible and for those who are not. The sources that follow have all been subject to centuries of interpretation. You may well think that you *know* the story these selections relate. But read the sources as they are given—not in terms of how they are later interpreted. How these sources are interpreted and crafted into a narrative that defines the devil and his role in history will be addressed in subsequent chapters.

1. THE SERPENT AND THE FALL OF HUMANITY

The first five books of the Old Testament (known as the Pentateuch) trace the history of the Jewish people from God's creation of the cosmos at the beginning of Genesis to the time when the "children of Israel" approached the promised land in Deuteronomy. Though they were traditionally ascribed to the prophet Moses, modern textual criticism and other scientific methods make it clear that they were probably written by various contributors over many centuries.

The following passages come from the book of Genesis. The first deals with God's creation. The second deals with the temptation of Adam and Eve—the first humans—by a creature called the serpent (Hebrew: nachash*), and with the consequences of this event. The account is generally read by later Christians through the lens of the New Testament as the opening act in the drama of sacred history that necessitated the coming of Christ and will culminate in the grand conflagration between good and evil described as occurring at the end of time in the book of Revelation. Significantly, the Old Testament contains no further references to the temptation story.*

Hebrew, probably seventh to fifth centuries BCE.

Source: trans. Gregory Martin et al. from the Latin Vulgate, The Holy Bible (Douay-Rheims version) (Douay: The English College, 1609–10), rev. Richard Challoner (1749–52); rev.

Genesis

1.1. In the beginning God created heaven, and earth.

2. And the earth was void and empty, and darkness was upon the face of the deep; and the spirit of God moved over the waters.

3. And God said, "Be light made." And light was made.

4. And God saw the light that it was good; and he divided the light from the darkness.

5. And he called the light "day," and the darkness "night"; and there was evening and morning one day.

6. And God said, "Let there be a firmament made amidst the waters: and let it divide the waters from the waters."

7. And God made a firmament, and divided the waters that were under the firmament, from those that were above the firmament, and it was so.

8. And God called the firmament, "heaven"; and the evening and morning were the second day.

9. God also said, "Let the waters that are under the heaven, be gathered together into one place: and let the dry land appear." And it was so done.

10. And God called the dry land, "earth"; and the gathering together of the waters, he called "seas." And God saw that it was good.

11. And he said, "Let the earth bring forth the green herb, and such as may seed, and the fruit tree yielding fruit after its kind, which may have seed in itself upon the earth." And it was so done.

12. And the earth brought forth the green herb, and such as gives up seed according to its kind, and the tree that bears fruit, having seed each one according to its kind. And God saw that it was good.

13. And the evening and the morning were the third day.

14. And God said, "Let there be lights made in the firmament of heaven, to divide the day and the night, and let them be for signs, and for seasons, and for days and years:

15. To shine in the firmament of heaven, and to give light upon the earth." And it was so done.

16. And God made two great lights: a greater light to rule the day; and a lesser light to rule the night: and the stars.

17. And he set them in the firmament of heaven to shine upon the earth.

18. And to rule the day and the night, and to divide the light and the darkness. And God saw that it was good.

19. And the evening and morning were the fourth day.

20. God also said, "Let the waters bring forth the creeping creature having life, and the fowl that may fly over the earth under the firmament of heaven."

21. And God created the great whales, and every living and moving creature, which the waters brought forth, according to their kinds, and every winged fowl according to its kind. And God saw that it was good.

22. And he blessed them, saying, "Increase and multiply, and fill the waters of the sea: and let the birds be multiplied upon the earth."

23. And the evening and morning were the fifth day.

24. And God said, "Let the earth bring forth the living creature in its kind, cattle and creeping things, and beasts of the earth, according to their kinds." And it was so done.

25. And God made the beasts of the earth according to their kinds, and cattle, and everything that creeps on the earth after its kind. And God saw that it was good.

26. And he said, "Let us make man to our image and likeness: and let him have dominion over the fishes of the sea, and the fowls of the air, and the beasts, and the whole earth, and every creeping creature that moves upon the earth."

27. And God created man to his own image: to the image of God he created him: male and female he created them.

28. And God blessed them, saying, "Increase and multiply, and fill the earth, and subdue it, and rule over the fishes of the sea, and the fowls of the air, and all living creatures that move upon the earth.". . .

31. And God saw all the things that he had made, and they were very good. And the evening and morning were the sixth day. . . .

3.1. Now the serpent was more subtle than any of the beasts of the earth which the lord God had made. And he said to the woman, "Why has God commanded that you should not eat from every tree of paradise?"

2. And the woman answered him, saying, "We do eat the fruit of the trees that are in paradise.

3. But of the fruit of the tree [of the knowledge of good and evil] which is in the middle of paradise, God has commanded that we should not eat, and that we should not touch it, lest perhaps we die."

4. And the serpent said to the woman, "No, you shall not die the death.

5. For God knows that when you eat of it, your eyes shall be opened, and you shall be like gods, knowing good and evil."

6. And the woman saw that the tree was good to eat, and fair to the eyes, and delightful to behold, and she took the fruit from it, and ate it, and then gave it to her husband who ate.

7. And the eyes of both of them were opened, and when they perceived themselves to be naked, they sewed together fig leaves, and made themselves aprons.

8. And when they heard the voice of the lord God walking in paradise at the afternoon air, Adam and his wife hid themselves from the face of the lord God, among the trees of paradise.

9. And the lord God called Adam, and said to him, "Where are you?"

10. And Adam said, "I heard your voice in paradise, and I was afraid, because I was naked, and I hid myself."

11. And God said to him, "And who told you that you were naked? Have you eaten from the tree from which I commanded that you should not eat?"

12. And Adam said, "The woman whom you gave me to be my companion gave me the fruit from the tree, and I ate it."

13. And the lord God said to the woman, "Why have you done this?" And she answered, "The serpent deceived me, and so I ate."

14. And the lord God said to the serpent, "Because you have done this thing, you are cursed among all cattle, and beasts of the earth. Upon your breast you shall go, and you shall eat earth all the days of thy life.

15. I will put enmity between you and the woman, and your seed and her seed. She shall crush your head, and you shall lie in wait for her heel."

16. To the woman he said, "I will multiply your sorrows, and your conceptions. You shall bring forth children in sorrow, and you shall be under your husband's power, and he shall have dominion over you."

17. And to Adam he said, "Because you listened to the voice of your wife, and have eaten from the tree, from which I commanded that you should not eat, cursed is the earth in your work; with labor and toil shall you eat from it all the days of your life.

18. Thorns and thistles shall it bring forth to you; and you shall eat the herbs of the earth.

19. In the sweat of your face shall you eat bread till you return to the earth, out of which you were taken, for you are dust, and into dust you shall return."

20. And Adam called the name of his wife "Eve," because she was the mother of all the living.

21. And the lord God made for Adam and his wife garments of skins and clothed them.

22. And he said, "Behold Adam has become like one of us, knowing good and evil. Now, therefore, lest he put forth his hand and take also from the tree of life and eat, and live forever."

23. And the lord God sent him out of the paradise of pleasure, to till the earth from which he was taken.

24. And he cast out Adam and placed Cherubim before the paradise of pleasure, and a flaming sword which turned every way, to keep the way of the tree of life.

Questions: What is the nature of God's creation? When did he create the devil? What is the serpent? Can it be evil? What is humanity's transgression? Can Adam and Eve's actions be evil?

2. THE SONS OF GOD AND THE GIANTS

Some stories in the Old Testament describe creatures and characters who seem to come from the realm of the divine and whose origin is never explained. Although the narrative generally makes clear that they are not gods, they are not identified as demons either. Chief among these are the giants (or nephilim*). From a textual perspective, the inclusion of such creatures may represent some sort of "spill-over" from earlier Near Eastern and Egyptian legends.*

The first excerpt comes from Genesis 6. Its placement, coming immediately before the account of Noah and the great flood, seems to imply that the two stories were intended to be read together. The second comes from the book of Numbers. Moses has sent out spies—including Caleb mentioned here—to ascertain the political situation in the promised land before taking the children of Israel there.

Hebrew, probably seventh to fifth century BCE.

Source: trans. Gregory Martin et al. from the Latin Vulgate, The Holy Bible (Douay-Rheims version) (Douay: The English College, 1609–10), rev. Richard Challoner (1749–52); rev.

Genesis

6.1. And after that, men began to be multiplied upon the earth, and daughters were born to them.

2. The sons of God, seeing that the daughters of men were fair, took wives of all which they chose for themselves.

3. And God said, "My spirit shall not remain in man forever, because he is flesh, and his days shall be a hundred and twenty years."

4. Now giants [*nephilim*] were upon the earth in those days. For after the sons of God went in to the daughters of men, and they brought forth children, these are the mighty men of old, men of renown.

5. And God, seeing that the wickedness of men was great on the earth, and that all the thoughts of their hearts were bent upon evil all the time,

6. Repented that he had made man on the earth. And being touched inwardly with sorrow of the heart,

7. He said, "I will destroy man, whom I have created, from the face of the earth, from man even to beasts, from the creeping thing even to the fowls of the air, for I regret that I made them."

8. But Noah found grace before the lord.

Numbers

13.31. In the meantime Caleb, to still the murmuring of the people that rose against Moses, said, "Let us go up and possess the land, for we shall be able to conquer it."

32. But the others that had been with him, said, "No, we are not able to go up to this people, because they are stronger than us."

33. And they spoke badly about the land which they had viewed in front of the children of Israel, saying, "The land which we have viewed, devours its inhabitants; the people that we behold are tall in stature.

34. There we saw certain monsters of the sons of Enac, of the giant kind, in comparison to whom, we seemed like locusts."

Questions: Who created these giants and when? Are they evil? At what is God angry? How do the children of Israel use the notion of giants?

ONE: SOURCES FOR THE MEDIEVAL DEVIL

3. SATANS AS GOD'S AGENTS

Among the supernatural beings that populated the Old Testament were angels. As with many other semi-divine creatures, the Bible does not spell out when they were created. Their function, though, can be surmised from the text's description of their activities. Their sudden appearance could be terrifying to unsuspecting humans. Among the angels of the Old Testament is a certain type referred to as a satan, a Hebrew term that translates into English as "opponent" or "adversary."

The first excerpt below comes from the book of Numbers. The story centers on Balaam, a non-Israelite prophet summoned by the king of Moab to curse the children of Israel as they approached his land. It includes the first use of the term satan in the Bible, although most European languages translate the Hebrew word as "angel of the lord" or something similar.

The final two selections come from the letters of Saint Paul, in which he offers advice and guidance to the various early Christian communities scattered around the Mediterranean basin.

Numbers: Hebrew, probably seventh to fifth century BCE.
Thessalonians and Corinthians: Greek, 50–57 CE.

Source: trans. Gregory Martin et al. from the Latin Vulgate, The Holy Bible (Douay-Rheims version) (Douay: The English College, 1609–10), rev. Richard Challoner (1749–52); rev.

Numbers

22.20. God therefore came to Balaam in the night, and said to him, "If these men come to call you, arise and go with them: but you must do what I shall command you."

21. Balaam arose in the morning, and saddling his ass went with them.

22. And God was angry. And an angel of the lord [a *satan*] stood in the road against Balaam, who sat on the ass, and had two servants with him.

23. The ass, seeing the angel standing in the road with a drawn sword, turned herself off the road, and went into the field. And when Balaam beat her, and had a mind to bring her again onto the road,

24. The angel stood in a narrow place between two walls which enclosed the vineyards.

25. And the ass seeing him, thrust herself close to the wall, and bruised Balaam's foot. But he beat her again.

26. And nevertheless the angel going further [went in] to a narrow place, where there was no way to turn aside either to the right hand or to the left, stood to meet him.

27. And when the ass saw the angel standing, she fell under Balaam's feet, who being angry beat her sides more vehemently with a staff.

28. And the lord opened the mouth of the ass, and she said, "What have I done to you? Why do you strike me now this third time?"

29. Balaam answered, "Because you have deserved it, and have served me badly. I wish I had a sword so that I could kill you."

30. The ass said, "Am not I your beast, on which you have always been accustomed to ride until this present day? Tell me if I ever did the like thing to you." But he said, "Never."

31. At that the lord opened the eyes of Balaam, and he saw the angel standing in the way with a drawn sword, and he worshipped him falling flat on the ground.

32. And the angel said to him, "Why do you beat your ass these three times? I have come to withstand you, because your way is perverse, and contrary to me.

33. And had the ass not turned off the road, giving place to me who stood against you, I would have slain you, and she would have lived."

34. Balaam said, "I have sinned, not knowing that you stood against me, and now if it displeases you that I go, I will return."

35. The angel said, "Go with these men, and see that you speak no other thing than what I shall command you." Balaam went therefore with the princes.

1 Thessalonians

2.13. Therefore, we also give thanks to God without ceasing because, when you had received the word of God which you heard from us [Paul], you received it not as the word of men, but (as it is indeed) the word of God, who works in you who have believed.

14. For you, brethren, have become followers of the churches of God which are in Judea, in Christ Jesus. You also have suffered the same things from your own countrymen as they have from the Jews,

15. Who killed both the lord Jesus and the prophets, and have persecuted us, and who do not please God, and are adversaries to all men,

16. [who] prohibit us to speak to the Gentiles so that they may be saved, to fill up their sins always: for the wrath of God will come upon them to the end.

17. But we, brethren, being taken away from you for a short time, in sight if not in heart, have hastened more abundantly to see your face with great desire.

18. For we would have come to you, I Paul indeed, once and again, but Satan hindered us.

2 Corinthians

12.7. And lest the greatness of the revelations [I preach] should exalt me, there was given me a sting of my flesh, an angel of Satan, to buffet me.

8. Because of this thing [the angel] I sought the lord thrice, so that it might depart from me.

9. And he said to me, "My grace is sufficient for you; for [my] power is made perfect in infirmity. Gladly therefore will I glory in my infirmities, so that the power of Christ may dwell in me.

10. For this reason, I please myself in my infirmities, in reproaches, in necessities, in persecutions, in distresses, for Christ. For when I am weak, then am I powerful."

Questions: Who or what are the satans in these texts? What are they doing? Where do they come from? Are they evil? How do the satans of Paul's letters differ from those of Balaam?

4. THE FALL OF LUCIFER?

The Old Testament books of Isaiah and Ezekiel are prophetic works informed by the turbulent circumstances in which God's people found themselves at the time of their composition. Isaiah was a politically engaged prophet at the court of the kings of Judah at the end of the eighth into the early seventh century BCE. In 701, Judah was attacked by the powerful Assyrian Empire; many towns were destroyed, and Jerusalem was besieged. Unsurprisingly, Isaiah came to understand these events as divine punishments, configuring the Assyrians as instruments of God. Ezekiel, by contrast, was a priest who was probably among those who were transported to Babylon in 597 by Nebuchadnezzar, the Babylonian king (r. 605–562 BCE), in the wake of the king's capture of Jerusalem. Ezekiel's whole prophetic career took place in the heart of the Babylonian Empire, where he likely heard reports of Nebuchadnezzar's campaign against the city of Tyre, an affluent center for maritime trade, and a region synonymous with idolatry to the Israelites.

The name Lucifer comes from the Latin words "lux" (light) and "fer" (from the verb "ferre," meaning "to bring" or "to bear").

Hebrew, seventh century BCE.

Source: trans. Gregory Martin et al. from the Latin Vulgate, The Holy Bible (Douay-Rheims version) (Douay: The English College, 1609–10), rev. Richard Challoner (1749–52); rev.

Isaiah

14.3. And it shall come to pass in that day, that when God shall give you rest from your labor, and from your vexation, and from the hard bondage, in which you served before,

4. You shall take up this parable against the king of Babylon, and shall say, "How has the oppressor come to nothing, and the tribute ceased?

5. The lord has broken the staff of the wicked, the rod of the rulers,

6. That struck the people in wrath with an incurable wound, that brought nations under in fury, that persecuted in a cruel manner.

7. The whole earth is quiet and still, it is glad and has rejoiced.

8. The fir trees also have rejoiced over you, and the cedars of Lebanon, saying, 'Since you have slept, there has come no one to cut us down.'

9. Hell below was in an uproar to meet you at your coming, it stirred up the giants for you. All the princes of the earth have risen up from their thrones, all the princes of nations.

10. All shall answer, and say to you, 'You also are wounded as well as we [are], you have become like us.

11. Your pride is brought down to hell, your carcass has fallen down: under you the moth shall be strewn, and worms shall be your covering.

12. How you have fallen from heaven, O Lucifer, who did rise in the morning? How are you fallen to the earth, you who wounded the nations?'

13. And you said in your heart, 'I will ascend into heaven, I will exalt my throne above the stars of God, I will sit in the mountain of the covenant, in the sides of the north.

14. I will ascend above the height of the clouds, I will be like the most high.'

15. But yet you shall be brought down to hell, into the depth of the pit.

16. They that shall see you, shall turn toward you, and behold you. Is this the man that troubled the earth, that shook kingdoms,

17. That made the world a wilderness, and destroyed the cities thereof, that opened not the prison to his prisoners?

18. All the kings of the nations have all of them slept in glory, every one in his own house.

19. But you have been cast out of your grave, as an unprofitable branch defiled, and wrapped up among those that were slain by the sword, and have gone down to the bottom of the pit, as a rotten carcass.

20. You shall not keep company with them, even in burial, for you have destroyed your land, you have slain your people: the seed of the wicked shall not be named for ever.

21. Prepare his children for slaughter for the iniquity of their fathers: they shall not rise up, nor inherit the land, nor fill the face of the world with cities.

22. And 'I will rise up against them,' said the lord of hosts: and 'I will destroy the name of Babylon, and the remains, and the bud, and the offspring,' said the lord.

23. And 'I will make it a possession for the ericius [hedgehog], and pools of waters, and I will sweep it and wear it out with a besom [broom],' said the lord of hosts."

Ezekiel

28.11. And the word of the lord came to me, saying, "Son of man, take up a lamentation upon the king of Tyre:

12. And say to him, 'Thus says the lord God: You were the seal of resemblance, full of wisdom, and perfect in beauty.

13. You were in the pleasures of the paradise of God: every precious stone was your covering: the sardius, the topaz, and the jasper, the chrysolite, and the onyx, and the beryl, the sapphire, and the carbuncle, and the emerald: gold the work of your beauty: and your pipes were prepared in the day on which you were created.

14. You [were] a cherub stretched out, and protecting, and I set you on the holy mountain of God, you have walked in the midst of the stones of fire.

15. You were perfect in your ways from the day of your creation, until iniquity was found in you.

16. By the multitude of your merchandise, your inner parts were filled with iniquity, and you sinned: and I cast you out from the mountain of God, and destroyed you, O covering cherub, out of the midst of the stones of fire.

17. And your heart was lifted up with your beauty: you have lost your wisdom in your beauty, I have cast you to the ground: I have set you before the face of kings, that they might behold you.

18. You have defiled your sanctuaries by the multitude of your iniquities, and by the iniquity of your traffic: therefore I will bring forth a fire from the midst of you, to devour you, and I will make you as ashes upon the earth in the sight of all that see you.

19. All that shall see you among the nations, shall be astonished at you: you are brought to nothing, and you shall never be any more.'"

Questions: To whom are the authors of the texts referring in their descriptions? Are they describing the same thing? When did or will these events occur? Why are these figures punished? Are they demonic?

5. GOD AS THE CREATOR OF EVIL?

Genesis 1 (doc. 1) asserted unambiguously that the creation God fashioned was good. This fact, however, was at odds with the experience of misfortune and suffering evident in the world. While the account of Adam and Eve's temptation in paradise and the demonization of the serpent would be used by Christians as a way of accounting for the problem of evil, Old Testament authors did not make use of the story. Instead, there are a number of texts that seem to suggest that God himself is the creator of evil—a firm assertion of monotheism in reaction to the Israelites' interactions with polytheistic cultures.

The selection from 3 Kings (1 Kings in non-Catholic Bibles) concerns God's dealings with Achab, the evil king of Israel, and his queen, Jezebel, who have refused to listen to the prophets of God, preferring instead to heed the advice of those who would tell them what they wanted to hear. Ramoth-Gilead is a neighboring kingdom.

While traditionalists have argued that the Old Testament book of Isaiah was written by a single author named Isaiah, modern scholars generally agree that it is the work of multiple writers. The section below comes from a later portion of the book (sometimes referred to as Second Isaiah), likely written after the freeing of the Jews from Babylon by the Persian king Cyrus the Great (r. 557–530 BCE). In Babylon, the Jews had encountered dualism—the idea that good and evil in the world are a consequence of the actions of two morally juxtaposed divine principles.

3 Kings: Hebrew, seventh to sixth century BCE.

[Second] Isaiah: Hebrew, mid-sixth century BCE.

Source: trans. Gregory Martin et al. from the Latin Vulgate, The Holy Bible (Douay-Rheims version) (Douay: The English College, 1609–10), rev. Richard Challoner (1749–52); rev.

3 Kings

22.18. (Then the king of Israel said to Josaphat, "Did I not tell you that he prophesied no good to me, but only evil things?")

19. And he added and said, "Hear therefore the word of the lord. I saw the lord sitting on his throne, and all the army of heaven standing by him on the right hand and on the left.

20. And the lord said, 'Who shall deceive Achab king of Israel so that he may go up and fall at Ramoth Galaad?' And one [of the army there present] spoke words in this manner, and another otherwise.

21. And there came forth a spirit and stood before the lord, and said, 'I will deceive him.' And the lord said to him, 'By what means?'

22. And he said, 'I will go forth and be a lying spirit in the mouth of all his prophets.' And the lord said, 'You shall deceive him, and shall prevail. Go forth, and do so.'

23. Now therefore, behold, the lord has put a lying spirit in the mouth of all your prophets that are here, and the lord has spoken evil against you."

Isaiah

45.5. I am the lord, and there is no other. There is no God besides me. I girded [armed] you and you have not known me,

6. That those may know who are from the [region of the] rising of the sun, and they who are from the west, that there is none besides me. I am the lord, and there is no other.

7. I form the light and create darkness. I make peace and create evil. I, the lord, do all these things.

8. Drop down, you heavens, from above, and let the clouds rain justice. Let the earth be opened, and bring forth a savior, and let justice spring up with it. I the lord have created it.

9. Woe to him who strives with his maker—a shard of the earthen pots. Does the clay say to the craftsman that made it, "What are you making," and "your work is without skill?"

10. Woe to him that says to his father, "What do you beget?" and to the woman, "What have you brought forth?"

Questions: How do these texts deal with the problem of evil? Is the lying spirit demonic? What do these texts imply about the nature of God? Is a devil necessary?

6. SATAN AS SPY AND TESTER

The book of Job is a fundamental source for the construction of the Christian devil. Unlike other Old Testament books that focus on the history of the Hebrew people, Job follows the sufferings of its titular character, a wealthy and pious landowner from the land of Hus, at the hands of a character identified as Satan—the first time the figure is given a "leading role" in scripture.

Like [second] Isaiah (doc. 5), Job seems to have been written after the return of the Jews from Babylon and reflects their experience there, for Satan together with God's other mysterious advisors—the so-called "sons of God"—seem to resemble officials of the Persian royal court called "the king's eyes." These were functionaries hired to gather intelligence for the monarch, not unlike modern espionage agents.

Hebrew, probably sixth century BCE.

Source: trans. Gregory Martin et al. from the Latin Vulgate, The Holy Bible (Douay-Rheims version) (Douay: The English College, 1609–10), rev. Richard Challoner (1749–52); rev.

1.1. There was a man in the land of Hus, whose name was Job, and that man was simple and upright, and fearing God, and avoiding evil.

2. And there were born to him seven sons and three daughters.

3. And in his possession were seven thousand sheep, and three thousand camels, and five hundred yoke of oxen, and five hundred she asses, and an exceeding large family: and this man was great among all the people of the east. . . .

6. Now on a certain day when the sons of God came to stand before the lord, Satan also was present among them.

7. And the lord said to him, "Where are you coming from?" And he answered and said, "I have gone round about the earth, and walked through it."

8. And the lord said to him, "Have you considered my servant Job, that there is none like him on the earth, a simple and upright man, and fearing God, and avoiding evil?"

9. And Satan answering, said, "Does Job fear God in vain?

10. Have you not made a fence for him, and his house, and all his substance round about, blessed the works of his hands, and his possessions have increased on the earth?

11. But stretch your hand a little further, and touch all that he has, and [then] see if he blesses you to your face any longer."

12. Then the lord said to Satan, "Behold, all that he has is in your hand, only do not put forth your hand upon his person." And Satan went forth from the presence of the lord.

13. Now upon a certain day when his sons and daughters were eating and drinking wine in the house of their eldest brother,

14. There came a messenger to Job, and said, "The oxen were ploughing, and the asses feeding beside them,

15. And the Sabeans rushed in, and took all away, and slew the servants with the sword, and I alone have escaped to tell you."

16. And while he was yet speaking, another came, and said, "The fire of God fell from heaven, and striking the sheep and the servants, it has consumed them, and I alone have escaped to tell you."

17. And while he also was yet speaking, there came another, and said, "The Chaldeans made three troops, and have fallen upon your camels, and taken them, moreover they have slain the servants with the sword, and I alone have escaped to tell you."

18. He was still speaking, and behold another came in, and said, "Your sons and daughters were eating and drinking wine in the house of their elder brother.

19. A violent wind came on suddenly from the side of the desert, and shook the four corners of the house, and it fell upon your children and they are dead, and I alone have escaped to tell you."

20. Then Job rose up, and rent his garments, and having shaven his head fell down upon the ground and worshipped,

21. And said, "Naked came I out of my mother's womb, and naked shall I return there. The lord gave, and the lord has taken away. As it has pleased the lord so is it done. Blessed be the name of the lord."

22. In all these things Job sinned not by his lips, nor did he speak any foolish thing against God.

2.1. And it came to pass, when on a certain day the sons of God came, and stood before the lord, and Satan came among them, and stood in his sight,

2. That the lord said to Satan, "Where are you coming from?" And he answered and said, "I have gone round about the earth, and walked through it."

3. And the lord said to Satan, "Have you considered my servant Job, that there is none like him in the earth, a man simple, and upright, and fearing God, and avoiding evil, and still keeping his innocence? But you have moved me against him, that I should afflict him without cause."

4. And Satan answered, and said, "Skin for skin, and all that a man has he will give for his life.

5. But put forth your hand, and touch his bone and his flesh, and then you shall see whether he will bless you to your face."

6. And the lord said to Satan, "Behold he is in your hand, but yet spare his life."

7. So Satan went forth from the presence of the lord, and struck Job with a very grievous ulcer, from the sole of the foot even to the top of his head.

8. And he [Job] took a potsherd and scraped the corrupt matter, sitting on a dunghill.

9. And his wife said to him, "Do you still continue in your simplicity? Bless God and die."

10. And he said to her, "You have spoken like one of the foolish women. If we have received good things at the hand of God, why should we not receive evil?" In all these things Job did not sin with his lips.

Questions: Why does God allow Satan to test Job? What is the relationship between Satan and God? Is Satan's power legitimate? Is he good? Does this image of the character Satan presented here accord with the satan in the story of Balaam (doc. 3)?

7. THE DEMONS OF ANCIENT GREECE

Plato (425–347 BCE) is one of the founders of the western philosophical tradition. A product of Athens's intellectual flowering, he wrote on a wide range of topics, including mathematics, biology, pure philosophy, and ethics. The first selection comes from the Symposium. *The work is set at a sumptuous dinner party—a symposion—and describes various famous Athenians offering an* encomium *(a speech of praise) to Eros, the god of love. Toward the end of the dialogue, Plato has the great teacher Socrates offer his views on the subject. The character Diotima, mentioned in the text, is one of the dinner-guests, the only woman mentioned by name.*

Plato wrote the Laws *toward the end of his life. The work is also framed as a dialogue, this time between representatives of Athens, Sparta, and Crete as they walk toward the temple of Zeus.*

Greek, mid-fourth century BCE.

Source: trans. Benjamin Jowett, from Plato, *The Symposium* and *The Laws* from *The Dialogues of Plato* (Oxford: University Press, 1892), vol 1, pp. 572–75, and vol. 4, pp. 241, 244; rev.

The *Symposium*

"What then, is Love [Eros]?" I [Socrates] asked, "Is he mortal?"

"No."

"What, then?"

"As in the former instance, he is neither mortal nor immortal, but in a mean between the two."

"What is he, Diotima?"

"He is a great demon, and like all demons he is intermediate between the divine and the mortal."

"And what is his power?" I said.

She replied, "He interprets between gods and humans, conveying and taking across to the gods the prayers and sacrifices of human beings, and to human beings the commands and replies of the gods. He is the mediator who spans the chasm which divides gods and mortals; thus, in him everything is bound together. Through him, the arts of the prophet and the priest find their way, as do their sacrifices and their mysteries and their charms. All prophecy and incantation find their way also. For god does not mingle with humans, but rather all intercourse, all correspondence between god and humans, whether it takes place while we are awake or asleep, is carried on through Love. The wisdom which understands this is spiritual. All other wisdom, such as that of the arts and crafts, is low and vulgar. Now these spirits or intermediate powers are many and diverse, and one of them is Love."

The *Laws*

There is a tradition of the happy life of mankind in days when all things were spontaneous and abundant. And the reason for this is said to have been as follows: Cronos . . . knew that no human nature invested with supreme power is able to order human affairs and not overflow with insolence and wrong. Which reflection led him to appoint not men but demi-gods, who are of a higher and more divine race, to be the kings and rulers of our cities; he did as we do with flocks of sheep and other tame animals. For we do not appoint oxen to be the lords of oxen, or goats of goats; but we ourselves are a superior race, and rule over them. In like manner God, in his love of mankind, placed over us the demons, who are a superior race, and they with great ease and pleasure to themselves, and no less to us, taking care of us and giving us peace and reverence and order and justice never failing, made the tribes of men happy and united. And this tradition, which is true, declares that cities of which some mortal man and not God is the ruler, have no escape from evils and toils.

Then what sort of action is agreeable to the God, and becoming in his followers? . . . Now, God is the measure of all things, in a sense far higher than any man could be, as the common saying affirms. And he who would be dear to God must, as far as is possible, be like him and such as he is. Wherefore the temperate man is the friend of God, for he is like him; and the intemperate man is unlike him, and different from him, and unjust. And the same holds of other things; and this is the conclusion . . . that for the good man to offer sacrifice to the gods, and hold converse with them by means of prayers and offerings and every kind of service, is the noblest and best of all things, and also the most conducive to a happy life, and very fit and meet. . . . next after the Olympian gods and the gods of the state, honor should be given to the gods below; they should receive everything in even numbers, and of the second choice, and of evil omen, while the odd numbers, and the first choice, and the things of lucky omen, are given to the gods above, by him who would rightly hit the mark of piety. Next to these gods, a wise man will do service to the demons or spirits, and then to the heroes, and after them will follow the sacred places of private and ancestral gods, having their ritual according to law.

Questions: What do Plato's demons do? What is their role in the cosmos? What is their relationship to God? Would Greeks have thought that demons were real or metaphorical?

8. RABBINICAL TEACHINGS ON THE DEVIL

The Aggadah—generally translated into English as "Legends"—is a large collection of narrative texts written by rabbis to help Jewish believers interpret the Tanakh (the Hebrew name for the Old Testament). It incorporates folkloric narratives, historical anecdotes, ethical writings, and doctrinal texts that supplement the biblical text. As such, it provides some sense of how these Old Testament narratives were being read and understood within the Jewish community at the time Christianity was emerging.
    Hebrew, second to eleventh centuries CE.

Source: trans. Henrietta Szold, *The Legends of the Jews*, vol. 1 (Philadelphia: The Jewish Publication Society of America, 1913), pp. 62–69, 71–74.

The Fall of Satan

The extraordinary qualities with which Adam was blessed, physical and spiritual as well, aroused the envy of the angels. They attempted to consume him with fire, and he would have perished, had not the protecting hand of God rested upon him, and established peace between him and the heavenly host. In particular, Satan was jealous of the first man, and his evil thoughts finally led to his fall. After Adam had been endowed with a soul, God invited all the angels to come and pay him reverence and homage. Satan, the greatest of the angels in heaven, with twelve wings, instead of six like all the others, refused to pay heed to God's command, saying, "You created us angels from the splendor of the Shekinah [the divine presence, or dwelling, of God], and now you order us to cast ourselves down before the creature which you have fashioned out of the dust of the ground!" God answered, "Yet this dust of the ground has more wisdom and understanding than you."

Satan demanded a trial of wits with Adam, and God consented, saying, "I have created beasts, birds, and reptiles. I shall have them all come before you and before Adam. If you are able to give them names, I shall command Adam to show you honor, and you shall rest next to the Shekinah of my glory. But if not, and Adam calls them by the names I have assigned to them, then you will be subject to Adam, and he shall have a place in my garden, and cultivate it." Thus spoke God, and he went off to Paradise, with Satan following him. When Adam saw God, he said to his wife, "O come, let us worship and bow down; let us kneel before the lord our maker." Now Satan attempted to assign names to the animals. He failed with the first two that presented themselves, the ox and the cow. God led two others before him, the camel and the donkey, with the same result. Then God turned to Adam, and questioned him regarding the names of the same animals, framing his questions in such a way that the first letter of the first word was the same as the first letter of the name of the animal standing before him. Thus Adam discerned the proper name, and Satan was forced to acknowledge the superiority of the first man.

Nevertheless, Satan broke out in wild outcries that reached the heavens, and he refused to do homage to Adam as he had been ordered. The host of angels following him did likewise, in spite of the urgent objections of Michael, who was the first to prostrate himself before Adam in order to show a good example to the other angels. Michael addressed Satan, "Give adoration to the image of God! But if you will not, then the lord God will break out in wrath against you." Satan replied, "If he breaks out in wrath against me, I will exalt my throne above the stars of God, I will be like the most high!" At once God flung Satan and his host out of heaven, down to the earth, and from that moment dates the enmity between Satan and man. . . .

The Fall of Man

Among the animals the serpent was notable. Of all of them he had the most excellent qualities, in some of which he resembled man. Like man he stood upright upon two feet, and in height he was equal to the camel. Had it not been for the fall of man, which brought misfortune to serpents, as well, one pair of serpents would have sufficed to perform all the work man has to do; moreover, they would have supplied him with silver, gold, gems, and pearls. As a matter of fact, it was the very usefulness of the serpent that led to the ruin of man and his own ruin. His superior mental gifts caused the serpent to become an infidel. It likewise explains his envy of man, especially of his sexual relations. Envy made the serpent think about ways and means of bringing about the death of Adam. He was too well acquainted with the character of the man to try and persuade him, so he approached the woman, knowing that women are easily beguiled. The conversation with Eve was cunningly planned, so she could not help but be caught in a trap. The serpent began, "Is it true that God has said, you shall not eat from every tree in the garden?" "We may," Eve answered, "eat fruit from all the trees in the garden, except from the one that is in the middle of the garden; we may not even touch that tree, lest we be stricken with death." She said this because, in his zeal to guard her against breaking God's commandment, Adam had forbidden Eve to touch the tree—even though God had mentioned only the eating of its fruit. The proverb remains true when it says, "Better a wall ten hands high that stands, than a wall a hundred ells high that cannot stand." It was Adam's exaggeration that provided the serpent with the opportunity to convince Eve to taste of the forbidden fruit.

The serpent pushed Eve against the tree, and said, "You see that touching the tree has not caused your death. It will hurt you just as little to eat the fruit of the tree. Adam's prohibition was prompted by nothing but malevolence, for as soon as you eat from it, you shall be like God. Just as he creates and destroys worlds, so will you have the power to create and destroy. Just as he slays and revives, so will you have the power to slay and revive. God himself ate the fruit of the tree just before he created the world. Therefore, he has forbidden you to eat from it, lest you create other worlds. Everyone knows that 'artisans of the same guild hate one another!' Furthermore, have you not noticed that every creature has dominion over the creature that was fashioned before it?"

The serpent began to shake the tree violently in order to bring down its fruit. He ate some of it, saying, "Just as I do not die from eating this fruit, so you will not die." At this, Eve could only say to herself, "Everything that my master (for this is what she called Adam) has commanded is a lie," and she decided to follow the advice of the serpent. However, she could not bring herself to disobey completely the command of God. Thus, she made a compromise with her conscience. First, she ate only the outside skin of the fruit, and then, seeing that death did not cut her down, she ate the fruit itself. Scarcely had she finished eating, when she saw the Angel of Death before her. Expecting her end to come immediately, she resolved to make Adam eat the forbidden fruit, too, lest he marry another wife after her death. With tears and lamentations, she prevailed upon Adam to take the baleful step. Still not satisfied, she gave the fruit to all the other living beings, that they, too, might be subject to death. They all ate the fruit, and they all became mortal. . . .

Adam spoke to Eve, "Did you give me fruit from the tree from which I forbade you to eat? You did give me some, for my eyes are opened, and the teeth in my mouth are set on edge." Eve responded, "Just as my teeth were set on edge, so may the teeth of all living beings be set on edge." The first result was that Adam and Eve became naked. Before, their bodies had been covered by a horny skin, and enveloped in a cloud of glory. No sooner had they broken God's command than the cloud of glory and the horny skin dropped away from them, and they stood there in their nakedness. They were ashamed. Adam tried to gather leaves from the trees to cover parts of their bodies, but he heard one tree after the other say. "There is the thief that deceived his creator. Nay, the foot of pride shall not rest upon me, nor the hand of the wicked touch me. Depart, and take no leaves from me!" Only the fig-tree granted him permission to take of its leaves. This was because the fig was the forbidden fruit itself.

Questions: Does God treat Satan justly? Why is Satan so hostile to humanity? How responsible is Eve for the fall? Does Satan have any role in the fall? Why might the author(s) of these passages have elaborated on the Genesis story?

9. SATAN REAPPEARS

Although the letters of Saint Paul are older, the first appearance of the devil in the New Testament in terms of the text's organization comes during the temptation of Christ in the wilderness. This episode is described in three of the four gospels. The gospel of Mark—chronologically the oldest of the four—relates merely that after his baptism, a spirit in the form of a dove descended upon Christ and then drove him into the wilderness, where he remained for forty days, during which time he was tempted by Satan. Matthew and Luke elaborate on this story, describing in more detail how Christ was tempted by Satan.

The fourth gospel is credited to a certain John and seems to have been composed at least a generation after the others. As such, it reflects the new realities of the early Church as they had developed by his day.

Luke: Greek, c. 70 CE.

John: Greek, late first century.

Source: trans. Gregory Martin et al. from the Latin Vulgate, The Holy Bible (Douay-Rheims version) (Douay: The English College, 1609–10), rev. Richard Challoner (1749–52); rev.

Luke

4.1. And Jesus being full of the holy spirit, returned from the Jordan, and was led by the spirit into the desert,

2. For the space of forty days; and was tempted by the devil. And he ate nothing in those days; and when they were ended, he was hungry.

3. And the devil said to him, "If you be the son of God, say to this stone that it be made bread."

4. And Jesus answered him, "It is written, that man lives not by bread alone, but by every word of God."

5. And the devil led him into a high mountain, and showed him all the kingdoms of the world in a moment of time;

6. And he said to him, "I will give to you all this power, and the glory of them; for to me they are delivered, and I will give them to whomever I wish.

7. If you therefore will adore before me, all shall be yours."

8. And Jesus answering said to him, "It is written, 'You shall adore the lord your God, and you shall only serve him.'"

9. And he [the devil] brought him to Jerusalem, and set him on a pinnacle of the temple, and he said to him, "If you are the son of God, cast yourself from here.

10. For it is written, that he has given his angels charge over you, that they will keep you.

11. And that in their hands they shall bear you up, lest perhaps you dash your foot against a stone."

12. And Jesus answering, said to him, "It is said, 'you shall not tempt the lord your God.'"

13. And all the temptation being ended, the devil departed from him for a time.

John

12.30. [Responding to an angel] Jesus answered, and said, "This voice came not because of me, but for your sakes.

31. Now is the judgment of the world: now shall the prince of this world be cast out.

32. And I, if I be lifted up from the earth, will draw all things to myself."

Questions: Why does Christ go into the desert? What power does the devil have? Does Christ question the devil's power and dominion? What does Jesus mean when he calls the devil "the prince of the world"? Has the devil done anything evil? What is the nature of Christ's victory over the devil? Does the text from John clarify the Luke story?

10. THE HOMICIDAL LIAR

The New Testament contains no sustained account of the devil, his powers, or his role in history. Instead, what it has to say about the devil is presented largely through asides or incidental remarks. While many of these comments add to the emerging portrait of the devil, when taken together, they implied a host of difficult questions for early Christian commentators.

Greek, second half of first century.

Source: trans. Gregory Martin et al. from the Latin Vulgate, The Holy Bible (Douay-Rheims version) (Douay: The English College, 1609–10), rev. Richard Challoner (1749–52); rev.

John

8.31. Then Jesus said to those Jews, who believed him, "If you continue in my word, you shall be my disciples indeed.

32. And you shall know the truth, and the truth shall make you free."

33. They answered him, "We are the seed of Abraham . . ."

39. Jesus said to them, "If you be the children of Abraham, do the works of Abraham.

40. But now you seek to kill me, a man who has spoken the truth to you, which I have heard of God. This Abraham did not."

41. . . . Therefore, they said to him, "We are not born of fornication: we have one father, even God."

42. Jesus therefore said to them, "If God were your father, you would indeed love me. For I proceeded from God and came; for I came not of myself, but he sent me:

43. Why do you not know my speech? Because you cannot hear my word.

44. You are of your father the devil, and the desires of your father you will do. He was a murderer from the beginning, and he stood not in the truth; because truth is not in him. When he speaks a lie, he speaks of his own: for he is a liar, and the father thereof."

Acts

13.6. And when they [the apostles Saul and Barnabas] had gone through the whole island, as far as Paphos, they found a certain man, a magician, a false prophet, a Jew, whose name was Bar-jesus:

7. Who was with the proconsul Sergius Paulus, a prudent man. Sending for Barnabas and Saul, he desired to hear the word of God.

8. But Elymas the magician (for so his name is interpreted) withstood them, seeking to turn away the proconsul from the faith.

9. Then Saul, otherwise [called] Paul, filled with the holy spirit, looking upon him,

10. Said, "O full of all guile, and of all deceit, child of the devil, enemy of all justice, you do not cease to pervert the right ways of the lord."

1 Corinthians

5.1. It is actually heard that there is fornication among you, a kind of fornication the like [of which] cannot even be found among the heathens; that a man should have his father's wife.

2. And you are puffed up [about such a thing]!; and have not rather mourned, that he who has done this deed might be taken away from among you.

3. I, indeed—[although] absent in body, but present in spirit—have already judged, as though I were present, on he that has so done,

4. In the name of our lord Jesus Christ, you being gathered together, and my spirit, with the power of our lord Jesus;

5. Deliver such a person to Satan for the destruction of the flesh, so that his spirit may be saved in the day of our lord Jesus Christ. . . .

7.1. Now concerning the matter about which you wrote to me: It is good for a man not to touch a woman.

2. But out of fear of fornication, let every man have his own wife, and let every woman have her own husband.

3. Let the husband render the debt to his wife, and the wife also in like manner to the husband.

4. The wife does not have power over her own body, but the husband [does]. And in like manner the husband also does not have power over his own body, but the wife [does].

5. Defraud not one another, except, perhaps, by consent, for a time, that you may give yourselves to prayer; and return together again, lest Satan tempt you for your incontinency.

2 Corinthians

11.3. But I fear lest, as the serpent seduced Eve by his subtlety, your minds should be corrupted, and fall from the simplicity that is in Christ.

4. For if he that comes preaches [about] another Christ, whom we have not preached; or if you receive another spirit, whom you have not received; or another gospel which you have not received; you might well bear with him. . . .

13. For such false apostles are deceitful workmen, transforming themselves into the apostles of Christ.

14. And no wonder: for Satan himself transforms himself into an angel of light.

15. Therefore, it is no great thing if his ministers be transformed [into] the ministers of justice, whose end shall be according to their works.

1 Timothy

5.3. Honor widows, that are widows indeed.

4. But if any widow have children, or grandchildren, let her learn first to govern her own house, and to make a return of duty to her parents: for this is acceptable before God.

5. But she that is a widow indeed, and desolate, let her trust in God, and continue in supplications and prayers night and day.

6. For she that lives in pleasures, is dead while she is living. . . .

11. But the younger widows avoid. For when they have grown wanton in Christ, they will marry. . . .

14. I wish therefore that the younger should marry, bear children, be mistresses of families, give no occasion to the adversary to speak evil.

15. For some are already turned aside after Satan.

1 John

3 5.8. He that commits sin is of the devil: for the devil sinned from the beginning. For this reason, the son of God appeared, so that he might destroy the works of the devil.

9. Whosoever is born of God, does not commit sin: for his seed abides in him, and he cannot sin, because he is born of God.

10. In this the children of God are manifest, and the children of the devil. Whosoever is not just, is not of God, nor he that loveth not his brother.

Questions: Who did the devil kill? When? What new powers do these selections give the devil? Are they consistent with each other? What do these passages imply about the devil's relationship to humanity? What does it mean if Satan is able to transform himself into an angel of light?

11. FALL OF LUCIFER REVISITED

While the books of Isaiah and Ezekiel (doc. 4) prophesied the fall of the kings of Babylon and Tyre respectively, passages from the New Testament suggested that these falls actually signal something different.

The Gospel of Luke, from which the first selection comes, seems to have been written by a companion of Saint Paul who accompanied him on his mission.

The Book of Revelation, the last book of the New Testament and the source of the second selection presented here, is attributed to a certain "John." He was sometimes confused with the gospel writer of the same name during the Middle Ages. Written on the Greek island of Patmos where the author seems to have been in exile, the visions related in the text are full of complicated, interwoven historical references about the end of days. The author's profound hostility to Rome suggests that it was composed in the context of the persecution of Christians under Emperor Domitian (81–96 CE).

Luke: Greek, c. 70 CE.

Revelation: Greek, late first century.

Source: trans. Gregory Martin et al. from the Latin Vulgate, The Holy Bible (Douay-Rheims version) (Douay: The English College, 1609–10), rev. Richard Challoner (1749–52); rev.

Luke

[Christ has sent out 72 followers to preach his message.]

10.17. And the seventy-two returned with joy, saying, "Lord, the devils also are subject to us in your name."

18. And he [Christ] said to them, "I saw Satan like lightning falling from heaven.

19. Behold, I have given you power to tread upon serpents and scorpions, and upon all the power of the enemy: and nothing shall hurt you.

20. But yet rejoice not in this, that spirits are subject unto you; but rejoice in this, that your names are written in heaven."

Revelation

12.7. And there was a great battle in heaven. Michael and his angels fought with the dragon, and the dragon fought and his angels:

8. And they prevailed not, neither was their place found any more in heaven.

9. And that great dragon was cast out, that old serpent, who is called the devil and Satan, who seduces the whole world; and he was cast down to the earth, and his angels were thrown down with him.

10. And I heard a loud voice in heaven, saying, "Now is come salvation, and strength, and the kingdom of our God, and the power of his Christ: because the accuser of our brethren is cast forth, who accused them before our God day and night.

11. And they overcame him by the blood of the lamb, and by the word of the testimony, and they loved not their lives unto death.

12. Therefore rejoice, O heavens, and you who dwell there. Woe to the earth, and to the sea, because the devil is come down to you, having great wrath, knowing that he has but a short time."

13. And when the dragon saw that he was cast down to the earth, he persecuted the woman who brought forth the man child:

14. And there were given to the woman two wings of a great eagle so that she might fly into the desert to the place where she is nourished for a time and times, and half a time, from the face of the serpent.

15. And the serpent cast out of his mouth after the woman, water as it were a river so that he might cause her to be carried away by the river.

16. And the earth helped the woman, and the earth opened her mouth, and swallowed up the river, which the dragon cast out of his mouth.

17. And the dragon was angry against the woman, and went to make war with the rest of her seed, who keep the commandments of God, and have the testimony of Jesus Christ.

18. And he stood upon the sand of the sea.

13.1. And I saw a beast coming up out of the sea, having seven heads and ten horns, and upon his horns ten diadems [crowns], and upon [each of] his heads [was a] blasphemous name.

2. And the beast, which I saw, was like a leopard, and his feet were as the feet of a bear, and his mouth was [like] the mouth of a lion. And the dragon gave him his own strength and great power.

3. And I saw one of his heads as it were slain to death: and his death's wound was healed. And all the earth was in admiration of the beast.

4. And they adored the dragon, which gave power to the beast: and they adored the beast, saying: "Who is like the beast?" and "Who can fight against him?"

5. And there was given to him a mouth speaking great things, and blasphemies: and power was given to him to do [act for] two and forty months.

6. And he opened his mouth to [utter] blasphemies against God, to blaspheme his name, and his tabernacle, and those that dwell in heaven.

7. And [the power] was given to him to make war against the saints, and to overcome them. And power was given to him over every tribe, and people, and tongue, and nation.

8. And all that dwell on the earth—whose names are not written in the book of life of the lamb, which was slain from the beginning of the world—adored him.

9. If any man have an ear, let him hear.

10. He that shall lead into captivity, shall go into captivity: he that shall kill by the sword, must be killed by the sword. Here is the patience and the faith of the saints.

11. And I saw another beast coming up out of the earth, and he had two horns, like a lamb, and he spoke like a dragon.

12. And he executed all the power of the first beast in his sight; and he caused the earth, and all those that dwell upon it, to adore the first beast, whose deadly wound was healed.

13. And he did great signs, so that he made also fire to come down from heaven onto the earth in the sight of men.

14. And he seduced those that dwell on the earth, for the signs, which were given him to do in the sight of the beast, saying to those that dwell on the earth, that they should make an image of the beast, which had the wound by the sword, and [yet still] lived.

15. And it was given [to the second beast the power] to give life to the image of the beast, and [to make] the image of the beast speak; and to cause whosoever will not adore the image of the beast to be slain.

16. And he shall make all men—little and great, rich and poor, freemen and bondmen—have a character on their right hand, or on their foreheads.

17. So that no man might buy or sell unless he has that character, or the name of the beast, or the number of his name [on his hand or forehead].

18. Here is wisdom. He that has understanding, let him count the number of the beast. For it is the number of a man: and the number of him is six hundred sixty-six. . . .

20.1. And I saw an angel coming down from heaven, having the key to the bottomless pit, and a great chain in his hand.

2. And he laid hold on the dragon the old serpent, which is the devil and Satan, and bound him for a thousand years.

3. And he cast him into the bottomless pit, and shut him up, and set a seal upon him, so that he cannot seduce the nations anymore, till the thousand years be finished. And after that, he must be loosed [for] a little time.

4. And I saw seats; and they sat upon them; and judgment was given unto them; and the souls of those who were beheaded for the testimony of Jesus, and for the word of God, and who had not adored the beast or his image, or had received his character on their forehead or on their hands; and they lived and reigned with Christ a thousand years.

5. The rest of the dead lived not, till the thousand years were finished. This is the first resurrection.

6. Blessed and holy is he that has a part in the first resurrection. In these the second death has no power; but they shall be priests of God and of Christ, and they shall reign with him a thousand years.

7. And when the thousand years has finished, Satan shall be loosed out of his prison, and shall go forth, and seduce the nations, which are over the four quarters of the earth—Gog and Magog—and shall gather them together to battle, the number of whom is as the sand of the sea.

8. And they came upon the breadth of the earth, and encompassed the camp of the saints, and the beloved city.

9. And there came down fire from God out of heaven, and devoured them; and the devil, who seduced them, was cast into the pool of fire and brimstone, where both the beast

10. And the false prophet shall be tormented day and night for ever and ever.

11. And I saw a great white throne, and one sitting upon it, from whose face the earth and heaven fled away, and there was no place found for them.

12. And I saw the dead, great and small, standing in the presence of the throne, and the books were opened; and another book was opened, which is the book of life; and the dead were judged by those things which were written in the books, according to their works.

13. And the sea gave up the dead that were in it, and death and hell gave up their dead that were in them; and they were judged every one according to their works.

14. And hell and death were cast into the pool of fire. This is the second death.

15. And whosoever was not found written in the book of life, was cast into the pool of fire. . . .

22.16 "I, Jesus, have sent my angel, to testify to you these things in the churches. I am the root and stock of David, the bright and morning star."

Questions: When does the war in heaven in Revelation take place? Who is Lucifer and how is he linked to the war? How might the passage from Revelation change a reader's interpretation of these earlier prophets?

CHAPTER TWO

DEVELOPMENT OF A NARRATIVE

Figure 2.1 School of Albrecht Dürer, "Archangel Michael Fighting the Dragon" (1450–70). This anonymous woodcut depicts one of the final actions of the war in heaven described by the book of Revelation (doc. 11). Early printing could not easily accommodate works printed in more than two colors, so at some point, the owner of this illustration had it colored by hand.

TWO: DEVELOPMENT OF A NARRATIVE

The first three centuries of Christianity were fundamental to the development not just of its rites and rituals but also of its understanding of the Church's place and role in sacred history. During this period, the new faith spread out from its humble beginnings in Jerusalem to take root in cities and towns across North Africa and Asia Minor, and into Europe. Lacking any centralized authority and hindered by poor communications, these early Christian communities developed more or less independently, finding answers to the pressing concerns facing their congregations through their own interpretation of the sacred text. Many modern scholars describe this period as characterized by the development of multiple *Christianities*.

One of the many problems facing these communities was to reconcile their experience of evil with the scriptural notion of a perfectly created world (doc. 1), for this period saw them subjected to occasional bouts of persecution. Though most of these were regional in scope, some were severe and saw professors of the faith put to death in humiliating and brutal ways. To Christians, their God's fundamental truth was under siege. The challenge for many of the faithful, then, was to explain how the forces of darkness had usurped the world—as they clearly seemed to have done. In this context, discerning the role of the devil and his relationship to God on one hand, and to the forces of malevolence on the other, was a crucial and immediate concern.

But if the devil was the cause of their travails, it was equally important to understand his origins and place in sacred history. After all, Genesis seems nowhere to describe the creation of a malevolent principal or hint at a benevolent power somehow turning bad. Different communities grappled with these issues in different ways, interpreting the Old Testament to admit the possibility of a principal whose power might explain their experience and turning to extra-scriptural texts to supplement what they gleaned there. Chief among these were the *apocrypha* and *pseudepigrapha*. These were texts believed to have been divinely inspired in some way but left outside what would become the accepted canon of scripture. Nevertheless, some of these apocryphal books helped to "flesh out" the devil, often embellishing allusions or anecdotes from the biblical narrative or reconciling tensions between canonical texts. Far from being discounted by medieval audiences, these extra-scriptural accounts were widely read and commented upon throughout the medieval period. Consequently, different Christianities developed different devils.

These communities were developing their conceptions of the devil as the Church based in Rome was beginning to assert its authority over all Christians. To these Roman Christians, the varying ideas about the devil only clouded and confused what they increasingly argued was their definitive interpretation of scripture. This was a concern, for obscuring truth was a hallmark of the devil. Some of the views of the devil that emerged in this period came to be among Christianity's earliest heresies.

12. THE SUBVERSION OF HUMANITY

Genesis 6.1–5 (doc. 2) posed a significant problem for Jewish and later for Christian scholars. Coming immediately after a long genealogy of the patriarchs, the account of the so-called "sons of God" and giants is unembellished and sparse on detail. Yet it presaged the story of Noah and the flood, and its location in the narrative implied that these events were formative in convincing God that the world should be destroyed. The Book of Enoch, *from which this reading comes, purports to be a series of revelations that explain in more detail why creation went so wrong.*

Attributed to an early patriarch named Enoch (Gen. 5.21–24), the work is a composite of various traditions from different periods. Because of the way in which it came together, there is still much debate on matters as fundamental as the text's original language; some scholars favor Hebrew, others Aramaic. Although fragments of the text in both these languages—along with Greek and Latin—have been discovered, the most complete version is in Ethiopic. The text seems to have been widely known in both Jewish and early Christian circles. The author of the epistle of Jude in the New Testament alludes to it explicitly.

Aramaic or Hebrew, 170 BCE (for the following section).

Source: trans. H.R. Charles, *Book of Enoch*, from The Apocrypha and Pseudepigrapha of the Old Testament, vol. 2 (Oxford: The Clarendon Press, 1913), pp. 191–94, 198; rev.

6.1. And it came to pass, when the children of men had multiplied, that in those days were born

2. beautiful and comely daughters to them. And the angels, the children of the heaven, saw and lusted after them, and said to one another, "Come, let us choose wives from among the children of men

3. and beget children." And Semjaza, who was their leader, said to them: "I fear you will not

4. indeed agree to do this deed, and I alone shall have to pay the penalty for this great sin." And they all answered him and said: "Let us all swear an oath, and all bind ourselves by mutual imprecations

5. not to abandon this plan but to do this thing." Then they all swore together and bound themselves

6. by mutual imprecations upon it. And they were in all two hundred; who descended in the days of Jared to the summit of Mount Hermon, and they called it Mount Hermon, because they had sworn

7. and bound themselves by mutual imprecations upon it. And these are the names of their leaders: Samlazaz, their leader, Araklba, Rameel, Kokablel, Tamlel, Ramlel, Danel, Ezeqeel, Baraqijal,

8. Asael, Armaros, Batarel, Ananel, Zaqiel, Samsapeel, Satarel, Turel, Jomjael, Sariel. These are their chiefs of tens.

7.1. And together, all the others with them took wives for themselves, and each chose for himself one woman, and they began to go unto them, and to defile themselves with them, and they taught them charms

2. and enchantments, and the cutting of roots, and made them acquainted with plants. And they

3. became pregnant, and they bore great giants, whose height was three thousand ells [a measure traditionally the length of an arm]. These giants consumed

4. all the acquisitions of men. And when men could no longer sustain them, the giants turned against

5. them and devoured mankind. And they began to sin against birds, and beasts, and reptiles, and

6. fish, and to devour one another's flesh, and drink the blood. Then the earth laid an accusation against the lawless ones. . . .

10.1. Then the most high, the holy and great one spoke, and sent Uriel to the son of Lamech,

2. saying to him: "Go to Noah and tell him in my name 'Hide yourself!' and reveal to him the end that is approaching, that the whole earth will be destroyed, and a deluge is about to come

3. upon the whole earth, and will destroy all that is on it. And now instruct him that he may escape

4. and his seed may be preserved for all the generations of the world." And again the lord spoke, saying to Raphael, "Bind Azazel hand and foot, and cast him into the darkness. Make an opening

5. in the desert, which is in Dudael, and cast him into it. And place upon him rough and jagged rocks, and cover him with darkness, and let him abide there forever, and cover his face so that he may not see light.

6. And on the day of the great judgment he shall be cast into the fire.

7. And heal the earth which the angels have corrupted, and proclaim the healing of the earth, that they may heal the plague, and that all the children of men may not perish through all the secret things that the

8. Watchers have disclosed and have taught their sons. And the whole earth has been corrupted

9. through the works that were taught by Azazel. To him ascribe all sin." And to Gabriel the lord said, "Proceed against the bastards and the reprobates, and against the children of fornication. Destroy [the children of fornication and expel] the children of the Watchers from among men. Send them one against the other so that they may destroy each other in

10. battle, for length of days they have not. And their fathers will make requests of you on their behalf, for they hope to live an eternal life, and

11. that each one of them will live five hundred years, but they shall not be granted." And the lord said to Michael: "Go, bind Semjaza and his associates who have fornicated with women and have defiled themselves. . . .

[Coming to appreciate their plight, the fallen Watchers plead with Enoch to intercede with God on their behalf as God told Gabriel he would. Enoch then falls asleep during which time he has a vision of God on his throne, surrounded by flames. God speaks to him.]

15.1. And he said to me, and I heard his voice: "Fear not, Enoch, you righteous

2. man and scribe of righteousness. Approach here and hear my voice. And go and say to the Watchers of heaven, who have sent you to intercede for them, 'You should intercede for men, and not have men intercede

3. for you. Why have you left the high, holy, and eternal heaven, and lain with women, and defiled yourselves with the daughters of men and taken wives for yourselves, and behaving like the children

4. of earth, begetting giant sons? And though you were holy and spiritual, living eternal life, you have defiled yourselves with the blood of women, and have begotten children with the blood of flesh. And, like the children of men, you have lusted after flesh and blood like those who die

5. and perish also do. That is why I gave them wives, so that they might impregnate them, and beget

6. children by them, so that nothing might be wanting to them on earth. But you were formerly

7. spiritual, living the eternal life, and immortal for all generations of the world. That is why I have not appointed wives for you. For the spiritual ones of the heaven, their dwelling is in heaven.

8. And now, the giants, who are produced from [the union of] the spirits and flesh, shall be called evil spirits upon

9. the earth, and their dwelling shall be on the earth. Evil spirits have proceeded from their bodies.

10. They shall be evil spirits on earth, and evil spirits shall they be called because in their beginning and primal origin they are born from men and from the holy Watchers.

11. As for the spirits of heaven, heaven shall be their dwelling, but as for the spirits of the earth which were born upon the earth, the earth shall be their dwelling. And the spirits of the giants afflict, oppress, destroy, attack, do battle, and work destruction on the earth, and cause trouble. They take no food, but nevertheless

12. hunger and thirst, and cause offences. And these spirits shall rise up against the children of men and against the women, because they have proceeded from them.

16.1. "From the days of the slaughter and destruction and death of the giants, from the souls of whose flesh the spirits, having gone forth, shall destroy without incurring judgment, thus shall they destroy until the day of the consummation, the great judgment in which the age shall be

2. consummated, upon the Watchers and the godless, yea, shall be wholly consummated." And now as to the Watchers who have sent you to intercede for them, who had been previously in heaven, (say

3. to them): 'You have been in heaven, but all the mysteries had not yet been revealed to you, and you knew worthless ones, and these in the hardness of your hearts you have made known to the women, and through these mysteries women and men work much evil on earth.'

4. Say to them therefore: 'You have no peace.'"

Questions: When are these events supposed to have taken place? What have the Watchers done that is so offensive? Does this account of the giants supplement Genesis 6.1–4 (doc. 2)? How and when is the angel Azazel to be punished? What is the origin of evil spirits?

13. *MASTÊMÂ* THE DEVIL?

The Book of Jubilees *is an apocryphal Jewish text that expands upon the narrative of Genesis and Exodus, reorganizing it according to cycles of 49 years—a jubilee. The text purports to be an account of a series of revelations about the history of creation given directly by God to Moses while he was on Mount Sinai and then recorded by an angel. Likely written down in the last quarter of the second century BCE by an author familiar with the* Book of Enoch *(doc. 12), the text seems to have enjoyed some currency within Judaism, for fragments from at least twelve different copies of the text were found among the Dead Sea scrolls. The text also seems to have been well known to early Christians.*

The name Mastêmâ *might be translated as* enmity. *The abbreviation* A.M. *used in the text denotes* Anno mundi—*the year as counted from creation.*

Hebrew, between c. 140 and 104 BCE.

Source: trans. H.R. Charles, *Book of Jubilees*, from The Apocrypha and Pseudepigrapha of the Old Testament, vol. 2 (Oxford: The Clarendon Press, 1913), pp. 18–20, 27–28; rev.

4.15. . . . in his days the angels of the lord descended on the earth, those who are named the Watchers, that they should instruct the children of men, and that they should do judgment and uprightness on the earth.

16. And in the eleventh jubilee [512–518 A.M.] Jared took a wife for himself, and her name was Baraka, the daughter of Râsûjâl, a daughter of his father's brother, in the fourth week of this jubilee [522 A.M.], and she bare him a son in the fifth week, in the fourth year of the jubilee, and he called his name Enoch.

17. And he was the first among men that were born on earth who learned writing and knowledge and wisdom, and who wrote down the signs of heaven according to the order of their months in a book, so that men might know the seasons of the years according to the order of their separate months.

21. And he [Enoch] was moreover with the angels of God these six jubilees of years, and they showed him everything which is on earth and in the heavens, the rule of the sun, and he wrote down everything.

22. And he testified to the Watchers who had sinned with the daughters of men; for these had begun to unite themselves, so as to be defiled, with the daughters of men, and Enoch testified against [them] all.

5.1. And it came to pass when the children of men began to multiply on the face of the earth and daughters were born to them, that the angels of God saw them on a certain year of this jubilee, that they were beautiful to look upon; and they took wives for themselves from all whom they chose, and they had sons and they were giants.

2. And lawlessness increased on the earth and all flesh corrupted its way, alike men and cattle and beasts and birds and everything that walks on the earth—all of them corrupted their ways and their orders, and they began to devour each other, and lawlessness increased on the earth and every imagination of the thoughts of all men [was] thus continually evil.

3. And God looked upon the earth, and saw that it was corrupt, and that all flesh had corrupted its orders, and that everything that was on the earth had wrought all manner of evil before his eyes.

4. And he said that he would destroy man and all flesh on the face of the earth which he had created.

5. But Noah found grace before the eyes of the lord.

6. And against the angels whom he had sent upon the earth, he [God] was exceedingly angry, and he gave a commandment to root them out from all their dominion, and he told us to bind them in the depths of the earth, and behold they are bound in the midst of them, and are [kept] separate.

7. And against their sons went forth a command from before his face that they should be smitten with the sword, and be removed from under heaven.

8. And he said "My spirit shall not always abide on man; for they also are flesh and their days shall be one hundred and twenty years."

9. And he sent his sword into their midst so that each person should slay his neighbor, and they began to slay each other till they all fell by the sword and were destroyed from the earth.

10. And their fathers were witnesses [of their destruction], and after this they were bound in the depths of the earth forever, until the day of the great condemnation, when judgment is executed on all those who have corrupted their ways and their works before the lord.

11. And he destroyed all from their places, and there not one of them was left whom he judged not according to all their wickedness.

12. And he made for all his works a new and righteous nature, so that they should not sin in their whole nature forever, but should be all righteous each in his kind always.

13. And the judgment of all is ordained and written on the heavenly tablets in righteousness—even [the judgment of] all who depart from the path which is ordained for them to walk in; and if they walk not on this path, judgment is written down for every creature and for every kind.

14. And there is nothing in heaven or on earth, or in light or in darkness, or in Sheol [doc. 50] or in the depth, or in the place of darkness [which is not judged]; and all their judgments are ordained and written and engraved. . . .

19. And as for all those who corrupted their ways and their thoughts before the flood, no man's person was accepted except that of Noah alone; for his person was accepted on behalf of his sons, whom [God] saved from the waters of the flood on his account; for his heart was righteous in all his ways, as it was commanded regarding him, and he had not departed from anything that was ordained for him.

20. And the lord said that he would destroy everything which was on the earth, both men and cattle, and

21. beasts, and fowls of the air, and that which move upon the earth. And he commanded Noah to make him an ark, so that he might save himself from the waters of the flood. . . .

10.1. And in the third week of this jubilee the unclean demons began to lead astray the children of the sons of Noah, and to make them err and to destroy them.

2. And the sons of Noah came to Noah their father, and they told him about the demons which were leading astray, blinding and slaying his sons' sons.

3. And he prayed before the lord his God, and said . . .

4. "bless me and my sons so that we may increase and multiply and replenish the earth.

5. And you know how your Watchers, the fathers of these spirits, acted in my day: and as for these spirits which are living, imprison them and hold them fast in the place of condemnation, and let them not bring destruction to the sons of your servant, my God; for these are malignant, and created in order to destroy.

6. And let them not rule over the spirits of the living; for you alone can exercise dominion over them. And let them not have power over the sons of the righteous from this time forth and for ever more."

7. And the lord our God bade us to bind all.

8. And the chief of the spirits, Mastêmâ, came and said: "Lord, creator, let some of them remain before me, and let them obey my voice, and do all that I shall say to them; for if some of them are not left to me, I shall not be able to execute the power of my will on the sons of men; for they are meant for corruption and leading astray before my judgment, for the wickedness of the sons of men is great."

9. And he said: "Let the tenth part of them remain before him, and let nine parts descend into the place of condemnation." . . .

10. And one of us he commanded that we should teach Noah all their medicines; for he knew that they would not walk in uprightness, nor strive in righteousness.

11. And we did according to all his words: all the malignant evil ones we bound in the place of condemnation and a tenth part of them we left so that they might be subject to Satan on the earth.

12. And we explained to Noah all the medicines of their diseases, together with their seductions, how he might heal them with herbs of the earth.

13. And Noah wrote down all things in a book as we instructed him concerning every kind of medicine. Thus the evil spirits were precluded from [hurting] the sons of Noah. . . .

Questions: When are these events supposed to have taken place? What is the cause of the fall of angels? What does God want done with these angels? According to the bargain struck between God and Mastêmâ, where do evil spirits end up?

14. INTERROGATING GENESIS

Philo of Alexandria (c. 25 BCE–50 CE)—also sometimes known as Philo Judaeus—was a Hellenized Jew and one of the foremost theological writers of his day. He was one of the founders and leading exponents of what would become known as the Alexandrian school of biblical interpretation, which emphasized the allegorical reading of scripture and other sacred texts. In this, his primary goal was to harmonize the revealed truths of the Torah with Greek philosophy. While Philo's approach did not flourish within Judaism, it came to be embraced by Roman Christians and accepted as an important way to read and interpret the Bible.

Moses is traditionally credited as being the author of Genesis.

Greek, mid-first century CE.

Source: trans. Charles Yonge, from Philo Judaeus, *On the Giants*, from *The Works of Philo Judaeus: The Contemporary of Josephus*, vol. 1 (London, 1854), pp. 331–32; *Questions and Solutions to those Questions which Arise in Genesis*, vol. 4 (London, 1855), pp. 300–303, 307–8; rev.

Questions and Solutions to Those Questions which Arise in Genesis

Why does Moses say that the serpent was more cunning than all the beasts of the field?

It is probably true that the serpent is more cunning than any other beast. But it seems to me that the reason why he is described in these terms here is because of the natural propensity of humanity to vice, of which he is the symbol. And by vice, I mean physical pleasure, for those who are devoted to pleasure are more cunning, and invent stratagems and means by which to indulge their passions. . . . But it seems to me that since that animal, so superior in wisdom, was about to seduce man, it is not the whole species that is being described as exceedingly wise here—rather, it is only that single serpent. . . .

TWO: DEVELOPMENT OF A NARRATIVE

Why did the serpent accost the woman, and not the man?

The serpent, having formed his estimate of virtue, devised a treacherous stratagem against them, in order to cause them to become mortal. But the woman was more accustomed to be deceived than the man. For his judgment like his body are of masculine in nature, and capable of disentangling the notion of seduction; but the mind of the woman is more effeminate, so that through her softness she yields easily and is easily caught by the persuasions of falsehood, which imitate the resemblance of truth. . . .

Why the serpent tells the woman lies, saying, "God has said, you shall not eat of every tree in the Paradise," when, on the contrary, what God really said was, "You shall eat of every tree in the Paradise, except one"?

It is the custom for parties in an argument to speak falsely in an artful manner, in order to create ignorance of the real facts, as was done in this case, as the man and woman had been commanded to eat of all the trees but one. But this insidious prompter of wickedness intervening, says that the order which they had received the commandment was that they should not eat of them all. He brought forward an ambiguous statement as a slippery stumbling-block to cause the soul to trip. . . .

What is the meaning of the expression, "You shall be as gods, knowing good and evil"?

How was it that the serpent found the plural word "gods," when there is only one true God, and when this is the first time that he names him? But perhaps this arises from there being in him a certain prescient wisdom, by which he declared the notion of the multitude of gods which would be the case among men at a future time. Perhaps the sacred history relates this point correctly here to show that this idea [polytheism] was first advanced not by any rational being, nor by any creature of a higher order—but that it finds its origin with the most virulent and vile of beasts and serpents, since other similar creatures lie hidden under the ground, and their lurking places are the holes and fissures of the earth. Equally, it is an unambiguous sign of being endowed with reason to consider God as essentially one being whereas it is the sign of a beast to imagine that there are many gods, and to a creature utterly devoid of reason to create a god who has no existence at all. . . .

Why did the woman touch the tree and eat its fruit first and the man received it from her afterwards?

First of all, according their own literal meaning, the words used assert that it was appropriate that immortality and every good thing should be represented as under the power of the man, while death and every evil under that of the woman. Understood symbolically, though, the woman is a reference to sense and the man to intellect. The external senses necessarily touch on those things that are perceptible to them, but they then transmit these impressions to the mind. For the external senses are influenced by the objects which are presented to them, and the intellect by the external senses.

Why does God curse the serpent first, then the woman, and the man last of all?

The reason is that the order of the verses follows the order in which the offences were committed. The first offence was the deceit practiced by the serpent; the second was the sin of the woman which was caused by him when she abandoned herself to his seduction; the third thing was the guilt of the man in yielding to the woman's inclination rather than to the commandment of God. But this order is very admirable, for it contains within itself a perfect allegory, inasmuch as the serpent is the emblem of desire—as has been proven—the woman of the external senses, and the man a symbol of intellect. Therefore, desire becomes the infamous source of sin. It first deceives the external senses, and then the external senses captivate the mind.

On Giants

"And when the angels of God saw the daughters of men that they were beautiful, they took unto themselves wives of all of them whom they chose" [see doc. 2].

Those beings, which many philosophers refer to as demons, Moses usually calls angels; they are souls hovering in the air. And let no one suppose that this statement is a fable, since it is necessarily true that the universe must be filled with living things in all its parts. This is because every one of its primary and elementary places contains its appropriate animals, and these animals are consistent with each place's nature: the earth contains terrestrial animals; the sea and the rivers contain aquatic animals; the fire contains animals born from fire (however, it is said that these sorts of creatures are found primarily in Macedonia); heaven contains the stars. These are also entire souls which pervade the universe, being unadulterated and divine, inasmuch as they move in circles—which is the kind of motion most similar to the human mind, for every one of them is the parent mind.

It is therefore necessary that the air should also be filled with living creatures. These beings are invisible to us, in much the same way that the air itself is not visible to mortal sight. Nevertheless, because our sight is incapable of perceiving the forms of souls, it does not follow that there are no souls in the air. Instead, it must follow that these souls should be comprehended by the mind—in this way, souls are contemplated by something that is similar to them. What, therefore, ought we to say? . . .

Therefore, if you consider that souls, demons, and angels are things that differ in name but are identical in reality, then you will be able to discard that heavy burden: superstition. But, since people talk in general about "good" and "evil" demons and similarly about "good" and "evil" souls, so they also talk about angels—regarding some as worthy of their good name, calling them ambassadors of humanity to God and of God to humanity, because of this blameless and most excellent duty, and others as unholy and unworthy of any regard. And the expression used by the writer of the Psalm in the following verse attests to the truth of my assertion, for he says, "He sent upon them the fury of his wrath, anger, and rage, and affliction, and he sent evil among them" [Ps. 77.49]. These are the wicked who, assuming the name of angels, not being acquainted with the daughters of right reason—that is, with the sciences and the virtues—but which pursue the mortal descendants of mortal men—that is, the pleasures—which cannot confer genuine beauty. This is because real beauty is perceived by the intellect alone. The pleasures can only confer a bastard sort of elegance of form, one which beguiles the outward sense. And they do not take all the daughters of humankind in marriage; instead, some angels have taken some of that innumerable company to be their wives: some choosing them by sight, and others by the ear, others again being influenced by the sense of taste, or by the belly. Some have even been influenced by the pleasures below the belly. Many angels have also laid hold of wives whose dwelling place is established at a great distance, initiating various desires among one another. This is because the choices of all the various pleasures are necessarily various, that is, different pleasures are established in different places. . . .

Questions: How does Philo interpret the story of the serpent in paradise? Who are the giants and where did they come from? Why does the presence of giants cause God to destroy the world? How does Philo's cosmology work?

15. EVE'S PERSPECTIVE OF HUMANITY'S FALL

Although extant only in Greek, the Apocalypse of Moses, *from which the selection below is taken, is likely derived from a lost Hebrew original that also seems to have been the source for a related Latin text known as the* Life of Adam and Eve. *The central narrative of the* Apocalypse *begins with Adam close to death. Surrounded by his thirty sons and thirty daughters, Adam rebukes his wife for incurring the wrath of God and for bringing death to humanity. This serves as a cue for Eve to describe the circumstances of the fall from her perspective, fleshing out the narrative of Genesis 3 (doc. 1) in important ways. Both the* Apocalypse *and the* Life *were probably in existence by the early fifth century, although it is possible that the lost original was composed as early as 100 BCE.*
    Hebrew [?], before c. 400 CE.

Source: trans. H.R. Charles, *Apocalypse of Moses*, from *The Apocrypha and Pseudepigrapha of the Old Testament*, vol. 2 (Oxford: The Clarendon Press, 1913), pp. 145–48; rev.

15.1. Then Eve said to them: "Listen, all my children and children's children and I will tell you

2. how the enemy deceived us. It happened that we were guarding paradise, each of us a portion

3. allotted to us by God. Now I guarded the west and the south as my area. But the devil went to Adam's area, where all the male creatures were, for God divided the creatures—all the males he gave to your father and all the females he gave to me.

16.1. And the devil spoke to the serpent saying, "Rise up, come to me and I will tell you something

2. that will benefit you." And the serpent arose and came to him. And the devil said to him,

3. "I hear that you are wiser than all the other beasts, so I have come to counsel you. Why do you eat Adam's weeds and not foods of paradise? Rise up, and we will cause him to be cast out of paradise, just

4. as we were cast out through him." The serpent said to him, "I fear that the lord will be angry with

5. me." The devil said to him, "Fear not. Just be my vessel and I will speak words that will deceive him through your mouth."

17.1. And immediately he hung himself from the wall of paradise, and when the angels ascended to

2. worship God, then Satan appeared in the form of an angel and sang hymns like the angels. And I bent over the wall and saw him, like an angel. But he said to me, "Are you Eve?" And I said

3. to him, "I am." "What are you doing in paradise?" And I said to him, "God set us to guard and

4. to eat of it." The devil answered through the mouth of the serpent, "You do well but you do not eat

5. from every plant." And I said, "Yea, we eat from all of them except for one which is in the midst of paradise. Concerning that one, God charged us not to eat from it, for he said to us, on the day on which you eat from it, you shall die the death.

18.1. Then the serpent said to me, "May God live! But I am grieved on your account, for I would not have you remain ignorant. But arise. Come here, listen to me and eat—and see the value of that tree."

2–3. But I said to him, "I fear that God will be angry with me as he said to us." And he said to me, "Fear not, for as soon as you eat from it, you too shall be as God, in that you will know good and evil.

4. But God understood this—that you would be like him—so he envied you and said, You shall not eat from

5–6. it. But if you come to the plant, you will see its great glory." Yet I feared to take the fruit. And he said to me, "Come here, and I will give it to you. Follow me."

19.1. And I opened the way for him and he walked a little way, then turned and said to me, "I have changed my

2. mind. I will not let you eat until you swear to me to give [the fruit] to your husband also." And I said, "What sort of oath shall I swear to you? Yet what I know, I say to you, By the throne of the

TWO: DEVELOPMENT OF A NARRATIVE

3. master, and by the cherubim and the tree of life, I will also give [the fruit] to my husband to eat." And when he had received the oath from me, he went and poured upon the fruit the poison of his wickedness, which is lust—the root and beginning of every sin. And he bent the branch on the earth, and I took of the fruit and I ate.

20.1. And in that very hour my eyes were opened, and immediately I knew that I was naked of the righteousness

2. with which I had been clothed, and I wept and said to him, "Why have you

3. done this to me, for you have deprived me of the glory with which I was clothed?" But I wept also about the oath which I had sworn. But he descended from the tree and vanished.

4. And in my nakedness, I began to seek leaves in my area [of paradise] to hide my shame, but I found none, for, as soon as I had eaten, the leaves showered down from all of the trees in my area, except for the fig tree.

5. So I took leaves from that and made myself a girdle; the leaves were from the very same plant from which I had eaten.

21.1. And I cried out in that very hour, "Adam, Adam, where are you? Rise up, come to me and

2. I will show you a great secret." But when your father came, I spoke words of transgression to him, those

3. which brought us down from our great glory. For when he came, I opened my mouth and the devil was speaking, and I began to exhort him and said, "Come here, my lord Adam. Listen to me and eat the fruit of the tree which God told us not to eat, and you shall be as

4. a God." And your father answered and said, "I fear that God will be angry with me." And I said to

5. him, "Fear not, for as soon as you have eaten you will know good and evil." And speedily I persuaded him, and he ate. Straight away, his eyes were opened and he too knew his nakedness.

6. And he said to me, "O wicked woman! What have I done to you that you have deprived me of the glory of God?"

22.1. And in that same hour, we heard the archangel Michael blowing with his trumpet and calling to

2. the angels, saying, "Thus says the lord: Come with me to Paradise and hear the judgment with which I shall judge Adam."

3. And when God appeared in paradise, mounted on the chariot of his cherubim with the angels proceeding before him and singing hymns of praises, all the plants of paradise, both in your father's area

4. and in mine, broke out into flowers. And the throne of God was fixed where the tree of life was.

23.1. And God called Adam saying, "Adam, where are you? Can the house be hidden from the presence

2. of its builder?" Then your father answered, "We hide not because we do not want to be found by you, lord. Rather, I was afraid, because I am naked, and I was ashamed before your might,

3. my master." God said to him, "Who showed you that you are naked, unless you have forsaken my

4. commandment, which I delivered to you to keep." Then Adam called to mind the word which I spoke to him, saying, "I will make you secure before God." And he turned and said to me, "Why have you done this?" And I said, "The serpent deceived me." . . .

[God metes out the punishments described in Genesis 3.]

27.1–2. Thus God spoke and told the angels to have us cast out of paradise, and as we were being driven out amid our loud lamentations, your father Adam begged the angels and said, "Leave me a little time so that I may entreat the lord that he have compassion on me and pity me, for I only

3[–4]. have sinned." And they left off driving him and Adam cried aloud and wept saying, "Pardon me, O lord, for my deed." Then the lord said to the angels, "Why have you ceased driving Adam out from paradise? Why do you not cast him out? Is it I who have done wrong? Or is my judgment

5. badly judged?" Then the angels fell down on the ground and worshipped the lord saying, "You are just, O lord, and you give righteous judgment."

28.1. But the lord turned to Adam and said, "From this point forwards, I will not suffer you to be in paradise . . . but you have the war which the adversary has put into you, yet when you have gone out of paradise, if you should keep yourself from all evil, as one about to die, when again the Resurrection comes to pass, I will raise you up and then the tree of life shall be given to you."

Questions: What is the condition of paradise before the devil attempts to seduce Adam? Is the devil the inspirer or the alias of the serpent? How and in what form does the devil tempt Eve? Why does the devil insist upon an oath from Eve? Is God omnipotent?

16. GNOSTIC DUALISM

By the second century, Christianity comprised a multitude of different sects, each of which offered its own interpretation of the faith—various Christianities. One of the most important of these was gnosticism. The term gnostic comes from the Greek "gnosis," meaning "knowledge," for all gnostic sects believed to some degree that they had access to a special form of secret, revealed knowledge of God which served as the key to salvation. There was no single gnostic movement; different teachers offered different interpretations. Nevertheless, most gnostics understood creation as comprising a flawed and evil material world intermixed with a wholly good spiritual world. In the hands of some gnostic thinkers, this led to a form of dualism—a belief in two morally juxtaposed cosmic principles whose struggle played out across the breadth of creation; for them, this explains the presence of good and evil in the world.

Most of what is known of Saturninus comes from the writings of contemporary opponents. Chief among these was Irenaeus (c. 130–c. 202), bishop of Lyon at the end of the second century, who wrote Against Heresies. *Originally written in Greek but surviving only in complete form in a late-fourth-century Latin translation, the work is a detailed study that classified and countered what he saw to be the spread of unorthodox belief.*

Greek, c. 175–189.

Source: trans. Alexander Roberts and James Donaldson, from Irenaeus, *Against Heresies*, from *Ante-Nicene Fathers*, vol. 1 (Buffalo, NY: Christian Literature Publishing Co., 1885), pp. 38–39, rev.

Saturninus (who was from that Antioch which is near Daphne) and Basilides laid hold of some favorable opportunities, and promulgated different systems of doctrine—the one in Syria, the other in Alexandria. Saturninus . . . taught one father unknown to all, who made angels, archangels, powers, and potentates. The world and everything in it were made by a certain company of seven angels. Man, too, was a creation of angels, a shining image bursting forth below from the presence of the supreme power; and when the angels could not keep hold of this, he says, because it immediately darted upwards again, they exhorted each other, saying, "Let us make man after our image and likeness" [Gen. 1.26]. He was formed accordingly; however, he was unable to stand erect because the angels could not convey to him that power, so instead he wriggled like a worm. Then the power above took pity upon him as he was made in his likeness, and sent forth a spark of life, which gave man an erect posture, compacted his joints, and made him live. . . .

Saturninus has also laid it down as a truth that the savior was without birth, without body, and without figure, and only appeared in the form of a visible man. He maintained that the God of the Jews was one of the angels; and, on this account, because all the powers wished to annihilate his father, Christ came to destroy the God of the Jews, and to save those that believe in him—that is, those who possess the spark of his life. This heretic [Saturninus] was the first to affirm that two kinds of men were formed by the angels—the one wicked, and the other good. And since the demons help the wicked, the savior came for the destruction of the wicked men and of the demons, and for the salvation of the good. They declare also, that marriage and generation are from Satan [see also 1 Tim. 4.3]. Many of those, too, who belong to his school, abstain from animal food, and draw away many through this kind of feigned temperance. Moreover, they hold that some of the prophecies were uttered by those angels who made the world, and some by Satan of whom Saturninus represents as being an angel himself, the enemy of the creators of the world, and especially of the God of the Jews.

Questions: *Who made the world for Saturninus? What does this imply for the moral economy of the universe? What is the relationship between God, the "God of the Jews," the angels, and Satan? What is the function of these cosmic agents?*

17. DID GOD CREATE EVIL?

According to tradition, Tertullian (c. 160–225) was the son of a Roman centurion, although that is disputed. He was raised in the North African city of Carthage. There he received an excellent education, particularly in rhetoric, which may have led him to practice law as a young man. While in Rome around 197, he converted to Christianity. Tertullian was deeply engaged in the theological controversies of the day and produced an extensive corpus of apologetic, theological, and polemical works in Latin defending the faith and attacking its rivals. The following document comes from a treatise written against the dualist heretic Marcion (d. c. 160). According to Tertullian, Marcion seized upon Isaiah 45.7 (doc. 5) to argue that the God of the Old Testament and the God of the New Testament were different and contrary principles.

Latin, c. 208.

Source: trans. Richard Raiswell and David R. Winter, from Tertullian, *Adversus Marcionem*, ed. Ernest Evans (Oxford: Clarendon, 1972), pp. 114–18.

But if you transfer the blame for evil from man to the devil because he the instigator of sin then you [also] direct blame towards the creator—[that is] he who made spiritual angels [Ps. 103.4]—as the author of the devil. It follows therefore, that what was made by God ... must be the responsibility of he who made him. But [this cannot be the case, for] what was not made by God—that is, the devil as the accuser. He must have made himself by means of the false statement he made about God: first, that God had forbidden them [Adam and Eve] from eating from every tree and then, that they would not die if they did eat from it; and third, that God would envy their divinity [if they ate the tree's fruit].

Where, therefore, did this malice of lying and deceit toward men, and slander toward God originate? Not from God who created the angel [who would become the devil] good in the manner of his good works. Indeed, before he became the devil, this angel stood out as the wisest of all creatures—and wisdom is not evil. But if you turn to Ezekiel's prophecy [doc. 4], you will clearly see that this angel was made good in creation but became corrupt through choice. Through the figure of the prince of Tyre, it is said about the devil, "And the word of the lord came to me, saying, 'son of man, take up a lamentation about the prince of Tyre, and say [to him], the lord says this, you are the repudiation of the likeness,'" which is to say, you have repudiated the integrity of the image and likeness [in which you were made]. "You were born in the delights of the paradise of your God with a crown of beauty" (meaning as the highest of the angels, an archangel, the wisest of them all). It was there—in that paradise—that God made the angels in the form of the shape of animals during the second creation [day?]. "You were clothed in precious stone—the sardius, topaz, diamond, carbuncle, sapphire, jasper, tourmaline, agate, amethyst, chrysolite, beryl, onyx, and you filled your storehouses and treasure chambers with gold. From the day you were created, I placed you with a cherub on the holy mountain of God. You were in the mist of stones of fire. You were blameless in your days from the day of your creation up until your iniquities were discovered. You have filled your storehouse with the abundance of your merchandise, and you have sinned, etc."—all of which, it is clear, properly pertains to the humiliation of an angel not to that of the prince [of Tyre] because no human being was born in paradise, not even Adam, who was, rather, translated there. Nor was any person placed with a cherub on God's holy mountain, that is, in the heights of heaven, [the place] from which the lord testifies that Satan fell. Nor has any person been held among the fiery stones, among the glinting rays of the burning stars from which Satan was cast down like lightning [doc. 11].

Rather, it is the author of sin who is personified in the form of this sinful man—someone originally faultless from the day of his creation, created by God for goodness as [is fitting for] a good creator of faultless creatures, and adorned with every angelic glory, placed in the presence of God—good before the good—but who was later moved to evil on his own accord. "From which time," he says, "your wounds were evident" attributing to him those wounds by which he wounded man and broke him from his allegiance to God. From the moment he [the angel] sinned, he sowed sin, and from then he grew the "abundance of his merchandise"—that is, his wickedness—and the value of his sins, for he, although a spirit, was created with freewill no less [than the man had been], for God has ordained nothing close to him which does not have such freedom.

Nevertheless, by predestining him to damnation, God testified that the angel had departed from the form of his creation through the angel's freely conceived delight in wickedness. And by measuring out a term for the angel's operations, God acted in accordance with the reason of his own goodness, deferring the destruction of the devil as he has deferred the restitution of man. He has allotted a space [of time] for a conflict so that man might destroy the enemy by means of that same freedom of will which cut him down, proving that it was man's sin—not God's—so that he might regain his salvation appropriately by means of a victory, and the devil might be punished more bitterly by him who he had previously defeated. Moreover, God might be seen to be so much more good, waiting for a now more glorious man to return from this life to paradise, with permission to pluck from the tree of life.

Questions: How has Tertullian interpreted Ezekiel 28 (doc. 4)? When does Tertullian see the devil turning evil? Does he give any sense of Satan's motivation? How does this passage deal with the charge that God is the source of evil?

18. A WORLDLY PRINCE AS THE DEVIL?

Origen (c. 185–254) was likely born in Alexandria to Christian parents. According to a later authority, Origen received a thorough education in both the Greek philosophical tradition and Christian scripture. Having narrowly escaped martyrdom, he was invited by the bishop of Alexandria to train catechumens (recent converts), teaching them Christian doctrine in ways that would be readily understood. It was at this time that he became increasingly ascetic, keeping fasts and vigils, even castrating himself, following Christ's pronouncement in Matthew 19.12 that "there are eunuchs, who have made themselves eunuchs for the kingdom of heaven. He that can take, let him take it." Origen became a prolific biblical scholar, frequently reading the sacred page allegorically in search of higher meanings. His most important work, On First Principles, *from which the selection below is taken, is a wide-ranging theological text written in response to what he saw as the danger of heresy. In it, he investigated the nature of God and heavenly beings.*

Greek, 220–231 CE.

Source: trans. Frederick Crombie, from Origen, *De principiis* in Ante-Nicene Fathers, vol. 4 (Buffalo, NY: Christian Literature Publishing Co., 1885), pp. 240, 256–59, 265, 346; rev.

With respect to the devil and his angels, and the opposing influences, the teaching of the Church has laid down that these beings indeed exist; but what they are or how they exist has not been explained with sufficient clearness. However, this opinion is held by most: that the devil was an angel, and that, having become an apostate, he induced as many of the angels as possible to fall away with him, and these up to the present time are called his angels....

We know that every being which is endowed with reason, and transgresses its statutes and limitations, is undoubtedly involved in sin by swerving from rectitude and justice. Therefore, every rational creature is capable of earning praise and censure: of praise, if he conforms to that reason which he possesses, he advances to better things; of censure, if he falls away from the plan and course of rectitude ... he is justly liable to pains and penalties. And this is also to be held as applying to the devil himself, and those who are with him who are called his angels.

Now the titles of these beings have to be explained so that we may know what they are, and of whom we have to speak. The name, then, of *Devil*, and *Satan*, and *Wicked One*—who is also described as *Enemy of God*—is mentioned in many passages of scripture. Moreover, certain "angels of the devil" are mentioned, and also a "prince of this world," who, whether the devil himself or someone else, is

TWO: DEVELOPMENT OF A NARRATIVE

not yet clearly manifest. There are also certain "princes of this world" described as possessing a kind of wisdom which will come to naught. But whether these are those princes who are also the principalities with whom we have to wrestle, or other beings, seems to me a point on which it is not easy for anyone to comprehend. After the principalities, certain "powers" also are named with whom we have to wrestle, and carry on a struggle even against the "princes of this world" and the "rulers of this darkness." Certain "spiritual powers of wickedness" also, in heavenly places, are spoken of by Paul himself. What, moreover, are we to say of those "wicked and unclean spirits" mentioned in the Gospel? Thus, we have certain heavenly beings called by a similar name, but which are said to bend the knee, or to be about to bend the knee, at the name of Jesus; nay, even things on earth and things under the earth, which Paul enumerates in order. . . .

But that we may not appear to build our assertions on subjects of such importance and difficulty on the ground of inference alone, or to require the assent of our hearers to what is only conjectural, let us see whether we can obtain any declarations from holy scripture, by the authority of which these positions may be more credibly maintained.

[Origen critiques Ezek. 28 along the same lines as Tertullian in doc. 17.]

We have shown, then, that what we have quoted regarding the prince of Tyre from the prophet Ezekiel refers to an adverse power, and by that chapter, it is most clearly proved that that power was formerly holy and happy, and from that state of happiness it fell at the time that iniquity was found in it, and was hurled to the earth, and was not such by nature and creation. We are of the opinion, therefore, that these words are spoken about a certain angel who had received the office of governing the nation of the Tyrians, and to whom also their souls had been entrusted for care. But what Tyre—whether it is that Tyre which is situated within the boundaries of the province of Phoenicia, or some other of which this one which we know on earth is the model—and what souls of Tyrians—whether they are those of the former or those which belong to that Tyre which is spiritually understood—we ought to understand does not seem to be a matter requiring examination in this place. . . .

Again, we are taught as follows by the prophet Isaiah regarding another opposing power.

[He quotes Isa. 14.12–22; see doc. 4.]

Most evidently by these words he who formerly was Lucifer and who used to arise in the morning is shown to have fallen from heaven. If, as some think, he was a nature of darkness, how is Lucifer said to have existed before his fall? Moreover, how could he who had in himself nothing of the light arise in the morning? Nay! Even the savior himself teaches us, saying of the devil, "Behold, I see Satan fallen from heaven like lightning" [Luke 10.18], for at one time he was light. . . . He compares him to lightning, and says that he fell from heaven, so that he might show by this that he had been at one time in heaven, that he had had a place among the saints, and enjoyed a share in that light in which all the saints participate—the light by which they are made angels of light, and by which the apostles are termed by the lord, "the light of the world." In this way, then, did that being once exist as light before he went astray, and fell to this place, and had his glory turned into dust. This is peculiarly the mark of the wicked, as the prophet also says, for which reason, too, he was called the "prince of this world,"—this is, of an earthly habitation—for he exercised power over those who were obedient to his wickedness, since "the whole of this world"—for I term this place of earth, "world"—"lies in the wicked one" [1 John 5.19], and in this apostate. That he is an apostate—that is, a fugitive—even the lord in the book of Job says, "You will take with a hook the apostate dragon," that is, a fugitive. [Job 40.20] Now it is certain that by "the dragon" is understood the devil himself....

According to our view, there is no rational creature which is not capable both of good and evil. But it does not follow that because we say there is no nature which may not admit evil into it, we should conclude that every nature has admitted evil—that is, that every nature has become wicked. In the same way that we might say that the nature of every man allows him the possibility of becoming a sailor, it does not follow from this that every man will become so. Likewise, it is possible for everyone to learn grammar or medicine, but this is not proof that every man is either a physician or a grammarian. So, if we say that there is no nature which may not admit evil into it, it is not necessarily the case that it has done so.

In our view, not even the devil himself was incapable of good. But although capable of admitting good into his nature, he did not also desire to do so, or make any effort toward virtue. For, as we are taught by those quotations which we adduced from the prophets, there was once a time when he was good, when he walked in the paradise of God between the cherubim. As he possessed the power either of receiving good or evil but fell away from the virtuous course, turning to evil with all the powers of his mind, so also other creatures, as having a capacity for either condition, in the exercise of the freedom of their will, fled from evil and cleaved to good. There is no nature, then, which may not admit into itself good or evil, except the nature of God—the fountain of all good things—and of Christ....

The last enemy who is called "death," is said . . . to be destroyed, in such a way that there may not be anything left of a mournful kind when death does not exist, nor anything that is adverse when there is no enemy. The destruction of the last enemy is to be understood, not as if its substance—which was formed by God—is to perish, but because its mind and hostile will—which came not from God, but from itself—are to be destroyed. Its destruction, therefore, will not be its non-existence, but rather its ceasing to be an enemy, and to be death. For nothing is impossible to the omnipotent one, nor is anything incapable of restoration to its creator: for he made all things that they might exist, and those things which were made for existence cannot cease to be. For this reason also will they admit change and variety into their nature, so as to be placed, according to their merits, either in a better or worse position; but no destruction of substance can befall those things which were created by God for the purpose of permanent existence.

Questions: Why does the devil fall, and what is Origen's basis for this argument? How does he understand Isaiah 14 (doc. 4)? How does Origen's devil differ from that of dualists? What will inevitably happen to the devil and those other evil creatures at the end of time?

19. DEVIL AS KIDNAPPER

Refuting various forms of gnostic dualism forced some scholars of the early Church to begin to explore the role of the devil in salvation history in general and his relationship to humanity and Christ's mission. Saint Paul had argued that sinners would be saved "through the redemption, that is in Christ Jesus" (Rom. 3.24). But the Latin word here translated as "redemption" was usually applied to the buying back of a slave. The passage seemed to imply several tricky questions: To whom were sinners enslaved? When did they become enslaved? And if they were being somehow bought back out of slavery, had the slave master legitimate rights over his slave?

The first selection comes from Irenaeus's Against Heresies *(see doc. 16). The second comes from Gregory, bishop of Nyssa's (c. 330–c. 395)* Great Catechism, *a work intended as a comprehensive exposition of the Catholic faith against the criticisms of Jews, pagans, and heretics. Both texts see their authors trying to wrestle with the issue of the consequence of Adam and Eve's transgression and the need for Christ's saving mission.*

Irenaeus: Greek, c. 175–189.
Gregory of Nyssa: Greek, 386.

Sources: trans. Alexander Roberts and James Donaldson, from Irenaeus, *Against Heresies*, from *Ante-Nicene Fathers*, vol. 1 (Buffalo, NY: Christian Literature Publishing Co., 1885), pp. 455–56, 526–27; rev.; trans. William Moore and Henry Austin Wilson, from Gregory of Nyssa, *Great Catechism*, from *Nicene and Post-Nicene Fathers*, second series, vol. 5 (New York: Charles Scribner's Sons, 1917), pp. 494–96; rev.

Irenaeus

It was necessary, therefore, that the lord . . . should save that very man who had been created after his image and likeness—that is, Adam—filling up the times of his condemnation, which had been incurred through disobedience. . . . [This was necessary,] too, inasmuch as the whole economy of salvation regarding man came to pass according to the pleasure of the father, so that God might not be conquered, nor his wisdom lessened, [in the eyes of his creatures]. For if man had been created by God so that he might live, after losing life—through being injured by the serpent that had corrupted him—should not any more return to life, but should be utterly [and forever] abandoned to death, God would [in that case] have been conquered, and the wickedness of the serpent would have prevailed over the will of God.

But inasmuch as God is invincible and long suffering, he did indeed show himself to be long-suffering in the matter of the correction of man and the probation of all.... By means of the second man [Christ] God bound the strong man [the devil], stole his goods and abolished death, giving life to that man [Adam] who had been in a state of death. For at the beginning of time, Adam became a vessel in his [Satan's] possession, whom he held under his power, that is, by bringing sin on him iniquitously, and under the guise of immortality inflicting death upon him. For, while promising that they should be like gods—which was in no way possible for them to be—he brought death upon them; wherefore he who had made man captive, was justly captured in his turn by God; but man who had been led captive, was loosed from the bonds of condemnation.

... the mighty word and true man [Christ]—in redeeming us by means of his own blood in a manner consistent with reason—gave himself as a ransom for those who had been led into captivity. And since the apostasy [the devil] tyrannized over us unjustly, and—though we were by nature the property of the omnipotent God—alienated us contrary to nature, rendering us his disciples [the devil's disciples], the word of God, powerful in all things, and not defective with respect to his own justice, did righteously turn against that apostasy, and redeem from him his own property, not by violent means—in the way that the apostasy had obtained dominion over us at the beginning, when he insatiably snatched away what was not his own—but by means of persuasion, as is becoming a God of counsel, who does not use violent means to obtain what he desires, so that neither justice is infringed upon, nor the ancient handiwork of God goes to destruction.

Gregory of Nyssa

[T]hat the omnipotence of the divine nature should have had the strength to descend into the humiliation of a human [form], furnishes a clearer proof of that omnipotence than even the greatness and supernatural character of his miracles.... But his descent into the humility of a human form is a kind of superabundant exercise of power, which thus finds no check even when it operates in directions which contravene nature. It is the peculiar property of the essence of fire to tend upwards; therefore, no one deems it wonderful in the case of flame to see that natural effect. But should the flame be seen to stream downwards, like heavy bodies, such a fact would be regarded as a miracle, by virtue of the fact that the fire still remains fire, yet, by this change of direction in its motion, passes out of its nature in that it is being carried downward. Likewise, it is not the vastness of the heavens, and the bright shining of its constellations, and the order of the universe and the unbroken administration over all existence that so manifestly displays the transcendent power of the God, so much as this condescension to the weakness of our nature. . . .

It was not in the nature of the opposing power to come in contact with the undiluted presence of God, and to undergo his unclouded manifestation; therefore, in order to make sure that the ransom on our behalf might be easily accepted by him who required it, the deity was hidden under the veil of our nature, so that, as with ravenous fish, the hook of the deity might be gulped down along with the bait of flesh. In this way, life is introduced into the house of death, light is shining in darkness, so that which is diametrically opposed to light and life might vanish, for it is not in the nature of darkness to remain when light is present, or of death to exist when life is active. . . .

A person is, perhaps, induced to entertain the thought that it was by means of a certain amount of deceit that God carried out this scheme on our behalf. It was not by pure deity alone, but by deity veiled in human nature, that God—without the knowledge of his enemy—got within the lines of him who had man in his power. This is in some measure a fraud and a surprise, seeing that it is the peculiar way with those who want to deceive to divert the expectations of their intended victims in another direction, and then to effect something quite different from what the latter expected. . . .

That repayment, adequate to the debt, by which the deceiver was in his turn deceived, shows the justice of the dealing, while the object aimed at is a testimony to the goodness of him who effected it. . . . He who first deceived man by the bait of sensual pleasure is himself deceived by the presentment of the human form. But with respect to the aim and purpose of what took place, a change in the direction of the nobler is involved; for whereas he—the enemy—effected his deception for the ruin of our nature, he who is at once the just, and good, and wise one, used his device, in which there was deception, for the salvation of him who had perished, and thus not only conferred benefit on the lost one, but on him, too, who had wrought our ruin. For from this approximation of death to life, of darkness to light, of corruption to incorruption, there is effected an obliteration of what is worse, and a passing away of it into nothing, while benefit is conferred on him who is freed from those evils. It is similar to when some worthless material has been mixed with gold, and the gold-refiners burn up the foreign and refuse part in the consuming fire, and so restore the more precious substance to its natural luster. . . . In the same way when death, and corruption, and darkness, and every other offshoot of evil had grown into the nature of the author of evil, the approach of the divine power—acting like fire—makes that unnatural accretion disappear. Thus, the purgation of the evil becomes a blessing to [him of] that nature, though the separation is agonizing. Therefore, even the adversary himself will not be likely to dispute that what took place was both just and salutary.

Questions: What is the effect of the fall of humanity for both authors? How is it that God is said to suffer? How does Christ redeem humanity? Is Christ's incarnation a trick? Is the devil independent of God or subservient to him?

20. SYMPATHY FOR THE DEVIL

Some early Christian authors were influenced by the Neoplatonic idea of "emanationism," a theory which states that every created thing radiates out from God and ultimately participates, however imperfectly, in divinity; it also claims that, at some point, everything must "return" to God. However, the language of emanationism and the mechanisms by which it purports to operate are frustratingly vague. Nevertheless, those who hold this view insist that no created thing can be consigned to eternal damnation. For some emanationist theologians, this implied the ultimate redemption of the devil. Indeed, while most Hellenistic Christians recoiled in horror at the notion of the devil's salvation, a small number of theologians in Late Antiquity championed the controversial idea—or at least entertained it in their philosophical musings. Because such views tested the limits of what early Christians considered acceptable, those who embraced or mooted them had to be very careful about how they discussed the matter, couching their language and even retracting comments that may have been offered primarily as a "thought experiment." Origen of Alexandria (doc. 18) and Gregory of Nyssa (doc. 19) espoused varieties of emanationism at various points in their writings. While Gregory faced some scrutiny of his "universalism" (as his version of the theory is sometimes called), Origen was subjected to repeated attacks and accusations of heresy.

Origen: Greek, c. 225.
Gregory of Nyssa: Greek, 386.

Sources: trans. Frederick Crombie and Kevin Knight, from Origen, *De Principiis*, from *Ante-Nicene Fathers*, vol. 4 (Buffalo, NY: Christian Literature Publishing Co., 1885) 3.6.5–6, rev.; trans. William Moore and Henry Austin Wilson, from Gregory of Nyssa, *The Great Catechism*, from *Nicene and Post-Nicene Fathers of the Church*, series 2, vol. 5 (Grand Rapids, MI: Wm. B. Eerdmans Publishing Company, 1892), chap. 26, rev.

Origen, from *First Principles*

The last enemy is called death and it is said to be destroyed for the following reason, namely that nothing mournful can exist when death does not exist, nor can there be anything adverse when there is no enemy. It should be understood, moreover, that it is not as if the substance of the last enemy will perish when it is destroyed; instead, its mind and hostile will—which do not derive from God, but rather from itself—will be extinguished. This is because nothing is impossible to the omnipotent, nor is the creator incapable of restoring any thing, for he made all things so that they might exist, and those things which were made for existence cannot cease to be. For this reason also, it must be admitted that change and variety are real, and thus, things may be placed, according to their merits, in a better or worse position. However, there can be no destruction of a thing's substance when God created it for the purpose of permanent existence. Concerning those things which are commonly believed to perish, neither our faith nor truth itself will permit us to suppose them to be destroyed. Finally, ignorant people and unbelievers believe that our flesh will be destroyed after death. They suppose that it retains no relic of its former substance. However, we who believe in the resurrection understand that death only produces a change, but that our substance unequivocally remains. By the will of the creator, at the appointed time, the body will be restored to life. And a change will take place in the body a second time: thus, what had been flesh formed from earthly soil was afterwards dissolved by death—reduced to dust and ashes (for, as the Bible says, "you are dust, and to dust shall you return" [doc. 1]). This body will again be raised from the earth and will afterwards advance to the glory of a spiritual body, according to the merits of the indwelling soul.

We then suppose that all of our bodily substance will be brought into this condition, when all things are reestablished in a state of unity with God, and God is all and everything. And we must understand that this result will not occur suddenly, but rather, slowly and gradually. The process of improvement and correction will take place within individuals imperceptibly over the span of countless ages. Some will outstrip others and take a swifter course towards perfection, while others will follow close at hand and others still will lag behind. Thus, the last enemy, who is called death, is eventually reached after all other beings have passed through uncounted and numerous forms as they are reconciled to God. Only then may death be destroyed and no longer deemed an enemy. Indeed, when all rational souls have been restored to a condition of this kind, then the nature of our earthly body will undergo a change and adopt the glory of a spiritual body. For we see that it is not the case with rational natures that some of them have lived in a state of degradation because of their sinfulness while others have been allowed to live in a state of happiness on account of their merits. Instead, we see those same souls who had formerly been sinful, after they had been converted and reconciled to God, assisted into a state of happiness. With respect to the nature of the body, we ought also to consider that the one which we now use is in a state of abjection, corruption, and weakness. But it is not a different body from the one that we shall possess in incorruption, in power, and in glory. Instead, it will be the same body, but when it has cast away the infirmities in which it is currently entangled, it will be transmuted into a condition of glory. It will be rendered spiritual, so that what was once a vessel of dishonor may, when cleansed, become a vessel of honor and an abode of blessedness. We are also to believe that, by the will of the creator, it will abide forever without any change in this condition, for as the apostle has declared, "We have a house, not made by hands, eternal in the heavens" [2 Cor.

5.1]. For the faith of the church does not agree with the view of certain Greek philosophers, namely that, besides the human body, which is composed of the four elements, there is a fifth body which is different in all of its parts and that this other form is different from our present body. But no one can produce evidence for such an opinion from holy scripture, nor can one accept the idea from rational inference. This is particularly so when the holy apostle openly declares that those who rise from the dead do not receive new bodies, but rather, they continue to possess the ones that they had while living—albeit transformed from an inferior to a superior condition. For his words are: "It is sown an animal body, it will rise a spiritual body. It is sown in corruption, it will arise in incorruption. It is sown in weakness, it will arise in power. It is sown in dishonor, it will arise in glory" [1 Cor. 15.44]. Therefore, there is a kind of advancement in man. Initially, he is an animal being, without any understanding of what belongs to the spirit of God. By means of instruction, however, he reaches the stage of being a spiritual being. Then he judges all things, while he himself is judged by no one. Similarly, with respect to the state of the body, we are to believe that this current body, on account of its service to the soul, should be called an animal body. When the soul, by means of a certain progress, is united to God and shall have been made one spirit with him . . . it will attain to a spiritual condition and quality, especially since, as I have already pointed out, our bodily nature was formed by the creator. And it was done in such a way that it might pass easily into whatever condition he should wish, or whatever nature the situation demanded.

Gregory of Nyssa, Selections from *The Great Catechism*

He who first deceived man with the bait of sensual pleasure was himself deceived by the representation of the human form. But regarding the aim and purpose of what took place, an understanding of its nobility is required. For whereas he, the enemy, perpetrated his deception for the ruin of our nature, the lord, who is at once good and just and wise, used the enemy's device, in which there was deception, for the salvation of humanity, which had perished. Thus, he conferred benefit not only on the ones who were lost, but also on the one who had sought our ruin. Concerning this transition from death to life, from darkness to light, from corruption to incorruption, that which is evil in a thing is obliterated. The evil passes away into nothing, while benefit is conferred on him who has been freed from it. It is like when some worthless material has been mixed with gold. The goldsmiths burn up the foreign matter and dross in the consuming fire. They restore the more precious substance to its natural luster. Not that this separation is achieved without difficulty, for it takes time for the fire by its melting force to cause the dross to disappear. But in the end, this melting away of the baser material that had besmirched the gold is a kind of healing.

In the same way, when death and corruption and darkness and every other form of evil had grown to become like the author of evil himself, the approach of divine power—like a purgation—becomes a blessing, acting like a fire and making the unnatural accumulation disappear, even though the separation process is agonizing. Therefore even the adversary himself will likely not dispute that what has taken place was both salutary and just, particularly if he appears to gain a blessing for himself. This is because now it is like those who are subjected to the knife and cauterization for their cure: they are angry with the doctors and wince with pain at the incision. However, if they recover their health with this treatment, and the pain of the cauterization passes away, they will ultimately feel grateful to those who have performed this surgery on them. In a similar way, when, after long periods of time, the evil in our nature which is currently mixed up with it—and which has developed as it has developed—has been expelled, and when those who are lying in sin have been restored to their original state, all creation will rise in a harmony of thanksgiving. Both those who have been chastened in the process of purgation and those who never required any purgation at all will rise in thanks.

The great mystery of the divine incarnation bestows these and similar blessings. For in those points in which the lord mingled with humanity, passing as he did through all the contingent events appropriate to human nature, such as birth, childhood, maturity, even approaching the threshold of death, he accomplished all of the results previously mentioned. He not only freed man from evil, he also healed the author of evil himself. However painful, the chastisement of moral disease is a healing of its defects.

Questions: Why is it necessary for these authors that the devil be saved? Why might Origen and Gregory have found the idea of the devil's salvation appealing? Alternatively, why did other Christians find the idea so objectionable? Does God actually forgive the devil? To what extent is the idea of the devil's salvation a form of skepticism?

21. A PERVERSE POWER, HOSTILE TO TRUTH

Born in North Africa, Lactantius (c. 250–c. 325) was a skilled rhetorician, eventually being appointed a teacher of rhetoric at Nicomedia (modern İzmit in Turkey) by Emperor Diocletian (d. 311). It is not clear when he became a Christian, but he resigned his position when the legal rights of Christians were rescinded in the opening years of the fourth century, a process that culminated in the so-called "Great Persecution" (303–311). It was during this period that Lactantius wrote his most important work, Divine Institutes. *This was a long and sophisticated apologetic intended to convince learned Latin critics of the reasonableness and truth of Christianity.*

Latin, 305–311.

Source: trans. William Fletcher, from Lactantius, *Divine Institutes*, from *Ante-Nicene Fathers*, vol. 7 (Buffalo, NY: Christian Literature Publishing Co., 1886), pp. 41, 52–53, 64, 66–67; rev.

For what reason can we suppose this [apparent misfortune] to arise unless there is some perverse power which is always hostile to the truth, which rejoices in the errors of men, whose one and only task it is perpetually to scatter darkness, and to blind the minds of men, lest they should see the light—lest, in short, they should look to heaven, and observe the nature of their own body . . . ?

. . . I will bring to light all the deceptions of the pretended deity, by which men have been led very far from the way of truth. But I will retrace the matter far back from its source, so that if anyone, unacquainted with the truth and ignorant, shall apply himself to the reading of this book, he will be instructed, and will understand what in truth can be the source and origin of these evils—and having received light, he will perceive his own errors and those of the whole human race. Since God has the greatest foresight in planning, and the greatest skill in acting on such plans, before he commenced the business of the world—inasmuch as the fountain of full and most complete goodness was and always is in him—he produced a spirit like himself who was endowed with the perfections of God the father so that goodness might spring as a stream from him and might flow forth afar. . . . Then he made another being, in whom the nature of his divine origin did not remain. And so he was infected with his own envy as with poison and passed from good to evil; and at his own will—which was a free gift to him from God—he assumed for himself a contrary name. From this it appears that the source of all evils is envy, for he envied his predecessor, who being steadfast in God the father is acceptable and dear to him. This being, who from being good became evil by his own act, is called by the Greeks *diabolus*; we call him *accuser*, because he reports to God the faults to which he himself entices us. . . .

When, therefore, the number of men had begun to increase, God in his forethought sent angels for the protection and improvement of the human race, lest the devil, to whom he had given power over the earth from the beginning, should by his subtlety either corrupt or destroy men, as he had done at first; and because he had given them a free will, God warned these angels above everything else not to defile themselves with contamination from the earth and lose the dignity of their heavenly nature. That is to say, he prohibited them from doing that which he knew they would do which would cause them to lose any hope of forgiveness. And so, while they lived among men, that most deceitful ruler of the earth, by his very association, gradually enticed them to vices, and polluted them by intercourse with women. Then, not being admitted into heaven on account of the sins into which they had plunged themselves, these angels fell to the earth. Thus, the devil makes his satellites and attendants from God's angels. But they who were born from these unions, because they were neither angels nor men, but bearing a kind of middle nature, were not admitted into hell, as their fathers were not into heaven. Thus, two kinds of demons were made: one heavenly, the other terrestrial. These are the wicked spirits, the authors of the evils which are done, and the devil is their prince. . . .

And this is said on this account because God had sent them as guardians to the human race; but although they are the destroyers of men, they want themselves to be seen as their guardians, so that they might be worshipped and not God. . . . Also, the art and power of magicians consists entirely in their influences—having been invoked by them, they deceive the sight of men with deceptive illusions so that these people do not see those things which exist and think they see things which do not exist. These contaminated and abandoned spirits, as I say, wander over the whole earth, and console themselves for their own perdition in the destruction of men. And so they fill every place with snares, deceits, frauds, and errors, for they cling to individuals, and occupy whole houses from door to door, and assume for themselves the name of *genii* which is thus translated *demons* in the Latin language. People consecrate these in their houses and pour out wine for them every day; they worship the wise demons as if they are terrestrial gods and averters of the evils which the demons themselves cause and inflict. And since spirits are without substance and not to be grasped, they insinuate themselves into the bodies of men, and secretly working in their guts, they corrupt men's health, hasten diseases, terrify their souls with dreams, harass their minds with frenzies, so that as a result of these evils they may compel men to seek out their help. . . .

Someone may say, "Why, therefore, does God permit these things to be done, and not immediately remedy such disastrous errors—that evil fights against good, that vices are opposed by virtues, that he has some who he may punish and others who he may honor?" For he has determined to pass judgment on the living and the dead at the last times. . . . He delays, therefore, until the end of the times come, when he may pour out his wrath with heavenly power and might. . . .

But now he suffers men to err, and to be impious even toward him, just, mild, and patient as he is. . . . Whoever will have worshipped and followed these most wicked spirits, will enjoy neither heaven nor the light, which are God's. Rather, he will fall into those things which we have spoken of as being assigned in the distribution of things to the prince of the evil ones himself—namely, into darkness, and hell, and everlasting punishment. . . .

Questions: Why does the devil fall? Where does he derive his conception of demons? Why must there be two different sorts of demons? What is their connection to the devil? Is the devil's power legitimate?

22. A PROTO-DEMONOLOGY?

The Testament of Solomon from which the excerpt below is drawn is a complicated text, and its sense is not always clear. Though King Solomon reigned in the tenth century BCE, the document in the form in which it is known today is much more recent. While it seems to have some Christian elements to it—one modern scholar has suggested that whoever set the text down in its current form had at least a passing familiarity with elements of Origen's demonology (see doc. 18)—there is no scholarly consensus as to whether the text began as a Christian document or whether it represents a Christian reworking of an older Jewish story.

The text expands on the story of 3 Kings 6–7 (1 Kings in Protestant Bibles), which describes Solomon's building of the temple in Jerusalem.

Greek, likely third or fourth century CE.

Source: trans. F. C. Conybeare, "The Testament of Solomon," *Jewish Quarterly Review* 11.1 (1898): 1–45; rev.

1. Testament of Solomon, son of David, who was king in Jerusalem and mastered and controlled all spirits of the air, on and under the earth . . . which describes also the power they wield over men and the particular angels which can frustrate them.

2. When the temple of the city of Jerusalem was being built and the workmen were working on it, Ornias the demon came among them around sunset. He took away half the pay of the chief-workman's little boy, as well as half his food. . . . And the child grew thin, although he was very much loved by the king. . . .

5. Now when I—Solomon—heard this, I entered the temple of God, and prayed with all my soul, night and day, that the demon be delivered into my hands, and that I might gain authority over him. Through my prayer, the grace of the lord Sabaoth was given to me by Michael, his archangel. [He brought me] a little ring which had a seal on it consisting of an engraved stone. The angel said to me: "O Solomon, king, son of David, take this gift which the lord God, the highest Sabaoth, has sent to you. With it, you will be able to confine all the demons of the earth—male and female. Moreover, with their help you will be able to build up Jerusalem. [But] you [must] wear this seal of God. And the engraving on the seal of the ring which has been sent to you is a Pentalpha [5 A's interlaced to form a pentagram]."

6. And I—Solomon—was overjoyed at this, and praised and glorified the God of heaven and earth. . . .

[Solomon gave the ring to the boy, and when Ornias came the next day to steal his money, the boy threw the ring at the demon's chest. There it stuck, allowing him to bring the demon to the gates of the king's palace.]

9. And when Solomon heard this, he rose from his throne, and went outside into the vestibule of the court of his palace. There he saw the demon, shuddering

TWO: DEVELOPMENT OF A NARRATIVE

and trembling. He said to him, "Who are you?" The demon answered, "I am called Ornias."

10. Then Solomon said to him: "Tell me, O demon, to what sign of the zodiac are you subject?" And he answered: "To the water-pourer [Aquarius]. And I strangle those who are consumed with desire for noble virgins upon earth [there is a textual gap, a *lacuna*, here]. When a person has no disposition to sleep, I can change into three forms. Whenever men come to be enamored of women, I metamorphose myself into a beautiful female, and in this form, I take hold of these men in their sleep and play with them. And after a while I take to my wings once again, and fly to heavenly regions. I also appear as a lion, and I am commanded by all the demons. I am offspring of the archangel Uriel, the power of God."

11. I—Solomon—having heard the name of the archangel mentioned, prayed and glorified God, the lord of heaven and earth. And I sealed the demon and set him to work cutting the stones for the temple, which had been brought by the sea of Arabia and were now lying along the shore. But he, afraid to be chained, continued and said to me: "I beg you, King Solomon, let me go free and I will bring you all the other demons." Because he was not willing to be subject to me, I begged the archangel Uriel to come and assist me, and immediately I saw the archangel Uriel come down to me from the heavens.

12. And the angel commanded the whales of the sea to come out of the abyss. And he cast his fate upon the ground, and that fate made the great demon subject to him. And he commanded the great and bold demon Ornias to cut stones for the temple. And accordingly I—Solomon—glorified the God of heaven and maker of the earth. And he commanded demon Ornias to come with his fate, and I gave him the seal, saying to him "Go and bring the prince of all the demons to me."

13. Ornias took the finger-ring, and went off to Beelzeboul, king of the demons. He said to him, "Come here! Solomon is calling you." Having heard this, Beelzeboul said to him: "Tell me, who is this Solomon of whom you speak?" At this, Ornias threw the ring at Beelzeboul's chest, saying, "King Solomon is calling you." Beelzeboul cried out with a mighty voice, and shot out a great burning flame of fire. He then arose and following Ornias, he came to Solomon.

14. And when I saw the prince of demons, I glorified the lord God, maker of heaven and earth, and I said: "Blessed are you, lord God Almighty, who has given wisdom to Solomon your servant . . . and has made the power of the devil subject to me."

15. And I questioned the demon, and said, "Who are you?" The demon replied "I am Beelzeboul, the ruler of the demons. All the other demons have their principal seats close to me. And it is I who makes manifest the apparition of each demon." And he promised to bring to me in bonds all the unclean spirits. Again I glorified the God of heaven and earth, always giving thanks to him.

16. I then asked the demon if there were females among them. And when he told me that there were, I said that I wanted to see them. So Beelzeboul went off at high speed, and brought me Onoskelis who had a very pretty shape, and the skin of a fair woman. She tossed her head.

17. When she arrived, I said to her, "Tell me, who are you?" She said to me, "I am called Onoskelis, a spirit wrought [*lacuna*], lurking on the earth. I lie in a golden cave. But I have a nature that is always changing. Sometimes, I strangle men with a noose. Other times, I creep up on them from the nature to their arms [margin reads "worms"]. I most often dwell on precipices, or in caves or ravines. . . .

19. [Solomon then asked her,] "What angel is it that thwarts you?" And she said to me, "The one that is reigning in you." At this, I thought she mocked me and ordered a soldier to strike her. But she cried out, and said: "I am subject to you, O king, by virtue of the wisdom God has given you, and by the angel Joel."

20. So I commanded her to spin the hemp for the ropes used in the building of the house of God; and accordingly, when I had sealed and bound her, she was so overcome and confounded that she stood night and day spinning the hemp.

21. I commanded another demon to be brought to me, and immediately the demon Asmodeus approached, bound. I asked him: "Who are you?" But he shot a glance of anger and rage toward me, and said, "Who are you?" I said to him, "You dare answer me like that—you who are bound as you are?" With rage, he said to me, "How shall I answer you, for you are a son of man? Though I was borne by the daughter of man, I was conceived of an angel's seed. It is impossible, then, for one of my heavenly species to address an earth-born creature presumptuously. My star is bright in heaven. Some men call it the Wain, others the dragon's child. But I always keep near to this star. So do not ask me many things, for your kingdom will be short-lived and your glory last but a season. Your tyranny over us will be short and then we will have free range over mankind once more, and people will revere us as gods not knowing—men that they are—the names of the angels set over us.

22. On hearing this, I—Solomon—bound him more carefully, and ordered him to be flogged with leather lashes so that he might humbly tell me his name and his business. And he answered me in this way, "I am called Asmodeus among mortals and my business is to plot against newlyweds, so that they may not know one another. I force them apart by causing many calamities. I waste away the beauty of virgins, and cause their hearts to stray."

23. I said to him, "Is this your only business?" And he answered, "I transport married men into fits of madness and desire so that they leave their wives, and go off by night and day to women who belong to other men. With them they commit sin, and fall into murderous deeds."

24. And I adjured him by the name of the lord Sabaoth, "Fear God, Asmodeus, and tell me which angel thwarts you." He said, "Raphael, the archangel that stands before throne of God. But I can also be thwarted if the liver and gall of a fish smoked over ashes of the tamarisk is put to me." I again asked and said: "Hide not aught from me. For I am Solomon, David, king of Israel. Tell me the name of the fish which you respect." And he answered: "It is the Glanos, and is found in the rivers of Assyria. . . ."

[After condemning Asmodeus to fetch water for the making of clay for the temple binding him by means of the fumigation described above, Solomon returned to his interrogation of Beelzeboul.]

26. I said to him: "Why are you alone, prince of the demons?" And he said to me, "Because I am the only one of the fallen angels of heaven left. I was first angel in the first heaven, and called Beelzeboul. But now I control all those who are bound in Tartarus. . . .

27. I—Solomon—said unto him, "Beelzeboul, what is your role?" And he answered me, "I destroy kings. I ally myself with foreign tyrants. And I set my demons on men so that people will believe in them and be lost. I stir God's chosen servants—his priests and the faithful—to wicked sins and evil heresies, and lawless deeds. They obey me and I bear them off into destruction. I inspire men with envy and a desire for murder—and for wars and sodomy and other evil things. And I will destroy the world." . . .

29. I said to him, "Tell me what angel thwarts you?" And he answered, "By the holy and precious name of the almighty God, called by the Hebrews by a row of numbers, the sum of which is 644, and among the Greeks is called Emmanuel. And if one of the Romans adjures me by the great name of the power of Eleêth, I disappear at once." . . .

34. And I glorified God who gave me this authority once more, and ordered another demon to come before me. And there came seven spirits—all female, each beautiful and attractive, but all bound and woven together. Seeing them, I—Solomon—questioned them, and said, "Who are you?" And they with one accord and in one voice replied, "We are the 33 elements of the cosmic ruler of darkness." The first said, "I am Deception." The second, "I am Strife." The third, "I am Klothod, which is battle." The fourth, "I am Jealousy." The fifth, "I am Power." The sixth, "I am Error." The seventh, "I am the worst of them all. Our stars are in heaven—seven stars not bright but all together. We are called goddesses and we often change position all together. Together, we are sometimes in Lydia, sometimes in Olympus, sometimes on a great mountain."

35. So I—Solomon—questioned them one by one, beginning with the first, and going down to the seventh. The first said, "I am Deception. I deceive and weave snares here and there. I create and nurture heresies. But I have an angel who frustrates me, Lanzechalal."

36. Likewise the second said, "I am Strife—strife of strife. I bring timbers, stones, hangers, my weapons on the spot. But I have an angel who frustrates me, Bartchiachel."

37. Likewise also the third said, "I am called Klothod—battle—and I cause the well-behaved to scatter and fall foul of each other. Why do I say so much? I have an angel that frustrates me, Marmarath."

38. Likewise also the fourth said, "I cause men to forget sobriety and moderation. I separate and split them into parties, for Strife follows me hand in hand. I separate the husband from the one who shares his bed, children from parents, and brothers from sisters. But why am I telling you so much? I have an angel that frustrates me, the great Balthial."

39. Likewise also the fifth said, "I am Power. By power I raise up tyrants and tear down kings. I furnish power to all rebels. I have an angel that frustrates me, Asteraoth."

40. Likewise also the sixth said, "O King Solomon, I am Error. I will make you err, as I have done before when I caused you to slay your own brother [see 1 Kings 2.25]. . . . I lead errant souls away from piety, and many other evil traits are mine. But I have an angel that frustrates me, Uriel."

41. Likewise also the seventh said, "I am the worst, and I make you worse off than you were before, for I will impose on you the bonds of Artemis. The locust will set me free [*lacuna*]. Anyone who is wise should not turn his steps toward me.

42. Having heard and wondered, I—Solomon—sealed them with ring. Since there were so many of them, I ordered them to dig the foundations of the temple of God, for it was to be 250 cubits long. And I ordered them to work hard, and with one murmur of joint protest they began to perform the tasks I had set.

Questions: Are the descriptions of the demons, angels, and their powers biblical? How is Solomon able to gain control over demons? Does the text present any qualms about the idea of using demons to effect some higher purpose? What sort of people might have tried to use this text?

CHAPTER THREE
FORGING A COMMUNITY

Figure 3.1 Michael Wolgemut, "Witch of Berkeley," in *Nuremberg Chronicle* (c. 1493), f. 189v. The *Nuremberg Chronicle* is a history of the world from creation to the time of its publication based on an array of medieval historical and geographical sources. The text was illustrated with 1,804 woodcut images by Michael Wolgemut (c. 1434/37–1519) and Wilhelm Pleydenwurff (c. 1450–94), many to a page.

THREE: FORGING A COMMUNITY

In the wake of Christ's death, one of the pressing issues facing his early followers was the need to define the new faith's relationship with its major competitors: Judaism and Roman religious practices. Indeed, in the context of mid-first-century Palestine, it was not altogether clear whether the faith would survive as a distinct religion at all. Jesus, after all, had been Jewish and most of his early followers identified themselves as such. Therefore, there was the very real possibility that Christ's teachings might be subsumed as a sect under the umbrella of Judaism. On the other side, however, the pragmatic, syncretist approach to foreign gods and their worship adopted by the Romans risked Christianity degenerating into just another of the empire's many regional cults.

To distinguish themselves from rival religious practices, early Christians endeavored to draw a bright line between themselves and their competitors. Writing to the church of Corinth in the middle of the first century, for instance, Saint Paul advised those who adhered to the message of Christ to shun the region's idolaters. Justice, he asserted, has nothing to do with injustice, as light has nothing to do with darkness. "What concord," he asked, "has Christ with Belial? Or what part has the faithful with the unbeliever?" (2 Cor. 6.14–15). In the next generation, as historian Elaine Pagels has argued, gospel writers would draw a similar distinction between themselves and Judaism, attributing Christ's crucifixion not to the Roman authorities that ruled Palestine but to the Jewish mob inspired by the devil.

In this, early Christians defined themselves against their opponents not in ethnic but in moral terms—that is, in terms of absolute good and evil. As such, differences between Christianity and other religious traditions came to be ascribed a cosmological significance, viewed as part of the battle between God and the devil. Accordingly, accommodation with rival religions—even toleration—was all but impossible. Difference needed to be confronted and opposed directly. As Christianity expanded into areas dominated by the Germanic tribes after the collapse of imperial authority in the west, this tendency to construe religious difference in absolute moral terms conditioned the attitude of Christians toward popular magical and superstitious practices, too.

While demonizing difference in this way allowed Christians to make sense of the various religious, social, and cultural traditions they encountered as the faith expanded, as a corollary, the process fostered social cohesion. This was particularly important during the first millennium as Christianity sought to define its core tenets and rituals, as it sought to articulate authority within the community and its relationship with other sources of power. Differences and variations within the ranks of the faithful were as potentially pernicious as those on the periphery.

In asserting what they were not, Christians found that the idea of the devil helped them define who they were.

23. THE PROBLEM OF IDOLS

Jews and early Christians lived in a religious environment that was polytheistic, accommodating, and syncretic. Thus, the sacred writings of both traditions reflect contact with these other religious traditions. As such, these seminal texts provided Christians with a way to view and understand religious difference.
Exodus: Hebrew, thirteenth century BCE?
Psalms: Hebrew, tenth century BCE?
Wisdom: Greek, first or second century BCE?
Corinthians: Greek, first century CE.

Source: trans. Gregory Martin et al. from the Latin Vulgate, The Holy Bible (Douay-Rheims version) (Douay: The English College, 1609–10), rev. Richard Challoner (1749–1752); rev.

Exodus

20.1. And the lord spoke all these words. . . .

3. You shall have no strange gods before me.

4. You shall not make for yourself a graven thing, nor the likeness of any thing that is in heaven above, or in the earth beneath, nor of those things that are in the waters under the earth.

5. You shall not adore them, nor serve them: I am the lord your God, mighty, jealous, visiting the iniquity of the fathers upon the children, unto the third and fourth generation of them that hate me.

Psalms

95.4. Since the lord is great and worthy to be praised greatly, he is to be feared above all gods.

5. All the gods of the people are devils but the lord made the heavens.

Wisdom

14.8. But the idol that is made by hands, is cursed, as well it, as he that made it: he because he made it; and it because being frail it is called a god.

9. But to God the wicked and his wickedness are hateful alike.

10. For that which is made, together with him who made it, shall suffer torments.

11. Therefore, there shall be no respect had even to the idols of the Gentiles: because the creatures of God are turned to an abomination, and a temptation to the souls of men, and a snare to the feet of the unwise.

12. For the beginning of fornication is the devising of idols: and the invention of them is the corruption of life.

13. For neither were they from the beginning, neither shall they be forever.

14. For by the vanity of men they came into the world: and therefore they shall be found to come shortly to an end.

15. For a father being afflicted with bitter grief, made to himself the image of his son who was quickly taken away: and him who then had died as a man, he began now to worship as a god, and appointed him rites and sacrifices among his servants.

16. Then in process of time, wicked custom prevailing, this error was kept as a law, and statues were worshipped by the commandment of tyrants. . . .

20. And the multitude of men, carried away by the beauty of the work, took him now for a god that a little before was but honored as a man.

21. And this was the occasion of deceiving human life. . . .

22. And it was not enough for them to err about the knowledge of God, but whereas they lived in a great war of ignorance, they call so many and so great evils peace.

23. For either they sacrifice their own children, or use hidden sacrifices, or keep watches full of madness,

24. So that now they neither keep life, nor marriage undefiled, but one kills another through envy, or aggrieve him by adultery:

25. And all things are mingled together, blood, murder, theft and dissimulation, corruption and unfaithfulness, tumults and perjury, disquieting of the good,

26. Forgetfulness of God, defiling of souls, changing of nature, disorder in marriage, and the irregularity of adultery and uncleanness.

27. For the worship of abominable idols is the cause, and the beginning and end of all evil.

28. For either they are mad when they are merry: or they prophesy lies, or they live unjustly, or easily forswear themselves.

29. For whilst they trust in idols, which are without life, though they swear amiss, they look not to be hurt.

30. But for two things they shall be justly punished, because they have thought not well of God, giving heed to idols, and have sworn unjustly, in guile despising justice.

1 Corinthians

10.19. What am I saying, then? That an idol is something or that something is sacrificed to idols?

20. But what the people sacrifice they sacrifice to demons and not to God. But I do not want you to be an ally of demons. You cannot drink from the lord's cup and the cup of demons.

21. You cannot partake of the lord's table and the table of demons.

Questions: How is the devil connected to idols? Do these texts make any distinction between types of worship that involve images? How might these texts condition Christian attitudes toward other cultures and religious traditions?

24. THE BETRAYAL AND TRIAL OF JESUS

Like the other gospel writers, Luke was not concerned primarily with historical accuracy in any modern sense of the concept. Rather, his gospel reflects on the Christ story through the lens of some of the major issues dogging the new faith in this crucial formative period; chief among these was the relationship between Jesus's followers, mainstream Judaism, and Rome.

Luke was the only non-Jew among the gospel writers, and he goes to some lengths to present the Roman authorities in the most favorable light. This is particularly the case in his portrait of the governor of Judaea, Pontius Pilate (r. 26–36 CE), whom Philo of Alexandria (doc. 14) characterized as notoriously corrupt and given to the most ferocious passions and brutal savagery.

Greek, c. 70 CE.

Source: trans. Gregory Martin et al. from the Latin Vulgate, The Holy Bible (Douay-Rheims version) (Douay: The English College, 1609–10), rev. Richard Challoner (1749–52); rev.

Luke

22.1. Now the feast of unleavened bread, which is called the Passover, was at hand.

2. And the chief priests and the scribes sought how they might put Jesus to death: but they feared the people.

3. And Satan entered into Judas, who was surnamed Iscariot, one of the twelve.

4. And he went, and discoursed with the chief priests and the magistrates, as to how he might betray Jesus to them.

5. And they were glad, and agreed to give him money.

6. And he promised. And he sought opportunity to betray Jesus when his followers were absent.

[After dining, Christ went to the Mount of Olives with his disciples.]

47. As Jesus was speaking, behold a multitude; and he that was called Judas, one of the twelve, went before them, and drew near to Jesus to kiss him.

48. And Jesus said to him, "Judas, do you betray the son of man with a kiss?". . .

52. And Jesus said to the chief priests, and magistrates of the temple, and the ancients, that had come to him, "Have you come out, as it were against a thief, with swords and clubs?

53. When I was daily with you in the temple, you did not stretch forth your hands against me: but this is your hour, and the power of darkness."

54. And apprehending him, they led him to the high priest's house. . . .

63. And the men that held him mocked him, and struck him.

64. And they blindfolded him, and smote his face. And they asked him, saying, "Prophesy, who is it that struck thee?"

65. And blaspheming, many other things they said against him.

66. And as soon as it was day, the ancients of the people, and the chief priests and scribes, came together; and they brought him into their council, saying, "If you are the Christ, tell us."

67. And he said to them, "If I shall tell you, you will not believe me.

68. And if I shall also ask you, you will not answer me, nor let me go.

69. But hereafter the son of man shall be sitting on the right hand of the power of God."

70. Then said they all, "Are you then the son of God?" And Jesus said, "You say that I am."

71. And they said, "What need we any further testimony? For we ourselves have heard it from his own mouth."

23.1. And the whole multitude of them rising up, led Jesus to Pilate.

2. And they began to accuse him, saying, "We have found this man perverting our nation, and forbidding tribute to be given to Caesar, and saying that he is Christ the king."

3. And Pilate asked him, saying, "Are you the king of the Jews?" But he answered, saying, "You say it."

4. And Pilate said to the chief priests and to the multitudes, "I find no cause in this man."

5. But they were more earnest, saying, "He stirs up the people, teaching throughout all Judea, beginning from Galilee to this place." . . .

13. And Pilate, calling together the chief priests, and the magistrates, and the people,

14. Said to them, "You have presented this man to me, as someone who perverts the people; and behold I, having examined him before you, find no cause in this man, in those things of which you accuse him. . . .

16. I will chastise him therefore, and release him."

17. Now of necessity Pilate was to release to them one upon the feast day.

18. But the whole multitude together cried out, saying, "Away with this man, and release to us Barabbas:

19. Who, for a certain sedition made in the city, and for a murder, was cast into prison."

20. And Pilate again spoke to them, desiring to release Jesus.

21. But they cried again, saying, "Crucify him, crucify him."

22. And he [Pilate] said to them the third time, "Why, what evil has this man done? I find no cause of death in him. I will chastise him therefore, and let him go."

23. But they were instant with loud voices, requiring that he might be crucified; and their voices prevailed.

24. And Pilate gave sentence that it should be as they required.

25. And he released unto them him who for murder and sedition, had been cast into prison, whom they had desired; but Jesus he delivered up to their will.

Questions: Who is responsible for Jesus's arrest and execution? How does Luke see the conflict between Jesus and the Jewish authorities? How does this account help foster a sense of community among the followers of Jesus?

25. THE SUSCEPTIBILITY OF WOMEN TO THE DEVIL

On the Dress of Women was part of a trilogy of works written by Tertullian (doc. 17) in Carthage shortly after his conversion, around 200 CE. At that time, Carthage was a wealthy city whose citizens enjoyed all the benefits of Roman civilization—and all of its luxurious temptations. Together with a work on idolatry and another on public games, On the Dress of Women *was an attempt by Tertullian to address how newly converted Christians should live in a pagan society with all of its potential moral and sensual snares.*

Latin, c. 200 CE.

Source: trans. Richard Raiswell and David R. Winter, from *Tertullien, La toilette des femmes (De cultu feminarum)* (Paris: Les Éditions du Cerf, 1971), http://www.tertullian.org/latin/de_cultu_feminarum_1.htm.

Most beloved sisters, if a faith existed here on earth commensurate with the reward we anticipate in heaven, none of you from the time she had known the living God and discovered her condition—that is, the true condition of womankind—would seek a more luxurious and ostentatious manner of dress! So as not to appear proud, she would go about in humble clothing and, preferably, affect a lowly appearance. She would go about as Eve herself, mourning and doing penance so that she might more fully atone for those things she inherited from Eve—and she would do so in a penitential manner of dress. Her shame comes from that first sin, and dare I say it, her hatred comes from being the cause of humanity's fall.

Woman, you bear children in sorrow and anxiety. You are subservient to your husband, for he has dominion over you [Gen. 3.16]. Do you not know that you are Eve? The judgment of God on your sex lives on right up to the present age.

Your guilt lives on and is wholly deserved. You are the devil's gateway. You are the unsealer of the [forbidden] tree. You are the first deserter of divine law. You are the one who persuaded the man whom the devil was not strong enough to destroy. You readily smashed the image of God—that is, man. Because of your reward [for disobedience]—that is, death—the son of God had to die. Still, you think that you should have adornments beyond animal skin tunics?

Come now, if, from the beginning of time, the Milesians had sheared sheep, and the Chinese had woven trees, and the Tyrians had dyed cloth, and the Phrygians embroidered with the needle, and the Babylonians with the loom, if pearls had gleamed and onyx had glittered, if gold had already been brought to the surface of the earth for humanity's greed, and if the mirror were permitted to lie so freely, I suppose Eve would have coveted all of these things—once she had been expelled from paradise and was already doomed to die. Now, though, if she wishes to live again, she ought not to seek or covet what she did not have then, let alone desire what she did not know about when she lived [in the Garden of Eden]. Accordingly, all these things are baubles for woman in her condemned and damned state. They are arranged as though they are finery for her funeral.

And, those who made these things are condemned, consigned to the punishment of death—namely the angels who fell from heaven onto the daughters of men so that their dishonor might also attach itself to woman [see doc. 2]. For when the angels disclosed their secret knowledge of things not previously understood by people living in that far more ignorant age, they revealed tools and crafts that appealed particularly to womanly vanity, namely: the smelting of metals, the virtues of herbs, the power of incantations, and the interpretation of the stars. They conferred on humanity the means to produce objects of womanly vanity: the gems that glint on women's necklaces, the bands of gold that encircle their arms, the bright dyes that stain their woolen fabrics, and the jet-colored powders that outline and highlight their eyes.

The true nature of these things can be discerned from the character and quality of those who taught them to humanity. Sinners are unable to demonstrate or offer anything conducive to virtue. Forsaken spirits can reveal nothing about the appropriate fear of God. If such things are to be called "teachings," then only evil "masters" can have taught them evilly. If these are the wages of lust, they are a shameful reward, fit for nothing!

But why was it so important for them to show and grant such things to women? Was it because women, who, when they are unkempt and unmade up—one might even say rough and unpolished—were able to provoke angels to lust but not men? Certainly this appears not to have been possible without the splendid material adornments and tricks of beauty that [the fallen angels] conferred. Or was it because the angelic lovers [thought they] would appear sullen and scornful through their casual and repeated use if they gave nothing to the women they had lured into marriage? Of course, it is not possible to guess at such things. The women wanted nothing more than to have angels for husbands—for they had certainly made great marriages.

To be sure, those angels lamented about where they had fallen from, sometimes sighing toward heaven after their heated moments of lust were over. They also rewarded the very excellence of women, that is, their natural beauty, as the cause of evil; they did this so that [the women's] good fortune should not profit them at all. Indeed, in this way, they ensured that women, who had turned away from simplicity and sincerity, had also offended God, just like the angels themselves. They were certain that women's adornment, their ambition, and their love of carnal pleasure was displeasing to God. Assuredly, these are the angels that we are destined to judge. These are the angels that we renounce in baptism. These are the very things for which they deserve to be judged by man. What business, then, do their affairs have to do with their judges? What connection is there between those who will condemn and those who will be condemned? In my opinion, it is the same as that which exists between Christ and [the demon] Belial [see 2 Cor. 6.15].

With what conscience will we climb to the seat of judgment to pass sentence against those whose gifts we currently seek? Indeed, that same angelic nature is promised to you as your reward, women: you will be given the same sex as men and the same dignity of judging. However, if we prejudge here, if we pre-condemn the affairs now that we are meant to condemn later, they will rather judge and condemn us. . . .

What legitimate honor can clothes claim when they are adulterated with illegitimate colors? Those things which God did not make are not pleasing to him: as if he was unable to command purple or sky-blue sheep into existence! If he was able to command such things into existence, clearly he did not want to do so. Thus, it is not permitted to produce things that God does not want. Therefore, things are not the best by virtue of their nature when they do not come from God, who is the author of nature. Indeed, such things must be understood as coming from the devil—that is, from him who falsifies nature. They cannot come from anywhere else because whatever does not originate with God, must necessarily originate with his rival. And apart from the devil and his angels, there is no other rival of God. . . .

I am certainly not suggesting these things in order to persuade you to adopt a rough and unkempt appearance. I do not see virtue in squalor and filth. However, I want to teach you about the appropriate and righteous way to adorn your body. You should not want to go beyond the simple and sufficient elegance that pleases God.

For those women who smear their skin with cosmetics, pollute their cheeks with rouge, and line their eyes with antimony utterly fail him. Evidently, they are not satisfied with God's workmanship. Instead, they challenge and blame the divine craftsman of everything. Indeed, whenever they try to improve themselves, they cast doubt on God's work. Whenever they attempt to add to God's handiwork, they are using the artifice of a rival craftsman, that is, of the devil! For who else would give lessons on how to change a body except him who transformed the spirit of man through malice? He undoubtedly concocted tricks of this sort so that he might bring the hand of God upon us in a certain manner. Whatever is born is the work of God. Whatever has been modified is the devil's business. How wicked it is to apply the devil's tricks to a divine work! Our slaves borrow nothing from our enemies; soldiers desire nothing from their general's foe. It is a sin to demand the use of anything from the adversary of him in whose hands you lie. Can a Christian really be helped by the evil one? If he can, I do not know if he can continue to call himself a Christian, for instead he will belong to him whose teachings he desires.

But how alien are these things to your teachings and declarations! How unworthy it is to wear the name of "Christian" with a painted face, you from whom simplicity is demanded! How unworthy it is to lie with your appearance, you for whom it is not permitted to lie with your tongue! How unworthy it is to seek that which was not given, you to whom abstinence from others' possessions is taught! How unworthy it is to exercise adultery in your appearance, you for whom modesty should be a study! Ask yourselves, blessed sisters, how will you keep the commandments of God if you do not preserve the very appearance he has given you?

Questions: Why are women especially susceptible to the devil's influence? Who created the instruments of ornamentation and why? What power does the devil have to make things? To what extent does the devil use vanities to turn women into his subjects?

26. THE DEATH OF THE OLD RELIGION

Eusebius (c. 260–340) lived through the last great persecution of Christians under Diocletian at the beginning of the fourth century. After Christian worship was sanctioned, he rose to become bishop of Caesarea under Constantine. This selection comes from his Preparation for the Gospel, *a defense of Christianity against paganism, and quotes extensively from* On the Obsolescence of Oracles, *a dialogue by the influential Greek philosopher and biographer Plutarch (c. 50–120 CE), a work that set out to examine why so many Greek oracles had ceased to function by his day. Eusebius is especially interested in Plutarch's lengthy digression on daemons. Among these is the horned semi-bestial figure of Pan. Half man and half goat, in Greek mythology Pan was traditionally associated with the pastoral world and, by extension, with fertility.*

Greek, early fourth century.

Source: trans. E. H. Gifford, from Eusebius of Caesarea, *Praeparatio Evangelica* (*Preparation for the Gospel*) (Oxford, 1903), pp. 205–8; rev.

It seems appropriate here to add the words of Plutarch from the book which he has written entitled *On the Cessation of Oracles*. . . .

"The opinion," said Demetrius, "that those who preside over the oracles are not gods but daemons who are servants of gods, seems to me a fair assumption, for gods ought rightly to be kept free from earthly affairs. But to take, as it were, a handful out of the verses from [the Greek philosopher] Empedocles, and to lay sins and frenzies and heaven-sent wanderings upon these daemons, and to imagine them dying deaths like men, I consider too bold and barbaric a step." At this point, Cleombrotus asked Philip who the young man was, and where he came from. When he had learned his name and city, he said, "We are not ourselves unconscious, Heracleon, that we have entered upon strange arguments. But in dealing with great subjects it is not possible to arrive at a probable opinion without employing great principles."

"But you are yourself unconsciously taking back what you grant. For you admit that daemons exist. But in claiming that they are not wicked and not mortal, you no longer have daemons to defend. For in what do they differ from the gods, if they are both incorruptible with respect to essence, and free from passion and sin with respect to virtue?"

While Heracleon was silently pondering to himself some answer to this, Philip said to him, "No, Heracleon, that daemons are wicked was admitted not only by Empedocles, but also by [other Greek philosophers] Plato, Xenocrates, and Chrysippus; and, in addition, when Democritus prayed that he might meet favorable apparitions, it was clear that he knew of other daemons with certain perverse and mischievous propensities and impulses.

"Now with respect to the death of such beings, I have heard a story from a man who was neither a fool nor braggart. For the father of Aemilianus the rhetorician—to whom some of you have listened—was Epitherses, my fellow citizen and grammar-master. He said that once, on a voyage to Italy, he embarked in a ship carrying merchandise and many passengers. At evening off the Echinades Islands, the wind dropped, and the ship drifted and came near to [the Ionian island of] Paxi. Almost everybody was awake, drinking after having finished their dinner. Suddenly a voice was heard from the island Paxi, someone calling aloud to Thamus. Everyone was amazed, for Thamus was the pilot, an Egyptian, and few on board even knew his name. Thamus was called twice, but kept his silence. However, on the third time he answered. Raising his voice, the caller said, 'When you are opposite Palodes, announce that the Great Pan is dead.'

On hearing this, Epitherses said they were all astounded, and began to debate as to whether it was better to do what was commanded, or to refuse to meddle and let the matter pass. At this, Thamus decided that if there was a wind, he would sail past the island and keep quiet, but if the wind should fail and a calm come on about the place, he would announce what he had heard.

So when he came opposite Pelodes and there was neither wind nor wave, looking toward the land from the stern of the ship, Thamus repeated the words as he had heard them, 'The Great Pan is dead.' No sooner had he finished speaking than there came a loud cry of lamentation—not of one but of many people—mingled with exclamations of amazement.

Because there were many people on the vessel, the tale soon reached Rome and Thamus was summoned by Tiberius Caesar. Tiberius so fully believed the story that he made thorough inquiry and research about Pan. The great number of learned men present at his court conjectured that the tale referred to Pan, the son of Hermes and Penelope."

Philip had witnesses to his story in some of those who were present who had heard it from the aged Aemilianus. But Demetrius said that there were many sparsely populated islands scattered about among those off the coast of Britain, some of which were named after daemons and heroes. And that he himself, being sent by the emperor to make an investigation and survey of the region, sailed to the nearest of these islands, which had but few inhabitants and these all sacred persons inviolable to the Britons.

Very soon after his arrival, though, there arose a great commotion in the air: there were many portents in the sky, violent blasts of wind, and thunderbolts crashing to the earth. When these abated, the islanders said that one of the higher powers had been extinguished. 'For as a lamp while lighted does no harm, but being extinguished is hurtful to many,' they said, 'so great souls are benignant and harmless in their shining, but their extinction and dissolution often—as now—causes winds and storms, often infecting the air with pestilent diseases.' . . ."

So much for Plutarch. But it is important to observe the time at which he says that the death of the daemon took place. For it was the time of Tiberius, during which our savior, making his sojourn among men, is recorded to have been ridding human life of daemons of every kind, so that there were some of them kneeling before him and beseeching him not to deliver them over to the Tartarus that awaited them.

You have therefore the date for the overthrow of the daemons, of which there was no record at any other time—just as you had the abolition of human sacrifice among the gentiles as not having occurred until after the preaching of the doctrine of the Gospel had reached all mankind. Let then these refutations from recent history suffice.

Questions: What are daemons? What has happened to them according to Plutarch? According to Eusebius? How is Eusebius understanding Plutarch's story? Are daemons demons?

27. THE PROBLEM OF MAGIC

The ancient world was teeming with wonder workers (see Elymas the Magician in doc. 10). One of the problems confronting Christ and the early Christians, then, was to distinguish their miracle-working abilities from such popular magic. This tradition, however, could not simply be dismissed as fraudulent, for Exodus 7.9–25 described a wonder-working contest between Pharaoh's magicians, and Moses and his brother. While the story demonstrated the superiority of the patriarchs' power, in so doing, it also made clear that the Egyptians' conjurations were authentic.

Simon Magus (Simon the Magician) figures briefly in the book of Acts, where he is described as offering to purchase the power to dispense the holy spirit to work wonders from the disciples. For this he was rebuked by Saint Peter (Acts 8.9–24). Over the centuries, this story was embellished.

The Passion of the Holy Apostles Peter and Paul is traditionally credited to Marcellus, one of Simon Magus's followers, but it is clearly much later.

Latin, fifth or sixth century.

Source: trans. Richard Raiswell and David R. Winter, from *Acta Apostolorum Apocrypha*, ed. Richard Lipsius and Maximilian Bonnet (Leipzig, 1891), pp. 129–35, 139, 147, 161–67.

Stirred with zeal, Simon began to say many evil things about Peter, claiming that the apostle was a magician and a deceiver. But those who had been amazed by the wonders Simon had made believed him, for he made a bronze serpent move, made bronze and stone statues laugh and move—and running, he suddenly made it so that he seemed to be flying in the air.

To counter these things, Peter cured the sick through his word, made the blind see through prayer, put demons to flight through his command—even raising the dead themselves. He told the people not only that they should flee Simon's deception, but that they should expose him so that it did not seem that they were in league with the devil.

And so it happened that all pious men cursed Simon the magician, declaring him wicked. But through false testimony, Simon's followers—because they were with Simon—claimed that it was Peter who was the magician. Word of this reached emperor Nero, and he ordered Simon the magician to come to him.

After he had entered, standing before the emperor, Simon suddenly began to change forms: he suddenly became a boy and after that, an old man—and in another instant, a youth. Changed in sex and age, through these many forms, he raged in the devil's service. When Nero saw this, he assumed that Simon really was the son of God. But the apostle Peter said that he was a thief, a liar, a magician, shameless, accursed, and an apostate, an adversary to the truth of all God's commandments, and that there was nothing left to done except to expose Simon's manifest iniquity to everyone, as commanded by God.

Then Simon went to Nero and said, "Hear me, good emperor. I am the son of God who descended from heaven. Up to now, I have put up with Peter who calls himself the only apostle. Now, though, his evil has been doubled. Now Paul, who teaches the same thing and who is also prejudiced against me, is reported to be preaching together with him. With respect to them, unless you contrive their destruction, your kingdom will not survive." Filled with anxiety about this, Nero ordered Peter and Paul to be brought to him immediately.

When Simon the magician and the apostles of Christ Peter and Paul went in to see Nero the next day, Simon said, "These are the disciples of that Nazarene—and for them it is not so good a thing that they are from the lowest ranks of the Jews . . . this is the race of people who have corrupted all Judea so that they do not believe in me. . . ."

Then Peter said to Simon, "You have been able to trick everyone, but never me—but those you have deceived, God has recalled from their error through me. And since it has been proven to you that you are not able to defeat me, I am amazed at the way you boast about yourself before the king—as if you think that you can defeat the disciples of Christ through your magical skill."

Nero said, "Who is Christ?"

Peter said, "He is the one Simon the magician asserts himself to be. But Simon is a wicked man; his works are diabolical . . . this Simon is so full of lies and surrounded by deceit that he thinks he is what God is—even though he is a man. . . In that Simon, there are two substances, one of man and one of the devil—the devil who tries to ensnare men through a man.

Simon said, "I am amazed, good emperor, that you think this man to be of any importance—an ignorant man, a fisherman, a most deceitful liar, powerful neither in word nor rank nor in any other manner. But so I do not have to put up with this enemy any longer, I will order my angels to come and take my vengeance on him immediately."

Peter said, "I do not fear your angels—but they will fear me in the power and confidence of my lord Jesus Christ who you falsely claim yourself to be.". . .

[After being challenged by Peter, Simon is unable to read the apostle's thoughts. Frustrated, Simon summons a pack of dogs to devour the apostle, but at the sight of some bread Peter had blessed, the dogs vanish.]

Then Nero turned to Paul and said, "Why do you say nothing, Paul?" Paul replied, "Know this, Caesar, if you allow this magician to continue doing such things, great evil will grow in your country and your kingdom will be cast down from its present state."

Nero said to Simon, "What do you say, Simon?"

Simon said, "Unless I clearly show myself to be God, no one will give me the reverence I am owned. . . . Do you believe, good emperor, that I am a mere magician—even though I have died and risen again?"

The treacherous Simon had earlier acted through his own trickery, saying to Nero, "Order me to be beheaded in a dark place and the body removed immediately. If I do not rise again on the third day, you will know me that I was a magician. But if I do rise again, you will know that I am the son of God."

After Nero had ordered this done, Simon secretly arranged that a ram be beheaded through his magical art. This ram appeared to be Simon until it was beheaded. The animal was beheaded in the dark but when the man who had beheaded it brought the head into the light and examined it, he discovered that it was the head of a ram. However, the man did not want to say anything to the king about this in case doing so exposed Simon who had ordered all this to be done in secret. As a result, from that time forward Simon claimed that he had risen again on the third day because the head and limbs of the ram had been removed [after it had been killed, leaving] only the congealed blood. And on the third day, Simon showed himself to Nero and said, "Have my blood which was poured out wiped away because—behold—I who was beheaded have risen again on the third day, just as I promised." . . .

Simon said, "Listen, emperor Nero. So that you will know that these men are false and that I was sent from the heavens, tomorrow I will go to the heavens so that I may bless those who believe in me—but I will show my wrath to those who have dared deny me."

Peter and Paul said, "God once called us to his glory—but you who have been called by the devil are hastening to his torments."

Simon said, "Caesar Nero, listen to me. Separate yourself from these madmen so that when I come to my father in the heavens, I can be favorably disposed towards you."

Nero said, "And how can we prove that you are going into heaven?"

Simon said, "Order a tall tower to be made from wood and great beams so that I can ascend it. And when I have climbed it, my angels will come to me in the air—for they are not able to come to me on the ground among the sinners."

Nero said, "I want to see if you can do what you say."

So Nero ordered a tall tower to be built on the Campus Martius [Field of Mars] and ordered all the people and dignitaries to come together for this spectacle. The next day, Nero ordered Peter and Paul to be present at this spectacle too, and, before the entire gathering, said to them, "Now the truth will appear."

Peter and Paul said, "We are not exposing Simon—rather, this will be the work of our lord, Jesus Christ, the son of God, who Simon pretends to be.

And Paul turned to Peter and said, "It is for me to pray to God on bended knees; it is for you to act if you see him trying anything, for you were chosen first by the lord." And with knees bent, Paul prayed.

Staring at Simon, Peter said, "Begin what you have started, for your exposure and our calling are approaching—indeed, I see my Christ calling me and Paul."

Nero said, "Where will you be going against my will?"

Peter said, "To wherever our lord summons us."

Nero said, "Who is your lord?"

Peter said, "Lord Jesus Christ who I see calling us."

Nero said, "Are you both going to heaven, then?"

Peter said, "We are going to wherever it pleases the one who is calling us."

Simon said, "So that you may know, emperor, that these men are liars, as soon as I ascend into heaven, I will send my angels to you and I will make you come to me."

Nero said, "Do, therefore, what you say."

Then Simon climbed the tower in front of everyone and, crowned with a laurel wreath and with his hands outstretched, he began to fly. When he saw this, Nero said this to Peter, "That man Simon speaks the truth, and you and Paul are deceivers."

To this, Peter said, "Presently, you will realize that we are the true disciples of Christ. This man is not Christ—he is a magician and evil-doer."

Nero said, "Do you still persist in this? Look, you can see him entering into heaven."

Then looking at Paul, Peter said, "Paul, raise your head and look." And when Paul raised his head, his eyes full of tears, he saw Simon flying, and he said, "Peter, why are you hesitating? Finish what you have begun, for our Lord Jesus Christ is calling us even now."

And Nero, hearing them, smiled, and said, "Now these men see that they have been defeated and they are raving."

Peter said, "Presently, you will attest that we are not raving." Paul said to Peter, "Do now what you were doing."

And looking towards Simon, Peter said, "I order you, angels of Satan—you who bear Simon in the air in order to deceive the hearts of unfaithful men—through God, the creator of all things and through Jesus Christ who rose from the dead on the third day, to carry him no longer. Abandon him." And as soon as the angels abandoned him, he fell onto the place which is called the Sacra Via [Sacred Way]. Having been broken into four pieces, he was turned into four stones. These remain up to the present day as evidence of the apostles' victory.

Then Nero had Peter and Paul bound in chains. But he ordered Simon's body to be guarded carefully for three days, thinking that he would rise again on the third day.

Peter said to him, "He will not rise now, for he is truly dead and condemned to eternal punishment."

Questions: Why is the accusation of magic so contentious for both Simon and the apostles? Why is it important that this wonder-working contest be public? Does Simon's magic work? How does Peter's supernatural power work? Is there a danger for Christians in connecting wonder working with demons? What does this story suggest about non-Christian wonder working?

28. SURVIVAL OF THE OLD RELIGION

Born in the Pannonia (modern Hungary), Martin of Braga (c. 520–580) spent a number of years in the Holy Land before traveling to Galicia (modern Portugal), where King Ariamir had recently converted from Arian to Catholic Christianity. Martin may well have played a significant role in spreading the new faith among the Germanic Suevi. He attended the first Council of Braga in 563 as bishop of Dumium (modern Dumio), and his conception of the devil's fall in the piece below is informed by the council's teachings on the devil against dualist heresies.

Latin, c. 572.

Source: trans. Claude W. Barlow, from Martin of Braga, *Reforming the Rustics*, in *Iberian Fathers*, vol. 1 (Washington, DC: Catholic University of America, 1969), pp. 71–85.

Bishop Martin, to my most blessed and beloved brother in Christ bishop Polemius.

I have received your kind letter, in which you write me that I should send you something on the origin of idols and their sins, or, if I like, a few selections from the abundant material available, in order to chastise the rustics who are still bound by the old pagan superstition and offer more veneration to demons than to God. Since it is necessary to offer them some small explanation for these idols' existence from the beginning of the world to whet the appetite, as it were, I have had to touch upon a vast forest of past times and events in a treatise of very brief compass and to offer the rustics food seasoned with rustic speech. . . .

In the beginning, when God created the heavens and the earth, in his celestial habitation he created spiritual creatures, that is, angels, who should stand in his presence and praise him. One of these, who had been appointed archangel, chief of them all, seeing himself so radiant and glorious, did not pay honor to God his creator, but said that he was equal to him; and for this act of pride he, along with many other angels who had agreed with him, was cast from that celestial abode into the air which is beneath the heavens; and he who had formerly been the archangel lost the light of his glory and became the devil, full of gloom and horror. Likewise, the other angels who had agreed with him were thrown out of heaven with him, lost their splendor, and became demons, while the rest of the angels, who had remained subject to God, still persevere in the glory of their brightness in the lord's presence; and they are called holy angels, while those who were thrown out with their leader, Satan, because of their pride are called rebellious angels and demons.

After this fall of the angels, it pleased God to form man from the mud of the earth and place him in paradise; and he said to him that if he obeyed the precept of the lord, he might succeed without death to that celestial region from which those rebellious angels had fallen, but if he acted contrary to the precept of God, he should suffer death. Then the devil, seeing that man had been created to succeed to the place in the kingdom of God from which he had fallen, was induced by envy to persuade man to disobey the commands of God. For this offense man was cast from paradise into the exile of this world, where he should endure many labors and pains. . . .

After the flood, the human race was again restored through the three sons of Noah, who had been saved with their wives. And when the multitude began to increase and fill the world, again men forgot God the creator of the world and when they had abandoned the creator they began to worship creatures. Some paid homage to the sun, others the moon and stars, others fire, others deep water and springs of water, believing that all of these had not been created by God for the use of man, but had sprung up as gods from themselves.

Then the devil or his ministers, the demons who had been cast out of heaven, seeing that ignorant men had dismissed God their creator and were mistaking the creatures, began to appear to them in various forms and speak with them and demand of them that they offer sacrifices to them on lofty mountains and in leafy forests and worship them as God, assuming the names of wicked men who had spent their whole lives in crime and sin, so that one claimed to be Jupiter, who had been a soothsayer and involved in so many adulteries that he had taken his own sister, Juno, to wife and had corrupted his daughters, Minerva and Venus, and had even committed foul incest with his nieces and all his female relatives. Another demon called himself Mars, who had sown quarrels and discord. Then another demon chose to name himself Mercury, who had been the crafty inventor of all theft and deceit; to him as though to God men anxious for gain heap up piles of stones for a sacrifice whenever they pass a crossroads. Another demon took for himself the name of Saturn, who had lived amid all sorts of cruelty, even devouring his own sons at their birth. Another demon claimed to be Venus; she had been a prostitute and not only participated in innumerable adulteries, but had even committed incest with her father, Jupiter, and her brother, Mars.

Lo, such was the nature in the days of those perverse men, whom the ignorant rustics basely honored by their own evil conduct, and whose names the demons had assumed in order that the rustics might worship them as gods and offer them sacrifices and imitate the deeds of those whose names they invoked. The demons even persuaded them to build temples to them and to place therein images or statues of wicked men and to set up altars to them, upon which they should pour out for them blood both of animals and even of men. Furthermore, many of the demons who had been expelled from heaven now preside over the sea or streams or fountains or forests, and in similar fashion ignorant men who do not know God worship them as gods and offer them sacrifice. In the sea, they call upon

Neptune; in the streams, the Lamias; in the fountains, the nymphs; in the forests, the Dianas, which are all worthless demons and evil spirits, who trouble and harm infidels who do not know how to fortify themselves with the sign of the cross. They do not harm them without God's consent, however; for the infidels have angered God and do not believe wholeheartedly in the faith of Christ, but are such disbelievers that they place the very names of the demons on each day of the week, and speak of the day of Mars and of Mercury and of Jupiter and of Venus and of Saturn, who never created a day, but were evil and wicked men among the race of the Greeks. . . .

Now what must we say with sorrow of that very foolish superstition by which they observe days for moths and mice; when, if it be right to mention it, a Christian man worships mice and moths instead of God? If the bread or cloth is not taken away from them and protected in a little box or basket, they will never spare what they find simply for your dedicating a holiday to them. It is without justification that wretched man sets up practices by which he may assure himself through the whole year of being as prosperous and successful in all things as he is at the beginning of the year. These are all pagan practices, thought up through the inventiveness of demons. Woe to that man who does not have God in his favor and does not possess sufficient bread and security of life granted by him! Yet you perform these idle superstitions either secretly or openly, and you never cease from these sacrifices to demons. Why, then, do they not help you to be continually prosperous and safe and happy? Why is it that, when God is angry, these idle sacrifices do not defend you from the locust, from the mouse, and from the many other tribulations which an angry God sends you?

Don't you clearly understand that the demons are lying to you in these superstitious practices which you vainly observe, and that they are making fun of you in the auguries which you frequently witness? As the most wise Solomon said: "Divinations and omens are unreal"; the more a man fears in these things, the more his heart is deceived. "Fix not your heart on it. For they have led many astray." Lo, this is what the holy scripture says, and it is most certainly true, for as long as unhappy men entice demons through birds' songs, as long as they destroy their faith in Christ in frivolous and idle ways, so long will they continue to rush unexpectedly to their own final destruction. God did not order man to know the future, but that he should always live in fear of him and ask him for guidance and help in his life. God alone possesses foreknowledge of events; but demons delude silly men with various fables, until they cause them to offend God and drag their souls with them to hell, just as they did in the beginning for envy, lest man enter the kingdom of heaven from which they were expelled.

For this reason also, when God saw that wretched men are so deceived by the devil and his wicked angels that they forget their creator and worship demons instead of God, He sent his son, that is, his wisdom and his word, to recall them to the worship of the true God from the error of the devil. . . .

When the end of this world comes, all nations and every man who has his origin from those first human beings, that is, from Adam and Eve, shall arise, both the good and the bad; and all shall come before the judgment of Christ. . . . Those who have been unbelievers or have not been baptized or, even though baptized, have after their baptism returned to idols and homicide and adultery and perjury and other wicked ways and who died without repentance; all who have been found such shall be condemned with the devil and with all the demons whom they worshipped and whose works they performed and shall be sent in the flesh to eternal fire in hell, where that inextinguishable fire lives forever and that flesh now recovered at the resurrection suffers eternal torments and groaning. It wants to die again that it may not feel the punishment, but it is not permitted to die that it may suffer everlasting torments. . . . Henceforth, it is up to you, my dear sons, to remember the words that we have spoken, and either by doing good to hope for future repose in the kingdom of God, or (and may this not come true!) by doing evil to await the perpetual fire to be found in hell. Both the life eternal and death eternal lie within man's choice. Whatever each one chooses for himself, that shall he have. . . .

Lo, such is the guarantee and confession of yours that God holds against you! How is it possible that some of you who have renounced the devil and his messengers and his worship and his evil ways turn again to the worship of the devil? To light candles beside rocks and beside trees and beside fountains and at crossroads, what else is this but worship of the devil? To observe divinations and auguries and days for idols, what else is this but worship of the devil? To observe Vulcan's day and the kalends, to set out tables, to put up laurel wreaths, to watch the foot, to pour fruit and wine on a log in the hearth, to throw bread into a fountain, what else is this but worship of the devil? For women at their weaving to call on the name of Minerva and to observe the day of Venus in weddings and to be careful about the day on which one commences a journey, what else is this but worship of the devil? To chant over herbs to make poisons, and to invoke the names of demons in incantations, what else is this but worship of the devil? And many other things which it would take too long to mention here. Lo, you do all these things after renunciation of the devil, after baptism, and by returning to the worship of demons and to the evil works of idols you have transgressed your faith and have broken the pact which you made with God. You have given up the sign of the cross, which you received in baptism, and pay attention to other signs of the devil, such as the flight of birds and sneezing and many other things. Why is it that augury does no harm to me or to any proper Christian? Because where the sign of the cross precedes, there is no sign of the devil. Why does it harm you? Because you despise the sign of the cross and fear what you yourselves make into a sign. Similarly, you have given up the sacred incantation, I mean the creed you accepted in baptism, which is: "I believe in God the father almighty," and the lord's prayer, that is, "Our father who art in heaven," and you retain the devil's incantations and charms. Whoever, then, scorns the sign of the cross of Christ, but looks for other signs, has lost the sign of the cross which he received in baptism. Similarly, he who clings to other incantations invented by magicians and evil-doers has lost the incantation of the holy creed and of the lord's prayer, which he received in the faith of Christ, and has trodden under foot that faith of Christ, for God and the devil cannot be worshipped together.

Questions: How has Martin modified the story of the devil? What is the devil worship about which he complains? To Martin's mind, how has it come about that so many people are worshipping the devil? In his view, what sorts of people worship the devil? How Christianized are they?

29. ALEXANDER ENCOUNTERS GOG AND MAGOG

Alexander of Macedonia—or Alexander the Great—(356–323 BCE) conquered an enormous swath of territory running from the Greek world up to northwestern India. In the centuries after his death, a body of legendary material came to supplement the more contemporary historical accounts of his exploits that Alexander had promoted during his lifetime. By the third century, this material came to form the core of the so-called Alexander Romance, *erroneously attributed to Callisthenes (fl. fourth century BCE), one of Alexander's historians. Although the Pseudo-Callisthenes version of the* Romance *was composed in Greek, it was translated into Latin in the next century. It survives in some 80 different versions in 24 different languages.*

The following section is a metrical discourse on a portion of the second book of the Romance and is attributed to the Christian Syriac writer Jacob of Serugh (451–521). While the section highlights the assimilation of various Christian apocalyptic elements into the story, it may be significant that his description of the physical features of the peoples of Mâgôg echoes those of classical historians such as Ammianus Marcellinus (c. 330–c. 400) in their account of the Huns who flooded out from the Caucasus at the end of the fourth century.

Syriac, sixth century.

Source: trans. E. A. Budge, *A Discourse Composed by Jacob of Sĕrûgh upon Alexander*, in *The History of Alexander the Great* (Cambridge: University Press, 1889), pp. 175–78, 182–87, 193–95, 198; rev.

[Traveling east toward India, Alexander gathers 300 old, grey-haired men to learn the secrets of the land.]

> And in his wisdom Alexander began to ask questions, saying,
> "What are these nations who are beyond you? Has the king obtained sovereignty in this land?"

The wise men looked upon this king full of wisdom and saw
How joyful he was at the advice of the old men and nobles of the country.
The old men replied, "This is the dominion of Tûbarlîkâ
The great king of the house of the Persians and of the Âmôrâyê.
Within it are the peoples of the house of Japhet and of the house of Mâgôg,
A cunning nation, a flayed nation, an uprooted nation."
The king said, "Are there mountains from here onwards?"
The old men replied, "As far as the river Kallath and as far as Halôrîs are
Fearful, savage and lofty mountains with great terror,
And beyond them terrible mountains—a great boundary
Which God has set between us and them for all eternity."
The old men replied, "It is altogether a difficult land
In which there are dragons, wild beasts, and serpents,
And unless men pass the sentence of death upon their lives
They are not able to dwell with dragons and snakes.". . .
And wonder seized the great king at this counsel of the old men,
And he began to ask questions to learn more about everything.
The king said, "Who are these kings
And the terrible peoples who are beyond this mountain?"
The old men replied, "Listen, O Master and king, and we will tell you.
Behold, the family of Âgôg and the family of Mâgôg are beyond us,
Terrible of aspect, hateful of form, of all heights,
The stature of each one of them is between six and seven cubits;
Their noses are flat and their foreheads hateful.
They bathe in blood, and in blood wash they also their heads;
They drink blood and eat the flesh of men;
They wear skins, sharpen weapons and forge wrath,
And are more ferocious and have more wars than all other nations.
Wherever the wrath of the lord rises, he sends them.
They overturn the land, uproot mountains, and devour men."
Then the son of Philip was grieved because he had heard these things,
And he marveled at this greatly within himself a long time.
Little by little he learned and understood everything which he asked,
And thought that he would make a great gate there. . . .

[Alexander wins a great victory against the Persians.]

Then he courageously took pains and made a door
Against Âgôg and the family of Mâgôg, and bound them inside.
He took a great quantity of iron and brass and prepared it
For the making of the door so that he could shut it in the face of these
    people.

He gave commands to twelve thousand skilled, ready workmen. . . .
He measured the ground of the narrow pass between the mountains,
So that he might shut in the peoples of the house of Mâgôg until the end of time.
The king in his wisdom measured from mountain to mountain,
Twelve cubits in the strength of his power.
The king said, "Make a threshold for the whole pass,
And let it be sunk in the mountain on this side and on that." . . .
He made a lintel over the door above the entire pass,
And sunk it in the mountains on both sides for the whole width of the door. . . .
The hosts erected and fixed the door there
In all the threshold, above and below, as in clay.
He put bolts into the threshold and into the door,
And sunk them in so that no man could tell where they fitted together. . . .
The king fixed doors and beams and bolts in the two sides of the mountain,
And another bolt of brass and iron, in his wisdom.
He fixed the door, and then wonder and quietness and rest and silence
Came over the peoples of the house of Mâgôg who had not perceived the building.
King Alexander made haste and made the door
Against the north, and against the spoilers and the children of Mâgôg.
In the sixth month, he finished building the whole door.
[After giving thanks to God, Alexander receives a vision from a watcher angel.]
The lord spoke by the hand of the angel, saying "I will magnify you
More than all the kings and governors in all the world.
This great gate which you have made in this land
Shall be closed until the end of times come.
Jeremiah also prophesied concerning it and the earth has heard,
'The gate of the north shall be opened on the day of the end of the world,
And on that day evil shall go forth on the wicked.
There shall be woe to those who are with child and to those who give suck' [Jer. 1.14]. . . .

[Inspired by the spirit of the lord, Alexander then records what has been revealed to him.]

Alexander the king, the son of Philip, said,
"Let the kings and their ranks and their dominions tremble,
On the day on which these people [Âgôg and Mâgôg] go forth over the earth at the end of times.

And men and all the quarters of the earth will anger the lord of hosts,
And his anger will rise and blot out the earth with an evil desolation. . . .
The seas shall roar, the earth shall cry out, and the mountains shall shriek,
The valleys shall fear, and towns and villages shall be desolated.
The vineyards shall be destroyed and stupor shall fall upon their planters,
Joy shall come to an end, and the power of all the mighty men shall fall.
Beautiful things shall perish, riches shall fail, and power shall vanish,
Fountains shall fail, streets shall be destroyed, and the valleys shall be useless.
The hosts and filthy assemblies of the children of Mâgôg shall stand up,
And all creation shall become and remain a ruin. . . .
That great nation which is perverse in its works,
And bears woe and is full of wrath and slaughter and death,
For evil captivity and destruction do they prepare with great wrath,
For spoil and slaughter are they entirely ready without ceasing.
They threaten with power and there is wrath in their cursings,
Mountains and valleys and plains tremble at them.
And great woe shall be upon those who are with child and those who
    give suck,
And mourning and pain upon young men and maidens,
Weeping for the children being slain through the cutting off of hope,
And for the youths also being cut off by the baleful ones.
The heavens and earth will put on pain and sadness,
And the assemblies of celestial beings will be astonished in those days.
Quaking will fall upon the living and the dead at that time,
Through the slaughter and blood of the children of Mâgôg before the end.
A renowned people will stir up strife in the lands,
And cast tumult among cities and towns,
An ugly people, a people flayed and uprooted and full of blemishes,
Of the children of Âgôg and of the house of Mâgôg with their fellows.
In abundance will they come to Palestine madly,
They will uproot and destroy its cities and slay its people.
The race of men, nation after nation, will roar and cry out,
Joy and gladness shall cease and woe will reign,
Weeping and spoiling and wickedness and all sadness shall increase . . .
Then the hosts of Âgôg and of the house of Mâgôg shall go forth,
And man shall fall upon his fellow man, and nation upon nation,
And the quaking of the earth and the sword of anger shall be there.
On the skirts of Zion the bodies of the dead shall lie in heaps.
And after these things, the earth shall be desolated of mankind,
Villages shall be destroyed and all towns and cities;
The scattered ones only remain in the earth as a remnant.

Then shall Antichrist rise upon the whole earth,
Through the gate shall that rebel go forth and come;
That lying one shall overthrow Christ as is promised.
There demons and spirits and wicked devils shall stand up before him,
And they shall gather together all creation to their cursed master.
The earth shall cry out, 'I entreat you, O lord, to spare me in your mercy,
For, behold, I am sick and persecuted with all wounds.'
These things which I have spoken shall come to pass before the end of the world,
And let anyone who has an ear of love listen to them."

Questions: What peculiarities has the author added to the story of Alexander's conquests? Why and where does Alexander build his gate? How does the author describe the people of Âgôg and Mâgôg? What are the signs of the end times?

30. DEALING WITH UNORTHODOX VIEWS

Wynfrith (c. 675–754)—better known as Saint Boniface—was one of a number of Anglo-Saxon missionaries engaged in the eastern part of the Frankish empire. With the support of the papacy and mayor of the palace, Charles Martel (d. 741)—the real power operating behind the throne of the last of the Merovingian kings—Boniface devoted much of his life to converting the peoples of the Rhineland. He was also concerned with re-establishing papal discipline across the empire, for religious practice during this era was often irregular or unorthodox.

The following section details Boniface's encounter with a cleric named Aldebert, likely active in Neustria. An earlier letter from Boniface dated 743 described him as a "new Samson" and claimed that he preached foolishness and never refrained from carnal lust. Here, Boniface outlines to a papal synod Aldebert's unorthodox practices.

Latin, 25 October 745.

Source: trans. Richard Raiswell and David R. Winter, "Akten der römischen Synode vom Jahre 745," from *Die Briefe des heiligen Bonifatius und Lullus*, MGH Epistolae selectae I (Berlin, 1916), pp. 108–20.

[A letter of Boniface to Pope Zacharias is read aloud to the Synod.]

Boniface, a poor servant of the servants of God, sends greeting of love to Pope Zacharias, the most exalted father and apostolic pontiff, made master by the authority of Saint Peter, the prince of the apostles . . .

Let it be known to your paternity that after you had ordered my unworthiness to oversee a council of priests and a synodal gathering in the province of the Franks—as they had asked—I suffered many wrongs and persecutions, chiefly from false priests, adulterous ministers, deacons, and fornicator clerics.

My chief work has been against two known wicked heretics, blasphemers against God and against the catholic faith. One—who is called Aldebert—is a Gaul by birth; the other is an Irishman called Clemens. They differ in type of error, but they are equal in terms of the weight of their sins. Against them, I entreat your apostolic authority to protect and help my mediocrity, and to correct the people of the Franks and Gauls through your writing, so that they do not follow the fables of the heretics, and the false wonders and signs of the precursor of Antichrist, but may rather be turned to church law and the way of the true doctrine. And so that these two heretics may be sent to prison—if that seems just to you—I will tell you about their life and doctrine. Let no one speak or have communion with them lest any perish, corrupted by their corrupt doctrine. But let them live separated, according to the word of the apostle, "such ones are handed over to Satan for the destruction of the flesh so that the spirit may be saved on the day of the lord" [1 Cor. 5.5; doc. 10], and according to the gospel precept, "if they do not hear the church, let them be heathens and sinners to us" [Matt. 18.17] until they learn neither to blaspheme nor to rend the tunic of Christ. Through them, I suffer the persecutions, enmity, and curses of many people, and the church of Christ is held back in the spread of right faith and doctrine.

As to Aldebert, the Franks and Gauls say that I have taken from them the holiest apostle, and robbed them of a patron and intercessor, a doer of great deeds and a worker of miracles. But hearing of his life, your piety may judge from the fruit whether he is a rapacious wolf dressed in sheep's clothing or not. In his youth, he was a hypocrite, saying that an angel of the lord in the form of a man brought him relics from the furthest ends of the earth of wonderful but uncertain sanctity and that through these he was able to obtain from God everything for which he asked. And then, at length, by this deception—just as the Apostle Paul warned—"he crept into the houses of many people and led captive silly women laden with sins, led away with various desires" [2 Tim. 3.6], and a multitude of peasants said that he was a man of apostolic sanctity and that he had performed many miracles and prodigies. After this, he paid unlearned bishops who ordained him utterly against the precepts of the canons. Eventually, he was raised in such pride that he likened himself to the apostles of Christ. Contemptuously, he refused to consecrate a church in honor of any of the apostles or martyrs, asking why men would want to visit the houses of the holy apostles. Later, he dedicated oratories in his own honor—or, as I should say more correctly, "defiled." He set up small crosses and oratories in fields and at springs or wherever seemed good to him, and there he ordered public prayers to be performed, until multitudes of people—spurning other bishops and abandoning their old churches—worshipped in such places, saying "The merits of Saint Aldebert will help us." He gave his toenails and hair to be honored and carried with the relics of Saint Peter, the prince of the apostles. Finally, he performed the greatest wickedness and blasphemy against God: with people coming, wanting to confess their sins, and prostrating themselves at his feet, he said, "I know all your sins because your secrets are known to me. There is no need to confess. Your past sins are forgiven you. Return to your homes in peace, absolved and untroubled." Everything which the holy gospel relates about hypocrites, he imitated in his dress, step and habits. . . .

When Boniface's letter had been read, the most holy and blessed Pope Zacharias, said, "Dearest brothers, you have heard what has been read out in that letter about these blasphemers who have proclaimed themselves apostles of the people—to their own condemnation." The most holy bishops and venerable priests replied, "We assuredly heard everything; they are not apostles but ministers of Satan and precursors of Antichrist. For what apostle or saint ever gave people his hair or toenails as holy things in the way that this sacrilegious and pernicious Aldebert has tried to do? Let this wickedness be cut out by your holiness . . . they must receive an appropriate sentence according to their deeds and transgressions. . . ."

[After a break, the session reconvenes with a chaplain named Theophanius charged with reading an account of Aldebert's life.]

In the name of our Lord Jesus Christ. Here begins the life of bishop Aldebert, holy and blessed servant of God, splendid and wholly fair, born a saint by the will of God. He was born to simple parents and crowned by the grace of God because while he was in his mother's womb the grace of God took hold of him and before his blessed nativity, his mother saw as if in a vision a calf coming out from her right side. The calf denoted that grace which he had received from an angel before he come out from the womb. . . .

[The text of the book is not reproduced.]

When this book had been read through to the end, the most holy and blessed Pope Zacharias said, "How do you respond to these blasphemies, most holy brothers?" Epiphanius, the most holy bishop of the holy church of Silva Candida said, "Certainly, O apostolic lord, the apostolic heart of your holiness was moved by divine inspiration when you commissioned the aforesaid Boniface, our most holy brother and the chiefs of the Franks, to call a council of the priests in those parts after such a long time so that these schisms and blasphemies might no longer be concealed from your apostolic holiness." . . .

[A new session begins.]

After the holy gospels had been placed in the middle in the presence of the deacons and the rest of the clergy, Gregory—a regional notary and numenculator [an official charged with taking care of widows and orphans]—said "Following the order given by your apostolic holiness in the previous conclave, that the pious priest Denehard should be present today for your consideration, he is waiting by the doors. What do you order?" To which, it was said, "Let him enter." And when he had entered, the most holy and blessed Pope Zacharias said, "Do you have more of their sacrilegious writing that you must present to the council for reading?" The pious priest Denehard replied, "My lord, I have a prayer which Aldebert himself labored to compose and which I am holding in my hands. Order it to be received." Receiving it, he read the prayer in these words, the beginning of which follows:

"Oh lord God omnipotent, father of Christ, the son of God, our Lord Jesus Christ, and alpha and omega, who sits on the seventh throne above the cherubim and seraphim, such great kindness and sweetness are with you. The father of the angels, you who made heaven and earth, the sea and all the things that are in them, I invoke, cry out and summon you to wretched me because you have condescended to say, "whatever you sought the father in my name, I gave to you. To you I pray; to you I cry out, to Christ the lord I entrust my soul" [John 16.23–24].

And when he had read through the order, he came to the place where it said, "I pray, I conjure and I kneel down before you, Angel Uriel, Angel Raguel, Angel Tubuel, Angel Michael, Angel Adinus, Angelus Tubuas, Angelus Sabaoc, Angelus Simiel."

When this sacrilegious prayer had been read through to the end, the most holy and blessed Pope Zacharias said, "How do you respond to this, most holy brothers?" The most holy bishops and venerable priests replied, "What else can be done except to have everything which was read to us be consumed utterly by fire, and the authors punished with the constraints of anathema? The eight names of angels which Aldebert invokes in his prayer are not angels—except Michael. Rather, in his prayer, he has invoked great demons to order to assist him. As we are taught by your apostolic holiness and as is handed down by divine authority, we know no more than the names of three angels: that is, Michael, Gabriel, and Raphael. Accordingly, he has introduced the names of demons under the pretext of summoning angels." The most holy and blessed Pope Zacharias said, "It is thought rightly by your holiness that all his writings should be consumed by fire. But it is fitting that for their refutation they be preserved for their perpetual shame in our holy archive. Now, indeed, because everything about the matter has been brought forward, it is fitting that sentence be given upon those whom mention has been made above."

The whole council decreed, "Aldebert whose deeds and nefarious schemes have been read to us—because he supposed to call himself an apostle and presented his hair and toenails to the people as holy things, seducing the people by means of many errors, and who invokes demons under the guise of angels to assist him—let him be deprived of all priestly duty, doing penance for his sins, and let him seduce the people no more. If he persists in his errors and continues to seduce people, let him be anathema, condemned by the eternal judgment of God, and all alike who agree with him or follow his teaching or are associated with him."

Questions: Was Aldebert popular? Why? How does the council deal with Boniface's claims? Why? If it is licit to invoke saints, why might invoking angels be problematic?

31. POLICING PRACTICE

Penitentials were manuals intended to guide priests when dealing with private confessions. They were fundamentally practical works, listing a wide variety of specific sins and their requisite penance. Penitentials first appeared in the Irish Church in the 500s but were brought to the Continent by Celtic and British missionaries. Penitentials varied enormously in terms of the kinds of sins they treated and the penalties assessed. However, they left confessors with little room to consider the particular circumstances around a sin or to offer reduced or modified penances.

The penitential of Columban is associated with the great Celtic missionary of that name who traveled to Gaul in the late sixth century to re-establish Christianity there. The anonymous Burgundian penitential seems to have been produced in Gaul about a century later. The penitential of Theodore is traditionally associated with Theodore of Tarsus, archbishop of Canterbury from 668 to 690. Burchard of Worms's "Corrector and Physician" comes from a large compendium of canon law he produced in the early eleventh century.

Council of Arles: Latin, 524.
Penitential of Columban: Latin, c. 600.
Penitential of Theodore: Latin, c. 668–690.
Burgundian Penitential: Latin, c. 700–725.
The Corrector and Physician: Latin, c. 1008–12.

Sources: trans. Richard Raiswell and David R. Winter, "Council of Arles," from Ivo of Chartres, *Decretum* (Migne, PL 161: 0758B–0759A); trans. John T. McNeill, *The Penitential of Columban, The Penitential of Theodore, Burgundian Penitential,* and *The Corrector and Physician,* from *Medieval Handbooks of Penance: A Translation of the Principal* libri poenitentiales *and Selections from Related Documents* (New York: Octagon, 1965), pp. 179–215, 249–57, 273–77, 321–45.

Council of Arles

Laymen who keep funeral watches should do so in reverence, fear, and trembling. Let no one presume to sing diabolical songs, perform games or dances there—things the pagans have invented through diabolical teaching. Who does not know that it is devilish—not only foreign to the Christian religion but contrary to human nature—to sing, to be drunk, to rejoice there, and to laugh unrestrainedly, neglecting all piety and the inclination to charity, as if rejoicing at his brother's death when grief and lamentation in tearful voices for the loss of a dear brother ought to be heard.

Indeed, we read in many places in the Old and New Testaments that the dead fathers of holy men wept with tears but nowhere are they said to have rejoiced because these men had passed on from this world. For 70 days, all Egypt mourned for the patriarch Jacob. And Joseph and his brothers brought their father for burial into the land of Canaan, celebrating the funeral rites at the threshing floor of Atad—which is situated beyond the River Jordan—celebrating the funeral rites with a great and vehement lamentation for seven days. So great was this lamentation that the place took that name from that point forth. And we read about Saint Stephen that God-fearing men cared for and buried him, and made great lamentation over him [Acts 8.2].

And so for that reason such foolish delights and pestilential songs ought to be thoroughly forbidden on the authority of God. If anyone wishes to sing, let him sing "Lord, have mercy upon me." But if he would sing otherwise, let him be entirely silent. But if he does not want to be silent, let him be so [severely] chastised the next day that others will be afraid [to do the same].

The Penitential of Columban

24. But if any layman eats or drinks beside [pagan] sacred places, if he does it through ignorance he shall promise thenceforth that he will never repeat it and do penance for forty days on bread and water. But if he does this through contempt, that is, after a priest has warned him that this was sacrilege, and has afterwards communicated at the table of demons, if he repeats that is as well through the vice of gluttony, he shall do penance for three forty-day periods on bread and water. If, indeed, he has done this for the sake of the worship of demons or in honor of their idols, he shall do penance for three years.

The Burgundian Penitential

25. If any soothsayer (those whom they call diviners) makes any divinations, since this is also of the demons, he shall do penance for five years, three of these on bread and water. . . .

29. If anyone takes a vow or absolves from one by trees or springs or lattices or anywhere except in church, he shall do penance for three years on bread and water; for this also is sacrilege or of the demons. He who eats or drinks in these places shall do penance for a year on bread and water. . . .

36. If anyone is a wizard, that is, takes away the minds of men by the invocation of demons or renders them mad, he shall do penance for five years, three of these on bread and water.

Penitential of Theodore

Of Those Who Are Vexed by the Devil

1. If a man is vexed by the devil and can do nothing but run about everywhere, and if he slays himself, there may be some reason to pray for him if he was formerly religious.

2. If it was on account of despair, or of some fear, or for unknown reasons, we ought to leave to God the decision of this matter, and we dare not pray for him.

3. In the case of one who of his own will slays himself, masses may not be said for him; but we may only pray and dispense alms.

4. If any Christian goes insane through a sudden seizure, or as a result of insanity slays himself—there are some who celebrate masses for such a one.

5. One who is possessed of a demon may have stones and herbs, without the use of incantation.

The Corrector and Physician

61. Have you observed the traditions of pagans, which, as if by hereditary right, with the assistance of the devil, fathers have ever left to their sons even to these days, that is, that you should worship the elements, the moon or the sun or the course of the stars, the new moon or the eclipse of the moon; that you should be able by your shouts or by your aid to restore her splendor, or these elements [be able] to aid you, or that you should have power with them—or have you observed the new moon for building a house or making marriages? If you have, you shall do penance for two years on the appointed fast days, for it is written "All, whatsoever you do in word and in work, do all in the name of our lord, Jesus Christ."

63. Have you made knots, and incantations, and those various enchantments which evil men, swineherds, plowmen, and sometimes hunters make, while they say diabolical formulae over bread or grass and over certain nefarious bandages, and either hide these in a tree or throw them where two roads, or three roads, meet, so that they might set free animals or dogs from pestilence or destruction and destroy those of another? If you have, you shall do penance for two years on the appointed days.

64. Have you been present at or consented to the vanities which women practice in their woolen work, in their webs, who when they begin their webs hope to be able to bring it about that with incantations and with the beginning of these the threads of the warp and of the woof become so mingled together that unless they supplement these in turn by other counter-incantations of the devil, the whole will perish? If you have been present or consented, you shall do penance for thirty days on bread and water. . . .

68. Have you ever believed or participated in this perfidy, that enchanters and those who say that they can let loose tempests should be able through incantation of demons to arouse tempests or to change the minds of men? If you have believed or participated in this, you shall do penance for one year on the appointed fast days. . . .

70. Have you believed that there is any woman who can do that which some, deceived by the devil, affirm that they must do of necessity or at his command, that is, with a throng of demons transformed into the likeness of women (she whom

common folly calls the witch Hulda), must ride on certain beasts on special nights and be numbered with their company? If you have participated in this infidelity, you should do penance for one year on the appointed fast days.

Questions: What sins are especially egregious? Are the sinners envisioned by these texts Christian? Are they devil worshippers? Are the texts concerned only with practice? How does the style of Burchard's penitential differ from the others?

32. THE POSSIBILITY OF DEMONIC NIGHT FLIGHT?

The canon Episcopi *first appears as part of a collection of canon (ecclesiastical) law compiled by Regino (c. 850–915), abbot of Trier, in the early tenth century. He attributed it to the Council of Ancyra (modern Ankara), which took place in 314. It was included in a number of subsequent canonical collections, including those of Burchard of Worms (c. 950–1025) and Gratian of Bologna (fl. 1150). Although Gratian compiled his work for teaching purposes and to reconcile apparent contradictions between points of church law, it quickly came to be widely used by canonists as an authoritative legal source. Consequently,* Episcopi's *conclusions about night flight proved exceptionally influential and were later a significant stumbling block for witchcraft theorists in the fifteenth century and beyond.*
   Latin, c. 910.

Source: trans. Henry C. Lea, *Materials Toward a History of Witchcraft*, vol. 1 (Philadelphia, 1939), pp. 178–80; compared with Regino of Prüm, *De ecclesiasticis disciplinis* (Migne, 132: 0352–3053); rev.

Bishops and their officials must labor with all their strength to uproot from their parishes the pernicious art of *sortilegium* [sorcery, but also the casting of lots] and *maleficium* [malicious magic] invented by the devil thoroughly, and if they find a man or woman follower of this wickedness to eject them foully disgraced from their parishes. For the apostle says, "Avoid a man that is a heretic after the first and second admonition" [Titus 3.10]. Those are held captive by the devil who, leaving their creator, seek the aid of the devil. And so the holy church must be cleansed of this pest.

It is also not to be omitted that some wicked women, perverted by the devil, seduced by the illusions and phantasms of demons, believe and profess themselves, in the hours of night, to ride upon certain beasts with Diana, the goddess of pagans, and an innumerable multitude of women, and in the silence of the dead of night to traverse great spaces of earth, and to obey her commands as of their mistress, and to be summoned to her service on certain nights. But I wish it were they alone who perished in their faithlessness and did not draw many with them into the destruction of infidelity. For an innumerable multitude, deceived by this false opinion, believe this to be true and, so believing, wander from the right faith and are involved in the error of the pagans when they think that there is anything of divinity or power except the one God. For this reason, the priests should preach through their churches to the people with all urgency so that they may know this to be false in every way and that such phantasms are imposed on the minds of infidels and not by the divine but by the malignant spirit. Accordingly, Satan—who transforms himself into an angel of light—holding the mind of a foolish woman, will subjugate it to himself through infidelity and unbelief, immediately transforming himself into the appearance and likeness of various people, deluding the mind which he holds captive in dreams, showing joyful and mournful things and people known and unknown, leading it away through devious means. And while the spirit suffers this alone, the unbelieving mind thinks this happens not in spirit but in body.

Who is there that is not led out of himself in dreams and nocturnal visions, and sees much when sleeping which he had never seen waking? Who is so stupid and foolish as to think that all these things which are only done in spirit happen in the body, when the Prophet Ezekiel saw visions of the lord in spirit and not in the body, and the Apostle John saw and heard the mysteries of the Apocalypse in the spirit and not in the body, as he himself says, "I was in the spirit" [Rev. 4.2]. And Paul does not dare to say that he was rapt in the body. It is therefore to be proclaimed publicly to all that whoever believes such things or things like them loses the faith, and he who has not the right faith in God is not of God but of him in whom he believes, that is, of the devil. For it is written about our lord "All things were made by him" [John 1.3].

Therefore, whoever believes that anything can be made, or that any creature can be changed for better or worse or can be transformed into another appearance and likeness, except by the creator himself who made everything and through whom all things were made, is beyond doubt an infidel.

Questions: What role does the devil play here? What about the goddess Diana? Why do people believe that they have flown? What does the author think this belief says about those who accept it? Can this canon be reconciled with the powers of the devil implied in docs. 9 and 27?

33. A SORCERESS AND HER DEMONS

William of Malmesbury (c. 1095–1143) was a Benedictine monk and historian. He developed his keen interest in history while acquiring books for the monastic library at Malmesbury, sometimes spending his own money to purchase copies of the works of foreign historians. Yet he found few of these had anything to say about English affairs, and this inspired him to write so that he might illuminate matters that would otherwise have been lost in the "rubbish heap of history." The Deeds runs from the death of the Venerable Bede in 735—the last great English historian by William's reckoning—to around 1125. Alongside the historical

material, the work is punctuated with tales intended to pique his readers' curiosity. The following comes after an account of the miraculous burial of Pope Gregory VI in 1048, placing it around that time.
Latin, c. 1130.

Source: trans. Richard Raiswell and David R. Winter, from William of Malmesbury, *Gesta Regum Anglorum atque historia novella*, vol. 1 (London, 1840), pp. 351–54.

In those days, something similar [to the miraculous burial of Pope Gregory VI] occurred in England, but not caused by heavenly miracle but rather by infernal deception. When I have finished relating it, the accuracy of the story will not be doubted—although the minds of listeners may well be incredulous. I heard this story from a man who swore that he had seen it himself, a man so excellent that I would be ashamed not to believe him.

A woman who dwelt in Berkeley was accustomed to using sorcery and quite familiar with the ancient auguries—as later became clear. She was a patron of gluttony and a mistress of impudence. She placed no limit on the extent of her shameful acts, for she was still on this side of old age—although she was knocking on its door. One day, while this woman was feasting, a small crow which she had among her pets spoke to her more loudly than usual—although I do not know what it said. On hearing this, the knife which the woman had in her hand fell to the ground and immediately her face turned pale. She let out a long groan, and said, "Today my plow has completed its final furrow. Today I will receive and hear news of a great disaster."

As soon as she had finished saying this, the messenger of her misfortunes arrived. Grimacing and with hesitation, he approached her. "I bring word to you," he said, "from that town"—and he named the place—"of the death of your son and of the whole of his family from a sudden, untimely accident." At this sorrowful news, the wounded woman immediately took to her bed. And feeling sickness creeping toward her bowels, she summoned her surviving children—a monk and a nun—with hastily written letters.

After they had arrived, she spoke to them, her voice sobbing, "Children, I have always dealt with the wretchedness of my life through the demonic arts. I have been a cesspit of every iniquity, the teacher of all allurements. Nevertheless, while I was perpetrating all these evils, it was my hope in your sanctity that flattered my wretched soul. Without hope in myself, I am relying on you two, setting you forward as my defenders against the demons, my protectors against these, the cruelest of enemies. Now, therefore, because I have come near to the end of my life and those exacters of punishment will have me—those who lured me into sin—I ask you by your mother's breast that, if you have any fidelity, any tenderness, you at least try to alleviate my torments. You may not be able to revoke the sentence that has been passed on my soul, but perhaps you will be able to save my body in the following way: Sew me into a stag's hide and then lay it on its back in a stone coffin; seal the lid tight with lead and iron. Place a stone on top of it and wrap it around with three weighty iron chains. Let psalms be sung for fifty nights and masses for the same number of days—which may relieve me of the cruel attacks of my adversaries. If I have lain there safely for three nights, on the fourth day bury your mother in the earth—although I am afraid that the earth which has been so often oppressed by my wickedness will not receive or maintain me in its bosom."

And so it was done as she had instructed with her children taking to their task with great enthusiasm. But alas what wickedness! No pious tears, vows or prayers could prevail—so great was the wickedness of the woman, so great the violence of the devil! For the first two nights, while choirs of clerics were singing psalms around the body, one by one demons, breaking through the entrance of the church—which had been closed up with a great bolt—severed the outer chains [around the tomb]. However, the middle one which had been more expertly worked remained intact.

On the third night, around cockcrow, the entire monastery seemed to be moved from its foundations by the crash of the advancing enemies. One demon, greater in size and with a face more terrifying than the others, smashed through the gates, shattering them to pieces with his great strength. The clergy became stiff with fear. Their hair stood on end and their voices stuck fast in their throats. The demon approached the tomb with an arrogant swagger, as it seemed, and, having called out the dead woman's name, ordered her to arise. She replied that she could not move on account of the chains. "You will be released," he said, "to your misfortune." Immediately, he broke the chain which had frustrated the ferocity of the other demons without any effort—as if it was just flaxen rope. He forced away the lid of the tomb with his foot, and then, taking her by the hand, before everyone, he dragged her from the church. There, before the doors a proud, black horse appeared neighing. Iron hooks protruded across its whole back. The demon placed the wretched woman on these and soon the whole fellowship disappeared from the eyes of those watching. Nevertheless, her wretched cries begging for help were heard for the space of some four miles.

Questions: What do we know about the woman's social station? What are the features of her sorcery? Why has she resorted to such measures? Why are these demons able to prevail against her counter-measures? Upon what tropes from earlier selections does this text draw? Why would anyone have trusted William's account?

CHAPTER FOUR

THE EARLY MONASTIC DEVIL

Figure 4.1 "Antony Attacked by Demons" (c. 1474). This anonymous woodcut modelled after the work of a mid-fifteenth-century German engraver known only by his monogram, "E.S." depicts the various means by which demons endeavored to assail Saint Antony (doc. 34). This particular copy of the woodcut was hand colored and fixed to the cover of a book.

FOUR: THE EARLY MONASTIC DEVIL

The Early Middle Ages were characterized by a series of profound social and political realignments. The period saw the ebbing away of Roman public power, even as the idea of Rome continued to linger in the imagination. During this era, two successive waves of invasions (the first between c. 350 and 500, the second between c. 700 and 1000) caused significant levels of political instability as well as social upheaval and anxiety throughout Western Europe.

During these centuries, town life all but disappeared; infrastructure and communications broke down under the weight of the attacks. The political response became increasingly local, voluntary, and contingent; it was organized around personal bonds of loyalty rather than any kind of centralized plan. That is, it became a feudal response (see Chapter 5). In this fraught situation, learning and erudition declined. Militant Christianity sought refuge behind the walls of the monastery; indeed, in many respects, the monastic cloister was Christianity's "big idea" of the first millennium. Between roughly 700 and 1050, the great monasteries of Europe became the chief repositories of learned culture. However, as Europe began to regain its equilibrium toward the eleventh century, the church gradually relinquished its posture of being at siege in the world and started to assert its authority into geographical regions and spheres of life where it had previously been unable. A series of reforming popes, many of them trained in the Cistercian or Cluniac tradition, sought to purge the Church of the corruption and vice that gathered about its core during its nadir in the tenth century.

The devil that emerges in this period was, in many respects, a creature forged from this deep instability. The difficulty in reconciling biblical sources into a single, coherent figure of absolute evil meant that the devil's nature and activity tended to be supplemented in practice by people's actual experience of misfortune and suffering in the face of an unstable world. As much as the text of scripture itself, it was this lived experience of malevolence that fleshed out the bald assertions about the devil provided by the New Testament.

While the majority of the population eked out a subsistence existence in the face of seemingly incessant violence, disease, famine and death, no direct record was left of their views on personified evil. The intellectual agenda of the period was defined by monks. It is the experience of these men and women, the desert fathers and mothers—people who had decided to flee to the wilderness in imitation of Christ's temptation in the desert (doc. 9) to do battle there against the devil—that animates the extant literature of the period. The result is a "monasticized" devil—that is, the devil almost as anti-monk, a personification of the preoccupation of monks with avoiding vice and shunning temptation. Consequently, the devil is pressed into service as the primary villain in the tales and legends of the monks, his character shaped to correspond with the spiritual priorities of those communities, whether in Scetis or Nitria in the Egyptian desert, in the wilds of the Roman Campania, or in the Celtic hinterland.

34. A "PROTO-MONK" IS ASSAULTED BY DEMONS IN THE WILDERNESS

According to tradition, the Egyptian Antony (251–356) was one of the very first monks (from the Greek monos, *meaning "alone") in the Christian tradition. Born near Faiyum on the west bank of the Nile River, Antony was raised in an atmosphere of late-Roman privilege at a time when Christianity was gaining public respectability. Antony's life was changed forever when, around age 20, he heard a preacher proclaim the gospel passage in which Jesus told a rich man, "If you would be perfect, go, sell what you possess and give to the poor . . . and come, follow me" (Matt. 19.21). Taking this injunction literally, Antony gave away all his belongings and fled into the desert to live a life of poverty and self-abasement. In so doing, he inaugurated a tradition of monastic observance that has continued, in various forms, to the present day. Antony's* vita *(that is, the account of the saint's life and holy deeds) was composed shortly after his death, probably by Bishop Athanasius of Alexandria (d. 373). In it, the bishop related Antony's many struggles with demonic agents. The* Life of Antony *established a template for battles between demons and Christian holy figures that would be repeated in countless sources throughout the Middle Ages and beyond.*

Greek, between 356 and 362.

Source: trans. H. Ellershaw, from Athanasius, *Life of Antony*, from *Nicene and Post-Nicene Fathers*, 2nd series, vol. 4 (New York, 1892), pp. 188–221; rev.

Athanasius the bishop to the brothers in foreign lands.

Now since you asked me to give you an account of the blessed Antony's way of life . . . I very readily accepted your request, because the merest recollection of Antony is a great addition of help. And I know that, when you have heard what I have to relate, apart from your admiration of the man, you will want to emulate his determination. This is because the life of Antony is a full model of discipline for monks. . . .

[From the time he became a monk, Antony demonstrated great aptitude for the ascetic life.]

But the devil, who hates and envies what is good, could not stand to see such conviction in a young man, and instead endeavored to carry out against Antony the stratagems that he had tried to use against others. First of all, he tried to lead Antony away from the monastic discipline, whispering to him about the memory of his wealth, concern for his sister, concerns about his family, love of money, love of glory, the various pleasures of the table, and the other joys of life. Finally, he whispered to him about the difficulty of virtue and the labor it entailed; he also suggested the infirmity of the body and the length of the time. In a word, the devil raised in Antony's mind a great whirlwind of debate, wishing to deter him from his set purpose. But when the enemy realized that he was too weak for

Antony's determination, and that he rather was conquered by the man's resolve, overthrown by his great faith, and failing on account of his constant prayers, he finally put his trust in the weapons which are "below the waist" and taking pride in them—for they are the devil's first snare for the young—he attacked the young man, disturbing him by night and harassing him by day, so that even onlookers could see the struggle which was going on between them. The devil would suggest foul thoughts and Antony would counter them with prayers. The devil would fire him with lust, and Antony—who seemed to blush at wickedness—would fortify his body with faith, prayers, and fasting. And the devil, that unhappy spirit, one night even took the form of a woman and imitated all her actions simply to beguile Antony. But with his mind filled with Christ and the nobility inspired by him—and reflecting on the spirituality of the soul—Antony quenched the embers of the devil's deceit....

Finally, when the dragon could not conquer Antony even in this way, but instead saw himself thrust out from his heart, he gnashed his teeth—as it is written—and was beside himself. He then appeared to Antony as a black boy, taking a visible form that accorded with the color of his mind. And cowering, as it were, he no longer assaulted Antony with obsessions, for as clever as he was, he had been defeated. But at last he spoke in a human voice and said, "I have deceived many; I have cast down many. But now, after attacking you and your labors in the same way as I have many others, I have proven myself weak." When Antony asked, "Who are you that speaks to me in this manner?" He answered with a lamentable voice, "I am the companion of whoredom, and I have taken up the allurements which lead the young to their ruin. I am called 'the spirit of lust.' How many have I deceived who desired to live soberly! How many are the chaste whom I have readily persuaded with my allurements! The prophet warns the fallen about me, saying, 'the spirit of whoredom has caused you to err' [Hosea 4.12]. For they have been tripped up by me. I am the one who has so often troubled you and who has been overthrown by you." But Antony, after giving thanks to the lord, with good courage said to him, "You are quite despicable, then, for you are as black-hearted and weak as a child. From now on I will have no more trouble from you, 'for the lord is my helper, and I shall look in triumph upon my enemies' [Ps. 118.7]." After hearing this, the black boy immediately fled, shuddering at the words and dreading the idea of approaching the man.

This was Antony's first struggle against the devil, or rather, this victory was the savior's work through Antony.... But, although the evil one had fallen, Antony did not relax his vigilance, nor did he cease despising him. Neither did the conquered enemy stop laying snares for Antony. For once again he went about like a lion looking for an opportunity against him....

Tightening his hold upon himself in this way, Antony departed for the tombs, which happened to be some distance from his village. And, after asking an acquaintance to bring him bread every few days, he entered one of them and had his acquaintance secure the door behind him, leaving him alone inside it. And when the enemy could not stand it, fearing that in a very short while Antony would fill the desert with the monastic discipline, he came one night with a multitude of demons and cut the saint with lashes so that he lay on the ground speechless from excessive pain. For Antony acknowledged that the torture had been so severe that no blows inflicted by a human could ever have caused him so much torment. However, by God's providence—because God never overlooks those who put their hope in him—the next day his acquaintance came to bring him loaves of bread. After opening the door of the tomb and seeing Antony lying on the ground as though he were dead, the acquaintance lifted him up and carried him to the village church, and there laid him upon the ground. . . . Around midnight, Antony came to his senses and stood up, and when he saw everyone asleep around him—except for his comrade who was keeping watch—he motioned with his head for his comrade to come near, asking him to carry him back to the tombs without waking anyone.

So the man carried him, and, as was his custom, when the man shut the door, Antony remained alone within. And though he could not stand up because of his injuries, he prayed as he lay upon the ground. After he prayed, he said with a shout, "Here am I, Antony! I will not flee from your lashes, for even if you inflict more nothing shall separate me from the love of Christ!" [Rom. 8.35]. Then he sang, "Even though an army sets up camp against me, my heart will not be afraid" [Ps. 27.3]. These were the thoughts and words of the ascetic. However, the enemy, who hates good, marveled that, after the blows he dared to return. He called together his hounds and burst forth, "You see," he said, "that neither by the spirit of lust, nor by blows did we stop this man; instead, he defies us. Let us attack him in another way." Changes of form for evil purposes are easy for the devil, so, in the night the demons made such a racket that the entire place seemed as if it had been shaken by an earthquake; and almost as if breaking the four walls of the tomb, they seemed to enter through them. They came in the shape of beasts and creeping things. The place was suddenly filled with the form of lions, bears, leopards, bulls, serpents, asps, scorpions, and wolves; and each of them began moving according to its nature. The lion roared, wishing to attack. The bull seemed to toss its horns in the air. The serpent writhed, but was unable to approach the saint. The wolf, struggling to rush forward, seemed restrained. With their angry raging, the noises of these apparitions were altogether dreadful. But, stricken and harassed by them, Antony endured these bodily agonies all the more. He lay watching, groaning from physical anguish, but his soul was unshaken. His mind was clear. In mockery, he said, "If there was any power in you, one of you would have sufficed. But since the lord has made you weak, you attempt to terrify me by your numbers. A proof of your weakness is that you take the forms of wild animals!" In addition to this, he said boldly, "If you've been given power over me, and you're able, don't delay your attack. But if you're not able, then why trouble me in vain? Faith in our lord is an assurance and a wall of safety for us." And so, after many attempts, they gnashed their teeth at Antony, because they were deceiving themselves rather than him.

Nor did the lord forget Antony's struggle, but was there to help him. Gazing upward, it looked as though the roof were open, with a shaft of light descending toward him. The demons suddenly vanished. The pain in his body immediately ceased. Then the tomb once again seemed whole. And Antony, feeling God's help, and getting his breath again, and being released from pain, beseeched the vision which appeared before him, saying, "Where were you? Why did you not appear at the beginning of my torments to make my suffering cease?" And a voice answered him, "Antony, I was here, but I waited to see your contest. Because you have endured, and have not been beaten, I will forever be a companion to you, and I will make your name known everywhere." After hearing this, Antony got up and prayed, and he received such strength that he believed that he had more power throughout his body than he had beforehand.

[Desiring to get further from civilization, Antony took up residence in an abandoned military fort.]

But since he did not allow the friends who followed him to enter the fort, they often used to spend their days and nights outside. When they did, they heard crowds clamoring inside the fort, shouting, and shrieking with piteous voices, "Depart what is ours! Why have you come into the desert?! You cannot endure our attacks!" At first, those staying outside the fortress thought there were men fighting with Antony, and that they had entered the place using ladders. But when they stooped down and peered through a hole in the wall, and saw that no one was there, they realized these were demons, and were afraid. Thus, they called on Antony. Antony heard his friends' voices immediately, even though he had given no heed to those of the demons. Opening the door of the fortress, he told his friends not to worry and begged them to leave. He said, "This is because the demons attack those who are cowardly. Therefore, sign yourselves with the cross and depart bravely. Let them make sport for themselves." So, fortified with the sign of the cross, Antony's friends departed. However, Antony was not harmed by the evil spirits, nor did he tire of the contest with them, not only because he was aided by visions from above, but also because his enemies' weakness relieved him of his troubles and armed him with great zeal. For his friends often used to visit, expecting to find him dead. Instead, they would hear him singing. . . .

If demons see any Christians—particularly monks—laboring cheerfully and advancing in the service of God, they first attack through temptation and place hindrances to hamper us in our way—that is to say, they stir us to evil thoughts. But we need not fear their suggestions, for by prayer and fasting, and through faith in the lord their attacks immediately fail. But even when they do, they the demons do not stop, but knavishly by means of subtlety try again. For when they cannot deceive the heart openly with foul pleasures they approach in different guise, creating illusions intended to strike fear. They change their shapes, taking the forms of women, wild beasts, creeping things, giants, even troops of soldiers. But not even then should one fear their deceitful displays, for they are nothing and quickly disappear, especially if a man has fortified himself beforehand with faith and the sign of the cross. Yet demons are bold and utterly shameless, for if one of their assaults is beaten back, they make a new onslaught in another way: they might pretend to prophesy and foretell the future; show themselves in a form as tall as the roof and as wide as the room. By such displays, they hope to catch through stealth those who could not be deceived by their arguments. But even here, if they encounter a soul strengthened by faith and a hopeful mind, they are rebuffed—at which point, they bring their leader to their aid.

Questions: Why does Antony take up residence in a tomb and then later in a fort deep in the wilderness of the desert? Who is provoking whom? What sort of values does the devil find most abhorrent? Is the devil a spirit or a physical being? Why might living alone in the wilderness promote such experiences?

35. SAINT MARTIN OF TOURS FIGHTS THE DEVIL

Martin of Tours (c. 320–397) was born in Pannonia to a late-Roman military family. Though his parents were pagans, Martin adopted Christianity in childhood. Despite this, he resolved to follow in his father's footsteps and join the cavalry (some traditions state that he simply could not escape military service). After soldiering with distinction for many years, he informed his superiors that he could no longer commit violence for Rome. He is thus one of history's first recorded conscientious objectors. Martin retired from the military and eventually became a monk and saintly bishop in Tours in Gaul. After his death, Sulpicius Severus (d. 420) wrote Martin's vita. The Life of Saint Martin *has become a touchstone of western hagiographic writing. One of the recurrent themes in Sulpicius's work is Martin's struggle with the devil. Just as Antony worked to free himself of Satan's influence in the wastes of Egypt, so Martin brought his military training to bear in his fight against the unholy specters and demons of Gaul.*
    Latin, late fourth century.

Source: trans. Alexander Roberts, from Sulpicius Severus, *Life of Saint Martin*, from Nicene and Post-Nicene Fathers, vol. 11 (New York, 1894), pp. 14–16; rev.

Martin Encounters Angels and Devils

It is also well known that Martin very often saw angels and that they spoke to him in turns using formal discourse. As for the devil, Martin was able to see him and keep him under observation whether he maintained his proper form or transformed himself into different shapes. Martin was able to perceive him regardless of whatever disguise he used. Knowing that he could neither escape detection, nor beguile Martin, the devil relentlessly insulted him. Once, the devil rushed into Martin's cell making a great noise and brandishing the bloody horn of an ox. He held it out to Martin in his blood-covered right hand, and exulted in the crime he had committed. He exclaimed "Where, O Martin, is your power? I have just killed one of your people!" Hearing this, Martin assembled the brothers and related what the devil had told him. He then ordered them to search all the cells of the monastery carefully in order to discover who had been afflicted by this calamity. They reported that none of the monks were missing, but that a peasant, whom they had hired to go into the forest to fetch wood in his wagon, had gone missing. Upon hearing this, Martin instructed a few of them to go and meet the man. Upon doing so, they found him, almost dead, just outside the monastery. As he was drawing his last breath, the peasant told the brothers the cause of his wounds and death. He said that, while he was yoking the oxen, one of them, throwing his head free, had wounded him in the groin with his horn. Shortly after this, the man died. You see what power has been given to the devil by the lord's judgment. This was a marvelous ability given to Martin. Not only on this occasion, but at other times as well, he frequently had foreknowledge of events. Things were disclosed to him that were not revealed to any of the other brothers.

Martin Preaches Repentance Even to the Devil

Now, while he tried to confound the saint using a thousand different stratagems, the devil often attacked him visibly, using various shapes and forms. Sometimes he presented himself in the guise of Jupiter. Often, however, he took the form of Mercury or Minerva. Frequently, Martin heard disembodied insults, as crowds of demons scolded him with scurrilous accusations. But knowing that all of this was false and baseless, he was unmoved by the slanders brought against him. In fact, some of the brothers confirmed that they too had heard a demon reproaching Martin in abusive terms. The demon asked why Martin had rehabilitated certain brothers who, at some point in the past, had lost their baptism by falling into various errors—even though they had subsequently repented. The demon listed the crimes of each of the sinning brothers. However, those who heard this encounter added that Martin steadfastly resisted the devil and answered him, stating that bygone sins were washed away by the resolution to lead a better life. Martin said that, through the mercy of God, those who had been absolved of their sins had given up their evil ways. The devil responded that the guilty men about whom he spoke did not merit forgiveness, and that the lord did not extend mercy to those who had fallen away. To this, Martin responded by crying out words to this effect: "Wretched creature, with every confidence in the lord, I promise you that, if you refrained from attacking humanity and repented of your sins, even now with the day of judgment at hand, Christ would show you his mercy." . . .

Martin Is Tempted by the Wiles of the Devil

Around this time, there was a young man in Spain who, because he performed wonders, had gained authority among the people. He was so arrogant that he started calling himself Elias [Elijah]. And when the crowds eagerly accepted this, he went further and said he was actually Christ. This delusion was so successful that a certain bishop named Rufus began to worship the boy as the lord. On account of this, we have heard that this bishop was some time later removed from his office. Many of the brothers have also told me that, at about the same time, a prophet rose in the east, claiming that he was John [the Baptist]. We infer from this that, because so many false prophets have appeared, the coming of Antichrist must be at hand. For it seems that he is already rehearsing the mysteries of iniquity in these deceivers. And truly, I should not pass over this point: it was at this time that the devil sorely tempted Martin. For on a certain day, after Martin had begun his prayers, the fiend appeared to him in a circle of purple light. And, in order to deceive people more easily by the brilliance of his splendor, he also clothed himself in a royal robe, placed on his head a diadem encrusted with precious stones, and he donned shoes inlaid with gold. He appeared with a tranquil countenance, and a generally joyful mien. He did all of this so that no one would suspect he was the devil. Then he stood at Martin's side as he was praying in his cell. At first, the saint was dazzled by the devil's appearance, so they both maintained a long and deep silence. The silence was broken by the devil, who said, "Martin, accept who it is that you behold: I am Christ! I am about to descend to earth, but before I do, I want first to manifest myself to you." When Martin did not speak upon hearing these words, and instead gave no response whatsoever, the devil was emboldened to repeat his audacious declaration: "Martin, why, when you can see me, do you hesitate to believe? I am Christ!" However, the holy spirit had revealed the truth to Martin, so that he understood that this was the devil, and not God. Thus, he replied as follows: "The Lord Jesus did not predict that he would come clothed in purple, with a glittering crown upon his head. I will not believe that Christ has come unless he appears in the form in which he suffered, openly displaying the marks of his wounds upon the cross." On hearing these words, the devil vanished like smoke. He filled the cell with such a disgusting odor that he left unmistakable proof of his real nature. This event that I have just described happened in the way I have related it. My information regarding these events came from the lips of Martin himself. Therefore let no one regard the story as fabulous.

FOUR: THE EARLY MONASTIC DEVIL

Questions: Why does Sulpicius place such emphasis on Martin's ability to discern the devil? How does Martin's experience with the devil align with Antony's? How would a reader respond to the notion of the devil's repentance?

36. WHY CAN DEMONS DO SUCH GREAT THINGS?

Augustine of Hippo (354–430) is perhaps the most important Christian thinker between the time of Saint Paul and Martin Luther (1483–1546). As a young man in Roman North Africa, Augustine moved restlessly between a number of belief systems (including a type of dualism and Neoplatonism) before abruptly converting to Catholic Christianity around the age of 31. After taking holy orders, Augustine rose to become bishop of Hippo Regius—one of the great episcopal offices in Roman Africa. Despite his high office, he lived a monastic life until his death. He related much of this story in the Confessions, *still one of the classics of spiritual autobiography. In addition to this work, Augustine wrote voluminously on matters of faith, often seeking to defend the emerging Catholic tradition against the theological claims of heretical sects.*

His On the Divination of Demons, *from which the excerpt below comes, was written in response to a claim that the pagan priests of the Temple of Serapis in Alexandria had been able to predict accurately its destruction following the establishment of Christianity as the official religion of the empire.*

Latin, early fifth century.

Source: trans. Ruth Wentworth Brown, from Augustine of Hippo, *The Divination of Demons*, from *Treatises on Marriage and Other Subjects* (New York, 1955), pp. 421–40, compared with Augustine, *De divinatione daemonum liber unus* (Migne, PL 40: 0354–0430).

The nature of demons is such that, through the sense perception proper to an aerial body, they readily surpass the perception possessed by earthly bodies. In speed, too, because of the superior mobility of the aerial body, they incomparably surpass not only the movement of men and beasts but even the flight of birds. Endowed with these two faculties, insofar as they are the properties of an aerial body—that is, keenness of perception and speed of movement—they foretell and declare many things that they have recognized far in advance. Men wonder at this because of the sluggishness of earthly perception. Moreover, by virtue of the long period over which their life is extended, demons have gained a far greater experience of events than accrues to men over the brief span of their lives. Through these faculties which are allotted to the nature of the aerial body, demons not only predict many future things but also perform many wondrous acts. Since man can neither tell nor perform these things, certain individuals think it proper to serve the demons and to render them divine honors. They are prompted to this service particularly out of the vice of curiosity, because of their desire for a false happiness and for earthly and temporal success.

Those, however, who cleanse themselves from these desires . . . should not regard demons as far superior to themselves because demons have an advantage through their keener bodily perception, namely the aerial—that is, one that is derived from a more subtle element. As a matter of fact, in the case even of earthly bodies, men do not think that beasts, whose sense perceptions are in many respects keener than their own, should be preferred to themselves. For example, because the keen-scented dog uncovers the hiding quarry with a sense of smell so very keen that he affords to man a certain guidance for capturing his prey, they do not for that reason regard him as possessed of wiser intellect, but of keener bodily sense. Nor do they so highly esteem the vulture, because, when a corpse is exposed, he flies to it from an unforeseen distance. . . . Nor do they so regard many other kinds of living creatures who, while pasturing, stray among herbs hurtful to their well-being and do not touch any of those by which they may be harmed. Man, on the other hand, has barely learned by trial to avoid poisonous herbs and fears many harmless varieties because they have not been tested. From these examples it is easy to infer how much keener may be the sense in aerial bodies. Nevertheless, no wise man would conclude that demons who are endowed with such perception should be preferred to good men.

This argument I would also make with respect to their swiftness of body. In this excellence, too, men are also surpassed, not only by birds but by many quadrupeds as well, that in comparison with those creatures men may be regarded as heavy as lead. Despite that, human beings do not think classes of animals are superior to themselves. . . .

Now, that third faculty of demons—namely, that by long experience in events they have learned to prognosticate many events and to announce them in advance—is lightly esteemed by those who take diligent pains to discern these circumstances according to the validity of the most true light. Even so, it comes about that honorable young men do not think that evil old men excel them by having undergone many experiences and being wiser on this account, so to speak. Likewise, men do not think themselves superior to doctors, sailors, and farmers—men whose wills are perverted and whose characters depraved—on the ground that they respectively make such predictions in advance about diseases, storms, and the phases of orchards and fruits that they seem to one inexperienced in matters of the kind to prophesy.

Given that demons not only predict some future things but can even perform certain wonders by virtue of the superiority of their body, why is this fact ignored by wise men? It is true that many sinful and lost men so train their bodies that, by various skills, they can perform such remarkable feats that those who do not know about them and have never seen them can hardly believe what they see even when it is explained to them. How much have rope-dancers and other theatrical performers done that has caused wonderment! How much have artisans—especially mechanics—done likewise? Are they for that reason better than men who are good and endowed with holy piety?

I have mentioned these matters so that he who regards them without stubbornness and without the vain arrogance of controversy may consider this likewise: if, while each one uses the somewhat gross material that is at hand—either that of his own body, or of earth and water, namely stones and wood, and various metals—certain men can produce such great works that those who are unable to do the same are commonly amazed, calling the producers "divine" in comparison to themselves—this despite the fact that while some of the producers are actually superior in the arts some of the admirers are superior in character—how much greater and more wonderful deeds in proportion to the faculty and facility of their most subtle body—that is, the aerial—can demons perform!

For all that, because of the depravity of their will—and especially because of the haughtiness of their arrogance and the malice of their envy—they are unclean and perverted spirits! How effective the element of air is—in which their bodies have efficacy—for producing invisibly many visible results, for moving, changing, and manipulating things is too long a story to set forth now. I think that it will occur readily to one who deliberates on the subject even to a moderate extent.

Since the divination of demons is the subject at hand, one must know in the first place that they very often foretell acts which they themselves intend to perform. They often use their power to induce diseases, to render the very air unhealthy by corrupting it, and to counsel evil deeds to men who are perverted and greedy for earthly gains. They are aware from the character of such men that they would agree with them were they to counsel such acts. They persuade them, however, through wondrous and invisible ways, penetrating by means of the subtlety of their own bodies into the bodies of these men unaware, mingling themselves with their thoughts through certain imaginary visions whether they are awake or asleep.

Yet sometimes they foretell not the things which they themselves do, but future events which they recognize by means of natural signs which cannot reach the senses of men. Surely if the physician foresees that which those ignorant of his art do not foresee, he ought not to be considered divine. So what is strange if a demon in the state and condition of the atmosphere (known to him but unknown to us) can predict future storms or if a physician is able to predict future good or bad health through disturbances or changes in the temperature of the human body? At times, too, they are able to discern the intentions of men with complete ease, not only as these are expressed through the voice but also as they are conceived in thought when certain mental signs are expressed physically through the body. In this way, they predict many future things which are clearly wonders to those who do not know the circumstances under which they were made. For just as violent emotions cause the movements of the mind to be apparent in the face, so that which is expressed inwardly can also be discerned by men externally—thus, it ought not be incredible if even lighter thoughts produce some signs throughout the body which cannot be known through the blunt sense perception of men but can be grasped through the keen perception of demons.

By this faculty and faculties of this kind, demons predict many things. Yet, far above them is the loftiness of that prophecy which God works through his holy angels and prophets.... Nevertheless, in their other predictions, demons are usually deceived and deceive. Indeed, they are deceived because when they announce their own intentions, something can be ordered from on high which unexpectedly throws all their plans into confusion.... They are deceived also with respect to natural phenomena. Like doctors, sailors, and farmers, they prognosticate but they do so more keenly and much more excellently through the more dexterous and practiced perception of their aerial body. But these natural things can be changed suddenly and unexpectedly by angels faithfully serving God on high according to another plan unknown to the demons—just as something unexpected might befall and kill a sick man whom a doctor had promised would survive because earlier signs pointed to his recovery, or some sailors who, having foreseen from the quality of the air predicted that the wind would blow for a long time, even though our lord Christ, sailing with his disciples ordered that the wind be still and there was great calm [see Matt. 8.26]. Or a farmer, considering the nature of the soil and the number of his seeds, might promise that a grapevine would bear fruit at the end of the year—yet during the year an unexpected disturbance in the heavens might break down the vine or some command of a local official might cause it to be rooted out. Thus, many things pertaining to the foreknowledge and prediction of demons which are foreseen in advance in lesser and more ordinary cases are changed and hindered through hidden and greater causes.

In any event, demons deceive with an eagerness for deception and malevolent will through which they delight in the error of men. Lest they lose the weight of their authority among their worshippers, they see to it that any failure to discern the future correctly is divided between those who read their signs and those who interpret them, claiming that these men were either deceived or lied.

How is it a wonder, then, if—with the destruction of the temples and their images imminent as the prophets of the highest God had foretold so long ago—the demon Serapis betrayed this fact to some of his worshippers so that he might still show his divinity, even while yielding and fleeing?

Demons are put to flight or rather, bound they are dragged off by higher commands and alienated from their own places so that with respect to those powers by which they ruled and for which they were worshipped, the will of God—who predicted such a thing would happen so long ago among all people and commanded that it be accomplished through his faithful servants—can be accomplished. Why, then, should the demon not be allowed to predict this event [the destruction of the temple] since he knew already it was going to happen to him and the prediction had also been attested to by the prophets? . . . For a long time before then, the demons had been silent in their temples about these coming events even though they could not have not known about them because the matter had been predicted by the prophets. Later, when the time of the temple's destruction began to draw near, they wanted—as it were—to predict the matter lest they be deemed ignorant and vanquished. Passing over other examples for the moment, long ago, it was predicted and written that which the Prophet Sophonias says, "the lord will prevail against them and will cast out all the gods of the gentiles of the earth. They will adore him, every man from his own place, all the islands of the gentiles" [see Zeph. 2.11]. But those who worshipped in the temples of the gentiles did not believe that these events would happen to them, and on that account they did not want these things repeated through their seers and diviners. Therefore, either the demons (that is, the powers of the air) doubted that those things which they knew had been predicted by the prophets could happen to them—and for that reason they did not want to advertise their prediction (and from this, something of their character may be deduced!)—or they knew that these things would assuredly come to pass, but kept silent through their temples lest they come to be distained and abandoned by understanding men because those prophets who forbade that they be worshipped attested that their temples and images would be destroyed. Now, however, after the time when the prophecies of the prophets of the one God—who calls their gods false and who warns most vehemently that they not be worshipped—has come, why should not even demons be allowed to declare what has been proven? Therefore, it should be more apparent that either demons did not believe these prophecies at all before they came to pass, or they were afraid to reveal them to their worshippers.

In the end, then, with nothing more that they could do, the tricks which for so many years they had performed to imitate divinity, they now wanted to present as examples of their power of divination.

Questions: Why are demons able to do amazing things? Are these miracles? Under what circumstances can demons actually predict future things? Is the source of demonic foreknowledge divine? Do demons operate within or above the realm of nature? What complications—intellectual and practical—might arise for people like Augustine who believe in the real existence of demons at work in the world?

37. BISHOP NARCISSUS SEES A HORRIBLE DEMON

The following story is taken from the anonymous vita *of Saint Afra, a young pagan woman who converted to Christianity and was martyred during the Great Persecution (303–313) of the Roman emperor Diocletian (d. 311). It presents us with an early and vivid portrait of the Christian devil. Though originally from Cyprus, Afra and her family moved to Augsburg in the Roman province of Raetia (southern Germany). It was there that the events described in the following selection are said to have taken place. Narcissus was a Christian bishop from Spain. He and his deacon Felix had been exiled from their homeland and found themselves in the German town. Hilaria is the mother of Afra.*

Latin, late eighth century.

Source: trans. Richard Raiswell and David R. Winter, from *Conversio et Passio S. Afrae*, from MGH *Scriptores rerum Merovingicarum*, vol. 3 (Hanover, 1896), pp. 57–60.

[To the questions of Narcissus, the bishop of Gerona] Hilaria responded, "My parents were of the Cyprian race. They came from that place [as followers of] the rites of Venus—although Venus is not worshipped, except by women who are prostitutes. At length, after consecrating my daughter to the rites of Venus, I permitted her [to stay] in a brothel, enslaved to the goddess and made pleasing for harlotry. I believed that Venus might favor me if I enlisted my daughter in imitation of her divinity. For the more lovers a woman has, the more pleasing she is to Venus. The priests of Venus affirm that this is how a woman serves the goddess." Hearing this, the man of God, bishop Narcissus, sighed and wept, and then he said to his deacon, "Rise, brother, and let us lament over such a cursed cult and beseech the lord that, where iniquity has abounded, grace should abound the more."

And it happened that, when they prayed, an Egyptian, blacker than a raven, appeared [to them]. He was naked and his whole body was covered with elephant wounds, and then he began to groan and say, "O holy bishop Narcissus, what business is my house to you? What business are the handmaids who I have always kept in my household to you? Your God loves cleansed souls and cleansed bodies. Those women are already mine; they cannot be anything else. Is it possible for me to enter where chastity rules? Is it possible for me to find the place where there is the spirit of chastity? [Do you know] what sort of place you have entered, [a place] where bodies are defiled and souls are polluted?"

Then Narcissus the holy bishop said to him, "I command you, unclean spirit, that you answer this question. Tell me, damned thing, do you know that my lord Jesus Christ of Nazareth was held, beaten, spat at in the face, violated, crowned with thorns, mocked, bound, dragged, was fed gall and vinegar, was fixed to the cross, died, and was buried and rose from death on the third day? Do you know that this happened?" The demon responded and said, "If only I was not allowed to know this, for out of that mouth [Judas's mouth] by which Jesus was crucified, our prince fled from his presence. He sent himself into the temple of God and on that account the curtain of the temple was ripped because he was not able to bear the power of Jesus's attack. Then, the solid stones were split, and the graves were opened, and holy men rose up [Matt. 27.50–53]. They witnessed our prince being seized by him who was crucified; they saw our prince being bound with burning chains."

Narcissus the holy bishop responded and said, "What is the name of your prince?" The demon said to him, "His name is Satan, which is translated as 'the beginning of death'" [compare this to doc. 3]. Narcissus the bishop said to him, "Tell me, how did the Lord Jesus Christ sin that he should suffer so greatly?" The demon said to him, "He never sinned." Narcissus the bishop said to him, "And why should he who has never sinned suffer so much?" The demon answered, "He did not suffer for his own sin, but for those of others." Narcissus the bishop said to him, "You are condemned by your own mouth, unclean spirit! Indeed, since you know that my Lord Jesus Christ died not for his own sins but for those of others, depart from these two women! Because he suffered for them, they have taken refuge in his faith and grace."

The demon said to him, "Does not holy law teach and command that a person ought not take the things of others? You, who are holy, why do you take my things? Why are you taking the souls I have gained?" Narcissus the bishop said to him, "From the beginning, you are a housebreaker and thief, damned and unchanging, for you separated those souls from their lord and creator. I bind you now thief: restore his creature to its creator!" The demon answered him, saying, "Am I not his creature? Therefore, restore me to my creator." Bishop Narcissus said to him, "You confessed with your own mouth that Christ suffered for the sins of men. If how he suffered for the sins of men is also how he suffered for the impieties of demons, I have [already] restored you to your creator. But now, because he died for the sins of men so that he might bind your prince, go to your prince yourself."

The demon said to him, "Pity me and give me power over just one soul." Narcissus the bishop said to him, "If I give you power over a soul, what will you do with it?" The demon said to him, "I will kill the person and gain their soul." Bishop Narcissus said to him, "If you stay until first light, I will give you the power to do this." The demon said to him, "Swear to me before God, that I will gain a soul enclosed within a body." Narcissus said to him, "Before my God, I am giving you a soul enclosed within a body, one which eats and drinks and sleeps and wakes again." The demon said to him, "Order me now to stay here for the night." Narcissus said to him, "Stay—if you are able to." The demon said to him, "If you do not reach up your hands toward heaven, and do not genuflect, and do not sing to your God, I will be able stay here." Narcissus said to him, "It should never be easy for you, O unclean spirit! Not only I, but all those with me, will genuflect to our God through the whole night and sing praises to him, all of us as one." Then, emitting a loathsome shriek in a dreadful voice, the demon disappeared.

After the fast, the holy bishop restored Afra to her mother. Her children were trembling on account of what they had heard and seen, so he comforted them through his teachings and prayers. But the bishop did not return to his deacon, the holy Felix, at that time, knowing he was about to have another struggle with the demon in the morning. And so he spent the whole night in prayers and singing psalms. At sunrise, the demon appeared saying, "Remember, holy bishop, the promises you made before God. Give me the soul, whose body I may kill and whose soul I may keep with me." And answering him, Narcissus the holy bishop said, "And swear to me in the name of my God, that you will immediately kill whomever I give to you. And swear to me now [this oath]: 'If I do not kill, God may order me into the abyss.'" And the demon said to him, "Three times! He has conquered us together with our prince; thus he will not order me into the abyss because I will immediately kill whomever you give me."

And Bishop Narcissus said to him, "Go to the spring in the Julian Alps from which no one is able to drink water, neither man, nor cattle, nor any wild beast because a dragon dwells there. That dragon kills all those who approach the spring with his breath. Go and kill that dragon and claim his soul." Then the demon exclaimed, saying, "O what a lying bishop! He has bound me by an oath to kill my friend. If I do not kill him, I will be compelled into the abyss!" Then the demon assented and killed the dragon and the spring was liberated for use by everyone, up to the present day.

Questions: How and why is the demon constrained? Why did the demon ask Narcissus to order him to remain with the Christians throughout the night? What elements of this story might have appealed to Christians during the Carolingian era?

38. STABLE HANDS PRAY TO THE DEVIL

The following story concerning the power of relics to defeat demonic forces comes from the Life and Miracles of Saint Maurus. *Maurus (d. 584) was a disciple of Benedict of Nursia and was reputed to be the founder of Glanfeuil monastery (near Angers in northwestern France). While the story of Maurus's life appears to be a ninth-century forgery by the abbot of Glanfeuil, it nevertheless reveals much about attitudes and cultural mores during the Carolingian Renaissance.*

Latin, ninth century.

Source: trans. John Wickstrom, *The Life and Miracles of St. Maurus, Disciple of Benedict, Apostle of France* (Collegeville, MN: Cistercian Publications, 2008), pp. 137–38; rev.

The stable hands once tried to carry off by force from Glanfeuil monastery some wine that belonged to the honorable Gerelmus—a man who had always lived a virtuous life in the house of Abbot Agelwine. Some of the brothers came running. A struggle broke out and the thieves started to attack the servants who were standing against them and objecting to their actions. When he heard the news, Abbot

Theodradus himself came up. He had begun rebuking their insolence with a mild reproach when one of them—bolder than the others—began attacking the abbot with insults. But Abbot Theodradus struck the man on the forehead with a small relic container which he carried close to his heart. He exclaimed, "Through the merits of blessed Maurus and the other saints—whose relics are hidden away in this capsule that we venerate—may almighty God reserve for himself vengeance and punishment on those who insult his relics and his servants! May he reserve punishment especially for you, who encourage the evil of plundering by assuming leadership over such thieves!" After this, the abbot ordered they be ejected from the monastery. The ringleader then commandeered a fishing boat that was reserved to the brothers' use, intending to cross the Loire River. Asverus, one of the brothers, went up and said, "This is not right! That all the ills you inflicted on the servants of blessed Maurus should not have been enough for you. Now you're trying to steal the boat set aside for their needs." When he made no impression on them by pursuing such issues, he added, "The boat belongs to the holy Maurus, and you have no right to make off with it." The thief answered him: "I will leave behind for the holy Maurus just as much as I leave for his woman [possibly a joke about his celibacy]." He had not yet finished these words when he was suddenly seized by a demon and thrown headlong into the Loire. He surfaced once from the depths, gnashing his teeth and calling, "O Satan, come to my aid!" Snatched away again by the waves, he appeared no more. Three days later, some fishermen discovered his body between two islands: his belly ripped open and the intestines missing. The fishermen were filled with fear by the mad shouting forced from the dead man's mouth by demons, and took flight. Tumbling off their boat, they entrusted themselves to the waters and swam to safety.

Questions: What role did the relic container play in dispersing demonic influences? Is the writer of this account suggesting that some people in early medieval Europe actually prayed to the devil? If not, to whom might the stable hand have been praying?

39. DEMONIC STRATAGEMS IN THE CAROLINGIAN WORLD

The political world of Carolingian Francia was gradually unified under the principle of Christian kingship. The embodiment of this idea was Charlemagne (r. 768–814), the second king of the Carolingian dynasty and the first western monarch since the collapse of Roman imperial government (in 476) to claim the title of emperor. While the Carolingians were not always able to live up to this ambitious ideology, they did engage in ventures designed to increase the borders of their world. One of the consequences of this worldview was that Carolingian Franks increasingly viewed government in cosmological terms. If the Carolingian king was indeed God's agent, then those pitted against him were, therefore, diabolical. The monk Notker "the

Stammerer" (c. 840–912) was an important courtier in the household of one of Charlemagne's grandsons, the emperor Charles the Fat (d. 888). He regaled the later Carolingian monarch with stories about his illustrious forbearer in his biography The Deeds of Charles the Great. As the two stories below suggest, even the Frankish royal and episcopal courts were sometimes subject to diabolical visits.

Latin, ninth century.

Sources: trans. Richard Raiswell and David R. Winter, from Notker Balbulus, *Gesta Karoli Magni*, from MGH *Scriptores rerum Germanicarum*, vol. 12 (Berlin, 1959), pp. 27–29; trans. Arthur James Grant, *Early Lives of Charlemagne by Einhard and the Monk of Saint Gall* (London, 1905), p. 142.

A Monstrous Devil Appears to a Frankish Bishop

In Neustria, there was a certain bishop of marvelous sanctity and abstinence, as well as incomparable generosity and kindness. The old enemy, who hates all types of justice, was exasperated by the virtue of this man. Thus, he aroused in him a desire to eat meat during the 40 days of Lent. The impulse was so great that the bishop thought he might die of weakness and want if he were not restored to vigor by having meat. Taking the counsel of many holy men and venerable priests, the bishop accepted that he must eat meat in order to recover his health, and then mortify himself for the entire year. However, driven by ultimate necessity, he submitted to their authority, for if he failed to obey them, he might have been considered a traitor. So, he placed a morsel from a quadruped into his mouth. When he began to chew it and to taste it tentatively on his palate, he was immediately seized by a revulsion or loathing, not only for meat and for all other types of food, but also for the light of the world, and for his very life itself. On account of this, he no longer wanted to eat or drink and he placed his only hope in the savior of the lost.

After the first week of Lent had passed, the previously mentioned fathers suggested to him that, because he knew that he had been deceived by a diabolical illusion, he should make an effort to rid himself of his momentary sin, that he should make amends for it and wash it away with harsher fasts, more generous alms, and heartfelt contrition. He obeyed their counsel, as it was the best possible advice. As he attempted to confound the malice of the devil, and to gain pardon from the one who restores innocence, he afflicted himself with fasts lasting two or three days. He fled from the peaceful repose of sleep, and he ministered daily to pilgrims and the poor. He washed their feet, gave them clean clothing, and money to the extent of his means. He wished he could go beyond his means! On the holy day of the sabbath of Easter [Saturday], he gathered wine-casks from the whole city and ordered that hot baths be established for all of the poor folk from dawn to sunset. With his own hand, he shaved the necks of each of them; with his fingernails, he picked purulent scabs and growths from their hairy bodies. He then anointed them with balms and clothed them in white robes as a sign of their rebirth.

When the sun began to set, and there was no one remaining who needed such services, the bishop himself stepped into one of the hot baths. When he emerged, his conscience was clean and so he donned a spotless vestment. He did this so that, with the approval of all the holy bishops, he might celebrate solemnities with the people. As he proceeded toward the church, the cunning adversary wanting to overturn what the bishop had done, assumed the form of a fetid and dirty leper, with running sores and filthy rags gone stiff with putrefaction, so that it seemed as though the bishop had sent away some pauper unattended against his vow. He came to meet the bishop at the threshold of the church, palsied with a tottering gait, and also with the hoarse voice of a man in complete misery. Then, turning around by divine instinct, the holy bishop recognized the enemy to whom he had recently succumbed. He took off his white clothing and ordered that more water should be heated without delay and that the "poor man" be placed in the tub. Then, he took hold of a razor and began to shave the miscreant's exceptionally filthy throat. And when he had finished shaving all of the hair from his neck from one ear to the middle, he began again at the other ear, and shaved until he came back to the same spot. The marvelous thing, though, is that when he returned to the middle with the razor a second time, he discovered that the long hairs which he had previously shaved had grown back. And though he did not stop shaving, this happened several times. At last, lo, under the hand of the bishop, an eye of extraordinary size was exposed at the center of the devil's throat! I shudder even to think of it. The bishop, terrified at such a monstrous sight, leapt to his feet with a shout. He then crossed himself while invoking the name of Christ. The fraudulent old enemy was unable to disguise himself any longer and, so, disappeared in a puff of smoke just before the invocation. As he receded, he said, "This eye was carefully watching you when you ate meat during the Lenten fast!"

King Pippin Dispatches a Diabolical Visitor to the Royal Baths

Not only was [Charlemagne's father's] courage shown against beasts and men, but he also fought an incredible contest against evil spirits. The hot baths at Aix had not yet been built, but hot and healing waters bubbled from the ground. He ordered his chamberlain to see that the water was clean and that no unknown person was allowed to enter into them. This was done and the king took his sword and, dressed only in linen gown and slippers, hurried off to the bath, when lo! the old enemy met him, and attacked him as though he would slay him. But the king, strengthened with the sign of the cross, made bare his sword, and, noticing a shape in human form, struck his unconquerable sword through it into the ground so far, that he could only drag it out again after a long struggle. But the shape was so far material that it defiled all those waters with blood and gore and horrid slime. But even this did not upset the unconquerable Pippin. He said to his chamberlain, "Do not mind this little affair. Let the defiled water run for a while, and then, when it flows clear again, I will take my bath without delay."

Questions: Are Notker's devils spiritual creatures? Why do they attack? How do the methods used by Pippin and the cleric to defeat the devil differ? Is this significant? Why do both stories stress the importance of ritual and pollution? Why might it be significant that the first story takes place between Good Friday and Easter Sunday?

40. THE MONASTERY AS A FORTRESS AGAINST THE DEVIL

Bernard of Clairvaux (1090–1153) was one of the intellectual and spiritual titans of the twelfth-century reform movement. Though a nobleman by birth, he entered the austere and struggling Cistercian Order of monks around 1112. Until then, the order had failed to fire the imagination of Christians. Upon establishing a reformed monastery in the remote vale of Clairvaux, however, Bernard almost single handedly revived Cistercian fortunes and made the order one of the most influential voices of twelfth century. He also promulgated the Second Crusade, helped to establish the Order of the Poor Soldiers of the Temple of Solomon (the Knights Templar), and encouraged the cult of the Virgin Mary. He was canonized by Pope Alexander III in 1174 and was later declared a Doctor of the Church. In this selection, Bernard applied the values of the nobility to the cosmic struggle against evil. He conceptualized Clairvaux as a military outpost garrisoned against the forces of evil.

Latin, before c. 1153.

Source: trans. Richard Raiswell and David R. Winter, from *In dedicatione ecclesiae* (Migne, PL 183: 0523D–526B).

On the threefold preparation which we should make for the protection of God.

Brothers, this house of the eternal king is a fortress but one besieged by enemies. We who have sworn to bear arms for its sake and who have given our names in its service know that our work in defense of this castle will be threefold: namely, fortification, armament, and provisioning. What, therefore, is fortification? "Zion is the city of our strength, a savior," said the prophet, "a wall and bulwark will be placed in it" [Isa. 26.1]. The wall is continence; the bulwark is patience. The wall of continence which surrounds and girds the fortress on all sides is good, so that no entrance is given to death either through the windows of the eyes or through the other senses. The bulwark of patience which holds back the enemy's initial attacks is good and allows us to stand valiantly in the midst of so many temptations and continuously persevere unshaken. Indeed, the only remedy when continence is shaken and falters is to block the way with patience, and however much our sense of sin may burn, to refuse to give in to that sense of sin in every way. "In your patience," says the apostle, "you will possess your souls" [Luke 21.19]. The savior himself is placed in his city as a wall and bulwark made for us by God the father in justice and through the patience of the prophet [David], for, as he said, "you are my patience, lord" [Ps. 70.5]. The wall is built by our manner of life, the bulwark by our suffering, abstaining from all the allurements of the flesh and those of this present age, resisting steadfastly against all adversities.

It is also necessary to prepare arms, but they should be spiritual arms, powerful for the sake of God, suitable not only for resistance but also for attacking and fighting the enemy valiantly. "Put on the armor of God etc." said the Apostle [Eph. 6.11]. What do we think, brothers? The temptation of the enemy is indeed weighty upon us, but weightier by far is our prayer. His iniquity and cunning wound us—but our simplicity and mercy torment him much more. He cannot endure our humility. He is burned by our charity. He is crucified by our obedience and meekness.

Indeed, we are no longer pressed by hunger to hand over the castle to our enemies since—thank God—that terrible threat of hunger and thirst that the prophet (or rather, the lord through the prophet) has not come upon us: not bread and water but the word of God [Amos 8.11]. For thus we read, "A man does not live by bread alone but by every word that proceeds from the mouth of God" [Deut. 8.3; Matt. 4.4]. And so, are we lacking in food who hear sermons often and the sacred readings more often still—we who also, from time to time, taste the delights of spiritual devotion like little dogs eating the scraps which fall from the table of their lords? We who are celestial guests, I say, who are filled up by the abundance of the house of God. We also have the bread of tears which, although less pleasant, nevertheless best strengthens the heart of man. We have the bread of obedience, too, about which the lord speaks to his disciples, saying "my nourishment is that I do the will of my father" [John 4.34]. Above all, we have the living bread from heaven, the body of the lord, our savior whose power assuredly drives out that of every sort of adversary.

The strength of the lord's castle is established in this way so that, if we act faithfully and valiantly—and are clearly found to be neither traitors, cowards, nor idlers—we ought to fear nothing. Whoever attempts to introduce God's enemies into the lord's castle are traitors, such as the detractors, hateful to God, who sow discord and foster scandal among the brothers. Just as the place of the lord was made in peace so it is evident that that of devil was made in discord. Do not be surprised, brothers, if I seem to speak harshly because truth flatters no one. Let him know himself to be a traitor if he, by chance—God forbid—tries to introduce any sin into this house and turn the temple of God into a cave of demons. Thanks be to God, we do not find many of this sort here.

However, now and then, we detect some by chance who confer with our enemies and strike a pact with death; that is, they try—because it is in them—to weaken the discipline of the order, to incite the passions, to disturb the peace and offend charity. Indeed, let us be aware of such men as much as we can, just as it is written about certain of them, "But Jesus did not trust himself with them" [John 2.24]. But I say to you, although they may be being sustained at the present time, they will soon bear a heavy judgment—like the heavy damage they have tried to inflict—unless they quickly mend their ways. What do you say, brother? Do you serve the faith through your works out of vanity or in tepidness or for the sake of some other vice? Are you lying to God through your tonsure? You will assuredly have robbed Christ of an excellent castle if you hand Clairvaux over to his enemies. Each year, he receives that income from here which is the best and most precious in his eyes: the many spoils which he seizes from his enemies, usually depositing them in this fortified place, having great confidence in its strength. Behold those he redeemed from the hand of the enemy and gathered together from all regions from the rising to the setting sun, from the north wind to the [southern] sea. After he has been seized and apprehended, to what punishments do you think a betrayer of the castle ought to be subjected—for such a man cannot hide nor flee? He will not be condemned to the same death as others of the community, for it is necessary that he die in exquisite torments. But I will not linger any longer on such things. I believe it is better henceforth that we be wary of this accursed treason, busying ourselves with other, greater concerns—not attracting, but repelling sins, whatever they might be, whether carnal, or only worldly, so as not to incur the stigma or punishment of traitors.

In the second place, it is necessary to beware lest anyone, overcome by cowardice, flee from the fortress shaking in fear where there is nothing to fear; likewise it is necessary to beware of remaining in a rash and foolish security, where there is the greatest danger. Anyone who flees, places himself in the enemies' hands—and at the point of their swords—as if he did not know that the enemies are entirely without mercy, cruel indeed to strangers, but crueler still to their allies since the enemies' allies are cruelest to themselves.

Now, since time is running short, I will speak briefly about the third danger, for while I greatly desire your salvation—as is fitting—I seek various cures for various afflictions of character. If you wish neither to betray nor surrender the castle, what use is it to remain there sluggish and idle? Let us work with all our soul and all our power, dearest brothers, to hold the castle our lord and king has given us, wary of the enemy's cunning, prepared against all his machinations, just as it is written "resist the devil, and he will flee from you" [James 4.7]. But since we know who said, "if the lord does not guard the city, whoever guards it, watches in vain" [Ps. 126.1], let us be humbled under the powerful hand of the almighty, coming together into that house with full devotion to his mercy so he may preserve us from all the enemies' snares entirely, to the praise and glory of his name, which is forever blessed. Amen.

Questions: What metaphors does Bernard use to describe a monastery? Where might this view have come from? What does this suggest about how monks see their work? Why are monks so vulnerable to demonic attacks?

41. BESIEGED BY DEMONS

Largely as a result of the influence of Bernard of Clairvaux (doc. 40), Cistercian monasticism grew dramatically in the twelfth century. By the time of Bernard's death in 1153, there were more than 300 Cistercian monasteries scattered across Europe. Anxious to avoid a descent into the sort of worldliness that had corrupted other monastic orders, the Cistercians stressed a strict and literal interpretation of the Rule of Saint Benedict. *Among other things, this meant a renewed emphasis on the importance of humility and manual labor in monastic life. Predictably, the order's success set it at odds with the older orders, who accused the Cistercians of regarding themselves as superior to others despite the* Rule's *teachings on humility.*

The monk Richalm rose to become abbot of the Cistercian abbey of Schöntal in southern Germany in 1216, a position he held until his death. His Book of Revelations Concerning the Deceit and Cunning of Demons Against Men *is a strange text. It begins as a lively dialogue between the abbot and an unnamed novice—complete with interjections and asides—but around halfway through, the structure changes, becoming instead just a catalogue of the abbot's observations and experiences with demons. In this respect, Richalm's work reflects a high medieval tradition of demon-seeing that is almost unique to the Cistercians.*

Latin, thirteenth century.

Source: trans. Richard Raiswell and David R. Winter, from Richalm von Schöntal, *Liber revelationum* (Hannover: Hahnsche Buchhandlung, 2009), pp. 31–36, 39, 58–59, 76–78.

Richalm: I'll tell you another wonderful thing. Wicked demons have been keeping a man who had died recently in some kind of motion—as if he were alive—for one or two and even more days, so that he was not supposed dead, even though he was.

Novice: So what is it they're doing? What do they intend by doing this?

R: Clearly that men become tormented and disconcerted by [the sight of] him.

N: How do you know this?

R: In a nearby village, a certain man lay in a struggle for seven days—I don't know, maybe more—neither able to die nor to appear dead. Having been called to him, I entered the house and heard demons saying, "We must leave. We won't be able to do anything more." So very soon after I arrived, the man was at rest.

I had a vision about Brother William in which he was dead before any of us could have known about it. The demons showed me such great wickedness in his suffering. As you know, this same William had lost his speech and couldn't talk. One day, when I had gone to attend the [monastic] reading, the demons wanting to prevent me from doing this called the name of my office [that is, "Prior"] through the mouth of this same William. Having heard this, immediately one of my assistants ran towards me shouting because William had called me. But I knew what was happening. Nevertheless, I went, but in vain, for neither then nor at any previous time had he said anything. However, the demons were tossing his arms and other enfeebled limbs here and there, just as we often see being tossed about in the infirm. . . .

Those demons who always accompany us report all our words and deeds back to other demons who've been placed at certain stations. Behold! Soon we'll go off for *nones* [afternoon prayers] and those demons who are always clinging to us will report to those who are located in the choir about how I have said this and that to you. O, if you could hear everything they're going to tell them!

N: I wonder whether demons really do accompany us everywhere—never leaving us entirely—as you say.

R: You've been deceived and are mistaken. Do you think that they're only with us on feast days? They are always with us—always!

Tonight, during the reading, as I read, I repeated a word twice, as you heard. But I say to you truly that I said that word but once. The other time it was said by a demon.

When I was reading in the scriptorium before *nones* in the usual way, the demon who clings to me forced me to spit up at a certain point so that the other demons who were further away could hear me spit and come together at this sign to frustrate me further. Knowing that this was the case, I tried as much as I could not to spit.

Demons fuss about at night to prevent us from sleeping so that during the day we might fall asleep at the reading. If we stay awake at night profitably in good contemplation, they suffer much on this account—but they're happy to keep us awake unprofitably. Sometimes, though, they don't know whether I'm awake or asleep unless they see some sign such as the raising of a hand or some other motion. And they also frustrate me in the repetition of my readings. They spread themselves over a man like clouds, and amass themselves everywhere around him, rendering his senses blunted and dull.

What great power there is in books! When I am sitting in conversation with the monks, it is always my habit to bring a book with me. As long as I have it open, the conversation between the monks concerns good and worthwhile things. But if, however, I close it and place it next to me, immediately useless chatter breaks out among them—more correctly, demons close the book using my hands and they push it away. Then, the good spirits say to me, "Pick it up! Pick it up! Open the book!" When I've done that, the chatter begins to subside and profitable discussions begin again. See, therefore, what power there is in books!

But you see that I'm always making the sign [of the cross] on myself—I never stop signing myself. Assuredly, I experience great grace on that account and I cannot live otherwise. You should do the same, most beloved one—especially upon your heart and inside [your clothing] upon your skin, because if demons set a reed or straw against the cross, they do it so that they might perceive its power less.

N: I thought that wherever the cross is made it has such power that nothing blocks it—not even clothing.

R: Those [demons] who are within do not know what the man is doing on the outside—and vice versa. Once I made thirty crosses under my clothes on my flesh and those demons that were on the outside [of my clothing] did not pester me any the less. But when I withdrew my hand and signed myself outside, they all fled.

Like specks in the sunlight such is the multitude of them that surround every man—perhaps even more. And I've seen them in such forms, that is, as specks. And this multitude gathered together out of many creates a single body. And they move the body and limbs of a man on which they settle toward every evil and dishonor. They turn up the noses of men; they contort their lips. If anyone has a handsome nose, in order to disfigure it, they often make it contract into wrinkles. If they see someone wanting to put their lips together modestly, they disfigure them, making the lower lip sag. Look, one demon was hanging on that lip for twenty years so that he alone made it droop and be deformed.

N: O that demon who has been hanging there in this way has done his work well!

R: What do you want? In a wondrous way, evil spirits watch for any and every enmity—and they pursue us for that reason. So it is amazing that any of us is alive were it not for the fact that divine grace protects us. Look, I am in the habit of pulling up my hood because exterior light blocks interior illumination. You would not believe how much they resist me in this—how much they scratch me on the head, and when my head is irritated, I pull back my hood . . .

I saw the ears of lay brother N. covered over and blocked with a bandage while he was listening to the Rule [of Benedict] being expounded to him in the Chapter House. I understood this to be a demon—one of many—whose job it is to block the ears [of monks] from hearing the word of God . . .

I've been tempted by a spirit of lust, and while I didn't succumb, this same demon appeared to me in the form of a nubile woman. And I wondered to myself why a demon would assume such a form—as if the mere temptation and mental suggestion were not enough for him. I realized that they assume the physical forms of those things through which they tempt us so that they will have a greater effect. Likewise, when demons are tempting me to restlessness in my bed, I make things difficult for them by signing and resisting. I heard a demon saying to himself,

"I am the strongest demon," rousing and urging himself to try to finish his tasks through these words. Two things should be noted from this: namely, that demons assume [physical] forms, and that they call out to themselves to be stronger and of greater efficacy. Right now, I don't feel myself coughing, but I always feel a demon. Never—or hardly ever—do they allow me to sleep through the night. They throw me here and there. They toss me one way and then the other. They place my feet over there—and then they move them back again.

Behold. That word which was repeated twice while I was speaking to you? The second time was a demon [speaking]. As you have heard, I often suffer from a hacking cough while speaking—they do this.

Sometimes, while our lord abbot is speaking, I have heard a demon anticipating and pre-speaking the very words which later were spoken from the abbot's mouth. . . .

Today, when we were going to Boxberg [20 km north of Schöntal], it was thundering. I heard voices coming from the thunder which said this, "the brothers are going there." These words didn't so much come from the thunder as they were the thunder itself. Then the thunder was joined with other voices, [saying], "Where are they going?" And they replied, that is, the demons who were accompanying us, "They are going to Boxberg. The lady sent for them." and [the thunder asked] "Who are they?" And [the accompanying demons replied] "The prior who hears everything we are saying." This often happens to me—that I hear voices asking who we are—when I travel from the monastery.

N: I am greatly amazed at that thunderous voice.

R: It is certain, on the authority of the scriptures—because demons are allowed to move and stir up the air and the elements. Concerning this, I must tell you about a miracle which an honest man [named] N—a canon of Würzberg—told me. He said, "Once, when we arrived at a certain port we were delayed there for a long time, not able to go any further. Then, behold. After we'd been there for some time, a woman arrived. We bought a wind from her for an agreed upon price. This wind would lead us to a certain specified place, but no further." I heard this most truly from the mouth of the aforesaid canon, and I'm thoroughly amazed by it—nor have I heard anything like this before. But such are the tricks and skills [of demons]—their action so subtle that it is indescribable. We consider ourselves sensible, wise and clever. But all the ingenuity of humanity is nothing compared to their cunning and trickery.

Did you hear that sound?

N: I see that you're scratching yourself between your shoulder blades.

R: Do you not hear a sound which issues forth as if from the scratching?

N: I hear it.

R: This sound is the sound of demons. They made it. Do you hear the same sound proceeding not from my movement, but as if it were coming from within me?

N: I do hear the sound! It is wondrous indeed, but not unusual. It seems to me to come from some condition of the stomach or wind in the bowels, such as we suffer daily.

R: It's the sound of a demon—not as you suggest, some condition of the stomach.

N: I readily believe you, given the particular quality of that sound.

Questions: What sort of troubles do demons cause? Why do they focus their efforts on such schemes? Why does Richalm see demons—and why does the novice not see them? What do the activities of these demons suggest about the ideals of monastic life at Schöntal? How has the monastic struggle against demons changed from the times of Saint Antony and Bernard of Clairvaux? Do such beliefs make his worldview more rational or irrational?

CHAPTER FIVE

THE DEVIL AND FEUDAL SOCIETY

Figure 5.1 Albrecht Dürer, "Knight, Death, and the Devil" (1513). This is one of Dürer's more famous engravings and features a knight being greeted by death (with an hourglass) and the devil (represented in the garb of a *lansquenet*, a mercenary). Copies of this print would have sold for around 54 pfennigs, about three days' wages for an unskilled worker.

Medieval society is often described as "feudal." Although "feudalism" was not a term that medieval people used themselves—it was coined in the nineteenth century—it denotes a system of reciprocal obligations between a lord and a vassal. While there was enormous variation in the system between regions and across the period (with some historians questioning whether it can be called a "system" at all), stripped down, feudalism operated at the highest levels of society and involved a vassal pledging his loyalty and service to an immediate overlord in exchange for maintenance and protection. By the High Middle Ages, the system was generally understood as the exchange of a parcel of land (known as the "fief") for military or some other highly skilled service. Lords and vassals entered into this relationship through the three-fold ritual of homage, fealty, and investiture, which saw each party formally articulate his obligations to the other, sealing the relationship by means of an oath. With no abstract sense of a nation-state, loyalty was conceived through most of this period in terms of personal relationships.

From roughly the fifth century, the relationship between the devil and his followers was construed in a fashion that mirrored the development of that between lords and vassals. Like a powerful terrestrial lord, the devil often sought a formal, binding pact with his subjects, demanding loyalty and service from them in exchange for a measure of maintenance, or the realization of their desires. After all, as Luke 4 implied (doc. 9), the devil did seem to have a patrimony of his own and from which he could reward his vassals. Justification for this was found in Isaiah 28.15: "We have entered into a league with death, and we have made a covenant with hell."

The formalization of this relationship between the devil and his vassals had a number of curious consequences, for it implied that the devil had something analogous to a legally enforceable expectation of fidelity and faithful service from his vassals. In this sense, the devil could legitimately complain to have been wronged should one of his servants renege on his obligations and betray him by defecting to his enemy. Indeed, in some authors' hands, the devil himself could be seen as a vassal who has been wronged by God.

42. THE DEMONIC PACT OF SAINT CYPRIAN

Gregory Nanzianzus (c. 329–389) was Patriarch (archbishop) of Constantinople and a theologian who much preferred the monastic life to ecclesiastical politics. Though he engaged in a number of theological debates throughout his time in office, he eventually resigned and returned to pastoral duties (teaching and preaching) in his hometown. In the document below, taken from one of his sermons, Gregory discusses the early Christian martyr Saint Cyprian of Carthage, who died in 258 during the Valerian persecutions. However, it seems that, at certain points in the story, Gregory confuses Cyprian the martyr with another Cyprian, a reformed sorcerer who had dabbled with demons and was executed in 304. This story was popular

through the Middle Ages, reproduced most influentially in Jacobus de Voragine's thirteenth-century Golden Legend, *where the virtuous maiden is named as Justina.*
Greek, October 379.

Source: trans. Martha Pollard Vinson, from Gregory of Nazianzus, *Oration 24*, from *Selected Orations*, Fathers of the Church vol. 107 (Baltimore: Catholic University of America, 2004), pp. 145–50; rev.

The man who later was a disciple of Christ [Cyprian] was [originally] a worshipper of demons; the great champion of the truth was a persecutor of the most vicious sort; the man who once applied his formidable powers of both eloquence and action toward confusing our path, later enlisted both to the utmost in the service of Christians. How very wicked, too, was his use of sorcery (the unmistakable trademark of his misdeeds) in carrying out these nefarious activities! And what a still more terrible thing was his voracious appetite for carnal pleasure, which can drive mad even those otherwise sane and which cannot but affect their minds adversely by galloping off with their wits like some frisky colt!

We have now come to the heart of the sermon. . . . There was a young woman of good family and high morals. Hear this and join in rejoicing, young women and, more, all you matrons, too, who are chaste and love chastity. Our tale is a source of pride that both of you can share. And the young woman was very beautiful. . . . It was with this thoroughly irreproachable and virtuous maiden that the great Cyprian was somehow taken, I know not why or how. Of all the parts of the body, the eyes are the most difficult to control and appease; in their lust, they manage to touch even the untouchable. Well, Cyprian was not merely taken with her, but he actually made an attempt on her virtue. What idiocy to think that he could ravish her! Or rather, what shamelessness on the part of him who takes such liberties and encourages others to do the same! He is the very one who first crept into paradise itself to plot against the first creature; who comes to stand in the company of angels to demand that Job be handed over to him; who reaches the point of challenging the lord himself, who will destroy and make an end of him; and who, because God made manifest was in his sight merely another Adam, parades temptation before the one who is beyond temptation as if to wrestle even him to the ground. Little did he know that in attacking humanity he would come afoul of divinity. Why then should it surprise that Cyprian too was his chosen instrument in the attempt on her sainted soul and virginal body?

Anyway, make an attempt on her he did. For a go-between, he selects not an old hag from among those who practice the trade, but one of the demonic devotees of carnal delights, for the spiteful hosts of apostasy, constantly on the lookout for large numbers of recruits to share in their fall, are quick to offer their services in such affairs. The price of procurement consisted of sacrifices and libations, and the kinship that is born of bloodshed and smoke: exactly the kinds of payment that those who bestow such benefits require. But when the young girl sensed the evil and realized what was afoot—souls that are pure and God-like very quickly ferret out the schemer, no matter how clever or varied his attack—what does she do? What strategy does she devise to counter the artificer of evil? In utter desperation she seeks refuge with God and takes as champion against the loathsome infatuation her bridegroom, the one who rescued Susanna from cruel elders and saved Thecla from a tyrant suitor and even more tyrannical mother [an allusion to the apocryphal *Acts of Paul and Thecla*]. Who might this be? Christ, who rebukes spirits and buoys up those who are drowning and walks on the sea and consigns a legion of spirits to the deep; who rescues from the lions' den a just man who, thrown to them for food, vanquishes the beasts by stretching out his hands, rescues the fugitive prophet swallowed by a whale, because he maintained his faith even in its belly, and preserves the Assyrian children in the fire by sending an angel to quench the flame and adding him as fourth to their three.

Invoking these and still other models and beseeching the Virgin Mary to help a virgin in distress, she takes refuge in a regimen of fasting and sleeping on the ground. Since it was her beauty that placed her in this predicament, she tries by these means to ravage her looks and so pull the kindling from the flame and dissipate what fuels our passions. At the same time, she tries to win God's favor through her faith and self-denial, for nothing at all serves God so well as mortification and he rewards tears with his mercy. I know you are impatient to hear the rest of the story because you are anxious for this girl but equally for her lover, and fear that his ardor will end by destroying both. Take heart. His ardor becomes an ally of faith and the lover who seeks to win the maiden's hand is himself won over by Christ. Thus, the flame of the passions is stamped out and that of truth set ablaze. How? In what way? I have now reached the most gratifying part of the tale. The young girl conquers; the demon is conquered. The tempter goes up to the lover; he concedes defeat. He is scorned; he is furious at the slight; he takes his revenge upon the one who slights him. What is his revenge? He ensconces himself in his erstwhile servant that evil might dislodge evil and frenzy be cured by frenzy. He rebounds from the girl like an engine of war from a mighty rampart, put to flight by her words and prayers; and he wrestles with the one who had sent him, miraculously rallying against his attacker and choking him. . . .

What does he do next, the mad lover, his madness now checked? He seeks a release from his wickedness; he finds it: hardship is ever the mother of invention. How does he win his release? He takes refuge in the maiden's God, as Saul once did in David's melodious harp. He goes to her pastor and, just as he was cleansed of his passion by the blow, so he is cleansed of the evil spirit by his faith in Christ and he transfers his passion to him. For a long time his change of heart is considered suspect, and he is turned away because it seemed a thing in the realm of odd and incredible that Cyprian of all people should ever be counted a Christian.

Yet transfer it he does and the proof of his conversion is clear to see: he takes his books of magic and exposes them to public display; he stands triumphant over his evil and pathetic store; he preaches against the foolishness they contain, he makes a flame leap up brightly from them, he destroys in the fire their deceit that had been powerless to support a single spark of carnal desire; he parts company with the demons, he assimilates himself to God.

Questions: What was Cyprian's occupation before his conversion? What are the terms of his arrangement with demons? How is Cyprian's agreement with demons terminated? Why does the girl invoke pious examples?

43. THE POPE MAKES A PACT WITH THE DEVIL

Gerbert of Aurillac (c. 945–1003), better known as Pope Sylvester II, was a wonder of his age. Though born to a humble family in Auvergne in central France, Gerbert was thoroughly educated in the mechanical and liberal arts. Gerbert was a scholar who adopted Hindu-Arabic numbers early, and he is often credited with reintroducing the abacus and armillary sphere into Europe. He rose swiftly through the ranks of the ecclesiastical hierarchy, becoming first archbishop of Rheims, then of Ravenna, before finally being elevated (not without controversy) to the bishopric of Rome in 999. A fierce partisan in early efforts at church reform (as well as the first Frenchman to serve as pope), Gerbert opposed moral failings among the clergy such as simony, nepotism, and incontinence. His rapid rise through the ranks of the prelacy, and his connection to Arab learning in Spain, probably exposed him to charges of being involved in sorcery and learned magic. Stories began to circulate about his prowess as a necromancer and his ability to manipulate natural forces. Before long, no story concerning him was too outlandish. The document below comes from William of Malmesbury's The Chronicle of the Kings of England *(see doc. 33).*
Latin, c. 1135–40.

Source: trans. Richard Raiswell and David R. Winter, from William of Malmesbury, *Gesta Regum Anglorum atque historia novella*, vol. 1 (London, 1840), pp. 271–84.

It would not be out of place if we relate some well-known facts about [Pope] Sylvester who is also called Gerbert. He was born in Gaul and was raised from childhood as a monk at Flory. At some point, though, either because he became bored of the monastic life or because he was seized by a lust for worldly glory, he arrived at the double path of Pythagoras [one which leads to heaven and one which leads to hell]. Escaping from the monastery one night and travelling to Spain, he desired to learn astrology and other related arts of that sort from the Saracens. . . . Just as Toledo is the main city of the Christians [in Spain], so is Hispalim which is commonly called Seville [the main city of the Saracens]. There they busy themselves with divinations and incantations, according to the custom of those people. Therefore, when Gerbert reached that place he satisfied his desire. There he surpassed the wisdom of Ptolemy [c. 98–170] in the astrolabe, Alcandraeus [Al-Kindi?, 801–873] in cosmic ratios, and Julius Firmicus [fl. 340] in [astrological] predictions. There he learned what the song and flight of birds portend. There he learned to summon [minor] spirits from hell. And finally, he came to learn whatever noxious or healthy things human curiosity has discovered....

He was received into the house of a certain Saracen philosopher, whose favor he tried to win first through lavish spending and after that with promises. The Saracen had no objection to selling his knowledge, frequently associating with Gerbert, talking with him about both serious and trivial matters, and he would even lend him books to transcribe. There was one codex, though, which contained the whole of his art that he could not coax [from him] in any way. As a result, Gerbert was inflamed by desire to obtain the book by whatever means possible....

And after making little progress through promises and entreaties, he prepared a nocturnal ambush [for the Saracen]. Plying him with wine, he grabbed the book from under [the sleeping Saracen's] pillow and fled. The Saracen, waking from his slumber, consulted the stars, in which art he was skilled, and pursued the fugitive. Looking back, the fugitive understood the danger he was in by that very same art, and so he hid himself underneath a wooden bridge which was nearby. Grasping at the bridge, Gerbert hung down so that he was touching neither the water nor the ground. In this way, he eluded his keen pursuer, who eventually returned home.

Then Gerbert, hurrying along the road, reached the sea. There, by means of incantations, he summoned the devil, pledging perpetual homage to him, if he protected him from the Saracen who had renewed his pursuit, and if he carried him to the other shore. And the devil did this. But some may consider these things made up because common people are often in the habit of undermining the reputations of the learned. They say that a man who works any kind of excellence must have been taught by a demon.... But the unheard of manner of his death makes me believe it. For why else, when he was dying—as we describe below—did his horrible teacher [that is, the devil] mutilate his body unless it was because Gerbert was aware of his own extraordinary crime?

Gerbert returned to Gaul where he became master of arts. Among his students were some noble men of extraordinary talent, including Robert, son of [Frankish king] Hugh Capet [r. 987–996] and Otto, son of the [Holy Roman] Emperor Otto [II, r. 973–983]. When Robert later became king of France [r. 996–1031], he repaid his former master, appointing him archbishop of Rheims. In that church proof of his knowledge still remains, including a mechanical clock and a hydraulic organ.... When Otto succeeded his father as emperor of Italy, he made Gerbert archbishop of Ravenna and soon after Roman pontiff.

Under the devil's patronage, Gerbert advanced his worldly fortune further, so that nothing that he had ever desired remained unfinished. Using the art of necromancy, he discovered the treasures previously buried by the inhabitants [of Rome] and, after discarding all the rubbish, used the rest to further his own desires. This is how poorly disposed the wicked are toward God. . . .

There was a statue in the Campus Martius near Rome. I do not know if it was made of iron or bronze. It had the index finger of its right hand extended. On its head was written "Strike here!" The men of earlier times understood by this that they might find treasure there. They battered the harmless statue with repeated blows of the ax. But Gerbert refuted them of their error, solving the problem in a very different way. He noted where the shadow of the statue's finger fell at noon, when the sun was at its highest point. There he placed a wooden stake. Later, when the night came, he proceeded to that place accompanied only by a servant carrying a lantern. There the earth, splitting open by means of his customary arts, revealed a wide entrance. They saw a huge palace with golden walls and golden paneled ceilings. Everything was made of gold: golden soldiers with golden dice as if they were entertaining themselves; a king of the same metal reclining with his queen; food placed before them; servants standing by; serving dishes of great weight and value. The work surpassed even nature itself.

In the inner part of the palace there was a carbuncle, a stone that was small in appearance but precious; [shining], it put the darkness of the night to flight. In the opposite corner a boy stood holding a bow with an arrow drawn. While the exquisite craftsmanship of everything captured the eyes of the onlookers, they could touch none of it. Though they could see it, if anyone stretched out his hand to touch an object, immediately all the other figures appeared to rush forth to drive off the presumptuous attack.

Overwhelmed by fear, Gerbert restrained his desire—but his servant could not restrain his. He tried snatching at a knife of wonderful craftsmanship that he saw set upon the table. He judged that from such enormous booty, such an insignificant theft would escape notice. Immediately, though, with all the figures arising with a groan, the boy fired his arrow at the carbuncle and plunged [the entire chamber into] darkness. If he had not heard the warning of his master and thrown the knife back, they would both have suffered severely. Thus, with their insatiable greed unfulfilled, they left, their lantern leading the way.

The common people agreed that Gerbert had been able to discover such a thing only by means of illicit tricks. Nevertheless, if anyone were to investigate the truth of the matter thoroughly, he would discover that Solomon to whom God gave his wisdom was not ignorant of such matters. As Josephus the historian says, Solomon with his father buried vast treasures in coffers which were—he says—hidden underground by means of some mechanical contrivance. Nor was [the Jewish high priest] Hyrcanus, illustrious in prophecy and valor, ignorant of this. So that he might be freed from the damage of a siege, he dug up 3,000 gold talents from [the prophet] David's tomb paying part to the besiegers, and building a hospital with the rest. . . . Besides, when I hear the Lord Jesus saying, "My father works in this manner up to the present day—and so do I" [John 5.17], I believe that he who gave Solomon the power over demons to such a degree would also have been able to give this knowledge to Gerbert—but I do not know whether he did or not. For Josephus says that there were men even in his time who were able to expel demons from the bodies of demoniacs, by placing a ring in the nostrils of the patient bearing the sign of Solomon. . . .

[William goes on to relate several other stories concerning Gerbert's abilities.]

Gerbert cast for himself the head of a statue, having first assessed the position of the stars carefully—that is, after he considered when all the planets were beginning their orbit. This head would not speak unless it was spoken to but then would declare the truth, either in the affirmative or negative. For example, if Gerbert asked "Will I be pope?" the statue would reply "Yes." [If he asked] "Will I die before I sing mass in Jerusalem?" [it would respond], "No." They say that Gerbert was deceived by this ambiguity so that he did not think about penance, instead, being deluded in his mind that he would live a long life. [After all,] why would he consider going to Jerusalem if it would cause his death? Nor did he foresee that there was a church in Rome called "Jerusalem.". . . The pope celebrates mass in this church on three Sundays, which are called "The Station at Jerusalem." On one of those days, Gerbert was preparing himself for the mass when he was suddenly struck with an illness. When it got worse, he took to his bed. After consulting his statue, he [finally] understood the deception and his [pending] death. Summoning his cardinals, he wept for a long time on account of his sins. Struck by sudden fear, the cardinals were unable to reply. Because of this, Gerbert began to rave, and losing his reason because of his excessive pain, he ordered himself to be torn to pieces and thrown outside limb by limb. He said, "Let him who sought the homage of men have service of my limbs! My mind never consented to that abominable oath and sacrilege!"

Questions: What are the terms of the agreement between the devil and the pope? Can Gerbert be freed from his pact? What kind of knowledge is deemed suspicious? Why? Does the text make any distinction between naturally worked wonders and demonic ones? What demonic tropes does the author draw upon? Could this text be construed as part of the twelfth-century debate over clerical reform?

44. THE MAN OF SIN

According to the New Testament Acts of the Apostles, Saint Paul established a church in Thessalonica (modern Thessaloniki in northeastern Greece). After returning to Athens, however, Paul became concerned about the development of the community and so sent the apostle Timothy to offer them encouragement. Based on what he heard from Timothy, Paul wrote to the Thessalonians. He encouraged the community to remain steadfast in faith and morality, reminding them to be ready lest they suddenly find judgment day upon them, for, he wrote, "the day of the lord shall so come, as a thief in the night" (1 Thess. 5.2). The Thessalonians seem to have interpreted this as a warning that judgment was imminent, and so, to correct this misconception, Paul wrote this second letter to them shortly afterwards.

Greek, c. 52–53 CE.

Source: trans. Gregory Martin et al. from the Latin Vulgate, *The Holy Bible* (Douay-Rheims version) (Douay: The English College, 1609–10), rev. Richard Challoner (1749–52); rev.

2 Thessalonians

2.1. And we beseech you, brethren, by the coming of our Lord Jesus Christ, and of our gathering together to him,

2. That you be not easily troubled in your senses, nor terrified by spirit nor by word, nor by [any] epistle [allegedly] sent from us, [asserting] that the day of the lord is at hand.

3. Let no man deceive you by any means, for [that day will not come] unless there first comes a revolt, and the man of sin is revealed—the son of perdition

4. Who opposes and is lifted up above all that is called God, or who is worshipped so that he sits in the temple of God showing himself as if he were God.

5. Do you not remember that, when I was yet with you, I told you these things?

6. And now you know what holds him back so that he may be revealed at his [appropriate] time.

7. For the mystery of iniquity [is] already working; only that he who now holds [it back], holds [it] until he is taken out of the way.

8. And then that wicked one shall be revealed whom the Lord Jesus shall kill with the spirit of his mouth, and shall destroy with the brightness of his coming—he

9. Whose coming is according to the working of Satan, in all power and signs, and lying wonders,

10. And in all seduction of iniquity to them that perish, because they did not receive the love of the truth so that they might be saved. Therefore, God shall send them the operation of error [a powerful delusion so that they] believe lying:

11. That all may be judged who have not believed the truth, but have consented to [delighted in] iniquity. . . .

14. Therefore, brethren, stand fast and hold the traditions which you have learned, whether by word or by our epistle.

Questions: Who is the "man of sin"? When and under what circumstances will he appear? What is his relationship to Satan? What bands his followers together? How does Christ respond to his coming? How does God respond?

FIVE: THE DEVIL AND FEUDAL SOCIETY

45. DEMONIC VASSALAGE

Pope Gregory I (c. 540–604) is regarded as the last of the four great fathers (or "doctors") of the western church and a transformative figure in the history of western Christianity. Although he had begun his ecclesiastical career as a monk, after he became pope in 590 he set about aligning the institution with the new political, cultural, and intellectual realities of the day. He centralized its administration, reorganized its finances, oversaw the papal mission to reconvert England, and set about finding new ways to communicate the central message of the faith to an increasingly illiterate population. Yet Gregory was also a prolific writer in his own right. The selection below comes from his Commentary on Job. *Written primarily for a monastic audience, the work interprets the biblical text both literally and allegorically. It was widely read through the Middle Ages.*

Latin, c. 578–595.

Source: trans. Richard Raiswell and David R. Winter, from Gregory I, *Moralium Libri, sive Expositio in Librum Job* XXV.16.34 and XXIX.7.15 (Migne, *PL* 76: 0343B–0344A and 0484A–0487C).

[Job 34.30 asks] "Who makes a man who is a hypocrite rule because of the sins of the people?" This must refer to Antichrist, the chief of all hypocrites. That seducer feigns piety so that he can draw others into iniquity. He is allowed to rule because of the sins of the people, though, because these people are doubtless predestined to be under his control. Because of subsequent later sins, though, they are foreknown from before the beginning of time to be fitting subjects for him, and so placed under Antichrist's authority on the basis of this anticipatory judgment. That Antichrist rules over the ungodly is not because of the injustice of the judge but rather because of the sins of the sufferer.

While most of these people are not aware that they are under Antichrist's rule, they are enslaved to his command because they are sinners. They worship him through their perverse way of living even though they are clearly not aware that he is governing them. Are those who try to appear to be what they are not by feigning sanctity not his very limbs? Although Antichrist is a damned man and an evil spirit, he assumes a pretended piety, falsely claiming to be God. Clearly, though, those who hide their iniquities under a cloak of sacred honors—those who try to seem to be of that profession which they clearly reject in their actions—are now coming forth out of his body. Because it is written, "everyone who commits a sin is a servant of sin" [John 8.34], however more freely such people do the evil things they desire, the more tightly they are bound to Antichrist's service. But let no one who endures such a ruler find fault with him who suffers because such a person most assuredly deserves to be subjected to the power of this wicked ruler. Rather, let such a person blame the fault of his own work rather than the injustice of the ruler. . . .

There are some who truly believe the eternal truths they hear but who nevertheless contradict the faith they hold by living evilly. Although these people act perversely [despite the fact that] they understand correctly about God, there is light in their darkness—the shining light [of the divine] illuminates them just a little so that they are not entirely immersed in darkness. While these people love earthly things more than heavenly ones, and love what they see more than what they hear, when faced with persecution, they lose that which they had rightly believed. This happens especially—and to a greater degree—during the final persecution of the holy church when, with the very head of the wicked himself rising up, Antichrist advances his power through unrestrained violence. Then everyone's heart is laid bare and whatever was hidden is exposed—and with their wickedness made public, those who are now pious in mouth but impious in heart are ruined, and lose that small light of faith which they had appeared to hold. But during these times, it is necessary that each of us returns to the hidden place of his heart, fearing the condemnation of his deeds, lest through the strict justice of God's judgments he falls into the company of such men—as his merits demand.

[Gregory turns to consider Job 38.15, "their light will be taken away from the wicked, and the high arm will be broken."]

Let no one unwisely flatter himself and believe that he is exempt from such a fall, thinking that he will not be included in the storm of this tempest. O how many people have not seen the times of that temptation but are nevertheless tossed about in that storm of his temptation! Cain did not see the time of Antichrist but nevertheless was deservedly a limb of Antichrist [Gen. 4.1–18]. Judas did not know the savagery of that persecution, yet he succumbed to the violence of Antichrist's cruelty, persuaded by greed [Matt. 26.15]. Simon [the Magician] lived long before the time of Antichrist, yet he yoked himself to Antichrist's pride by seeking the power to work miracles in a perverse fashion [Acts 8.19 and doc. 27]. In this way a wicked body is joined to its head—in this way are limbs joined to limbs. While they may not actually know each other in person, these people are nevertheless bound to each other by virtue of their depraved action ... because shared traits make a single perverted body even if they are separated from each other in time or place. From this, it is clear that every wicked person who has already died lives on through their perverted imitators, and that the very author of iniquities—who is yet to come—can be found in those who do his works. Hence John says, "Now many Antichrists have been made" [1 John 2.18] because all wicked people are already his limbs which—having been raised up perversely—anticipate their head through their perverse living. Hence Paul says, "so that he may be revealed in due time; for the mystery of iniquity is already at work" [2 Thess. 2.6 and doc. 44]. It is as if he were saying, "then the visible Antichrist will be seen, for the hidden Antichrist now works his secrets in the hearts of the wicked."

Let me pass over in silence Antichrist's more overt crimes. But consider a man who silently envies another in his heart and tries to trip him [this enviable man] up when given the chance. Of who else can such a person be said to be a limb unless it is of him about whom it is written, "death came into the world through the envy of the devil" [Wisd. of Sol. 2.24]? Consider another: a person who thinks he is a man of great merit—preferring himself to all others on account of his swollen heart, believing everyone else inferior to him. Of who else is he a limb unless it is of him about whom it is written, "he sees every high thing and is a king over all the children of pride" [Job 41.25]? Another seeks the power of this world not for the benefit of others but so that he may not be subject to anyone else. Of whom else is he a limb but of him about whom it is written, "he who said, 'I will sit on the mountain of the covenant on the north sides; I will rise above the height of the clouds. I will be like the almighty'" [Isa. 14.13]? Only the almighty rules over all things in this way, unable to be subject to anyone else. Perversely, the devil wants to imitate him, for in seeking his own kingdom he refused to be subject to the almighty. Therefore and for this reason, whoever seeks his own power imitates the devil because he refuses to be subject to the one who has been placed above him by heavenly commandment. . . .

Nor are the temptations of Antichrist lacking even within the peace of the church. Therefore, let no one recoil in terror at the thought of the age of the last persecution—as if it is the only one—for the business of Antichrist is being done daily among the wicked because the hidden Antichrist works his mystery in their hearts even now. And even if many people who are now established within the church—as least in terms of external appearance—feign themselves to be what they are not, what they are will nevertheless be revealed at the coming of the judge, about whom Solomon rightly says, "I saw the wicked buried who, even when they lived here were in a holy place, and were praised in the city, as if they were men of just works" [Eccles. 8.10]. And after that, it was said about the wicked, "the seal will be restored as clay, and it will stand as a garment, and the light will be taken away from the wicked" [Job 38.14–15], which will certainly take place during Antichrist's persecution.

But to console us about the destruction of that same Antichrist, he goes on to say, "and the high arm will be broken." What else can that "high arm" be unless it is the haughty arrogance of Antichrist which is raised above the reprobate minds of men by means of the pride of worldly glory so that that sinful man—that man who hates being esteemed as such—pretends that he is God over men. On this account, the apostle Paul says, "so that he sits in the temple of God, showing himself as if he were God" [2 Thess. 2.4]. And to show Antichrist's pride more fully, Paul said before this, "[he] who opposes and is lifted up above all that is called God or that is worshipped" [2 Thess. 2.4]. A man can sometimes be called "God" according to what the lord said to Moses, "Behold, I have made you a God of Pharaoh" [Exod. 7.1]. But a simple man cannot be worshipped as God. Indeed, because Antichrist exalts himself above all holy men and above the power of the divinity himself, he tries to surpass that which is called "God" and that which is worshipped as God by demanding the name of glory for himself.

But it must be noted into what deep a pit of pride he has fallen, for he did not remain in that state of ruin into which he originally fell. Obviously, the devil and man fell from their original condition through pride, as the devil says in one place "I will ascend above the highest clouds and I will be like the almighty" [Isa. 14.14] and man hearing him in another believes "your eyes will be opened and you will be like gods" [Gen. 3.5]. For this reason, therefore, both fell not for the sake of justice but for the sake of power because they both aspired to be like God. But man who fell for perversely seeking the image of God was freed by grace. Realizing himself to be far from equal to God by virtue of the guilt of his crime, he shouted out, "Lord, who is like you?" [Ps. 88.9]. The devil, though, having been cast down justly for his criminal lapse remained in this state of ruin only for a short time—indeed, the longer he was deprived of the almighty's grace, the more he added to the guilt of his crime. For he who fell because he wanted to be like God in a perversion of the natural order was led so far that, entering into Antichrist, he disdained to seem to be like God and—having been condemned—believes him to be his inferior who his pride would not let him have as his equal. For when this (which we have already stated) is said about him, "lifting himself above all that is called God or that which is worshipped" [2 Thess. 2.4], it is shown clearly that by originally seeking the likeness of God, he wanted to be exalted as much as God. But with the sin of pride growing, he now extols himself as above all that is called "God" or that is worshipped. Therefore, because his pride will be slain by the coming of the severe judge as it is written, "the Lord Jesus will kill by the spirit of his mouth and destroy through the brightness of his coming" [2 Thess. 2.8], it is rightly said "and the high arm will be broken."

Questions: How has Gregory modified the idea of the "man of power" (doc. 44)? What is Antichrist? What is his relationship to sinners? To Satan? Is he a metaphor, a personification, or is he real? Is he one or many? What is the difference between his hidden and manifest forms?

46. THE DEVIL AS FEUDAL LORD

The tenth-century Junius Manuscript contains some of the finest surviving examples of Anglo-Saxon poetry. Among these is an Old English paraphrase of Genesis 1–22 known as Genesis A. However, between lines 235 and 851, the style of the poetry is markedly different. Scholars now recognize this as a slightly later interpolation added by a scribe, presumably to supplement the narrative. This section, known as Genesis B, deals with the fall of the rebel angels and the temptation of humanity in a unique way. In Genesis B, *for instance, humanity is tempted not by Satan but by a lesser demon who appears first to Adam—not Eve—in the form of an angel of God, telling him that God had commanded him to eat from the hitherto forbidden tree of knowledge. After failing to convince Adam, the disguised demon turns to Eve, who eats from the tree not out of pride but in an attempt to save Adam from retribution for failing to obey God's command. The most striking thing about* Genesis B *is its portrait of the devil, who becomes a central character with his own voice.*

Old English, tenth century.

Source: trans. R. K. Gordon, *Genesis B*, from *Anglo-Saxon Poetry* (London: J. M. Dent & Sons, 1922), pp. 100–104; rev.

The ruler of all, the holy lord, by the might of his hand had established ten tribes of angels in whom he greatly trusted to bear him true allegiance . . . one he had formed very strong, very mighty in thought; he let him have sway over many things, and placed him next under himself in the kingdom of heaven. . . . God let him possess his power for long, but the angel turned it to a worse issue, and began to stir up strife against the most high ruler of heaven. . . . He could not find it in his heart to serve God, the lord, with allegiance; it seemed to him that he had greater strength and skill than holy God, the companion in war, could have. The angel uttered many words in his pride; thought how by his single strength he should set up for himself a stronger throne, higher in heaven. He said that his heart prompted him to work westwards and northwards; he set up a building; he said it seemed doubtful to him whether he would be God's disciple.

"Why am I to toil?" said he. "I have no need of a master; I can work as many wonders with my hands [as God]. I have great power to prepare a better throne, higher in heaven. Why am I to wait upon his favor, bow before him with such homage? I can be a God like him. Strong comrades, bold-hearted heroes who will not fail me in the fight, stand by me. They, brave men, have chosen me for their master. With such comrades, a man can lay a plan, carry it out with such companions in war. They are keen in their friendship to me, loyal in their hearts; I can be their leader, rule in this kingdom. Thus it does not seem right to me that I need to flatter God any more for any benefit. No longer will I be his follower."

When the ruler of all things heard all this—that his angel began to set up great pride against his master and that he presumptuously uttered haughty words against his lord—[he knew that] the angel had to atone for the deed, suffer the affliction of war, and he must have his penalty, the heaviest of all punishments—as does every man who tries to fight against his ruler, wickedly against the glorious lord. Then the mighty one, the most high ruler of heaven, was angered. He cast the angel off his lofty throne. He had won hate from his master; he had forfeited his favor. The righteous one was angry at him in his heart. Accordingly, he was doomed to seek the abyss of bitter hell-torment, because he warred against the ruler of heaven.

God rejected him then from his favor and hurled him to hell, to the deep valleys, where he became the devil, the fiend with all his followers. Then the angels fell from heaven on high into hell for as long as three nights and days, and the lord transformed them all into devils. . . . Henceforth, angels who were true before to God's allegiance held the height of heaven. The other fiends lay in the fire, who before in such numbers had strife with their ruler. They suffer torment, the hot fierce flame in the midst of hell, fire, and broad flames, likewise also the bitter fumes, vapor, and darkness, because they neglected the service of God. . . . The fiends saw that they had won countless torments through their haughty hearts and the might of God and most of all through pride. Then . . . God said that the [former] highest [angel] should henceforth be called Satan, and told him he had charge of the depths of dark hell, and by no means was he to fight against God.

Satan . . . spoke these words, "This desolate place is very different from that other which once we knew, high in heaven, which my lord gave me, though we could not hold it before the ruler of all, possess our kingdom. Yet God has not done right to hurl us to the fiery abyss, to hot hell, deprived of the heavenly realm. He has determined to people heaven with mankind. That to me is the greatest of griefs—that Adam, who was formed from earth, shall hold my mighty throne, dwell in bliss, and we suffer this torment, affliction in this hell. Alas! Had I but the strength of my hands, and could win free for one hour, but for a winter hour, then I with this host—! But around me lie iron bonds, the chain of the fetter is on me. I am powerless. The hard bonds of hell have seized me so closely. Here is a great fire above and beneath; never have I looked on a loathsome landscape; the fire ceases not, hot throughout hell. A chain of rings, a fetter severe, has barred my going, deprived me of movement. My feet are bound, and my hands pinioned. The passage through these doors of hell is closed. Thus I cannot at all free my limbs from these bonds. Huge bars of hard iron, forged in the heat, lie around me; with them God has shackled me by the neck. So I know that he knew my thought, and the lord of hosts knew also that Adam should strive with me for the kingdom of heaven, if I had the strength of my hands. But now in hell we suffer torments; there are darkness and heat-grim, bottomless. God himself has whirled us away to these gloomy mists. Though he can convict us of no sin nor prove that we did him hurt in that land, yet he has deprived us of the light, hurled us into the greatest of all torments. We cannot work vengeance, pay him back him with any hurt, for that he has deprived us of the light. He has now planned out a world where he has man, formed after his image, with whom he will again people the kingdom of heaven with pure souls. We must earnestly plan to satisfy our vengeance on Adam and on his children together with him—if ever we can—to deprive God there of his desire, if we can in any way devise it. No longer do I look to regain that light, that happiness, which God thinks long to enjoy with the host of his angels. We can never succeed in appeasing the wrath of mighty God. Let us snatch it from the sons of men, that heavenly kingdom, now that we may not have it, cause them to abandon his allegiance, to break the behest which he uttered. Then God will be angry at them in his heart, dismiss them from his protection; then they shall seek this hell and these dread depths. Then we can have them for our followers, the sons of men, in these firm bonds. Put now your thoughts to the warlike venture. If previously I gave princely treasures to any follower, while, blessed, we dwelt in that happy realm and held sway over our abodes, never at a time more desired could he pay back my gifts with offerings, if now any of my followers would be willing to pass out hence from this prison and had the strength to fly with pinions, wing his way up through the clouds, to where Adam and Eve stand created on the realm of earth with riches all round them, while we are hurled hither into these valleys profound. They are now far dearer to the lord and may own the wealth which we should have in the heavenly kingdom, the realm rightly ours: that good fortune is decreed for mankind. It is this that is such a grief to me in my heart, that causes sorrow to my mind, that they should hold the kingdom of heaven forever. If any of you can contrive in any way that they should forsake the command and teaching of God, straightway they will be the more hateful unto him. If they observe not God's charge, then he will grow angered against them, then will their weal suffer change and punishment be prepared for them, hard affliction. Do you all ponder this: how you may beguile them? Afterwards I shall be able to rest at ease in these fetters, if that kingdom be lost to them. For him who achieves that the reward is afterwards ever ready, what henceforth we can gain of benefits in this fire. I will let him sit with myself, whosoever comes in this burning hell to say that they in word and deed have ignobly forsaken the counsel of heaven's king."

Then God's foe began to prepare himself, ready in his trappings; he had a faithless heart. He set on his head a helmet which made its wearer unseen, and bound it full tightly, fastened it with clasps. He knew many speeches of wicked words. He winged his way from there, passed through the doors of hell. By the fiend's art the fire was cleft in two. He purposed to beguile God's followers, men, secretly by evil deeds, to mislead and allure them, so that they should grow hateful to God.

Questions: How does the mighty angel (later the devil) maintain the loyalty of his followers? In terms of feudal values, is the devil's rebellion justified? Is the devil a good ruler in his new kingdom? What comparisons might a tenth-century reader or listener draw between this recounting of the devil's rebellion and the political realities of his own day?

47. THE LIFE OF ANTICHRIST

Adso (c. 910–992), a monk and abbot in the monastery of Montier-en-Der (in the north-east of modern France), was a figure of the Carolingian revival. Thus he was well educated and comparatively well read for his day. Indeed, he bequeathed his personal collection of twenty-three manuscripts to Montier-en-Der's library. Adso was a prolific author, writing saints' lives, hymns, and a verse rendering of part of Gregory the Great's Dialogues. *This current selection comes from a letter he wrote to Gerberga, the wife of Louis IV, king of western Francia (r. 936–954), on the life and career of Antichrist.*

Latin, c. 950.

Source: trans. Bernard McGinn, Adso of Montier-en-Der, *Letter on the Origin and Time of the Antichrist*, in *Apocalyptic Spirituality: Treatises and Letters of Lactantius, Adso of Montier-en-Der, Joachim of Fiore, The Franciscan Spirituals, Savonarola* (New York: Paulist Press, 1979), pp. 89-96.

When you wish to be informed about the Antichrist then first thing you want to know is why he is so called. This is because he will be contrary to Christ in all things. . . . Christ came as a humble man; he will come as a proud one. Christ came to raise the lowly, to justify sinners; he, on the other hand, will cast out the lowly, magnify sinners, exalt the wicked. He will always exalt vices opposed to virtues, will drive out the evangelical law, will revive the worship of demons in the world, will seek his own glory [John 7.18], and will call himself Almighty God. The Antichrist has many ministers of his malice. Many of them have already existed, like Antiochus, Nero, and Domitian. Even now in our own time we know there are many Antichrists, for anyone, layman, cleric, or monk, who lives contrary to justice and attacks the rule of his way of life and blasphemes what is good [Rom. 14.16] is an Antichrist, the minister of Satan.

Now let us see about the Antichrist's origin. What I say is not thought out or made up on my own, but in my attentive reading I find it all written down in books. As our authors say, the Antichrist will be born from the Jewish people. . . . He will be born from the union of a mother and father, like other men, not, as some say, from a virgin alone. Still, he will be conceived [and] born in sin [Ps. 50.7; John 9.34]. At the very beginning of his conception the devil will enter his mother's womb at the same moment. The devil's power will foster and protect him in his mother's womb and it will always be with him. Just as the holy spirit came into the mother of our Lord Jesus Christ and overshadowed her with his power and filled her with divinity so that she conceived of the holy spirit and what was born of her was divine and holy [Luke 1.35], so too the devil will descend into the Antichrist's mother, will completely . . . encompass her, . . . so that with the devil's cooperation she will conceive through a man and what will be born from her will be totally wicked. . . . For this reason that man is called the "son of perdition" [2 Thess. 2.3], because he will destroy the human race as far as he can and will himself be destroyed at the last day. . . .

The Antichrist will have magicians, enchanters, diviners, and wizards who at the devil's bidding will rear him and instruct him in every evil, error, and wicked art. Evil spirits will be his leaders, his constant associates, and inseparable companions. Then he will come to Jerusalem and with various tortures will slay all the Christians he cannot convert to his cause. He will erect his throne in the holy temple, for the temple that Solomon built to God that had been destroyed he will raise up to its former state. He will circumcise himself and will pretend that he is the son of Almighty God.

He will first convert kings and princes to his cause, and then through them the rest of the peoples. He will attack the places where the lord Christ walked and will destroy what the lord made famous. Then he will send messengers and his preachers through the whole world. His preaching and power will extend "from sea to sea, from east to west" [Ps. 71.8], from north to south. He will also work many signs, great and unheard-of prodigies [Rev. 13.13]. He will make fire come down from heaven in a terrifying way, trees suddenly blossom and wither, the sea become stormy and unexpectedly calm. He will make the elements change into differing forms, divert the order and flow of bodies of water, disturb the air with winds and all sorts of commotions, and perform countless other wondrous acts. He will raise the dead in the sight of men in order to lead into error, if possible, even the elect [Matt. 24.24]. For when they shall have seen great signs of such a nature even those who are perfect and God's chosen ones will doubt whether or not he is the Christ who according to the scriptures will come at the end of the world.

He will arouse universal persecution against the Christians and all the elect. He will lift himself up against the faithful in three ways, that is, by terror, by gifts, and by prodigies. To those who believe in him he will give much gold and silver. Those he is not able to corrupt with gifts, he will overcome with terror; those he cannot overcome with terror, he will try to seduce with signs and prodigies. Those he cannot seduce with prodigies, he will cruelly torture and miserably put to death in the sight of all. . . .

The Apostle Paul reveals the time when the Antichrist will come and when judgment day will begin in the [second] Epistle to the Thessalonians [2.3]. . . . For we know that after the Greek Empire, or even after the Persian Empire, . . . at last after all the other empires there came into existence the Roman Empire, which was the strongest of all and had all the kingdoms of the earth under its control. All nations were subject to the Romans and paid tribute to them. This is why the Apostle Paul says that the Antichrist will not come into the world (unless) . . . all the kingdoms that were formerly subject shall have defected from the Roman Empire. This time has not yet come, because even though we may see the Roman Empire for the most part in ruins, nonetheless, as long as the kings of the Franks who now possess the Roman Empire by right shall last, the dignity of the Roman Empire will not completely perish because it will endure in its kings. . . . He will be in the last time and will be the greatest and the last of all kings. After he has successfully governed his empire, he will finally come to Jerusalem and will lay aside his scepter and crown on the Mount of Olives. This will be the end and the consummation of the Roman and Christian Empire.

Immediately, according to the saying of Paul the Apostle cited above, they say that the Antichrist will be at hand. And then will be revealed the man of sin, namely, the Antichrist. Even though he is a man, he will still be the source of all sins and the son of perdition, that is, the son of the devil, not through nature but through imitation because he will fulfil the devil's will in everything. The fullness of diabolical power and of the whole character of evil will dwell in him in bodily fashion; for in him will be hidden all the treasures of malice and iniquity.

"He is the enemy," that is, he is contrary to Christ and all his members, "and he is lifted up, that is, raised up in pride above everything that is called God" [2 Thess. 2.4], that is, above all the heathen gods, Hercules, Apollo, Jupiter, and Mercury, whom the pagans think are gods. Antichrist will be lifted up above these gods because he will make himself greater and stronger than all of them. He will be lifted up . . . "above everything that is worshipped," that is, above the holy trinity, which alone is to be worshipped and adored by every creature. "He will exalt himself in such a way that he will be enthroned in God's temple, displaying himself as if he were God."

As we said above, he will be born in the city of Babylon, will come to Jerusalem, and will circumcise himself and say to the Jews: "I am the Christ promised to you who has come to save you, so that I can gather together and defend you who are the diaspora." At that time all the Jews will flock to him, in the belief that they are receiving God, but rather they will receive the devil. Antichrist also "will be enthroned in God's temple," that is, in holy church, and he will make all Christians martyrs. He will be lifted up and made great, because in him will be the devil, the fountainhead of all evil "who is the king above all the sons of pride" [Job 41.25]. . . .

Since we have spoken about his beginning, let us say what end he will have. This Antichrist, the devil's son and the worst master of evil, as has been said, will plague the whole world with great persecution and torture the whole people of God with various torments for three-and-a-half years. After he has killed Elijah and Enoch and crowned with martyrdom the others who persevere in the faith, at last God's judgment will come upon him, as Saint Paul writes when he says, "The Lord Jesus will kill him with the breath of his mouth" [2 Thess. 2.8]. Whether the Lord Jesus will slay him by the power of his own might, or whether the Archangel Michael will slay him, he will be killed through the power of our Lord Jesus Christ and not through the power of any angel or archangel. . . .

Questions: Is Antichrist created evil or is he possessed? If he has been created evil, how does Adso envisage the power of the devil? If he is a human victim, can Antichrist be saved? How might knowing Antichrist's nature and future actions affect how people understood the progression of history and its plan? How does this Antichrist differ from that of Gregory the Great (doc. 45)?

FIVE: THE DEVIL AND FEUDAL SOCIETY

48. THE DEVIL'S CHURCHMEN

From 1309 until 1377, the papacy resided in Avignon in modern France. During this period, papal authority became increasingly centralized, allowing successive popes not only to collect the traditional income they were owed by lesser clergy but also to impose new taxes and exploit new sources of revenue, leading critics to castigate the Avignon papacy for its worldliness, extravagance, and obsession with wealth. Particularly open to abuse were papal provisions that permitted the pope to intervene in the appointment of clergy for his own political or financial benefit—a practice closely linked to the sin of simony, that is, the buying and selling of ecclesiastical offices. The great Italian poet Francesco Petrarch (1304–74) dubbed this the "Babylonian Captivity" of the Church, a reference to the period in the sixth century BCE during which the Jews were held captive by the Neo-Babylonians (or Chaldeans), while also evoking the specter of Antichrist predicted to rise from Babylon.

"Lucifer's Letter to the Clergy" was originally written in Latin by Peter Ceffons, a Cistercian theologian, in 1352, and was intended as a critique of the worst excesses of the Avignon papacy. Written in a style intended to mock the officious legalese of the papal bureaucracy, the letter sees Satan praise the clergy of the day for turning their backs on the simplicity of Christ and embracing vice. In the first decades of the fifteenth century, the letter was translated into Middle English, significantly reworked and greatly expanded. However, the Middle English translator's skills are not always up to the task.

Gehenna was originally the name for a region south of Jerusalem where the kings of Judah sacrificed their children and is described in 4 Kings 16.3 and 21.6. But by the time the New Testament was set down, the term was used to denote the place of eternal punishment.

Middle English, c. 1420–30.

Source: modernized by Richard Raiswell and David R. Winter, from Robert E. Raymo, "A Middle English Edition of the *Epistola Luciferi ad Cleros*," in *Medieval Literature and Civilization: Studies in Memory of G. N. Garmonsway* (London: Athlone Press, 1969), pp. 233–48.

Lucifer—lord and prince of the deep dungeon of darkness, ruler of the kingdom of the infernal empire, king of the country of evil, the wretches' justice and judge of all Gehennal subjects, duke of the vale of death, heir to the inheritance of hell—to all our dear fellows—each and every one cherished, and fellows worthy to be loved, brethren and children of pride, with the fruit of all falseness fulfilled in the current church through the fealty of your obedience to our imperial magnificence and infernal sovereignty to which ever yet we find you obedient and true lieges and subjects—health, wealth, and greeting, which we covet and desire for ourself and our subjects while you are obedient, ready, and well-willing to our wishes, precepts, and commandments, and—agreeably to us—enduring and fulfilling everlastingly your desire (begun and long-lastingly continued) for the laws of our lordship about whom our adversary, that very Jesus Christ, through his prophet, once said, "I have hated the church of evildoers" [Ps. 25.5].

Some time ago, some of the vicars, subjects, and disciples of that Jesus Christ—following his steps and tracing his ways, confident in the signs of his virtues, performing his will through their works, living under a poor manner of life by their preaching and works (in great disdain of our infernal kingdom and jurisdiction, and [in] contempt of our infernal majesty)—turned all the world from the yoke and servitude of the excellence of our tyranny to their doctrine, manner, and life (to the great injury, annoyance, and harming of our Gehennal jurisdiction), neither dreading nor ashamed to hurt, defile, or harm our dreadful power, or to offend the majesty of our infernal estate. In those days, through their wrongful agitating, we were violently precluded from the tribute of the our subjects' dues, and the gathering of our people at our mournful palace of the Gehennal empire was then miserably hindered and stopped—and the broad, light way "that leads to death" [Prov. 12.28] lay contemptuously undefiled, un-haunted, and unused (without any noise), and un-trampled by our subject people. On that account, the entire vanquished court of our wretched company, with every tearful wailed, mourned, and sorrowed complaint, was piteously despoiled of the right to our rueful region—so much so that the impatient fury of our breast could no longer bear it, nor could the hard cruelty of the heart of our demonic host and our sorrowful subjects suffer it any longer.

But now, using foresight from that time onwards, with careful consideration, we consciously developed for ourselves a clear solution to counter all such like perils: in the place and stead of those our harmful adversaries—that Jesus Christ's apostles and all their followers in doctrine or manners—by our mighty power and subtle boldness, we have now, in these days and modern times, made you feignedly shrouded rulers, prelates, and princes in the modern church—engaging substitutes in their place—as that very Christ said of you, "They have reigned but not of me" [Hosea 8.4]. Once before we promised him—that Jesus—all the kingdoms of the world if he, falling to his knees, worshipped our royal might [see Matt. 4.9], but he would not, saying, "My kingdom is not of this world" [John 18.36], fleeing and avoiding when the people would have chosen him for any temporal kingdom or lordship. In you—who have fallen and slid from the degrees, steps, and state of grace and truth, and continually serve us truly in our precepts, counsels, and arguments on the earth—this promise and pledge is fulfilled, and now by us and through us, you preserve all that which we have given to you as office holders in continuance of your true service. As you well know, that Jesus said this of you, "The Prince of this world has come [John 14.30] and he wills that you reign over all the children of pride" [see Job 41.25].

But those our aforesaid adversaries—the Christ's apostles and their followers—were subjects to the princes of the world, as they so taught, "Be subjects to every human creature for God is superior to the king, etc." [misquoted from 1 Pet. 2.13]

FIVE: THE DEVIL AND FEUDAL SOCIETY

and in another place, "you should obey your sovereigns" [Heb. 13.17]. So their master—that Jesus—did and told them to do this, saying, "Kings and princes of people have power over them and those that are rulers are called good, but you do not do so" [Luke 22.25–26].

And these our aforesaid adversaries all the while led a poor, miserable, and wretched life, but you, as we like it best, have not done so, but the venomous arrogance of pride—which we once produced and poured into you—has fully blossomed in you and has been inflated to a fulfilling satisfaction for our Gehennal majesty. Not only unlike but utterly contrary both in life and manners to the foresaid first fathers [of the Church]—raised up and elevated in pride above all others—having and keeping in possession all that you may catch and get, and neither, "delivering or yielding to Caesar what pertains to him, nor to God that which belongs to him" [Mark 12.17 and Matt. 22.21], but following the will and intent of our councils, precepts, and decrees, you exercise the jurisdiction and power of both the sword of temporality as well as that of spirituality, meddling under our guidance in all worldliness and interfering in every kind of secular business, always fleeing from wretchedness and every kind of misery of poverty, quickly ascending to the highest summit of estates and honors through every worldly wisdom and wit, subtleties, tricks, [false] glossings, lyings, perjuries, deceits, treasons, betrayals, dissimulations, and other contrived hypocrisies, and every other sort of worldly wickedness which all the inscrutable Gehennal wits and conceits can scarcely understand or conceive without proper order. And when you have been elevated and exalted to the profits of those honors, you are struck by a more dogged hunger than before, oppressing the poor and all your inferiors wickedly with a dogged rage, plundering everything that you can catch and hold, corrupting everything of this kind with a swelling of every sort of pride—as it best pleases us—putting all the cares and thoughts of your hearts into the desire for lecherous living, leading, and expending the days of your life in every delight, bodily desire, comfort, and satisfaction, taking to yourself the name of gods on earth and holy, cleverly, and hypocritically hiding—under a false face of holiness and visage of goodness—the secret superstitious pride as our well-beloved children of wickedness with all the skill of our stratagems, deceiving the world, pleasantly and continually earning the good will of our infernal majesty—but not that Jesus.

The gifts of the church—which you violently plunder or abuse, occupy or hold falsely, or are keeping tyrannically (as our well-beloved children) by false title, and those goods which were once distributed and provided for the sustenance of the poor people of that Jesus Christ (who we have and always have hated)—you spend and consume in your uses to our bodily accord and liking (as you should), feeding and maintaining strumpets, jokers and jugglers, harlots, whores, and their clients, proudly going and riding with them as princes of our infernal palace, living your days voluptuously (as you should)—not like those poor wretched people of that Jesus and his first church. You build your buildings as palaces with every manner of delight and worldly delicacy that can be seen, feeding your bodies with every manner of delicate meat, drinking all [manner of] exquisite wines aplenty, insatiably gathering, and hiding enormous quantities of treasure—not as that Peter said, "Silver and gold is not to me" [Acts 3.6].

O you, our dearest partners—once worthily and deservingly promised to us, the dukes of death, by the prophets (and condemned by them in olden times), while that Jesus called you the "Synagogue of Satan" and prefigured you in the common strumpet who fornicated with the kings and princes of the earth—have turned from a mother to a stepmother, from Christ's bride to a strayed strumpet, from chaste to a common whore. You have broken and destroyed your former chastity and virginity. You have lost your former benevolence. You have eagerly brought and given yourself to us. O to you, our worthily beloved citizens of our beloved Babylon, worthily we love you, heartily we rejoice in you—you (as our beloved children), who are always adhering to the agreeable laws of Simon the Magician, boldly using and applying them openly (as we approve), carefully buying and selling all the spiritual things of the church, and (against the precepts of that Christ) apportioning and dividing the benefices and estates of the church for prayer, price, service, or favor (wholly subverting ecclesiastical offices and laws), cunningly refusing to admit the worthy into that heritage of God's holy calling while warmly proclaiming the unworthy—such as your own children, relations, and others beloved to you such as your clerks and grooms—knowingly giving many prebends unworthily to a single child, denying [even] the very least of them to an able poor man, considering and accepting not his ability or inability, tending to the care of money and not of souls. You have made the house of that Jesus into a den of thieves, arranging among you all manner of abuses, extortions, wrongs, and immoralities—a hundredfold [more] exercised in your jurisdiction and court than under any secular tyrant's laws. . . .

And so laboring continuously in our service—for which we heartily thank you—most principally for the destruction of the Christian faith in which the lay people be uncertain and in doubt, for when any of the law of that Jesus is preached to them—although that is done rarely and negligently—they are not filled with belief, saying that each of you says one thing in your preaching but fulfils the contrary in your actions—saying one thing and doing another. For that reason, following in the footsteps of your actions, they constantly use the model of our customs and decrees which are before them as an example, sliding and falling irredeemably into the deep valley of vices, and a copious multitude of them are pulled and are coming to the dark desolation of the miserable star of the country of darkness.

You send us nowadays such a multitude of every sort of people that we could receive no more, were it not that the insatiable mansion of our dark region, in its boundless hunger and thirst for consuming more and more, can shelter, receive and devour those that come abundantly and willingly; and so because of you,

FIVE: THE DEVIL AND FEUDAL SOCIETY

the abundant return of our subjects (the way and path toward the house of the lordship and principality of the empire of our infernal realm which was once violently blocked by the poor wretched servants of that Jesus) is now fully restored by your industry and tireless labor, and these ancient, unbearable harms and losses are now fully overcome. For that reason, we commend to you infinite thanks. . . .

From day to day nowadays, we are busily occupied with the multitude and their arrival which you send and convey to us every day. For that reason, we cannot come to visit you on account of our constant business. Therefore, we entrust our power on the earth to you so you may continue the business of your foresaid occupation, wishing you to be our vicars and ministers in this place, keeping in mind the imminent coming of the Antichrist, for whom you have prepared the way as true harbingers of the best sort—not like John the Baptist who came before that Jesus, saying, "I am the voice shouting in the desert" [John 1.23], but as our true servants, always relying on your counsel as well-wishing servants of our infernal court whose suggestions, counsels, and doctrines you take and keep, and upon which you model yourself.

In addition, concealing you—who we have set in the highest estates and dignities—is a stratagem so that you may falsely propose and bring about eternal peace between worldly princes and powers but secretly feed all matters of discord between them (as you once boldly destroyed the rule of the Roman Empire), allowing no kingdom nor region to dwell or remain under the rule of peace or tranquility lest those temporal princes—strengthened under the ease and peace of tranquility for a long time—oppress you, robbing you of your possessions, treasures, and the temporal lordships which we have put in your care and keeping, stored for the imminent coming of Antichrist, for whom you busily prepare the way.

Furthermore, for that reason, we completely entrust each and every one in any order or sect we constitute to your protection and the power of the entire Gehennal lordship—chiefly and primarily our highly beloved children, the four begging orders [the mendicant friars: the Franciscans, Dominicans, Carmelites, and Augustinians], whose exploits and industry for our needs and yours they are laboring incessantly, as we have learned through clear proof, urging that you cherish and favor them for the sake of their great merits, encouraging them with such gifts that they may rejoice to have so labored for you and for us, and with a happier spirit be ready to continue the busy work to come. For through the keenness of their industry, many are diverging from the church's faith and led into many errors.

For that reason, we strongly urge you (under the threat of full repayment of the gifts of our infernal majesty and infernal lordship and for our love) that you do not stop offering them your hands in help and supporting them, and defend and maintain them completely in all their cursed works at the very least, so that they may know themselves completely bound, held, and indebted to you and us as their sincere and special friends, fully understanding that we are exceedingly troubled in our heart and wounded with a heavy, heaped sorrow that you—erring with the blindness of darkness—have not considered what the industrious action of the preaching servants of Jesus ask, for many now in these days rise against us [likely Lollards; see doc. 93], preaching the laws of that Jesus Christ, advancing them with all their might and strength, neither ashamed nor afraid to hinder the furtherance of our majesty. For that reason, with you opposing us wickedly, against our best council on this matter, you must endure this shame, contempt, and injury without letting the offense boil over, just as the contempt of our infernal majesty (which you, in contradistinction to your merits, have completely deserved) may attach to you more surely, and which—surrounded by deception—brings no advantage to our infernal power, domination, and majesty.

. . . you [should] punish them so zealously through the authority and power of our royal jurisdiction that they, out of fear of your censures and our power, will always be afraid to go against our prohibitions or incur your or our wrath thereafter, and they will have plain cause to remember your vengeance and punishment for the foresaid offense even after their life, having incessantly commended to your warm affection our dearest and most beloved daughters, pride, covetousness, envy, anger, lechery, fraud, deceit, sloth, gluttony, and each and every other one, namely—among others—our special daughter, simony, who you, with your own teats have nourished, milked, and brought forth, not calling our dear daughter "simony" since the sin is entirely yours.

Nothing can be said about what you sell, for everything that is paid is paid for what is yours, and you may not be said to be proud—whatever you do—for your estate deservedly requires such magnificence. Neither will reason allow you to be called covetous [for everything you] gather you keep for the patrimony of the church and Saint Peter. . . . And whoever preaches or teaches against your or our jurisdiction, chastise and violently oppress them, cursing fervently with our censures, condemning them as heretics and transgressors of our law. And so you sweat and labor industriously in the ministry of our service so you may worthily deserve to rejoice in that place which we have made ready and prepared for you under the surest certainty of abiding in the habitation of our infernal region, which we have also preserved for you, [a place] where none of our [followers] has been assigned to inhabit except for the principal officers or ministers of the kingdom of our Gehennal lordship.

You neither hope nor deserve the future reward of that Jesus, nor dread the eternal retribution of our tearful torment and therefore you rejoice in the use of the prosperity of this present life so that in worthy recompense for your merits you may deserve the retribution of eternal death which was prepared for you from the creation of the world, knowing this certainly while you lead the days of your life, fearing no earthly creature, not even that Jesus. Farewell now, live your days in that prosperity from which your bodily desires and comforts may best maintain and increase and in the full hope of that retribution which we, from the original and ancient time of the constitution of our infernal domination, have willed and fully planned to give you in final and lasting, enduring privation.

Given at the center of the earth in our dark palace in the presence of infinite legions of prince's potentates, ministers, and subjects specially summoned to our dolorous consistory, printed and sealed in witness of the lordship of these present letters.

Questions: According to Lucifer, what did the coming of Christ do to his power? How has he addressed this problem? What virtues does Lucifer identify in contemporary clergy? Why are the new "preaching servants of Jesus" a problem, and how does Lucifer propose they should be handled? What effect does placing this satire in the mouth of Lucifer have?

49. TRIAL BY LANDSCAPE

The Mongol conquests of the first half of the thirteenth century brought the region from the Genoese trading colony of Tana on the Sea of Azov to the eastern coast of China under a single political authority for the first time. In so doing, they also opened up the possibility of a direct, safe land route from Europe to the fabulously wealthy lands of the east. From the 1240s, hundreds of European missionaries and merchants made the arduous journey to China, bringing back with them Asian spices and accounts of these distant lands. Marco Polo (1254–1324) was the most famous of these merchant travelers.

One person who probably never made this trip was the author of the Book of John Mandeville. *Though he recounted all manner of natural oddities and peculiarities concerning the east, his account relies heavily on classical sources and material borrowed from the writings of various people who had actually made the trip there a generation earlier. The following section, for example, is adapted by the author from the account of an Italian Franciscan named Odoric of Pordenone (1286–1331), who was in western India and northern China between 1318 and 1330.*

English, between c. 1330 and 1350.

Source: [Anon], *The boke of Iohn Maunduyle* (London, 1496), sig. t.1v–t.2; rev.

A little from that place, on the left side, beside the river Phison [the Ganges] is a great marvel. There is a valley between two hills that is four miles long. Some call it the Enchanted Valley, some the Valley of Devils, some the Perilous Valley. And in that valley there are many storms, and great and hideous noises [can be heard] every day and night—sometimes it is the noise of drums, kettledrums, and trumpets, as if there were a great feast going on.

The valley is completely full of devils and always has been; men say that there is an entrance to hell there. In this valley, there is much gold and silver, and because of that many Christian men and pagans go there out of greed to get that gold and silver. However, few of them come out again, for they are immediately strangled by devils. On a rock in the middle of that valley, there is the face and head of a fiend which is very hideous and dreadful to see. Nothing can be seen of it but the head down to the shoulders. There is no Christian or pagan in the world so hardy that would not be filled with dread if he saw it, for it looks at each man so sharply and so cruelly—its eyes are so shifting and sparkling like fire, and it changes its expression often—and out of its mouth and nose comes much fire of various colors that no man dares come near it for all the world. Sometimes the fire stinks so much that no man can endure it. Nevertheless, a good Christian man who is secure in his faith can always pass through the valley without harm; if they confess themselves fully and bless themselves with the sign of the cross the devils have no power over them.

And you should understand that when my companions and I were in that valley we had a great discussion as to whether we should put our bodies at risk and go through the valley. Some of my companions agreed that we should go; some did not agree. There was in our company two friars minor [Franciscans] from Lombardy and they said that if any of us decided to go, they would go with us. We sang a mass and were confessed and took communion and fourteen of us entered the valley. But when we came out there were only ten. We did not know whether our companions were lost in the valley or if they turned back, but we saw no more of them. The rest of our companions who would not go with us into the valley went around by another way so as to be ahead of us [when we arrived], and so they were.

We went through the valley and saw many marvelous things there. There was gold, silver precious stones, and jewels in great quantities on many sides of us—but whether what I saw was as it seemed I do not know, for I did not touch them as devils are so subtle and cunning that they often make a thing appear which is not there in order to deceive men. Therefore, I would not touch anything out of fear of the devils that I saw in many forms and of the dead bodies that I saw lying in the valley—but I dare say that they were not all bodies; rather, they seemed bodies through the dealings of devils.

We were often knocked down to the ground by wind and thunder and storms, but God helped us continuously, and so we passed through that valley without any danger or harm—thanks be to God who kept us well.

Questions: Why is it appropriate for devils to populate this terrain? What is their role? Is this test a form of ordeal? If so, what kind of ordeal is it? Who is overseeing it and what is being tested? How might this section shape the understanding of European Christians who had not traveled to the east?

CHAPTER SIX

THE DEVIL'S DOMAIN

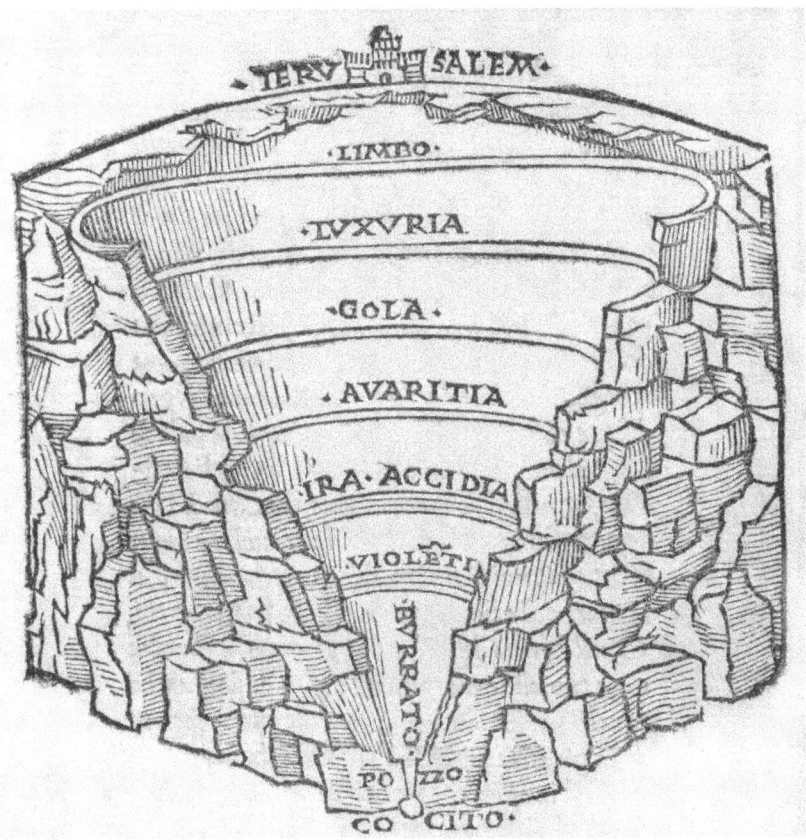

Figure 6.1 Antonio Manetti, "Overview of Hell" from *Dialogo di Antonio Manetti, Cittadino fiorentino, circa al sito, forma, & misure dello inferno di Dante Alighieri* (1506), sig. G.2r. This illustration is part of a series of seven woodcuts by the Italian Antonio Manetti (1423–97) depicting the structure of hell according to Dante (doc. 57). As a mathematician and architect, Manetti was especially interested in the location, structure, and measurement of the poet's hell. This illustration depicts the upper circles of hell, including limbo—where the unbaptized are held—and those reserved for the lustful, the gluttonous, the greedy, the wrathful, and the violent. Below this, the artist shows the ravine and shaft leading to Cocytus, the deepest level of hell.

SIX: THE DEVIL'S DOMAIN

The question of the devil's domain is complicated and fraught. The book of Job (doc. 6) described Satan as being in heaven, and it seems to be implied from his conversation with God that the creator did not consider him to be out of place there. By contrast, Luke's account of Christ's temptation (doc. 9) has the devil claim that he has been given dominion over all the kingdoms of the world, an assertion that Jesus does not contradict. Yet Isaiah (doc. 4) implies that there is—or will be at some point—a place into which the king of Babylon will be cast and where giants and the princes of nations can be found, a prophecy maybe confirmed by the description of Satan being cast down and sealed for a thousand years in a bottomless pit in Revelation (doc. 11) as part of the penultimate action of history.

Nevertheless, the idea of a place of cosmic punishment for those who offended God or who committed sinful acts was deeply embedded in Near Eastern religion and assimilated into Judaism particularly after the Babylonian captivity. With Christ's redeeming sacrifice implying a place of eternal bliss, the development of a Christian theology around its opposite was inevitable. But this was not without its problems, for if Satan was hell's jailor—running, ironically, for the master of chaos, quite a tight ship—in what sense could he also be its chief prisoner? And if he was imprisoned as a result of the just God's justice, how could he still be permitted to stalk the earth in search of souls to tempt into sin? As with the construction of the devil himself, many of these details were glossed over theologically and a premium placed instead on the accounts of those who claimed to have experienced hell at some level—either through a visionary experience or by traversing space.

But this idea of a place of torment had another consequence, too, for it implied that hell had a geographical location—one which presumably could be sought out and found. Landscape could be hellish.

As a concept, though, hell resonated as much as the devil himself. While human society may be a mixed realm, a place of tension and conflict, the two eternal kingdoms between which it was situated were morally unambiguous. As such, it functioned a place for the projection of anxieties—anxieties which shifted and evolved over the centuries according to intellectual and social priorities.

50. THE DEVELOPMENT OF HELL

As with the devil himself, the Old and New Testaments are remarkably vague—even contradictory—about hell. In part, this is a function of the development of traditions about an afterlife over the historical period during which the texts were written. This difficulty is compounded by the problem of translation. The Hebrew Old Testament distinguishes two underworlds. "Sheol" refers to the abode of the dead, a melancholy place where souls wander but are not tormented. However, the Latin Bible conflates these under the term "infernus," which is usually rendered as "hell" in English translations. Nevertheless, medieval Christians would have

drawn upon both Old and New Testament sources in formulating their conception of hell as a place of eternal torment for the reprobate.
Hebrew, from sixth century BCE.
Greek, first century.

Source: trans. Gregory Martin et al. from the Latin Vulgate, The Holy Bible (Douay-Rheims version) (Douay: The English College, 1609–10), rev. Richard Challoner (1749–52); rev.

Psalms

17.5. The sorrows of death surrounded me: and the torrents of iniquity troubled me.

6. The sorrows of hell [more literally translated from Hebrew as "the cords of Sheol"] encompassed me: and the snares of death prevented me.

7. In my affliction I called upon the lord, and I cried to my God: And he heard my voice from his holy temple: and my cry before him came into his ears.

8. The earth shook and trembled: the foundations of the mountains were troubled and were moved, because he was angry with them.

9. There went up a smoke in his wrath: and a fire flamed from his face: coals were kindled by it.

10. He bowed the heavens, and came down: and darkness was under his feet.

11. And he ascended upon the cherubim, and he flew; he flew upon the wings of the winds.

12. And he made darkness his covert, his pavilion round about him: dark waters in the clouds of the air.

13. At the brightness that was before him the clouds passed, hail and coals of fire.

14. And the lord thundered from heaven, and the highest gave his voice: hail and coals of fire.

15. And he sent forth his arrows, and he scattered them: he multiplied lightning, and troubled them.

16. Then the fountains of waters appeared, and the foundations of the world were discovered: At your rebuke, O lord, at the blast of the spirit of your wrath.

17. He sent from on high, and took me: and received me out of many waters.

18. He delivered me from my strongest enemies. . . .

20. And he brought me forth into a large place: he saved me, because he was well pleased with me.

21. And the lord will reward me according to my justice; and will repay me according to the cleanness of my hands:

22. Because I have kept the ways of the lord; and have not done wickedly against my God. . . .

25. And the lord will reward me according to my justice; and according to the cleanness of my hands before his eyes.

26. With the holy, you will be holy; and with the innocent man you will be innocent.

27. And with the elect you will be elect: and with the perverse you will be perverted.

28. For you will save the humble people; but will bring down the eyes of the proud.

Matthew

25.31. And when the son of man shall come in his majesty, and all the angels with him, then shall he sit upon the seat of his majesty.

32. And all nations shall be gathered together before him, and he shall separate them one from another, as the shepherd separates the sheep from the goats:

33. And he shall set the sheep on his right hand, but the goats on his left.

34. Then shall the king say to them who shall be on his right hand, "Come, you blessed of my father, you possess the kingdom prepared for you from the foundation of the world." . . .

41. Then he shall say to them also that shall be on his left hand, "Depart from me, you cursed, into everlasting fire which was prepared for the devil and his angels.

42. For I was hungry, and you gave me not to eat: I was thirsty, and you gave me not to drink.

43. I was a stranger, and you took me not in: naked, and you covered me not: sick and in prison, and you did not visit me."

44. Then they also shall answer him, saying, "lord, when did we see you hungry, or thirsty, or a stranger, or naked, or sick, or in prison, and did not minister to you?"

45. Then he shall answer them, saying, "Amen I say to you, as long as you did it not to one of these least, neither did you do it to me."

46. And these shall go into everlasting punishment: but the just, into life everlasting.

Luke

16.20. And there was a certain beggar, named Lazarus, who lay at the gate [of a rich man], full of sores,

21. Desiring to be filled with the crumbs that fell from the rich man's table which no one gave him; moreover the dogs came and licked his sores.

22. And it came to pass that the beggar died and was carried by the angels into Abraham's bosom. And the rich man also died: and he was buried in hell.

23. And lifting up his eyes when he was in torments, he [the rich man] saw Abraham afar off, and Lazarus in his bosom:

24. And he cried, and said, "Father Abraham, have mercy on me, and send Lazarus so that he may dip the tip of his finger in water to cool my tongue: for I am tormented in this flame."

25. And Abraham said to him, "Son, remember that you did receive good things in your lifetime, and likewise Lazarus [received] evil things, but now he is comforted; and you are tormented.

26. And besides all this, between us and you, there is fixed a great chaos: so that they who would pass from hence to you, cannot, nor from thence come hither."

27. And he said, "Then, father, I beseech you to send him to my father's house, for I have five brethren, so

28. That he may testify to them, lest they also come into this place of torments."

29. And Abraham said to him, "They have Moses and the prophets; let them hear them."

30. But he said, "No, father Abraham: but if one went to them from the dead, they will do penance."

31. And he said to him, "If they do not hear Moses and the prophets, they will not believe even if one rise again from the dead."

Revelation

[Taken up in the spirit, John describes the opening of a book with seven seals by a figure identified as "the lamb."]

6.7. And when he had opened the fourth seal, I heard the voice of the fourth living creature, saying: Come, and see.

8. And behold a pale horse, and he that sat upon him, his name was Death, and hell followed him. And power was given to him over the four parts of the earth, to kill with sword, with famine, and with death, and with the beasts of the earth. . . .

9.1. And the fifth angel sounded the trumpet, and I saw a star fall from heaven upon the earth, and there was given to him the key of the bottomless pit.

2. And he opened the bottomless pit: and the smoke of the pit arose, as the smoke of a great furnace; and the sun and the air were darkened with the smoke of the pit.

3. And from the smoke of the pit there came out locusts upon the earth. And power was given to them, as the scorpions of the earth have power:

4. And it was commanded them that they should not hurt the grass of the earth, nor any green thing, nor any tree: but only the men who have not the sign of God on their foreheads.

5. And it was given unto them that they should not kill them; but that they should torment them five months: and their torment was as the torment of a scorpion when he strikes a man.

6. And in those days men shall seek death, and shall not find it: and they shall desire to die, and death shall fly from them.

7. And the shapes of the locusts were like horses prepared for battle: and on their heads were, as it were, crowns like gold: and their faces were as the faces of men.

8. And they had hair as the hair of women; and their teeth were as lions:

9. And they had breastplates as breastplates of iron, and the noise of their wings was as the noise of chariots and many horses running to battle.

10. And they had tails like to scorpions, and there were stings in their tails; and their power was to hurt men five months. And they had over them

11. A king, the angel of the bottomless pit; whose name in Hebrew is *Abaddon*, and in Greek *Apollyon*; in Latin *Exterminans*,

12. One woe is past, and behold there come yet two woes more hereafter.

Questions: How do these accounts of hell differ? What is happening in these places—and when does this occur? Is there any governance in hell? Where are these hells located? Are these accounts consistent with that in Revelation 20 (doc. 11)?

51. THE HARROWING OF HELL

The non-canonical Gospel of Nicodemus *is the medieval name for two distinct texts. The first is attributed to a certain Ananias, who claims to have been a member of Pontius Pilate's bodyguard, and offers new light on the circumstances of Christ's trial, execution, and resurrection. The second centers upon the period between Christ's death and his resurrection during which he liberated the souls of the Old Testament patriarchs trapped in hell. This was necessary, for it was not possible for non-Christians to have been saved before this point in time, for they had had no opportunity to know Christ. Thus, in rescuing the souls of the virtuous from hell the story preserves the idea of God's perfect justice. The story of the harrowing of hell was very popular in Middle Ages, inspiring both artists and authors.*

This selection begins by describing how Christ resurrected others along with himself on Easter Sunday. Among these were Carinus and Leucius, the sons of Simeon, the Old Testament patriarch, who were taken to the Sanhedrin to explain how they had been brought back from the dead. The rest of the text follows their experiences.

The translation below derives from a Latin translation of an earlier Greek version of the text. Greek and Hebrew, fourth or fifth century; Latin translation, fifth century?

Source: trans. James Montague Rhodes, "Gospel of Nicodemus," also called "Acts of Pilate" (Latin B text) 2.2–9, *The Apocryphal New Testament* (Oxford, 1924) pp. 123–39; rev.

Carinus: O lord Jesus Christ, son of the living God, permit me to speak of the marvellous works which you did in Hades. Indeed, when we were confined in the darkness of hell, in the shadow of death, suddenly there shone a great light, and Hades trembled, along with the gates of death. And the voice of the son of the most high father sounded like thunder. It proclaimed loudly and began, "Draw back your gates, O princes! Remove your everlasting doors! Christ the lord, the king of glory, approaches and will enter in!"

Then, Satan, the prince of death, came fleeing in fear and saying to his ministers and to all the hells, "O my ministers, and all the hells, come together and shut your gates! Set in place the bars of iron and fight boldly and stand firm so that we who hold our captives will not be made captive ourselves in the bonds that we have made."

At this, Satan's evil ministers were troubled, so they began to shut the gates of death with all diligence. At last, they managed to secure the locks and bars of iron. Then they took up their weapons and began to howl with dreadful and hideous voices.

Then Satan said to Hades, "Prepare yourself to receive him whom I shall bring down to you."

To this, Hades responded, "That voice was none other than the cry of the son of the most high father! That is why the earth and hell quaked so greatly at it! On account of that voice, I think that I and all of my bonds are now wide open. But I adjure you, O Satan, chief of all evil, by your strength and mine, do not bring him down to me! I fear that when we try to take him, he will make captives of us! Indeed, if he can shake earth and hell with his voice alone, what will he be able to do to us when we are actually in his presence?"

Satan answered, "Why are you whining like this? Fear not, my evil old friend, for I have incited the Jewish people against him and commanded that they smite him with blows. I have contrived to have him betrayed by his disciple! Moreover, he is a man who fears death greatly, for in his fear he said, 'My soul is sorrowful even unto death' [Matt. 26.38]. Yet, I have brought him to the point of death and now he hangs upon a cross!"

Then Hades said to him, "If, by word of his command alone, he made Lazarus—who was dead for four days—fly up from my embrace like an eagle, then we must ask if he really is a man or if he is God in all his majesty? I beg you, do not bring him into my presence!"

Satan said to him, "Never mind. Prepare yourself and fear not. He is already hanging on a cross, and there is nothing else I can do."

Then Hades said to Satan, "If you can't do anything else, then woe to you. Your destruction is drawing near. And I shall finally be cast down and will remain without honor. You, however, will be tormented under my dominion."

Now, the saints of God heard the quarrel between Satan and Hades. However, at this time, they did not know each other—though the time of their acquaintance was drawing near. Our holy father Adam answered Satan in this way, "O prince of death, why are you fearful and trembling? Behold, the lord is coming and he will destroy all of your creatures, and you will be bound and imprisoned, world without end!"

When all of the saints heard the voice of father Adam, and how he valiantly responded to Satan, they were glad and felt comforted. They all ran toward father Adam and gathered around him in that place. Then our father Adam looked earnestly upon the multitude and marvelled that he was responsible for bringing them all into the world. He embraced those who stood around him and shed extremely bitter tears. Then, he said to Seth his son, "My son Seth, tell the holy patriarchs and prophets what the keeper of paradise said to you when I sent you to fetch the oil of mercy for me to anoint my body when I was sick."

Seth responded, "When you sent me to the gates of paradise, I prayed and sought the lord with tears. And I asked the keeper of paradise to give me the oil of mercy. And the archangel Michael approached me and said, 'Seth, why do you mourn? Know that your father Adam will not receive the oil of mercy now, but rather, after many generations of the world. For the most beloved son of God will come down from heaven and into the world. He will be baptized by John in the river Jordan. Then, your father Adam will receive the oil of mercy, as will all who believe in the son of God. . . .

[At this point, prophets and patriarchs rejoice and bear witness to the divinity of Christ.]

Then . . . all of the patriarchs and prophets cried out, saying "Hallelujah! Blessed is he who comes in the name of the lord!" [Matt. 21.9] When he heard this, Satan was afraid and tried to flee. However, he was unable to do so because Hades and his ministers bound him and fenced him in on every side.

Hades said to Satan, "Why are you afraid? We will not let you roam about. However, it is right for you to receive those things that you deserve. Moreover, you should receive them from the hands of the one you fought every day. If not, know that you will be bound by him and committed to my custody forever."

Again, the voice of the son of the most high father resounded like thunder, saying, "Lift up your gates, O princes! And be lifted up, you everlasting doors! The king of glory will enter in!" [Ps. 23.7].

Then Satan and Hades cried out, saying, "Who is the king of glory?"

And the lord answered them, "The lord strong and mighty! The lord mighty in battle! [Ps. 23.8]"

After this, there appeared before us a man who resembled a thief. He carried a cross upon his shoulder. He cried from outside the gates, "Open up to me so that I might enter!"

Satan opened the gate a little and brought him inside before closing the gates again. All the saints saw that he shone brightly, so they said to him, "You look like a thief. Can you show us what you are carrying on your back?"

He answered them humbly, "In truth, I was an out-and-out thief, and the Jews hanged me upon a cross with my lord, Jesus Christ, the son of the most high father. In the end, I have come ahead of him. However, he himself will appear immediately after me." . . .

And again there was a cry from outside, "Lift up your gates, you princes! And be lifted up, you everlasting doors! The king of glory is coming in!"

And again at the sound of that clear voice, Hades and Satan inquired, saying, "Who is this king of glory?" And the marvellous voice said to them, "The lord of hosts—he is the king of glory!"

And behold, Hades began to quake. The gates of death and the locks were shattered to pieces and the bars of iron were broken and fell to the ground. Everything was laid open. Satan remained in the midst of the confusion, cast down and bound with fetters around his feet. Behold, the lord Jesus Christ appeared in the light of glory, but also meek and humble. He held a chain in his hands that he wound around Satan's neck. It also bound his hands behind his back. Jesus threw him backwards towards Tartarus, and placed his holy foot upon Satan's throat and said, "Throughout the ages, you have done great evil without ceasing. Today, I will deliver you into the eternal fire."

And he summoned Hades quickly and commanded him, saying, "Take this most evil and wicked thing and hold him in your keeping until the day I tell you otherwise."

And Hades took Satan from beneath the lord's feet and they were cast down together into the depth of the bottomless pit. . . .

Then all the saints of God begged the lord to leave a sign of victory in hell—even the holy cross itself—to ensure that Satan's wicked ministers might not attempt to keep any of those souls whom the lord had absolved. So it was done: the lord set his cross in the midst of hell, as a sign of victory. It shall remain there forever.

Then, all the saints went out from that place with the lord, and they left Satan and Hades in Tartarus.

Questions: Who or what is Hades? Is he or it a fallen angel? Who is under his or its care—and why? What is his or its role in the universe? Is he or it a benign or malevolent force? How does he or it compare to the notions of hell described in the Old and New Testaments (doc. 50)? What is his or its relationship with Satan—with God?

52. THE GEOGRAPHY OF HELL

The Apocalypse of Paul—*also called the* Vision of Paul—*marks an early attempt to define the landscape of hell and to make explicit the fate of the wicked. The text takes as its starting point 2 Corinthians 12.2–5, where the apostle Paul describes how he was transported to what he called "the third heaven." This becomes a pretext for a description of paradise, culminating in Paul's entry into the celestial city of Christ. From there, Paul and an angel travel to hell.*

The Apocalypse *draws heavily on pre-Christian descriptions of an underworld particularly of Tartarus, a place described by Homer in the* Iliad *(c. 800 BCE) as an abode of punishment, lower than Hades. Virgil, in the* Aeneid *(late first century BCE), added that in the midst of Tartarus is a pit extending deep into the middle of the earth.*

The text was known in Latin in the west through the Middle Ages, although this translation was likely made from a lost Greek original composed by a monk in Egypt.

Greek, c. 400; Latin translation, c. 500.

Source: trans. Richard Raiswell and David R. Winter, from Marie-Françoise Damongeot-Bourdat, "Un nouveau manuscript de l'Apocalypse de Paul (Paris, BnF, nouv. Acq. lat. 2676)," *Bulletin du Cange* 67 (2009): 43–63.

When the angel had finished speaking to me, he led me outside the city, through the midst of a forest, away from the place of the land of the good, and he stood me on the other side of the river of milk and honey. Then he led me across the ocean which holds the foundation of heaven. . . . And when I was at the outer edge of the ocean, I looked, and there was no light in that place—only sadness, darkness, and grief. I sighed and saw there a boiling river of fire and a large number of men and women sunk in it up to their knees, other men up to the navel, others up to their lips, others—indeed—up to their hair. And I asked the angel, saying, "Lord, who are those in the fiery river?" Replying, the angel said to me, "They are neither cold nor hot, because they were found neither among the number of the just nor among the number of the impious. They spent the duration of their life on earth up to their death some days in prayer, other days in sin and fornication." And I asked, saying, "Who are those, lord, sunk up to their knees in fire?" Replying, the angel said to me, "They are those who, when they left church, would dispute, engaging in contrary speeches. Those who have been sunk up to the navel are those who—holding the body and blood of Christ in contempt—went out to commit fornication and would never refrain from sin up to the point at which they died. But those sunk up to the lips, these are those who belittled each other when gathered in the church of God. Those sunk up to their eyebrows—these are those who leave themselves open to envy and conspire against their neighbor.

And I saw to the north a place of various and diverse punishments full of men and women and into which a fiery river ran down. I looked and I saw pits enormous in depth and in which many souls were stacked together as one. And that place was almost 30,000 cubits in depth. And I saw those souls groaning and weeping, saying, "Pity us, lord." But no one pitied them. And I asked the angel, saying, "Who are those, lord?" Replying, the angel said to me, "These are those people who did not trust in the lord that they could have him as their helper." And I asked him and said, "Lord, were these souls to continue being stacked like this one on the other for 30 or 40 generations, I think the pit would not be able to hold them—unless they were sent down deeper." And he said to me, "The abyss has no measure, and it boils like a cauldron under the earth. Were some strong man to take up a stone and drop it into a very deep well and it only reached the bottom after many hours—that is what the abyss is like. For when souls are dropped in there, they only just come to the bottom after 500 years."

In truth, when I had heard this I cried and groaned on account of the entire human race. Replying, the angel said to me, "Why are you crying? Surely you are not more merciful than God? For although God is good, since he knows that there are punishments, he suffers the human race with patience, sending each one to do his own will for the time which he is dwelling on or about earth."

I looked again at the fiery river and I saw a man there being choked by Tartarian angels, who had in their hands a three-hooked piece of iron with which they ripped out the old man's guts. And I asked the angel, saying, "Lord, who is that old man to whom such torments are applied?" Replying, the angel said to me, "He whom you see was a priest who did not serve his ministry well. He offered the host to God at the holy altar while he was eating and drinking—and even while he was fornicating."

Not far away, I saw another old man whom four wicked angels led forth running hurriedly. They plunged him into the fiery river up to his knees and, pelting him with stones, wounded his face as if in a storm. And they did not allow him to say, "Pity me." And I asked the angel, saying, "Lord, who is that old man to whom such torments are brought to bear?" Replying, the angel said to me, "He whom you see was a bishop and he did not serve his bishopric well. Indeed, he accepted the great title, but through his whole life he did not enter into the holiness of he who gave the title to him—he did not give just judgment, and he was not merciful to widows or orphans. But now he is being rewarded according to his iniquity and deeds."

And I saw another man in the fiery river up to his knees. And his hands were extended and bloody. Worms were coming out of his mouth and nostrils. He was groaning and weeping, crying out, "Pity me, because I am being hurt more than the others who are in this punishment." And I asked the angel, saying, "Lord, who is this?" And he said to me, "He whom you see was a deacon who consumed the offerings and fornicated, and did never did right in the sight of God. On this account, he is paying that price unceasingly."

And I looked and I saw another man beside him, whom the angels took out hurriedly and threw into the fiery river so that he was up to his knees. And the angel who was in charge of these punishments came with a great fiery razor, and cut the man's lips with it, and his tongue likewise. And heaving a sigh, I wailed, and I asked the angel, saying, "Who is that, lord?" And he said to me, "He whom you see was a lector. He read to the people, but did not keep the commandments of God."

I also saw another multitude of pits in that same place. And in the middle of that river there was a multitude of men and women; worms were eating away at

SIX: THE DEVIL'S DOMAIN

them. I wept and I sighed, and I asked the angel, saying, "Lord, who are those?" And he said to me, "These are those who—exacting interest on top of interest, trusting only in their riches—did not place their hope in God as their helper. After that, I looked and I saw another very narrow place—it was like a mountain enclosed by fire. Inside it, I saw men and women chewing their tongues. And I asked the angel, saying, "Who are those, lord?" And he said to me, "These are they who disparage the word of God in church, paying no attention to it—behaving as if the lord and his angels were not worth mentioning. On this account, they are now paying the appropriate penalty."

I looked and I saw another old man lower down in the pit and his face was bloody. And I asked, saying, "Lord, what is this place?" And he said to me, "All punishments flow into this pit." And I saw men and women sunk up to their lips and I asked the angel, saying, "Who are they, lord?" And he said to me, "They are sorcerers who supplied evil magic to men and women, and did not stop until they died."

And again, I saw men and women with very black faces in the fiery pit, and sighing, I wept and I asked the angel, saying, "Who are they, lord?" And he said to me, "These are fornicators and adulterers who—having their own wives—committed adultery. Likewise, the women committed adultery in the same way, despite having their own husbands. For that reason, they are constantly paying the price."

And I saw girls there wearing black garments, and four dreadful angels. The angels had fiery chains in their hands and put them around the girls' necks, leading them into darkness. And again, weeping I asked the angel, saying, "Who are those, lord?" And he said to me, "These are those who, although they had been ordained virgins, polluted their virginity without the knowledge of their parents. On that account, they are constantly paying the appropriate price."

And again, I looked there and I saw men and women with their hands and feet cut off. They were naked and set in a place of ice and snow, and worms were eating away at them. Seeing them, I wept, and I asked the angel, saying, "Who are they, lord?" And he said to me, "These are those who harmed orphans, widows and paupers, and did not hope in the lord. For that reason, they are constantly paying their penalties." I looked back and I saw other men hanging over a watery ditch, and their tongues were parched. Many fruits had been placed in their sight but they were not allowed to eat them. And I asked the angel, saying, "Who are they, lord?" And he said to me, "These are those who broke the fast before the appointed hour. For that reason, they are constantly paying these penalties." And I saw other men and women hung by their eyebrows and hair, the fiery river drawing them toward it. And I said, "Who are they, lord?" And he said to me, "These are they who committed themselves not to their own husbands and wives, but to adulterers. On that account, they are constantly paying their penalties." I saw other men and women covered in dust, and their appearance was like blood, and they were in a pit with tar and sulfur, being carried down into the fiery river. And I asked the angel, saying, "Who are these, lord?" And he said to me, "These are the ones who committed the wickedness of Sodom and Gomorrah, male with male. On that account, they are paying their appropriate penalties continuously."

And I looked and I saw men and women dressed in bright clothes set in the pit, their eyes blinded. And I asked the angel, saying, "Who are they, lord? And he said to me, "These are from those gentiles who gave alms but did not know the lord God. On that account, they are paying the appropriate penalties continuously." And I looked and I saw other men and women upon a fiery spit. Beasts were tearing at them, but they were not permitted to say, "Pity me." And I saw an angel of punishments applying a very great punishment to them, saying "It is a great thing to know the son of God. It was foretold to you, but you did not hear. When the divine scriptures were read, you did not pay attention. On that account, the justice of God is just upon you. Your deeds have caught up with you in these punishments." And I sighed and wailed, and asked the angel, saying, "Who are these men and women who are assailed in fire and pay their penalties?" And he replied to me, "These are women who defiled God's creation while bringing forth infants out of the womb—and these are the men who lay with them."

But their infants called upon the lord God and the angels who oversaw the punishments, saying, "Wicked is the hour of our parents, for they have defiled the name of God, not observing his commandments. They gave us as food for dogs—and to be trodden on by swine. Others they tossed into the river." Those infants were handed over to the Tartarian angel who oversaw the penalties so that he might lead them into a spacious place of mercy. But their fathers and mothers were strangled in perpetual punishment. And after this, I saw men and women who were covered in rags full of tar and sulfur and fire, and dragons were coiled around their necks, shoulders, and their feet. And angels with fiery horns restrained them, pelted them, and closed up their nostrils, saying to them, "Why did you not know the time when it was right for you to do penance and give yourself to God—why did you not do it?" And I asked the angel, saying, "Who are they, lord?" And he said to me, "These are those who—taking up our habit—seemed to give up the world, but who the trappings of the world made wretched. They furnished no charity, showed no pity to widows or orphans, did not take in foreigner or pilgrim—nor did they bear any offering, or show pity to their neighbor. Not for a single day did their prayer ascend pure to the lord God. Many trappings and worldly things held them back and they could not do right in the sight of God.

And the angels enclosed them in the place of punishments. . . .

[The angel said,] "Follow me and you will see seven times greater punishments than these."

And he brought me to the north side and placed me above a well and I found it sealed with seven seals. And the angel who was with me said to the angel who had been placed in that place, saying, "Open up the mouth of the well so that Paul, the most beloved man of God, may look upon it, because the power has been given to him that he might see all the punishments of hell." And the angel said to me, "Stand back so you can stand the stench of this place." When he had opened the well, immediately there arose out of it a certain hard and very wicked stench which surpassed all the other punishments of hell. I looked again into the well and I saw fiery masses on every side, burning and tormenting. The mouth of the well was narrow, admitting only one man at a time. Replying, the angel said to me, "If anyone is sent into this well of the abyss and it is sealed over him, he will never be remembered in the presence of the father and son and holy spirit and holy angels. And I said, "Lord, who are those who are sent into this well?" And he said to me, "Whoever has not confessed that Christ has come in the flesh and that the Virgin Mary gave birth to him—and whoever says that the bread and chalice of the consecrated eucharist are not the body and blood of Christ."

I looked again toward the north into the west and there I saw the restless worm, and in that place there was a gnashing of teeth. The worm measured one cubit and there were two heads on it. And I saw men and women there in the cold, gnashing their teeth. And I asked the angel, saying, "Lord, who are these who are in this place?" And he said to me, these are those who say that Christ did not rise from the dead and that this flesh will not be restored." And I asked the angel again, saying, "Lord, is there no fire nor heat in this place? There is nothing other than cold and snow." And again, the angel said to me, "If the sun were to rise over them, they are not warmed on account of the abundant snow in that place." But hearing this, I extended my arms and wept and sighing once again I said, "It would be better for us had we never been born, for we are all sinners."

Questions: What types of sin are singled out for punishment? How are the relative degrees of sin differentiated? What are the worst punishments? Why are they deemed so bad? To what extent does this account build on the biblical accounts of hell (doc. 50)?

53. AN ANGLO-SAXON MONK RECOUNTS A VISION OF HELL

In 716, Saint Boniface (doc. 30), undertook a missionary journey to Radbod, king of the Frisians, who had recently broken from the Frankish church and had begun reviving traditional worship. The saint's efforts to restore Christianity were unsuccessful because, when he learned that his heathen ancestors were in hell, Radbod exclaimed that he would not deprive himself of their companionship to dwell in heaven with a small company of paupers.

Boniface was a prolific letter writer. The following is addressed to an abbess and dates from immediately after his failed mission.
Latin, c. 717.

Source: trans. Edward Kylie, from Boniface, Letter XIII, in *The English Correspondence of Saint Boniface* (London, 1911): 78–89; rev.

To the holy virgin and dear lady, Eadburga . . . Wynfrith, poor servant of the lord, sends love and greetings in Christ.

You asked me, dear sister, to send you an account as the venerable Abbess Hildelida gave it to me of the wonderful vision seen by the man who recently died and came back to life in the convent of Abbess Milburga. I thank God that now I can meet your wishes more fully, because I spoke with this brother recently myself, when he came back here from abroad. He set forth to me in his own words the marvelous spectacle which he beheld when carried away in spirit beyond the body.

He said that . . . As he left his body, angels of such dazzling brightness that he could scarcely look upon them for their splendor, bore him up. With sweet and harmonious voices they sang, "Rebuke me not, O lord, in your indignation; nor chastise me in your wrath" [Ps. 37.2]. "They raised me," he said, "high into the air, and circling the world I beheld a blazing fire, the mighty flame soaring terribly aloft, as though grasping the whole mechanism of the world in its embrace, had not the holy angel calmed it with the sign of Christ's holy cross. When he had made the sign of the cross before the threatening flame, it gradually retired. I was sorely tried by its terrible heat, while my eyes were burned, and my sight was shattered by the brightness of the gleaming spirits until an angel, splendid to behold, touched my head with a protecting hand, and brought me safe from harm in the flames.

He added that during the time that he was out of the body, such a multitude of souls leaving the body had gathered where he was as to exceed what he had thought before to be the numbers of the whole human race. An innumerable band of evil spirits and a bright choir of heavenly angels had also assembled; and there was the greatest dispute between the demons and the angels over the souls leaving the body, for the demons were accusing the dead and making heavy the burden of their sins, while the angels were excusing them and lightening their load. . . .

He told, too, how he had seen, as it were, in the depths of this earth many fiery pits, belching forth terrible flames, and as the awful blaze burst forth, the souls of miserable men, in the form of birds, flew through the flames lamenting and bemoaning their deserts and their present punishment, with human cries. They rested, hanging for a little time on the edges of the pits, and then screaming, fell into the depths. One of the angels said, "This moment of rest shows that almighty God means to grant these souls relief from punishment and eternal rest on the day of Judgment to come."

But under these pits in the lowest depths, in deepest hell, he heard the awful weeping and wailing of sorrowful souls, terrible, beyond the power of words to describe. And the angel said, "The lamentations and weeping which you hear in the depths come from those souls to whom the mercy of God will never come. But everlasting flame will torture them without end." . . .

He beheld also a river of fiery pitch, boiling and blazing, wonderful and terrible to behold. Across it a beam was set for a bridge, to which the holy and glorious souls hastened as they left the assembly, eager to cross to the other bank. Some crossed with certain step. But others slipped from the beam and fell into the hellish stream. Of these some were entirely immersed, while others were only partially covered, it might be to the knees, or to the waist, or merely to the ankles. And yet each one of those who fell climbed from the river onto the other bank brighter and more beautiful than he was before he had fallen into the river of pitch. And one of the blessed angels said of the souls who fell, "These are the souls who, after the end of their mortal lives, had a few trivial faults not entirely washed away, and needed bountiful castigation from a merciful God, that they might be worthily offered unto him."

Beyond the river he saw, shining with a great splendor, walls of astounding length and immeasurable height. And the holy angels said, "This is the holy and renowned city, the heavenly Jerusalem, in which these holy souls will find joy forever." He said that these souls and the walls of the glorious city to which they hurried after crossing the river, were resplendent with such a flood of dazzling light that the pupils of his eyes were shaken by the exceeding splendor, and he could no longer look upon them.

He told how to that gathering there had come among the other souls the soul of a man who had died while abbot. It was a fair and beautiful soul. The evil spirits seized it and claimed that it was under their rule and sway. Thereupon one of the choir of angels replied, "I will show you quickly, you abandoned and miserable spirits, that this soul is not proven to be under your power." And at these words there suddenly intervened a great throng of white souls who said, "He was our master and teacher, who, by his rule, has won us all for God. And by this price is his redemption purchased, and he is shown to be not of your law," and they made as though they would join the angels in the struggle against the demons. By the aid of the angels they snatched away the soul and freed it from the power of the evil spirits. And an angel, driving the demons away, cried, "You should know and understand that you took this soul unjustly; get you gone, spirits of evil, into eternal fire." When the angel had spoken, the demons raised a mighty lamentation and sound of weeping. In a moment, as in the twinkling of an eye, with baneful flight, they hurled themselves into the pits of burning fire. But after an interval they came forth again into the assembly to dispute about the merits of souls.

At that time, he also beheld the merits of different men who were still alive. Those who were not slaves to crime, but who, by relying on holy virtues, had clearly won the favor of the omnipotent God were kept safe by the angels and were joined to them in love and friendship. But those who were polluted with unspeakable vices and the stain of unclean lives were constantly accompanied by a hostile spirit always urging them on to sin. And whenever they sinned in word or deed, the spirit proclaimed it to the other abandoned spirits so that they might be glad and rejoice. And when a man sinned, the evil spirit made no delay by waiting until he should sin again but brought each error singly to the notice of the other spirits. At one moment he pressed sinful deeds upon the man and at the next announced among the demons their accomplishment.

Among other things, he described how he had seen a girl, still in this earthly life, grinding corn in a mill. She saw lying near her a new distaff adorned with carving which belonged to someone else. It seemed beautiful to her and so she stole it. Then, as if filled with a great joy, five loathsome spirits bore news of this theft to the others in the assembly declaring the girl guilty. . . .

And he bore witness likewise about Ceolred, king of the Mercians, who, there is no doubt, was still in the flesh when this vision was seen. He saw the king protected against the onslaught of demons by a screen of angels like a great book spread out above him. But the enraged demons kept demanding of the angels that their defense be taken away and that they be permitted to work their cruel will upon him. They accused him of a multitude of horrible and unspeakable crimes and threatened that he must be shut in the direst dungeons of hell and there, as his sins merited, be tortured with eternal torments. Whereupon the angels, more disheartened than was their wont, said, "Alas, that a sinner should not suffer his defense to stand, and that through his own fault we cannot afford him any aid." And they took away the bulwark from above him. Then the demons with joy and exaltation gathering from all over the universe—in numbers he thought beyond all men who drew the breath of life—harassed and tore him with infinite tortures.

Then the blessed angels enjoined him, who, carried outside the body, had seen and heard all these things in spiritual contemplation, to return without delay to his own body, and to declare without hesitation everything which had been shown him, to those who believed and asked with good intention, but to refuse word of it to scoffers. . . .

And that everything which had been revealed to him by the angels . . . he proved afterwards from their own lips. And the death of the wicked king, which soon followed, showed beyond doubt that what he had seen concerning him was true. . . .

SIX: THE DEVIL'S DOMAIN

At his request I have written these things carefully as he told them to me in the presence of my holy and venerable brethren, who also heard the story. They can be taken as witnesses to this letter.

Farewell. May you live the true angelic life as a virgin and with good repute reign eternally in heaven with Christ.

Questions: What is the purpose of this hell? How does the process of judgment work? Is this divine justice? Who rules over hell? Can people in hell be saved? How are the living and dead connected? Of what use was the concept of a corporeal hell to the Catholic Church?

54. HELL AT SEA

The historical Saint Brendan (c. 484–577/583) was born in Tralee on the southwestern coast of Ireland. Little is certain about his life beyond the fact that he appears to have established a number of monasteries, including Clonfert in Galway. He is best known, however, through the anonymous Voyage of Saint Brendan, *a work set down in the ninth or early tenth century. While it draws upon earlier accounts of Irish seafarers, the* Voyage *is framed as a pilgrimage by sea. The main characters journey from island to island across a sacralized seascape, impelled by divine forces. Throughout, Brendan and his monks hope to discover "the promised land of the saints."*

Many scholars have tried to identify the geographical location of some of the islands described in the text. The author, however, is clearly far more concerned with articulating a theological message than with communicating geographical realities.

Latin, between 795 and 950.

Source: trans. Richard Raiswell and David R. Winter, from *Navigatio Sancti Brendani Abbatis*, from *Early Latin Manuscripts* (Notre Dame, IN: University Press, 1959), pp. 61–70.

When eight days had passed, they saw an island not far off. It was very rough, stony, and covered in slag heaps, without trees and grass, full of the forges of smiths. The venerable father said to his brethren, "Truly, brothers, this island distresses me, because I do not want to land on it or even approach it, but the wind is drawing us on course there." When they had traveled a little further—as much as a stone is thrown—they heard the sound of the blowing of bellows—like thunder—and the striking of hammers against iron and anvils. Having heard these things, the venerable father armed himself making the sign of the lord's victory in the four cardinal directions, saying, "Lord Jesus Christ, deliver us from this island."

When the man of God had finished speaking, one of the inhabitants of that island came outside about to do some work. He was very hairy, fiery, and dark. When he saw the servants of God coming very close to that island, he turned back into his forge. The man of God armed himself again and said to the brothers,

"Little children, spread the sails higher and get underway as soon as possible, so we may flee that island." With this said, the aforesaid barbarian hurried quickly from that place to the shore carrying pincers in his hands with a fiery mass of great size and heat taken from the slag. Immediately, he threw the aforesaid mass at the servants of God, but it did not harm them. It missed them by more than a stade [185 meters]. Where it fell into the sea, it began to boil as if the debris of the mountain of fire was there, and smoke rose from the sea as if from a fiery furnace.

However, when the man of God had gone about a mile from the place where the mass fell, all those who were on that island hurried to the shore, each carrying a mass of slag. Some threw the slag after the servants of God; others threw theirs further. Going back into their forges, they set them alight and at once it seemed as if that whole island was burning like a single furnace, and the sea was boiling the way a cauldron full of meat boils when it has been well served by fire. And through the whole day the brothers heard a great howling coming from that island. For when they were no longer able to see it, the howling of the inhabitants on that island reached their ears and a mighty stench reached their nostrils. Then the saintly father comforted his monks, saying, "O knights of Christ, be strengthened in a faith unfeigned and in spiritual arms because we are at the edges of hell. On that account, watch and act courageously."

On another day, a high mountain appeared to them in the ocean toward the north not far away; it was almost covered with fine clouds, but very smoky at the top. And suddenly the wind drew them on a swift course all the way up to the coast of that island until the ship came to rest not far from land. The cliff was of such great height that they were scarcely able to see the top and was the color of coal and marvelously upright like a wall.

A certain monk . . . leaped outside off the ship and began to walk up to the base of the cliff. He began to cry out, saying, "Woe is me, father, for I am torn from you and I do not have the power to return to you." Immediately, the brothers led the ship back from the land and cried out to the lord, saying, "Pity us, lord, pity us." And the venerable father when he saw how the wicked man was led from his companions by a multitude of demons to the torments and how he was burning among them, he said, "Woe to you, my son, because you are receiving such an end to your life according to its merit."

Again, a favorable wind took hold of them driving them toward the southern sea. But when they looked back toward that island from afar, they saw the mountain uncovered by smoke, shooting flames up to the sky and breathing back the very same flames into itself again, so that the whole mountain resembled a lone funeral pyre in the sea.

Then, after Saint Brendan had sailed south for seven days, there appeared to them in the sea a certain form—like a man sitting on a rock—and there was a sail before him about the size of a cloak hanging between two iron forks, and

SIX: THE DEVIL'S DOMAIN

he was tossed about in the waves like a small ship at risk in a storm. Some of the brothers said that this was a bird, others that it was a ship. The man of God, when he heard them discussing such things among themselves, said, "Stop arguing. Set the ship's course for that place."

When the man of God had reached there, the waves, as if frozen, stood motionless around the rock. They found a man sitting on a rough and shapeless rock, and the waves flowed forth around him from every side, striking him up to the top of his head; and when they receded, the rock upon which that wretched man was sitting was exposed. Also, anytime the wind picked up the cloth which was hanging before him lashed him upon the eyes and forehead.

Blessed Brendan began to ask him who he was and for what sin he had been sent there, and what he had done to deserve such a punishment. The man said to him, "I am that most wretched Judas, that most wicked of merchants. I have this place not out of merit but rather out of the indescribable mercy of Jesus Christ. I do not consider this a place of punishment but rather an indulgence of the redeemer in honor of the lord's resurrection." For it was then the lord's day. "When I sit here, it seems to me as if I am in a paradise of delights because of the fear of the torments which are in store for me in the evening. For I burn day and night like a mass of molten lead in a cauldron in the middle of the mountain you saw. Leviathan is there with his attendants. I was there when he swallowed down your brother, and on that account hell was so joyful that it sent out enormous flames just as it always does when it devours the souls of the ungodly. But I have my relief here every Sunday from evening to evening, from Christmas to Epiphany, from Easter to Pentecost and from the Purification of the Virgin to Assumption. Before and after that, I am tormented in the depth of hell with Herod, Pilate, Annas, and Caiphas. Therefore, I entreat you through the redeemer of the world that you condescend to intercede with the Lord Jesus Christ so that I might be able to stay here up to sunrise tomorrow, and that on account of your coming here the demons do not torment me and lead me back to that evil inheritance which I bought at such an evil price." Saint Brendan said to him, "Let the will of the lord be done. Tonight, up until morning, you will not be the prey of demons."

Again the man of God spoke to him, saying, "What does that cloth signify?" Judas said to him, "I gave that cloth to a certain leper when I was chamberlain of the lord. Yet what I gave was not mine. It was of the lord and his brothers. On that account, I do not have any relief from it but rather greater hindrance. The iron forks on which the cloth hangs, I gave them to the priests of the temple for supporting their caldrons. I put that rock on which I am sitting in a ditch in a public road to go under the feet of passers-by [as a stepping stone?] before I was a disciple of the lord."

But when the evening hour had darkened the sea, an innumerable number of demons covered its surface in a circle, shouting and saying, "Get away from us, man of God because we cannot reach our companion unless you go away from him, we do not dare see the face or our prince unless we can return our friend to him. You have snatched our prey from us. Do not protect him tonight." The man of God said to them, "I am not defending him, but the Lord Jesus Christ has allowed him to stay here tonight until morning." The demons said to him, "How can you invoke the name of God over him when he is the lord's betrayer?" The man of God said to them, "I order you in the name of our Lord Jesus Christ that you may do him no evil until morning."

With the night having passed, when the man of God had begun to get underway at dawn, an infinite multitude of demons overwhelmed the face of the abyss sending out horrible noises, and saying "O man of God, cursed be your coming and going for last night our prince scourged us with the most unkind blows because we did not hand over that cursed captive." The man of God said to them, "Your abuse is nothing to do with us—but caused by you yourself. Blessed is he whom you curse; cursed is he whom you bless." The demons replied to him, "Because you defended him last night, wicked Judas will suffer double punishment over the next six days." The venerable father said to them, "From your position, you do not have that power—and nor does your prince. Rather, that will be in God's power." Then he added, "I order you and your prince in the name of our lord, Jesus Christ that you not subject him to more torments than before." They replied to him, "Surely you are not lord of everything that we should obey your words?" The man of God said to them, "I am his servant, and everything which will happen to Judas I will order in his name; I have the ministry which he gave to me." And so the demons escorted him until they could not see him any longer. The demons turned and grabbed up that wicked soul with them with great fury and shrieking.

Questions: Is the Island of the Smiths meant to be understood literally or figuratively as hell? How is Judas presented? Why is Judas permitted any respite from his punishment? How does the fact that this is a voyage to hell rather than a vision of hell change the nature of the account?

55. A MAIDEN VIEWS HELL

As the Middle Ages proceeded, Christian piety focused increasingly on the role of Mary, Jesus's mother, particularly her queenship over heaven and her intercessory power with her son. The Dominican preacher Johann Herolt (d. 1468) was especially devoted to the Blessed Virgin (as she is sometimes called) and assembled a large collection of preaching stories about Mary's interventions and wonders. Herolt was a prior of the Order's house in Nuremberg, Germany, and a friend and colleague of the noted reformer Johannes Nider, author of the Formicarius *(doc. 97).*

Latin, fifteenth century.

SIX: THE DEVIL'S DOMAIN

Source: trans. Richard Raiswell and David R. Winter, from Johannes Herolt, *Sermones discipuli in quadragesima* (Venice: Haeredes Melchioris Sessae, 1599), pp. 198–99.

A certain maiden was faithfully serving the Blessed Virgin Mary in chastity, and vowed to serve Mary and her son right up to her death. However, the ancient enemy hated her on account of her blessed deeds. He corrupted the eyes of a certain handsome man of wealth and power, into love of the maiden, throwing his whole mind into confusion. This man frequently seduced the maiden with flattery and promises so that he might win her as a wife. He promised her glory and riches, and all good things before God, and pressing her more urgently every day, the wicked devil roused her heart more intensely.

What more shall I say?

The maiden was worn down by the whirlwind of the enemy's repeated attacks, and so she went from being the bride of the eternal king to agreeing to become the wife of a mortal man! Renouncing Christ and eternal goods, she chose a mortal spouse and transitory goods.

The day of the nuptials was decided and on the night immediately before the wedding, when she was sleeping in her parents' house, she had a dream in which she saw herself taken over the mouth of the abyss. It was enormous in size, and in the depths of its mouth she saw hell. While she was there, it emitted fetid vapors that seemed to infect the air of the entire world. Dense clouds of smoke seemed to drive away the brightness of this world. The whole place seemed overrun with snakes and worms, and she constantly marveled in horror at the shouts of those being tormented within.

Suddenly, she saw certain fiery Ethiopians bursting forth from its midst and they were cruelly plunging the souls assigned to them into these torments without any respect for difference. She was seized by them and as she was being dragged into their midst, she came to understand her desperate situation. She looked around to see if there was anyone who could help her. She saw her former lady, the mother of God, the virgin Mary—but too far away and with her back to the maiden. But this sight, so far away, gave her very little hope. Eventually, with her whole heart and with great effort, the maiden turned toward the Virgin and shouted her name mightily. "O lady," she said, "rescue your handmaid who finds herself in such dire circumstances!" The Virgin came closer and asked, "Who are you?" "I am your handmaid, O lady," she said, "your slave, devoted to your memory." The Virgin said, "Be gone! You are not mine. No, indeed! You have chosen that which is contemptible to me and my son—he who could rescue you; he who could free you!"

Unable to bear these words of reproach, she said, "O, that my Lady should be so far from me, and my memory of her should be so far from my heart! Free your handmaid and do not delay, O lady! Even now, the abyss is swallowing me! Even now, the hellmouth threatens me!"

And as she apologized in this manner, hoping that the Virgin might assist her, her enemies, giving her no respite, dragged her down. However, the mother of piety, the holy receptacle of God, Mary, approached her. She took the maiden's hand and held it. Immediately her enemies were repelled. Nor did they dare to look at her when they saw the mother of the lord drawing near to her inheritance. Then, sweetly calling and gently consoling her, the virgin said, "These are the fruits of the flesh. This is the reward of lust. You gave yourself into this deep pit of perdition and you did not know it. But now, avoid such tests, and strive for the recovery of that grace which chastity deserves with all men, and I will help you with my prayers."

She said this and went away, restoring the maiden's soul to her.

At that point, the maiden awoke. The rich man's friends gathered around, asking what should be done. She said, "Get yourselves far from here, you ministers of death and inciters of eternal fire!" And to those whom she cast out with great indignation, and to her parents and everyone else gathered there, she revealed the whole affair. When they heard her, they released her to her liberty. And she returned to her old calling with full force in penitential mourning. By so doing she was able to regain the grace of our lady, the virgin mother of God, and her son, our Lord Jesus Christ.

And thus, she ended her life following the good and salubrious path.

Questions: How is this vision of hell different from those of men? Why is it granted to her? What values does this vision seek to impart?

56. AN URBAN HELL

By the thirteenth century, Verona was a thriving commercial center. With its location at the confluence of two major trade routes, Veronese merchants were well placed to reap the rewards of the medieval economic system at its height. The city's prosperity was epitomized by the large number of towers that dotted the cityscape.

"On Babylon, the Infernal City" is one of two poems by an otherwise unknown Franciscan cleric named Giacomino of Verona (fl. 1250) written during this period. Along with its companion piece, "On the Heavenly Jerusalem," the poems are part of a tradition of didactic vernacular poetry that seems to have been popular in northern Italy at this time. As such, they represent an attempt to bring contemporary conceptions of the afterlife to an illiterate and semi-literate urban audience.

Veronese, thirteenth century.

Source: trans. Robert Buranello, from Giacomino of Verona, *De Babylonia infernali*, from *The De Jerusalem Celesti and the De Babylonia Infernali* (London: Oxford, 1930), pp. 83–95.

SIX: THE DEVIL'S DOMAIN

For the honor of Christ . . .
. . . Let us now begin reading this, our new text,
With exempla and comments of the city hexed.
And the Master of Every Art, let's pray to him next
For divine assistance as our principal pretext.
I speak of the king of this land, yes, that fallen one,
Lucifer, who said: "In Heaven, second to none,
I will place myself just like the lord God on the throne,"
Whence he and his followers were cast to weep and moan.
The citadel is so large, and tall, and long, and wide
Full of every evil and every sadness inside.
For sure and for certain, as all the saints do confide,
Whosoever enters within must plan to abide.
In the deepest darkness of hell is where it is found
With so much pitch and sulfur it is always abound,
As much as there is water in the sea, all around,
It would immediately burn like wax dripping down.
Across the middle of it turbid torrents run through,
More bitter than evil itself, with poison accrue,
Bordered all around by nettles and thorns that outdo
The pointiest knives and sharpest swords, this is true.
Atop the city there was made a false rounded sky
All of steel and metal, pewter and bronze up on high;
Walled with stones and mountains, intended to fortify,
The sinner's eternal fate that he cannot deny.
At the very top there is a door with four watchmen,
Trifon and Macometo, Barachin and Satan,
Who, with revolting, cruel and vile indignation
Mete out pain and sorrow to their victims, forsaken.
And above the door there is a tower, very tall
With, on top, yet another patrol above it all.
As yet nobody has gone beyond its evil thrall,
No matter whence they come, they have not the wherewithal.
And, yet, although truly forbidding, a marvel great,
Never does he sleep but remaining wide-awake late
All night and day he signals the keeper of the gate
So that his people may forever there populate.
Then, from o'er the other side, they shriek, and they wail:
"Know that you are entering the great realm of betrayal!
Keep locked the door and observe carefully their trail

So not one of our souls can escape and prevail!"
But who comes toward you now, so important and great,
With a smile in your direction that will not abate,
Let the door be opened for him, and the drawbridge gate,
As he enters the city, with songs to jubilate.
Who else but King Lucifer, if you really must know,
Descends these dreadful depths in an attempt to farrow
This dark place that iniquity nurtures and makes grow
And where he is justly punished in this state of woe.
O wretched, yes, evil, deplorable, cursed one!
He who bears these titles merits this situation.
I must not speak of you as per my obligation
Never to praise him, else will he without cessation.
With both this mind and heart of mine I can clearly see
The message of our great lord God has not lied to me
That this place, so cruel and criminal, appears to be
Terrible to praise to its very extremity.
Perhaps he was already brought there, quick as ever
With his hands, feet, then body bound, so fast and clever
To be presented to the king of the endless never
And beaten fiercely without pardon whatsoever.
Such things must be done by some minister treacherous
Who, as written, puts him in a prison most heinous,
Where heaven permits a point most altitudinous
And torment and affliction remain continuous.
The stench is so great that comes from its very entrance
That mere words would provide a most useless resemblance
Even the man who will not touch but merely advance
Shall never be free of that foul, fetid fragrance.
Never have I ever seen, not even for a moment,
A place nor any other thing near so putrescent
That from o'er a thousand miles you cannot circumvent
The stench and the reek that come from that place fraudulent.
With so many snakes, lizards, toads, and serpents there are,
Vipers and basilisks and savage dragons alar,
That lacerate tongues and teeth worse than razors, by far.
They constantly eat, though their greedy maws stay ajar.
Here and there, demons, with enormous clubs and truncheon
To break your bones, shoulders, hip at any occasion,
More than a hundred of them, black like obsidian,
If we can believe the words of the holy sermon.

SIX: THE DEVIL'S DOMAIN

With the horrible faces of that cruel company
It would be a much greater pleasure, absolutely,
To be thrashed with thorns from Rome to far off Hispanie,
Than to meet up with just one of that grim assembly.
At all hours—all night and all day—do they expel
From their mouths horrible yellowish fire of hell.
Their heads are horned and hairy, and their hands are as well,
They howl just like wolves and bark like dogs when they yell.

But when a damned soul arrives, they do take such good care:
In icy water they throw him and leave him in there
Where one day seems a year, as said in the book of prayer,
Before they return him to heat and sulfurous air.
And when in the hot place, he wishes it were cold.
It is so long, violent, and cruel, if truth be told,
That he is never free, unrestricted, uncontrolled
As despair, pain, and punishment forever unfold.
Ensnared in that torment, a cook arrives suddenly,
That is, Beelzebub, among the worst there can be,
Who roasts him like a fat pig, over fire, easily,
On an enormous steel spit so he cooks speedily.
And then he takes water and salt, some soot and some wine,
Strong, awful vinegar, toxins, poisons to combine,
And he makes a sauce that is so good and so refined,
That every Christian may revere the king divine.
To the king of hell I send him as an offering,
Who cries out this message, with his full mouth watering
"I could not give a damn," as he sits there swallowing,
"If the meat is raw; the blood is nice and refreshing."
But then he very hurriedly turns back around,
And says to that foul cook that he is not very browned,
That he should cook him so much longer, turned upside down,
All day and all night in that hot, burning fire bound.
Even more greedily, he says, "In my opinion,
Do not send him back; leave him there, in my dominion.
Be not negligent nor lazy with this commission;
'Tis good to have that sinner and more in addition."
Of all those souls he is sent, he does not mind at all
If one is put in that harsh fire to burn and wrawl
That all the people in the world would never pall
If even one drop of saliva would down there fall.

I have never experienced, nor ever seen
Such a fire as that one, huge, fierce, and mean.
Not gold, silver, castle nor city as far as I can glean
Could escape that fire where dead sinners sing their keen.
The fire is so great—the intensity, the flame—
Beyond description, even in scripture, is its fame.
It radiates no light, remaining dark, just the same;
It is black, smelly, and all evil it can proclaim.
Just as paintings on paper, walls, or any location,
Are no match at all for the fire of this location,
Such would be the cursed soul in this damnation
From which God protects us with his fortification.
Just as water offers to the fishes all the food
So this fire to the vexatious vermin does good:
The sinners host them in their guts, it is understood,
As it eats eyes and mouths, thighs and hamstrings, as it should.
The devils cry out, with heads held high and voices cruel:
"Stoke the fire! Stoke it!" Woe to those souls who are its fuel!
But now you must know what kind of joyful accrual
Awaits the sinner, at this foul feast unusual.
As one evil devil cries out, another responds;
One hammers the metal; as another melts the bronze.
Some stoke the fire to still others' circumrotations,
Tormenting the sinner with unending tribulations.
And at the very end, there exits a great villain
From the very abyss, a companion of Satan
Thirty paces tall, a great truncheon in his hand,
To consecrate the shortcomings of the false Christian.
Yelling noisily, "All who choose to money follow
At the end of their days are left phony and hollow.
When they fall short, they are sure of ultimate sorrow
And the dangerous cost of their very last morrow."
"Let it be so! Let it be so!" all the devils reply.
"This is good news! Let us hope it turns out!" they all cry.
"You must go ahead, to be our guide, to show them why
Dreadful misfortune awaits the coward who will fly."
Among all those great devils, many run to the square.
Also those little ones, of whom nobody could care,
Each one crying out "Kill! Kill! Kill!" as the *cri de guerre*.
That thieving hypocrite cannot get away from there!

SIX: THE DEVIL'S DOMAIN

Some go in search of rakes while still others go get spades,
Some get fire pokers, yet others go get spears and blades,
They do not bother with shields, helmets, nor other aids;
Just shovels, pitchforks, and hammers are tools of their trades.
They are so cruel and used to committing wickedness
That one waits to join the other, these evil wretches:
Whoever is in front, he will have much more success,
As they run like demented hunting dogs, all breathless.
The sinner may very well think to exit the game
But all the devils come running at him just the same,
And by some miracle there is nowhere left to claim
That has no demons yelling, "Fire! Fire! Fire!" in the flames.
All of them doing this creates an infernal din
Enough to pain the poor soul condemned there for his sin:
If one devil is not enough, two make it worse when
God does smite the superior fiend there yet again.
Not the best, nor even the worst, could I separate
Since all devils and brethren of that infernal state
Are just as content for winter to initiate
As they torment man in the fire perpetuate.
Those involved in that business you will see most guilty;
Their places are found in the center of the city,
Where all others adore them just like a deity
As they genuflect at their feet and pledge fealty.
Wherefrom one is overcome by such great desire
To cause intense harm and have no one escape his ire.
Hence the sinner expresses his laments so dire
For he sees these rabid dogs surround him in the fire.
Those canines size him up and menacingly glower;
They seize him by the head and force him even lower,
Those who were staring from afar come right up before
Him with great fury to fulfil their rage even more.
Some flay his arms while others beat his legs brutally;
Some break his bones with cudgels and poles most cruelly;
With spades, shovels, axes, and trowels, most unduly
They cover his body with enormous wounds, truly.

On the ground, near death, the poor little bird collapses.
Do not make it worse with your compassion relapses!
A rope round his neck, a line through the narices [nostrils],

He is struck and dragged through hellish metropolises.
Whereupon there descends on the sinner deep despair
Whose hopes for release from that foul horde grow thin as air
Now pain and more pain, fire and imprisonment to bear
From that moment on all his hopes are dashed forever.
'Tis better for that miserable malefactor
To be dead a thousand than alive for one hour
Since he has no family, neither friend nor neighbor
Who could help him out since it would be useless labor.
Yet still this derision, as I have recounted now,
Of these people who repeatedly furrow their brow
And say to each other, "Oh, he deserves it, and how!"
"To honor God's work in life is to avoid sorrow!"
But the time did arrive when he was truly deceived
When doing good works would no longer be achieved
And even if a mountain of gold had been received
From this awful place, he will never ever be cleaved.
If he is not beaten well with the weapons at hand
With all those that are left we will make him understand."
Whereupon great sighs of the sinner again began
And he did holler with all the force of his weasand [throat]:
"O wretched, evil, and miserable soul am I
I feel these cruel ministers' beatings intensify!
May it please the creator that never born was I
And brought to this infernal station to mortify!
Most cursed be the hour, the night, the day, and the place
Where my mother and my father did meet and embrace
And whoever baptized me in criminal disgrace
And did not drown me at the Christian watering place!
How I arrived at this point I truly do not know—
Not on Christmas, Epiphany, nor at Easter, no!
Just deep, bitter anguish for the chance that I would blow,
And vain attempts to leave the dark I brought myself to."

Now most willingly that miserable wretch would flee
But he can do nothing for they have blocked his journey.
The devil's grip is so strong; he is at his mercy
And all the gold in the world could not set him free.
Now the sinner twists and now he turns, wretched, and poor.
He can find no rest, no beauty, nor any grandeur,
Now that he is in there—dead yet beaten with vigor,

SIX: THE DEVIL'S DOMAIN

Just like a goat, tormented with a club and dagger.
All the demons move toward him and they gather 'round
With metal clubs, heavier than lead, ready to pound
And they beat him so severely, all up and all down,
That this wretch was ever born only serves to confound.
They take from the sinner all his children and his wife,
His friends and family, his horse, and even his knife,
The castles and fortresses of which he was most rife,
And let him fend for himself, such a great lord in life!
Now the sinner is entrapped and my heart tells me so
If the Gospels of the lord God speak truth down below
So say Saints John, Luke, Mark, and, especially, Matthew
That the man condemned to hell cannot to and fro.
None of the sinners in hell offer help or support
Since each is busy with his own pain and discomfort
But one thing I would like to tell you, and I purport,
That he has no desire for laughing nor sport.
Since he is a man of the land, and so it must be,
Interred in the soil and consumed is his destiny
All the day, as well you should know, but then, presently
He will give back to the earth to grow it verdantly.
The worst suffering of that pathetic parasite
Is when he thinks about all the fires infinite
That rage through hell and his burning path without respite
In which he must be ablaze, all day, morning to night.
Still in that dreadful place we have often heard it said,
That son meets father where they fight, in the realm of dread.
He says: "Lord God in heaven, with a crown on his head,
Has cursed you father, body and soul, forever dead!

While I was alive on earth, you never chastised me.
My worst sins you condoned and encouraged mastery.
With gold and silver you did seduce and beguile me
So that now I am in embers, cruel and fiery.
And vividly I do remember how swift and quick
You would run up to me and beat me with a huge stick
As if I had asked for it, and laid it on me thick;
To mistake friend or neighbor would get me quite the snick!"
The father does then reply: "O cursed, dreadful son
I am here for my love for you and what I had done
Once I, the lord God did ultimately abandon,

I stole money, practiced usury and extortion.
All day and all night, these discomforts do continue
To overcome the fortresses, towers, and châteaux,
The woods and vineyards, mountains and idyllic venues
That, as terrestrial comforts, you chose to pursue.
Such were your thoughts and such was your exasperation,
Sweet, beautiful child, may God curse you with damnation!
May the poor souls of Christ beyond your recollection
Perish in the street from hunger and dehydration!
But right now I appear angry and ridiculous,
For crying and distressing is truly frivolous.
I got what I deserved for being so villainous
Here, where I pay four times my sin by divine process."
So immense and intense this dispute between the men,
As if by battle to the death they were condemned,
If the one could bite the other it still would not end
Until one's heart right out from his body he would rend.
The suffering is so great from that burning fire,
That if I had fifteen hundred mouths, they would not tire,
But rather speak all the day and all the night, entire
I still could not truly express what there does transpire.
These cruel people who these iniquities did commit,
To think of their punishments, would you ever admit?
When a mere toothache, becomes a daylong crying fit
How do you expect to tolerate pain infinite?

Questions: What sources does the author draw upon? How is the organization of hell different? What sins are especially singled out for punishment here? Why might the torments described earlier in the poem seem particularly humiliating to an urban audience? Does this version of hell have any purgative or purifying function?

57. DANTE'S VISION OF THE STRUCTURE OF HELL

The Divine Comedy, *written by the great Florentine poet Dante Alighieri (1265-1321), is a tour through the afterlife. Framed as a journey from hell, through purgatory and into paradise, the poem illustrates issues in contemporary theology by describing the fate of figures drawn from history, many of whom come from the turbulent political scene of thirteenth- and fourteenth-century Florence. For the first half of the journey, Dante, the central character of the* Comedy *(who is distinct from the author), is led by the Roman poet Virgil (70-19 BCE).*

SIX: THE DEVIL'S DOMAIN

The poem begins on the evening before Good Friday at a point where the character of Dante discovers himself lost in a dark wood, his path blocked by three wild beasts. Virgil appears and proposes another path along a "deep and rugged road." But immediately after they begin their journey, their way is barred by a gate.
Tuscan, 1314.

Source: trans. Henry Longfellow, *The Divine Comedy of Dante Alighieri* (Boston, 1867), pp. 9–10, 109–10; rev.

Canto III

"Through me the way is to the city dolent;
Through me the way is to eternal dole;
Through me the way among the people lost.
Justice incited my sublime creator;
Divine omnipotence—the highest wisdom
And the primal love—created me.
Before me there were no created things,
Only eternal ones, and I shall last eternally.
Abandon all hope, you who enter in!"
These words in somber color I beheld
Written upon the summit of a gate;
To which I, "Their sense, master, is cruel to me!"
And he to me, as one experienced,
"Here all suspicion must be abandoned,
All cowardice must be here extinct.
We to the place have come, where I have told you
You shall behold the people dolorous
Who have forgotten the good of intellect."
And after he had laid his hand on mine
With joyful mien, by which I was comforted,
He led me in among these secret things.
There sighs, complaints, and ululations loud
Resounded through the air without a star,
At which I, at the beginning, wept. . . .

[After traversing hell and witnessing the torment to which the souls of sinners are subjected (doc. 77), Dante and Virgil come to the center of the pit of hell, where they see Lucifer.]

Canto XXXIV

"*Vexilla Regis prodeunt Inferni*
[The banners of the king of hell advance]
Toward us; therefore look in front of you,"
My master said, "if you can discern him."
For, when there breathes a heavy fog, or when
Our hemisphere is darkening into night,
[There] appears far off a mill the wind is turning,
I thought that such a building then I saw;
And, for the wind, I drew myself behind
My guide, because there was no other shelter.
Now was I—and I fear to put it into verse—
There where the shades [souls] were wholly covered up,
And glimmered through like straws in glass.
Some prone are lying, others stand erect,
This with the head, and that one with the soles;
Another, bow-like, face to feet inverts.
When in advance so far we had proceeded,
That it my master pleased to show me
The creature who once had the beauteous semblance,
He from before me moved and made me stop,
Saying, "Behold Dis, and behold the place
Where you with fortitude must arm yourself."
How frozen I became and powerless then,
Ask it not, reader, for I write it not,
Because all language would be insufficient.
I did not die, but alive I remained not;
Imagine for yourself now, if you have any understanding,
What I became, being of both deprived.
The Emperor of the kingdom dolorous
From his mid-breast forth issued from the ice;
And better to a giant do I compare
Than do the giants with those arms of his;
Consider now how great must be that whole,
To which such a part conforms itself.
Were he as fair once, as he now is foul,
And lifted up his brow against his maker,
Well may proceed from him all tribulation.
O, what a marvel it appeared to me,
When I beheld three faces on his head!

SIX: THE DEVIL'S DOMAIN

The one in front, and that vermillion was;
Two were the others, that were joined with this
Above the middle part of either shoulder,
And they were joined together at the crest;
And the right-hand one seemed between white and yellow;
The left was such to look upon as those
Who come from where the Nile fall valley-ward.
Underneath each came forth two mighty wings,
Such as befitting were so great a bird;
Sails of the sea I never saw so large.
No feathers had they, but as of a bat
Their fashion was; and he was waving them,
So that three winds proceeded forth from there.
Thereby Cocytus wholly was congealed.
With six eyes did he weep, and down three chins
Trickled the tear-drops and bloody drivel.
At every mouth he with his teeth was crunching
A sinner, in the manner of a rake,
So that he three of them tormented thus.
To him in front the biting was as naught
Upon the clawing, for sometimes the spine
Utterly stripped of all the skin remained.
"That soul up there which has the greatest pain,"
The master said, "is Judas Iscariot;
With head inside, he plies his legs without.
Of the two others, who head downward are,
The one who hangs from the black jowl is Brutus;
See how he writhes himself, and speaks no word.
And the other, who so stalwart seems, is Cassius.
But night is descending, and it is time
That we depart, for we have seen it all."

Questions: What is new about the structure of hell described here? How has Dante imagined hell and Satan differently from earlier traditions? Does he rule over hell? Why does the poet reserve such an appalling fate for Judas, Cassius, and Brutus? What does this say about medieval social values?

CHAPTER SEVEN

VARIETIES OF POSSESSION AND EXORCISM

Figure 7.1 "Exorcism of the Gerasene Demoniac," Basilica of Sant'Apollinare Nuovo, Ravenna, Italy (early sixth century). This is the second in a series of thirteen mosaics depicting incidents in the life of Christ that line the upper portion of the left side of the nave of Sant'Apollinare Nuovo. It is juxtaposed on the right side with the same number of mosaics depicting the passion and resurrection. The church also features larger mosaics of various saints and figures from sacred history, along with depictions of the palace of the Ostrogoth Theodoric, who commissioned the building, and one of Emperor Justinian, which was added later. In this scene from the Gospels, Jesus sends the unclean spirits that have been afflicting a man into a herd of swine that were foraging nearby. They in turn jump off a high cliff into the Sea of Galilee, drowning themselves. It is one of the most famous demonic dispossession sequences in the New Testament (doc. 58).

Although the ability to expel demons was central to Christ's mission and helped seal his reputation as a powerful wonder worker, demon possession and its remedy raised many fundamental but difficult questions about the power of God, his relationship to the Church, and the nature and abilities of the devil. As the religion spread into new territories, encountering spiritual traditions that Christians understood as demonic, these questions took on a new immediacy.

The accounts of the exorcisms that Christ performed over the course of his ministry provided Christians with a basic inventory of the symptoms of demon possession. The gospels, however, gave believers no explanation as to why the devil had been granted the power to possess people—beyond the fact that casting out demons was an authenticating mark of Christ's divinity. Christ's death raised many other questions: To what extent was the power invested in Christ transferred to the apostles—and later to the saints? That is, did dispossession work *ex opere operantis* (on the basis of the work of the doer), by virtue of some charismatic power associated with the exorcist himself? Or did it work *ex opere operato* (on the basis of the work performed), that is, through regularized formulae involving a standard ritual, prayers, and biblically grounded invocations?

Nor was it entirely clear why dispossession worked. Could it be that demons were somehow bound and constrained by human commands when delivered under particular ritual circumstances? But if the opposite was the case—that demons were compelled to respond to the effects of human imprecations to God—then why were dispossessions not spontaneous? Indeed, why did they sometimes not work? Put differently, if dispossession was a miracle performed by God to relieve suffering, why did it not function like a sacrament?

While a formal order of professional exorcists seems to have come into existence by the fourth century, they never assumed a monopoly on the practice. Non-clerical healers sought and used natural remedies against demonic assaults and afflictions. In God's perfectly ordered creation, there was no noxious thing that did not have a neutralizing opposite. This left the door open to all manner of healing, blending elements of natural and preternatural lore with elements of dispossession.

Some have argued that the High Middle Ages experienced a crisis in exorcism: theologians bickered about how a demon could enter into a body, a position that challenged aspects of Aristotelian physics, which proposed that two things could not occupy the same space at the same time. They argued about whether demons could seize a demoniac's soul—and, if they could, what this implied for the doctrine of free will. Theologians also wondered whether it was licit for people to seek to expel demons, given that their possession of a body must, at some level, be a function of God's will.

Without standardized methods for diagnosing demon possession or helping those afflicted, all interactions with the spirit world were potentially hazardous.

Those claiming to have had mystical experiences were vulnerable to accusations of demon possession, and toward the end of the period, many mystics and hermits were viewed with suspicion by authorities.

58. BIBLICAL POSSESSIONS

To Christians, the reality of demon possession was firmly anchored in the New Testament, its successful relief through some form of dispossession central to Christ's mission and the propagation of the new faith. However, while these accounts of Christ's work exorcising demoniacs often overlapped with more general healing narratives, they helped to define the symptoms of possession and made it clear that demons were ultimately impotent when confronted. Scripture, however, defined no specific procedure as to how exorcisms could be accomplished, nor did it explain how they worked.

Greek, second half of first century CE.

Source: trans. Gregory Martin et al. from the Latin Vulgate, The Holy Bible (Douay-Rheims version) (Douay: The English College, 1609–10), rev. Richard Challoner (1749–52); rev.

Mark

9.16. One of the multitude [who saw Jesus] said, "Master, I have brought my son who has a dumb spirit to you.

17. And wherever it takes him, it dashes him, and he foams [at the mouth] and gnashes with [his] teeth, and pines away; and I spoke to your disciples to cast him out, and they could not."

18. Answering them, he [Jesus] said, "O incredulous generation. How long shall I be with you? How long shall I suffer you? Bring him to me."

19. And they brought him. And when he had seen him [the boy], immediately the spirit troubled him [the demoniac], and being thrown down upon the ground, he rolled about foaming.

20. And he [Jesus] asked his [the boy's] father, "For how long has this been happening to him?" But he said: "From his infancy.

21. And often it has cast him into the fire and into waters to destroy him. But if you can do any thing, help us, having compassion on us."

22. And Jesus said to him, "If you can believe, all things are possible to him who believes."

23. And immediately the father of the boy crying out in tears said, "I do believe, lord. Help my unbelief."

24. And when Jesus saw the multitude running together, he threatened the unclean spirit, saying to it, "Deaf and dumb spirit, I command you, go out of him; and enter not any more into him."

SEVEN: VARIETIES OF POSSESSION AND EXORCISM

25. And crying out, and greatly tearing [at] him, it went out of him, and he became as dead, so that many said, "He is dead."

26. But Jesus taking him by the hand, lifted him up and he arose.

27. And when he [Jesus] had come into the house, his disciples secretly asked him, "Why could not we cast him out?"

28. And he said to them, "This kind can go out by nothing but by prayer and fasting."

Luke

8.27. And when he [Jesus] had come forth into the land [of the Gerasenes], he was met there by a certain man who had had a devil [in him] now a very long time, and he wore no clothes, neither did he abide in a house, but lived instead in the sepulchers [tombs].

28. And when he saw Jesus, he fell down before him; and crying out with a loud voice, he said, "What have I to do with you, Jesus, son of the most high God? I beseech you, do not torment me."

29. For he had commanded the unclean spirit to go out of the man. For many times it seized him and he was bound with chains, and kept in fetters; and breaking the bonds, he was driven by the devil into the deserts.

30. And Jesus asked him, saying, "What is your name?" But he said, "Legion," because many devils had entered into him.

31. And they begged him not to command them to go into the abyss.

32. And there was there a herd of many swine feeding on the mountain; and they begged him that he would allow them to enter into them. And he allowed them.

33. The devils therefore went out of the man, and entered into the swine; and the herd ran violently down a steep place into the lake, and were stifled [drowned].

34. Which when they that fed them saw what had been done, they fled away, and told it in the city and in the villages.

35. And they went out to see what was done; and they came to Jesus, and found the man, out of whom the devils were departed, sitting at his feet, clothed, and in his right mind; and they were afraid. . . .

38. Now the man . . . asked him that he might be with him. But Jesus sent him away, saying,

39. "Return to your house, and tell how great things God has done to you." And he went through the whole city, publishing the great things Jesus had done to him. . . .

Questions: What symptoms do demons seem to cause in the bodies of those in whom they reside? What methods does Christ use to perform exorcisms? Do these texts make any distinction between casting out demons and curing diseases? Can other people cast out demons? Do their methods differ? Are the demons destroyed? How might most people have understood what Christ did in performing such acts?

59. EXORCISMS BY THE DISCIPLES

As is clear from the New Testament, early-first-century Palestine was teeming with people offering preternatural cures and relief from demonic affliction. While the gospel of Mark suggested that the power to exorcise demons lay exclusively with Christ, other New Testament texts and apocrypha suggested that this power had been diffused to Jesus's followers more generally—perhaps even to people beyond their ranks. These texts, however, are vague as to whether the power to dispossess was an inherent ability of the exorcist or whether exorcists were merely conduits for the manifestation of divine power.

Greek, second half of first century CE.

Source: trans. Gregory Martin et al. from the Latin Vulgate, The Holy Bible (Douay-Rheims version) (Douay: The English College, 1609–10), rev. Richard Challoner (1749–52); rev.

Luke

9.1. Then calling together the twelve apostles, he gave them power and authority over all devils, and to cure diseases.

2. And he sent them to preach the kingdom of God, and to heal the sick. . . .

6. And going out, they went about through the towns, preaching the gospel, and healing everywhere. . . .

49. [Later, John spoke to Christ, saying], "Master, we saw a certain man casting out devils in thy name, and we forbade him, because he did not follow with us.

50. And Jesus said to him, "Forbid him not; for he that is not against you, is for you."

10.1. And after these things, the lord appointed also [an]other seventy-two: and he sent them two and two before his face into every city and place whither he himself was to come. . . .

8. [And he said to them], "Into whatever city you enter and they receive you, eat such things as are set before you.

9. And heal the sick that are therein. . . ."

17. And the seventy-two returned with joy, saying, "Lord, the devils also are subject to us in your name."

18. And he said to them, "I saw Satan like lightning falling from heaven.

19. Behold, I have given you power to tread upon serpents and scorpions, and upon all the power of the enemy: and nothing shall hurt you."

SEVEN: VARIETIES OF POSSESSION AND EXORCISM

Acts

16.16. And it came to pass, as we went to prayer, a certain girl, having a pythonical spirit [a spirit of divination] met us, who brought to her masters much profit by divining.

17. This same [girl] following Paul and us, cried out, saying, "These men are the servants of the most high God, who preach to you the way of salvation."

18. And this she did many days. But Paul being grieved, turned, said to the spirit, "I command you, in the name of Jesus Christ, to go out from her." And he [the spirit] went out the same hour. . . .

19.11. And God wrought by the hand of Paul more than common miracles.

12. So that even there were brought from his body to the sick, handkerchiefs and aprons, and the diseases departed from them, and the wicked spirits went out of them.

13. Now some also of the Jewish exorcists who went about attempted to invoke over those who had evil spirits, the name of the Lord Jesus, saying, "I conjure you by Jesus, whom Paul preaches."

14. And there were certain men, seven sons of Sceva, a Jew, a chief priest, that did this.

15. But the wicked spirit, answering, said to them, "Jesus I know, and Paul I know; but who are you?"

16. And the man in whom the wicked spirit was, leaping upon them, and mastering them both, prevailed against them, so that they fled out of that house naked and wounded.

17. And this became known to all the Jews and the Gentiles that dwelt at Ephesus; and fear fell on them all, and the name of the Lord Jesus was magnified.

18. And many of them that believed, came confessing and declaring their deeds.

Questions: Who can perform dispossessions? Who cannot? Is there a difference between these dispossessions and those performed by Christ? What methods do the apostles use? Do these texts make any distinction between casting out demons and curing diseases? What defines a legitimate dispossession? Why does God allow demons to possess people?

60. TWO EARLY FORMS OF EXORCISM

By the second century, exorcism clearly had come to hold an important place among some Christians. Its successful public performance served as visible proof of the power of the new God and the veracity of his teachings. The idea of what constituted evidence of demonic possession was not confined to an array of seemingly unnatural physical symptoms. It was diagnosed in those whose behavior and beliefs were deemed perverse or contrary to the ordinary operation of nature. To be sure, Mark's gospel implied that self-harm could be a sign of possession, but in the hands of subsequent authors, religious or theological deviance might also be read as a token that an individual had become somehow overcome by the devil. Thus, despite dispossession's use as a vehicle for proselytizing, the variety of forms of possession ensured that many different methods were employed for its remedy. That said, there was still no standard method for casting out demons. Moreover, the processes employed to deal with demons were often indistinguishable from those used to cast out other impurities and thus overlapped closely with other forms of magical and preternaturally inspired healing.

Flavius Josephus was a Romano-Jewish historian. His Antiquities of the Jews is a history of the Jewish people from creation to the start of the Jewish War in 66 CE. Origen appears in doc. 18.

Josephus: Greek, c. 93/94 CE.
Origen: Greek, c. 248 CE.

Sources: trans. John Court, from Josephus, *History of the Antiquities of the Jews*, in *The Works of Flavius Josephus* (London: Penny and Janeway, 1733), p. 183, rev.; trans. Frederick Crombie, from Origen, *Contra Celsum*, in Ante-Nicene Fathers, vol. 4 (Buffalo, NY: Christian Literature Publishing Co., 1885), pp. 398–99, 612; rev.

Josephus

The wisdom and understanding with which God blessed Solomon exceeded that of the ancients. The Egyptians who were thought to excel all others in knowledge came infinitely short of him. Those Hebrews who in his time were reckoned men of penetration and had become renowned for their deep understanding were not to be compared with him. . . . God also gave him a power of driving out devils from possessed persons for the good of humanity. He invented incantations by which diseases were healed and left behind a method of exorcising whereby devils were so effectually cast out that they never returned again. This method of cure is much in vogue with our nation to this day. I myself have seen one Eleazar, a countryman of mine, dispossessing people of devils in the presence of [Emperor] Vespasian, his sons, captains, and army. The form of performing the cure was this: he touched the nostrils of the demoniac (or person possessed with a devil) with a ring, under the seal of which was placed a piece of one of those roots which Solomon had discovered. As the man was smelling this, Eleazar drew the devil out of his nostrils, upon which the demoniac suddenly fell down. Then, invoking at the same time the name of Solomon and the incantations composed by him, Eleazar adjured the devil never to return into the man again. After this, Eleazar set about persuading the people around him that he really had the power of casting out devils. To this end, he placed a pot or basin of water a short distance away from a demoniac and commanded the devil to come out of the man and then to overturn the vessel. He did this so that the spectators around him might know that the devil had actually left the person. Through this, the wisdom and knowledge of Solomon was made clear—and for this reason, we have been induced to relate these things so that everyone might be acquainted with his genius and excellence in all fields of knowledge.

Origen

Celsus asserts that it is by the names of certain demons, and by the use of incantations, that the Christians appear to be possessed of [miraculous] power; hinting, I suppose, at the practices of those who expel evil spirits by incantations. And here he manifestly appears to malign the Gospel. For it is not by incantations that Christians seem to prevail (over evil spirits), but by the name of Jesus, accompanied by the announcement of the narratives which relate to him; for the repetition of these has frequently been the means of driving demons out of men, especially when those who repeated them did so in a sound and genuinely believing spirit. Such power, indeed, does the name of Jesus possess over evil spirits, that there have been instances where it was effectual, when it was pronounced even by bad men, which Jesus himself taught (would be the case), when he said: Many shall say to me in that day, In your name we have cast out devils, and done many wonderful works. Whether Celsus omitted this from intentional malignity, or from ignorance, I do not know. And he next proceeds to bring a charge against the savior himself, alleging that it was by means of sorcery that he was able to accomplish the wonders which he performed; and that foreseeing that others would attain the same knowledge, and do the same things, making a boast of doing them by help of the power of God, he excludes such from his kingdom. . . . But even if it be impossible to show by what power Jesus wrought these miracles, it is clear that Christians employ no spells or incantations, but the simple name of Jesus, and certain other words in which they repose faith, according to the holy scriptures. . . .

It is said of the Pythian priestess, whose oracle seems to have been the most celebrated, that when she sat down at the mouth of the Castilian cave, the prophetic spirit of Apollo entered her private parts; and when she was filled with it, she gave utterance to responses which are regarded with awe as divine truths. Judge by this whether that spirit does not show its profane and impure nature, by choosing to enter the soul of the prophetess not through the more becoming medium of the bodily pores which are both open and invisible, but by means of what no modest man would ever speak of. . . . Moreover, it is not the part of a divine spirit to drive the prophetess into such a state of ecstasy and madness that she loses control of herself. . . . If, then, the Pythian priestess is beside herself when she prophesies, what spirit must that be which fills her mind and clouds her judgment with darkness, unless it be of the same order with those demons which many Christians cast out of persons possessed with them? And this, we may observe, they do without the use of any curious arts of magic, or incantations, but merely by prayer and simple adjurations which the plainest person can use. Because for the most part it is unlettered persons who perform this work; thus making manifest the grace which is in the word of Christ, and the despicable weakness of demons, which, in order to be overcome and driven out of the bodies and souls of men, do not require the power and wisdom of those who are mighty in argument, and most learned in matters of faith.

Questions: Who can drive out demons? Do dispossessions performed by non-Christians work? Do they work ex opere operantis *or* ex opere operato? *What are the main weapons of these exorcists? Which use oral formulae and which used defined rites? What is the purpose of each of these possessions and dispossessions? To what extent is exorcism a specialist service at this point? To what extent has the process been institutionalized?*

61. DISPOSSESSION BY PERSON

While the gospels and Acts of the Apostles made clear that Christ and his early followers could dispossess those afflicted by demons either in their own right or as conduits of divine power, the extent to which this power could be harnessed by others was an open question in the early church. Although doc. 59 contains passages which suggest that the name of Christ had adjurative powers in itself and could be used legitimately by those who were not among Jesus's followers, the ability to cast out demons was a service that came increasingly to be associated with especially pious men and women. The stories below come from Gregory the Great's (doc. 45) Dialogues, *a very popular narrative source from the early medieval period.*
Latin, late sixth century.

Source: trans. Richard Raiswell and David R. Winter, from Gregory I, *Sancti Gregorii papae dialogorum libri IV* (Migne, PL 77: 0168D–0169A, 0177A–0177B, 0196b–0197A, 0200B–0205A, and 0272B–0273A).

One day, a servant of God, one of the virgins from a monastery [under Abbot Equitius] entered its garden. Seeing a lettuce she desired, she ate it hungrily, having forgotten to bless it with the sign of the cross beforehand. Immediately she fell to the ground, seized by the devil. While she was being tossed around violently, word was immediately sent to Father Equitius asking that he come in all haste to help her with his prayers. As soon as the father entered the garden, the devil who had seized the woman began to shout through her mouth, as if justifying himself, saying, "What have I done? What have I done? I was sitting on that lettuce and she came and ate me!" At this, with grave indignation, the man of God ordered the devil to depart and to stay no longer in the body of the servant of almighty God. At that, the demon immediately left her, since it no longer had the power to harm her. . . .

[In 571], when the Lombards entered the province of Valeria, the monks fled from the monastery of that most reverent Equitius to his tomb in the chapel. When the savage Lombards entered the chapel, they dragged the monks outside to torture or slay them with their swords. One of the monks, groaning and moved by bitter pain, cried out, "Alas, alas, Saint Equitius. Do you approve of us being dragged out like this? You are not defending us." At the sound of his voice, an evil spirit immediately took possession of the savage Lombards. Falling to the ground, they were tormented for so long a time that the rest of the Lombards who were outside came to appreciate what was happening, realizing that they should not violate that holy place any more. Thus, while the holy man defended his disciples, he provided safety for many others fleeing to that place afterwards. . . .

Also, not long ago, a certain old cleric . . . related many things about him [Bishop Bonifacius of the city of Ferentino] that ought not to be kept in silence. He says that having gone into his garden on a certain day, the bishop found it covered with a large number of caterpillars. Seeing all the vegetables destroyed, he turned toward those caterpillars and said, "I adjure you in the name of our lord God, Jesus Christ: depart from here, and do not eat these vegetables anymore." At the word of the man of God, they all left immediately so that not one remained within the bounds of the garden. . . .

At another time, that same servant of the almighty God [Bishop Fortunatus] cast out an impure spirit from a certain possessed man. The wicked spirit, seeing that evening had fallen and that there was hardly anyone outside because it was so late, took the form of a stranger and began to wander around the streets of the city, shouting, "O holy bishop Fortunatus! See what he has done! He has driven a stranger from his home. I am looking for a place to rest but I can't find one in this city." Then a certain man who was sitting by the fire in his house with his wife and small boy heard this voice and, enquiring about what the bishop had done to him, invited the stranger into their lodgings, letting him sit with them by the fire. And while they were talking in turns about matters, the wicked spirit entered the small boy and threw him forth into the fire, where he promptly died. Then the bereaved, wretched man recognized who it was he had received and who the bishop had expelled.

Peter: What are we to say about the fact that the ancient enemy dared to kill in the house of a man who thought him a stranger and so had graciously offered him hospitality?

Gregory: Many things, Peter, seem good but they are not because they are not done with good intention. For this reason, the evangelist speaks the truth when he says, "if your eye is evil, your whole body will be in darkness" [Matt. 6.23]. When the intention which precedes an act is evil, every work which follows is depraved—even if it appears morally correct.

In my opinion, while the man who lost his child seemed to be practicing hospitality, he did not in fact act in the spirit of charity but did so rather for the bishop's derogation, for the punishment which followed made it clear that what he did was not without sin. There are some people who strive to do good things so that they might obscure the kindness of others. In such cases, they are not nourished by the good they do—rather, they feed on the praise they receive for their [apparently] good deeds which [in reality were done to] oppress others. In this matter, then, I think that the man who received the evil spirit in hospitality intended more a display than an action—he wanted to appear to have done better than the bishop, for he received a man whom [Bishop] Fortunatus, a man of the lord, had expelled.

Peter: It is as you say, for the result of his effort proves that the intention underlying the act was not pure.

Gregory: Also, at another time, a certain man who had lost his eyesight was brought to Fortunatus seeking and [then] obtaining his intercession. For after the man of God had prayed, he imprinted the sign of the cross on his eyes and immediately light was restored to them and the darkness of his blindness dissipated. Also, the horse of a certain soldier had become so mad that many men could scarcely hold it. The horse would attack anyone, biting their limbs with its teeth. Eventually, having been bound by many men in some way, it was led to the man of God. With his hand extended, he made the sign of the cross on the horse's head, and immediately all the horse's madness was turned into meekness so that afterwards it appeared gentler than it had been before the madness. . . .

In the city of Todi, a certain good man named Marcellus lived with his two sisters. Becoming sick in body, he died late on Easter Sunday evening. As his body had to be carried far away, it could not be buried that day. During the delay in burial, the man's sisters, distressed by Marcellus's death, hurried to the venerable Fortunatus weeping. With raised voices, they cried out to him, "We know you hold to the life of the apostles. You cleanse lepers. You give sight to the blind. Come and reawaken our dead brother." As soon as he knew that their brother was dead, the bishop also began to weep at his death. Then he replied, saying to them, "Go away and don't speak about this because it [his death] was a commandment of almighty God which no man can oppose." When they were gone, the bishop remained unhappy because of the man's death. But on the following day—a Sunday—before sunrise, he called two of his deacons to him and went to the house of the deceased. Coming to the place where the lifeless body lay, he gave himself over to prayer. Having completed his prayers, he got up and sat next to the body of the deceased, and in a quiet voice he called him by his name, saying, "Brother Marcellus." But even though his voice was restrained, the dead man was awakened, as if he had been sleeping lightly, and immediately opened his eyes. Seeing the bishop, he asked, "What have you done? O what have you done?" The bishop responded to him, saying, "What have I done?" The man replied, "Yesterday, two men came to me who took me out from my body and led me into a good place. But today, a man was sent who said, 'restore him because Bishop Fortunatus has come into his house!'" Having said these words, Marcellus immediately recovered from his illness and remained in this life long after. . . .

But why do we say so a many things about Fortunatus's life when even up to the present day we have examples of all his abilities at his tomb? For in the presence of his dead bones, he continues to free demoniacs and heal the sick as often as he is sought by the faithful—just as he was accustomed to do ceaselessly while he was alive. . . .

In the city of Spoleto, the daughter of a certain distinguished man, a girl of marriageable age, burned with desire to live a heavenly life. Her father, though, tried to oppose her desire to take up this way of life. But disregarding her father, she took up the habit of the holy way of life anyway. . . . On a certain day, Abbot Eleutherius, a man of virtuous living, came to her to offer encouraging and edifying words. He was sitting with her discussing the word of God when a peasant carrying a present suddenly arrived from the little parcel of land that she had received from her father. While the peasant was standing before them, he was seized by an evil spirit and fell to the ground. Completely overcome, he started hissing and making a kind of bleating sound. At this, the nun arose and with an angry countenance ordered him in a loud voice, saying, "Get out from him, wretched one! Get out from him, wretched one!" To this, the devil replied through the mouth of the possessed man immediately, saying, "And if I come out from him, into whom shall I go?" By chance, there was a small pig feeding nearby. Then the nun ordered him, saying, "Get out from him and go into that pig." Immediately, the devil left the man and entered the pig as she had ordered. He killed it and left.

Peter: I would like to know if she had the power to grant even a pig to an unclean spirit.

Gregory: The things that were done by truth (that is, Christ) should be our rule. Indeed, it was said to our redeemer by a legion of demons that possessed a man, "if you cast us out, send us into a herd of swine" [Matt. 8.31 and doc. 58]. Christ expelled the demons from the man and allowed them to go into the pigs which he sent into the sea. From this matter, it can be inferred that an evil spirit has no power against man without the permission of almighty God, for it was not able to enter into the pigs without permission. . . .

Questions: Who can exorcise? What can be exorcised? What methods do they use to expel demons? Is there any difference between the dispossession of demons and other forms of adjuration? What explanations do the texts provide to account for why people can become possessed? Are any of these demons actually good?

62. DISPOSSESSION BY OBJECTS

Amulets and talismans had long been used across the ancient world for their presumed protective and healing powers against both visible and invisible enemies. While early Christian authorities cautioned against the use of such devices because of their association with demonic power, Christians came to accept that certain objects connected to the divine might function in an analogous fashion. It was rarely clear, however, whether such objects were deemed to have power in themselves or whether they served as conduits for the transmission of divine power.

Quodvultdeus (c. 390–454) was bishop of Carthage from c. 437. Shortly afterwards, the city was conquered by the Vandals and he was forced to flee to Naples. There, he wrote his most important work, The Book of the Promises and Prophecies of God, *from which the selection below comes. This is a collection of 153 promises and predictions about the end times supplemented by accounts of the current state of the Church. The incident described here can be dated to 434. Some scholars have suggested that the unnamed bishop in this account is Quodvultdeus himself.*

Gregory of Tours (c. 535–594) was an aristocratic Gallo-Roman bishop. With privileged access to the Merovingian court, he is one of the foremost historians of the Frankish people. The selection below comes from his life of Saint Julian.

Quodvultdeus: Latin, 445–449.

Gregory of Tours: Latin, late sixth century.

Sources: trans. Richard Raiswell and David R. Winter, from Quodvultdeus, *Liber promissionum ac praedictorum dei*, in *Opera omnia*, in *Corpus Christianorum Series Latina*, vol. 60 (Turnholt: Brepols, 1976), pp. 196–97; trans. Richard Raiswell and David R. Winter, from Gregory of Tours, *De passione et virtutibus sancti Iuliani martyris*, in *MGH: SS rev. Merov.* 1.2 (Hannover: Impensis Bibliopolii Hahniani, 1969), pp. 112–34.

Quodvultdeus

Who in this country does not know about that monstrous and diabolical sign which also happened in our days when the famous Asper was made consul of Carthage?

When a certain young Arab girl wearing the habit of a servant of God was washing herself in the public baths she saw an immodest statue of Venus, and by imitating it, she presented herself a dwelling for the devil [see doc. 37]. Immediately, that roaring lion found what he sought and took possession of her. Having entered into her, occupying her throat so that she could take no food or drink for almost 70 days and nights, the devil showed his hunger through this captured, possessed vessel.

For many days, the girl's parents hoped that this monster might be taken away. When they could not endure this continuous evil any more, they went immediately to a priest with their daughter, telling him faithfully everything that had happened. The girl admitted only this: that in the middle of the night a certain bird appeared to her which poured something—she did not know what—into her mouth. It was a wonder for all to see: the wretched girl showed no signs of her long fast; she was made neither pale nor weak nor incapacitated from it, but rather robust in body and full in limbs. Although the things which were said sounded incredible, having taken counsel, the priest immediately enclosed the girl in the monastery of women in which the relics of Saint Stephen are located and commended her to the care of the prior. There she remarked that that bird appeared to her only on the first day and rebuked her because—being constrained by neither hunger nor thirst—she had taken herself to a place to which it was not allowed to come. She remained in the monastery for two full weeks, taking neither food nor drink.

With us rising with the priest so that the morning sacrifice might be offered there as usual, the prior led the girl to the altar with that approach and demeanor with which women are used to coming from feasting and drinking, overcome with redness. She prostrated herself before the altar with a clamor of weeping. This brought forth groans and tears from all present, causing them to beg the lord for such evil to be taken away. An unseemly murmur immediately arose from the people. With the sacrifice completed, she—along with the other women—received a small, moistened piece of the body of the lord from the priest. Chewing for half an hour, she was not able to swallow it, for he had not yet been put to flight about whom the apostle says, "What concord has Christ with Belial?" [2 Cor. 6.15] . . .

Therefore, with the priest holding her face with his hand so she could not spit out the holy morsel, a certain deacon suggested that the bishop apply the saving chalice to her throat. As soon as this was done, by the power of the savior, the place which the devil had blocked was immediately relinquished. In praise for the redeemer, the girl cried out that she had swallowed the sacrament that she had been carrying in her mouth. Hence everyone was full of joy and voices were raised in the glory of God because the devil had been expelled, and after 85 days the girl had been freed from the power of the enemy. And so an offering of thanks was again performed for her, and receiving a part of the host, she was restored to her original condition.

While these things were being done, the deacon—urged by the divine spirit—smashed the [immodest] statue of that name, breaking it entirely into dust. And so in this way the divine majesty overcame the cunning trap!

Gregory of Tours

After a certain man . . . had lost his eyesight as a result of a demonic assault, he remained unhappily in his lodging, deprived of light. Unable to work with his own hands, he had no hope of being able to look after himself. Then one night, a man appeared to him in a vision reminding him to go to the church of the blessed [Saint Julian]—and there, if he asked devoutly, the man promised that help would be found. And so, without delay, the blind man took hold of his cane and, with the support of a servant boy, went to the holy place. After he had said his prayer, he approached Publianus, the archpriest who managed the place, begging him to make the sign of the cross of Christ on his blind eyes.

Now Publianus was very pious and avoided the blind man because he did not want to appear to be showing off. But the blind man held on to him and would not let go until he carried out what he sought. So Publianus prostrated himself before the saint's tomb and prayed for a long time for the help of the martyrs. After that, he brought his hand close to the blind man's eyes so that he might make the sign of the cross and as soon as he did, the man's sight was restored.

Wonder—I beg of you—at the power of the martyr! While it may be a small thing for him to perform miracles, nowadays they are worked publicly even through the hands of his disciples, underscoring the goodwill of his power. But the merit of the disciple who is seen to perform these miracles was not inconsiderable. . . .

[Gregory takes some threads from Saint Julian's shroud and takes them to the shrine of Martin of Tours.]

Having placed the most holy relics down upon the altar and he had kept vigil with them through the night, they were transferred to the aforesaid church with a great singing of psalms. And behold: one of the possessed, having struck himself with his hands and spitting blood from his gaping mouth said, "Martin, why have you joined yourself with Julian? Why have you called him forth to this place? Your presence was punishment enough for us. Yet you have called upon someone like you to increase our torments. Why are you doing this? Why are you and Julian tormenting us together in this way?" While the wretched man was shouting these and other things, the ritual of the mass was performed. The man continued to strike himself before the altar for a very long time. But eventually, with blood pouring from his mouth, he was freed from the assaults of his raging devil. . . .

[Aridius, a priest from Limoges,] sent to one of his clerics, saying "Go to the church of the blessed Julian. After saying a prayer, ask that the caretakers condescend to grant you some wax and dust from his tomb so that I may receive them with a blessing when they have been brought here." Coming to the church, the cleric demanded and received what had been commanded of him. But when he tried to carry what he had received he was weighed down with such a weight that he could scarcely raise his neck. Shaken by a great shudder, he laid himself down on the pavement and, in tears, said a prayer once again. He arose unimpaired, understanding that he had been granted the freedom to leave.

Moving slowly down the road, he was seized by thirst on account of the great heat of the sun. Coming to a village by the side of the road, he went to a small cottage asking for water. A youth came out of the cottage to respond but when he saw the cleric and his men, he fell to the ground as if he was dead. At this, the boy's parents ran forth, falsely accusing the men who carried the relics, saying that they had killed the boy by means of their magical arts. The parents took hold of the boy and lifted him up, half alive—but he slipped from their hands. Then the boy clapped his hands together and raging, he began to shout, saying that he was inflamed with the power of Julian the martyr. Hearing this, the cleric placed the small container which contained the holy relics on the boy's head, and, filled with faith, he began to pray diligently. Having vomited blood and ejecting the demon, the boy went away delivered.

After that, the relic bearer, fortified in his faith, spent the entire journey singing psalms and giving thanks—and with the martyr's guidance he came to the desired place. Over the following years, so many demoniacs, fever-stricken people and those afflicted with various other illnesses were healed through the martyr's power that one cannot remember their names or work out how many there were. . . .

After the death of Properius, the keeper of the relics, at the time when deacon Urbanus was ordained caretaker of the church, a wonderful thing appeared at the saint's tomb. While the deacon was lying awake in his bed, he heard a sound as if the front door of the church was being opened. And truly, after the space of many hours, he heard it closed again. At this, he rose from his bed and, with a light in his hand, he approached the tomb of the saint. Wonderful to say! He saw that the pavement was strewn with bright red roses—they were very large and the fragrance of their odor was all-pervading. He was also amazed by the roses woven into the canopy of that enclosure, for it was the ninth month [November] and they were so fresh that you would think them to have been picked from living branches at the moment of that very hour. Then, having gathered up the roses with great reverence, he placed them in a secret place, distributing them as medicine to many sick people from that time forth. For a certain demoniac coming from Tours so that he might take up a draught steeped [in the roses] went away delivered, his demon having been cast out.

Questions: How are objects used in dispossessions? To what extent are possessing demons expelled spontaneously by the presence of these objects? To what extent do they have to be manipulated? What gives these objects their efficacy? What does Publianus's anxiety suggest about his sense of his own power?

63. BAPTISM

While a form of ritual washing had long been a part of Jewish practice, both Saint Paul's letters and Acts show that early Christians had come to adopt a form of these purification rituals on the basis of the precedent of Jesus's baptism in the River Jordan. Baptism established the means by which an initiate would enter the community of the faithful and was therefore central to Christian identity. From very simple beginnings, the rite became progressively more elaborate and complicated over the years, requiring candidates to undergo intensive instruction in the faith before renouncing their old life and entering the new.

John Chrysostom (c. 347–407) was a theologian and skilled preacher—hence his name, meaning golden-mouthed—who rose to become Patriarch of Constantinople. His many surviving homilies are concerned with instructing the faithful and eliminating pagan and other immoral practices in his city. The selection below comes from his second homily on baptism. Greek, 390.

Source: trans. Thomas M. Finn, from John Chrysostom, *Baptismal Homily 2*, in *Early Christian Baptism and Catechumenate*, vol. 1 (Collegeville, MN: Liturgical Press, 1992), pp. 72–78.

Today I am going to speak a few more words to those who have been enrolled among the household of Christ, to teach them the power of the weapons which they are about to receive and the indescribable goodness of the love God shows to the human race. I hope that as a result they may approach him with great faith and confidence and enjoy his generosity more liberally. . . .

Exorcisms

Since you are on the threshold of the time when you are to receive these great gifts, I must now teach you, as far as I can, the meaning of each of the rites, so that you may go from here with knowledge and a more assured faith. So you need to know why it is that after the daily instruction we send you off to hear the words of the exorcists. This rite is neither a simple one nor pointless. You are about to receive the heavenly king into your house. So those who are appointed for this task, just as if they were preparing a house for a royal visit, take you on one side after our sermon, and purify your minds by those fearful words, putting to flight all the tricks of the evil one, and so make the house fit for the presence of the king. For no demon, however fierce and harsh, after these fearful words and the invocation of the universal lord of all things, can refrain from flight with all speed. And, in addition, the rite imprints great reverence in the soul and leads it to great sorrow for sin. . . .

Such is the effect of these marvelous, awesome words and invocations. But something else is made known to us by the outward attitude—the bare feet and the outstretched hands. Just as those who suffer bodily captivity show by the appearance they present their dejection at the disaster that has struck them, so do those men who have been captives of the devil. As they are about to be freed from his tyranny and go beneath the yoke that is easy [see Matt 11.30], first of all they remind themselves by their appearance of their previous situation and try to understand what they are being saved from and what they are hastening to. This then becomes for them a reason for greater gratitude and thankfulness. . . .

Renunciation of Satan and Contract with Christ

I turn now to the sacraments and the covenant between yourself and the lord into which you are about to enter. In business, when a man wishes to entrust his affairs to another, it is necessary for a contract to be signed between the two parties. The same is true now, when the lord of all things is about to entrust to you affairs that are not mortal and passing away and decaying, but spiritual and heavenly. The contract is also called a pledge of faith, since we are doing nothing that can be seen but everything can be discerned by the eyes of the spirit. Meanwhile it is necessary for the contract to be signed, not with ink on paper but with the spirit in God. The words that you pronounce are inscribed in heaven, the agreement spoken by your lips remains indelibly before God.

Now consider once again the posture of captivity. The priests who introduce you first of all tell you to kneel down and pray with your hands raised to heaven, and by this attitude of body recall to your mind the one from whom you have been delivered and the other whom you are about to join. After that the bishop approaches each in turn and demands your contracts and confessions and instructs each one to pronounce those fearful and awesome words, "I renounce you, Satan."

Tears and deep sighs now force themselves upon me. I have recalled the day on which I too was judged worthy to pronounce these words. As I reckon up the weight of the sins which I have gathered from that day to this, I am confused in mind and stung in conscience as I reflect upon the shame with which I have covered myself by my subsequent negligence. And so I beg all of you to show some generosity towards me, and since you are about to approach our king—he will receive you with great alacrity, he will dress you in the royal robe [the white garment] and will grant every kind of gift that you desire, at least if you seek spiritual gifts—beg a favor for me too. Pray that God may not ask an account of my sins but grant me pardon, and for the future count me worthy of his support. I have no doubt that you will do this in your affection for your teachers.

But I must not allow myself to lose the thread of my argument any more. The priest then instructs you to say, "I renounce you, Satan, your pomp, your worship, and your works." There is great power in these few words. For the angels who are present and the invisible powers rejoice at your conversion and, receiving the words from your lips, carry them to the common master of all things, where they are inscribed in the books of heaven.

Have you seen the terms of the contract? After the renunciation of the evil one and all the works he delights in, the priest instructs you to speak again as follows: "And I pledge myself, Christ, to you." Do you see the overwhelming goodness of God? From you he receives only words, yet he entrusts to you realities, a great treasure. He forgets your past ingratitude; he remembers nothing of your past; he is content with these few words.

Questions: How is exorcism incorporated into the baptismal process? Why? To whom are these exorcisms addressed? Who can perform these exorcisms? Do the exorcist's character and moral condition matter? Does baptismal exorcism protect Christians from subsequent demonic action?

64. FORMALIZING DISPOSSESSION

While there developed an office within the ecclesiastical hierarchy that came to specialize in the casting out of demons, it is only from the eighth century that manuscripts containing formal liturgical rites for exorcism survive.

The Ambrosian Rite *from which the first selection is taken is associated with Saint Ambrose, bishop of Milan in the fourth century. Nevertheless, it is unlikely that the rite below was written by him, at least insofar as it is known today. In part, this is because in the eighth century, Charlemagne ordered the rite suppressed and the Gallican rite he favored used universally within the Latin Church. The* Ambrosian Rite's *defenders, though, petitioned the emperor to reconsider his decision, and eventually the advocates for the two rites agreed on a test whereby manuscripts of both rites would be left closed upon the altar of St-Peter in Rome for three days. When both were later discovered open, this was taken as a sign that God approved of both. Nevertheless, suppression of the* Ambrosian Rite *had been such that much of it had to be reconstituted from memory at that time.*

The "Paris Supplement" was originally part of the so-called Gelasian Sacramentary, *likely compiled in the south of France around 750. The association with Pope Gelasius (492–496) is undoubtedly spurious. While the* Sacramentary *does contain an exorcism probably adapted from use during baptism, the exorcism included in the "Supplement" is considerably more involved.*

Ambrosian Rite: *Latin, eighth century?*
"Paris Supplement": Latin, c. 750.

Sources: trans. Richard Raiswell and David R. Winter, from *Manuale ambrosianum*, vol. 2 (Milan, 1904–05), pp. 469–71; trans. Richard Raiswell and David R. Winter, from E. A. Lowe, "Vatican MS of the Gelasian Sacramentary and Its Supplement at Paris," *Journal of Theological Studies* 27.108 (1926): 360–65.

Ambrosian Rite

Almighty lord, the word of God the father, Christ Jesus, God and lord of all creatures, who gave to your holy apostles the power of trampling on serpents and scorpions, who among the other commands of your wonders condescended to say "drive out demons," by whose power Satan was beaten and fell from heaven like lightning, on bended knee I invoke your name with fear and trembling, that having forgiven all my sins, you may condescend to give me—your most unworthy servant—confidence and power so that I can oppose this cruel dragon faithfully and securely, strengthened by the might of your arm.

Prayer: Therefore, I order you, every most unclean spirit, every apparition, every attack of Satan, by the power of the name of Christ—who after baptism in the Jordan was led into the desert and conquered you in your own lands—that you cease to fight against the one who he formed from the mud of the earth for the honor of his glory, and that you come to fear in wretched man not human fragility, but the image of the power of God. Therefore, yield to God who reduced you to servitude in Job, his humbled servant. Yield to God who plunged you and your soldiers in Pharaoh and his army into the abyss through his servant, Moses. Yield to God who betrayed your presence in Bel through his servant Daniel, and struck you down in the dragon. Yield to God who through his most faithful David made you flee from King Saul by means of spiritual songs. Yield to God who damned you in the traitor Judas.

Now he drives you forth by means of divine scourges, in whose sight you—trembling with your legions—shout out, "What is it between us and you, Jesus, son of David? Have you come to torture us before our time?" He drives you with perpetual flames who, at the end of time, will say to the impious, "Go—cursed ones—into the eternal fire which my father prepared for the devil and his angels."

O impious one, the worm that never dies is for you and your angels. An inextinguishable fire has been prepared for you and your angels. For you, O cursed one, are the prince of murder; you are the author of debauchery, the source of sacrilege; you are the master of the worst arts, the teacher of heretics, inventor of all obscenities. Get out, therefore, O impious one. Get out, O criminal. Get out, with all your trickery, because God wants man to be his temple.

But why do you delay so long?

Give honor to almighty God to whom every knee is bent. Give place to Christ Jesus who shed his blood for man. Give place to the holy spirit who—through his blessed apostle Peter—revealed you in Simon, who condemned your trickery in Anania and Saphira, who struck you down in King Herod for not giving honor to God, who—through his apostle Paul—poured forth a mist of blindness on you in the magician Elymas [see doc. 10], and through the same person ordered you in a word to get out from the pythoness.

Therefore, depart now!

Depart seducer, for the desert is your land—the serpent is your habitation. Be humbled. Be prostrated. Now is not the time for wavering, for—behold—the lord and master is near. The fire will burn quickly before him and will burn his enemies all around. You may be able to trick man but you cannot mock God. He—from whose eyes nothing is hidden—casts you out! He—to whose power all things are subject—expels you. He—who has prepared an eternal Gehenna for you and your angels, from whose mouth a double-edged sword will come and who in the holy spirit will judge the world through fire—banishes you.

"Paris Supplement"

Exorcism over the Possessed

Lord God, God of the heavens, God of the angels, God of the archangels, God of the patriarchs, God of the prophets, God of the apostles, God of the martyrs, God of the confessors, God of the virgin, God of all the saints, God of Abraham, God of Isaac, God of Jacob, God who gave us life after death, almighty father, I have invoked you because you are worthy to be invoked. I offer you my fleshly hand. Send your holy spirit from heaven upon your servant [name] so this serpent—the enemy—may not lie hidden. Let him by struck down by the power of your glory as you struck down the two cities, Sodom and Gomorrah. Let that accursed seducer of the world be so struck down.

Reproacher of peoples, snare of death, son of darkness, obey the power and the majesty by which I adjure you. I adjure you by the king of heaven, by Christ the creator, by Jesus the savior of our souls—I adjure you by him, damned one. I do not adjure you by gold, silver, or precious stones. I adjure you by God who stretched out his hand to Peter as he sank [into the water; see Matt. 14. 29–31], and who found you hidden in the tomb. Prostrated, you worshipped him and said to him, "What have we to do with you, Jesus of Nazareth, son of the highest God? You came to destroy us before our time." And, "If you want to destroy us, send us into a herd of swine," and "Whenever we hear your name, we will come out groaning and shaking, and we will honor you."

Honor him, accursed Satan. Take yourself there—into the depths of the sea, into a herd of swine, into the deserted places which are neither plowed nor sown and where the power of his name is not invoked. Take yourself there, damned one. Let your wicked deeds cease. Let your lies cease. Let your alliances cease. Let your machinations cease. Let your pestilences cease. Let your delusions cease. Separate yourself from this form just as heaven was separated from the earth, light from darkness, justice from inequity, life from death. Separate yourself, damned one.

You will not communicate through food or drink, nor come upon him in wakefulness or in sleeping, nor while sitting or walking, nor through silence, not in public nor in private. You will not communicate. You will not do things every day, every third day, or every fourth day. You will not approach people at the intersection of two, three, or four roads. You will not enter the tongue, nor the throat, nor below the throat, nor the smaller nor larger intestine, damned one. Forbidden to you are the twelve hours of the day and the twelve night hours during which times you may not do what you wish.

Bloody multi-shaped mass, persuader of the wicked, accuser of truth, empty shadow, puffed up void, son of darkness, inequity of the angels, you were cast out from heaven, accursed Satan, according to your merits. Most foul of demons, you were defeated, damned one. He defeats you who cannot be defeated. He defeats you, alpha and omega. He defeats you who knows the number of hairs [on the heads] of his servants, male and female, and who knows the number of the stars. He defeats you who made the heaven and the earth, the sea, and everything in them.

He commands you, not by flesh and blood, nor by worldly ostentation. God commands you, father, son, and holy spirit. He commands you who fasted for forty days and forty nights and raised Lazarus from the tomb on the fourth day, and who said to his disciples, "Go in my name. Lay your hands upon them. Drive out demons. Heal the paralyzed. Raise the dead. Let the deaf hear. Let the lame walk. Cure every illness. Give freely because you have received freely" [see Matt. 10.8].

You do nothing with grace. Six thousand years have passed already and it is fitting to have an end of you, most foul of demons. Whether you flee into a herd of swine, into deserted places which are neither plowed nor sown, into your stomach and your breast, terrible one, you cannot evade the punishments that have been prepared for you. They come from the four corners of the world.

I command you by the power of he who opens what no one shuts and shuts what no one opens. I adjure you by the power of him who made the heaven and earth, who gives light to the blind man, hearing to the deaf, and speech to the mute. He commands you, most foul spirit, to whom you said, "make bread from stones." And he who said to you, "man does not live by bread alone but in every word of God." He commands you, accursed Satan, who made water into wine in Cana of Galilee, who fed five thousand men along with a number of women and children from five loaves and two fish and from which meal there were twelve baskets of fragments left over, foreshadowing the twelve apostles.

Obey the great power, the great majesty by which I adjure you. I adjure you by the king of heaven, by Christ the creator, by Jesus the savior of our souls. I adjure you by him, damned one. I adjure you not by gold, silver, or precious stones. I adjure you by God who stretched out his hand to Peter as he sank. Let it become unpleasantly clear that you have been adjured by such great glory and clarity, accursed Satan. You are reduced as this world is reduced as you are being exorcised.

You will not sing; there are no songs for you. I adjure you by the three witnesses. I adjure you by the father, son, and holy spirit so that once you have been exorcised, you will withdraw more quickly from here. Where will you hide when our Lord Jesus Christ descends with his multitude of angels? Four trumpets will sound from the four corners of the world. All the world will burn from east to west. The lord will descend from heaven to destroy the earth, and then the bodies of the saints will appear. Rocks will be moved from their very places and the sun will be turned to blood. And when the lord folds up heaven like a book in his hands, where will you hide, accursed Satan? Surely you will not say that you were not commanded. This should be a sign for you that on the day of judgment you will not be destroyed in eternity.

You came on the wind—go out on the wind. Leave completely. Get out from it as the raven left Noah's ark. Just as it left and did not return so you get out, accused Satan. You do not have a place here—nor rest. Torments upon torments, punishments upon punishments, blows upon blows have been set aside for you. Hot irons have been prepared to punish you with burning lashes according to your merits, accursed Satan.

Most wicked of demons, you should be afraid and tremble—you will not straddle nor impede the sought for life, that is, the life eternal. You will not persuade man to do evil. You will not persuade him to commit adultery. You will not do violence to him. You may not kill him. You may not bring to you the seven more wicked demons who do worse than you [see Matt. 12.45]. You may not resort to enfeebling sufferings in his limbs. You may not occupy that which is not yours. You may not dwell where the holy spirit dwells. I adjure you through our very same lord, Jesus Christ, who will come to judge the living and the dead and this world with fire.

Holy lord, almighty father, eternal God, hosanna on high. Father of our Lord Jesus Christ, you who assigned that tyrant and fugitive to hell, you who sent your only begotten son into this world so that he might crush that bellowing lion, give heed and hurry so you can rescue a man formed by your hands, from ruin and from the noon-day demon [see Ps. 90.6]. Lord, strike your terror upon the beast who destroys your vineyard. Give confidence to your servants so that they can stand firm against this most evil dragon lest he mock those hoping in you—lest he say with Pharaoh who once said, "I knew not God nor will I let Israel go" [Exod. 5.2]. Let your powerful right hand drive him from your servants, lord, so that he may no longer dare to hold captive man who you deemed worthy to make in your own image.

I adjure you, therefore, ancient serpent, by the judge of the living and the dead, by the maker of the world, by him who has the power to send you to hell, that you along with your army of rage leave [name] immediately, this servant of God who is running to the manger of the church. I conjure you—not by my own weakness—but by the power of the holy spirit that you abandon those whom almighty God made in his own image. Surrender—surrender not to me but to the mysteries of Christ. The power of him who subjugated you when he was affixed to his cross compels you. Tremble under his arm, for it is he who conquered the groans of hell and led souls to the light. Be afraid of the body of man. Dread the image of God. You cannot resist, nor delay in abandoning this man, for it has pleased Christ that he reside in man—lest you consider weakness despised.

The lord commands you. The majesty of Christ commands you. God the father commands you. The son and the holy spirit command you. The faith of Saints Peter and Paul and all the other apostles commands you. The blood of the martyrs commands you. The forgiveness of the confessors commands you. The sacrament of the cross commands you. The power of the mysteries commands you.

Get out, transgressor. Get out, seducer, full of tricks and deceit, enemy of truth, persecutor of the innocent. Give place, cruel one. Give place, impious one. Give place to Christ in whom you have found nothing of your works—Christ who stripped you of your power, who destroyed your kingdom, who conquered and bound you, who shattered all your tools, who hurled you into the outer darkness where destruction has been prepared for you and your servants.

Why do you reconsider now, turbulent one? Why do you draw back, reckless one? You are guilty before almighty God whose ordinances you have transgressed. You are guilty before his son, Jesus Christ whom you dared tempt and was emboldened to have crucified. You are guilty before the human race to whom death came as a result of your persuasions.

Therefore, I adjure you, most wicked dragon, in the name of the immaculate lamb who walked on the asp and the basilisk, who trampled the lion and dragon that you leave this man—that you leave the church of God. Tremble and flee. I invoke the name of that lord whom the infernal fear, to whom the heavenly virtues and powers and lordships are subject, whom the cherubim and seraphim praise in unending voice. The word made flesh commands you. He who was born of a virgin commands you. Jesus the Nazarene commands you who, when you mocked his disciples, shattered and humbled your pride and ordered you to leave a certain man. And when he had separated you from that man, you did not even dare to take possession of a herd of swine [without his permission]. Having been adjured, leave this man who God himself formed now. It is hard for you to resist Christ; it is hard for you to kick against the cause of your torture because the more reluctantly you come out the more your punishment grows. It is not a man whom you despise but he who is the ruler of the living and the dead—about whom the universe is silent—he who will come to judge this world with fire.

Nor does it escape you, Satan, that punishments threaten you, that torments threaten you—the day of judgment, the day of eternal punishment, the day which will come like a burning furnace on which the eternal destruction which has been prepared for you and your angels. And so, on account of your wickedness, you damned and future damned one, give honor to the living God. Give honor to Jesus Christ, his son. Whatever you are, unclean spirit, give honor to the holy spirit—the Paraclete—in whose power I command that you get out and leave this servant of God and give him back to his God, since our Lord Jesus Christ has deemed him worthy to be called to his grace and blessing.

We humble petitioners entreat you, lord, that you rouse [name] your servant through your holy blessing and that the adversary not be allowed to go so far as to tempt the soul, as in Job. Place a limit [on his power], lest the enemy begin to conquer his soul itself.

For this reason, therefore, accursed one, recognize your sentence and give honor to the living and true God and withdraw from [name] this servant of God. Therefore, I warn you, accursed one, filthy spirit, enemy of the human race, through God the almighty, invisible, incorruptible, and immortal father, who made heaven, earth, and the sea and all the things in them, that all the power of the adversary, the whole army of the devil, all the attacks of the enemy, and all the phantoms of Satan are eradicated and driven out from [name] this servant of God so that a mixture of contrary virtues may no longer reside in him.

But you, almighty God, be merciful so that those possessed in their bodies by demons may be cleansed of all diabolical wickedness through your power by the sign of the holy cross which we [now] make—that you, accursed devil, never dare violate—through our lord, Jesus Christ who will come in the form of the holy spirit to judge the living and dead and this world through fire.

Lord, holy father almighty, eternal God who does not want to lose sinning souls but would rather erase error, grant mercy to this servant [name] who having been expelled from your face according to his merit of sins is now subjected to the power of Satan. Remember your mercy, and drive out the whole infestation of the enemy and the tribulations of Satan from him. Restore him cleansed to his original undefiled state. May he be the undefiled holy temple he was in baptism. Through our Lord Jesus Christ who will come to judge this world with fire.

Almighty and merciful God, father of our Lord Jesus Christ, we humbly beseech you. Order the devil who possesses your servant [name] to draw back from him and free those who believe in the word of the deliverer, our Lord Jesus Christ, so that purged of all faults, these unworthy ones may devote themselves to your majesty with a pure mind, attending the holy spirit who will live and rule with the father and son forever, amen.

Questions: Do these rituals work ex opere operantis *or* ex opere operato? *What is the importance of the biblical allusions? Of repetition? What is the relationship implied here between the demoniac, exorcist, God, and the possessing demon? Is the exorcist commanding demonic and divine powers? Will this process necessarily work—why or why not?*

65. PROTECTION AND CHARMS AGAINST DEMONIC INCURSIONS

That Saint Benedict (c. 480–547) declared in his Rule for Monks *that provision must be made for the care of the sick in a monastery meant that the Middle Ages kept alive Antiquity's interest in the therapeutic uses of plants. Monasteries tended to have gardens in which plants were grown for their curative powers, and monks produced manuscripts that described their uses. Some of these plants—taken either individually or in combination—were also believed to have properties that might stifle, neutralize, or even eliminate demonic affliction and possession.*

Leechbook III, from which the selection below is taken, exists in a single copy, bound with two other leechbooks that the manuscript associates with an otherwise unknown man named "Bald." Unlike these other two texts which show the influence of continental Latin sources, scholars have argued that Leechbook III *likely better reflects contemporary Anglo-Saxon medical practice, for the remedies it describes draw upon only ingredients that would have been available in England, and they are given in the text according to their native names.*

Hildegard of Bingen (1098–1179), abbess of Rupertsberg, was one of the most accomplished women of the twelfth century. From a young age, she received visions that later came to be the subject of several treatises and established her reputation as a prophet with some of the most important ecclesiastical and secular figures of the day. The selection below comes from her Subtleties of the Divine Qualities of Created Things *(better known now as the* Physica, *or* Medicine*) and details the various properties bestowed by God in created things and their uses. The offerings below come from section 1, dealing with plants, and section 4 on stones.*

Leechbook III: *Old English, mid tenth century?*
Hildegard: *Latin, between 1151 and 1158.*

Sources: trans. T. O. Cockayne, in *Leechdoms, Wortcunning, and Starcraft of Early England*, vol. 3 (London, 1864), pp. 307, 335, 349–57, rev.; trans. Priscilla Throop, *Hildegard von Bingen's Physica: Complete English Trans of her Classic Work on Health and Healing* (Rochester, VT: Healing Arts Press, 1998), pp. 29–30, 119, 142–43, 148.

Leechbook III

Work a good drink against all temptations of the devil [in this way]. Take betony, bishopwort, lupins, githrife, attorlothe, wolfscomb, [and] yarrow. Lay them under the altar [and then] sing nine masses over them. Scrape the herbs into holy water. Give a full cup [to the afflicted person] to drink at night [after he has been] fasting, and put the holy water into all the food which the person eats. Work [in this way] a good salve against the temptations of the fiend: [take] bishopwort, lupin, vipers bugloss, strawberry stalk, the cloven wenwort, earth rime, blackberry, pennyroyal[, and] wormwood. Pound all the herbs [and then] boil them in good butter. Wring [them] through a cloth [and then] set them under the altar. Sing nine masses over them. [Then] smear the man with the mixture on the temples, and above the eyes, and on the head, and the breast, and the sides under the arms. This salve is very good for every temptation of the fiend, and for a man full of elfin tricks, and for spring fever. . . .

Work a salve against the elfin race and nightgoers, and for the people with whom the devil has intercourse [in this way]. Take the ewe [female] hop plant, wormwood, bishopwort, lupin, ashthroat, henbane, harewort, vipers bugloss, heathberry plants, cropleek, garlic, grains of hedgerife, githrife, fennel. Put these herbs into a vessel [and] set [them] under the altar. Sing nine masses over them [and then] boil [them] in butter and sheep's grease. Add a large amount of holy salt. Strain through a cloth, [and then] throw the herbs into running water. If any evil temptation occur to a man, or an elf or a nightgoer [should come], smear his face with this salve, and put it on his eyes, and where his body hurts, and cense him with incense, and sign him frequently with the sign of the cross. His condition will soon be better.

Write this [Latin] writing: It is written, king of kings and lord of lords, Veronica, Veronica, lurlure[?], iehe [?], aius, aius, aius [holy, holy, holy in transliterated Greek], holy, holy, holy, lord, God the ruler of all. Amen. Alleluia." Sing this over the drink and the writing, "Almighty God, father of our Lord Jesus Christ, through the application of this writing expel from your servant [insert name], every attack of castalides [elves] from the head, from the hair, from the brain, from the forehead, from the tongue, from under the tongue, from the throat, from the neck, from the teeth, from the eyes, from nostrils, from the ears, from the hands, from the neck, from arms, from the heart, from the mind, from the knees, from the thighs, from the feet, from the joints of all limbs—both internal and external. Amen." Then make up a drink [using] font water, rue, sage, hassock, dragonwort, the lower part of the smooth plantain, feverfew, a head of dill, three cloves of garlic, fennel, wormwood, lovage, [and] lupin in equal quantities. Write a cross three times with the oil of unction, and say [in Latin], "Peace be with you." Then take the writing, draw a cross with it over the drink and sing this [in Latin] over it, "Almighty lord, father of our Lord Jesus Christ, though the application of this writing and through its taste, expel the devil from your servant [insert name]," and [then say] the Credo and Paternoster. Wet the writing in the drink and write a cross with it on every limb and say, "may the sign of Christ's cross maintain you in eternal life. Amen." If you do not want [to do this], have [the man] himself or whoever is his closest relation [do it], and let him cross him as well as he can. This remedy is powerful against every temptation of the fiend.

A mild drink against a devil and dementedness. Put hassock, roots of lupin, fennel, ontre, betony, hindheal, marche, rue, wormwood, nepeta, helenium, elfthone, wolf's comb into ale. Sing twelve masses over the drink, and let [the patient] drink [it]. It will soon be well with him. A drink against temptations of the devil: [take] tuftythorn, cropleek, lupin, ontre, bishopwort, fennel, hassock, betony. Bless these plants. Put [them] into some holy water mixed with ale, and keep the drink therein where the sick person is, and every time before he drinks [it] sing [in Latin], "God! Save me in your name," three times over the drink.

Hildegard of Bingen

Fern is very hot and dry and has a little bit of juice in it. It holds within itself great power, namely such a power that the devil flees from it [another manuscript adds: and it even has certain energy which is like the power of the sun. As the sun lights up dark places, so the fern chases away apparitions, and evil spirits disdain it.] In the place where it grows, the devil rarely practices his deceptions. The fern avoids and shrinks back from any home or place where the devil resides. Thunder, lightning, and hail rarely fall near a home where there is fern. Hail also rarely falls in the field where it is growing. Magic and incantations of demons—as well as diabolic words and other phantasms—avoid a person who carries a fern with him. If any image is prepared for carrying out injury or death, it is not able to harm one who has a fern with him. For a person is sometimes reviled through an image in such a way that he is harmed by it and becomes mad.

In paradise, when the devil drew the human being to himself, a certain sign was made on the devil to remain on him, as a reminder, until the last day. When a person invokes the devil by some words, through which his deceptions are accomplished, the sign is touched. He is often invoked to injure a person, or to fulfil the will of a person over whom the words are spoken. Sometimes a person is blessed by the image which was made, and it furnishes him with prosperity and health. However, hatred and envy make evil, and evil is joined to evil. The wickedness of the devil always lies in wait for a person—looking at what evil has accumulated in him—and adds to it.

A human being has both good and evil knowledge, and good and bad herbs were created for him. Fern sap has been placed for knowledge, and in its honest nature, goodness and holiness are signified. All evil and magic things flee and avoid it. In whatever house it is, poison and phantoms are not able to complete their work. Whence, when a woman gives birth to a child, fern is placed around her, even around the infant in his cradle. The devil besieges the infant less since, when he first looks at the infant's face, he hates him intensely. . . .

Sapphire is hot and develops after noontime, when the sun burns ardently and the air is a bit obstructed by its heat. The splendor of the sun, from the extreme heat that it has, pierces through the air. The splendor is not as full as it is when the air is a bit cool. Sapphire is turbid, indeed, more fiery than airy or watery. It symbolizes a complete love of wisdom. . . .

If a person is in the power of an evil spirit, another person should place a sapphire on some earth, then sew that earth into a leather sack, and hang it from his neck. He should say, "O you, most wicked spirit, quickly go from this person, just as, in your first fall, the glory of your splendor very quickly fell from you." The evil spirit will be greatly tortured. He will depart from that person, who will be better, unless it is a very cruel and most good-for-nothing spirit.

If the devil should incite a man to love a woman so that, without magic or invocations of demons, he begins to be insane with this love, and if this is an annoyance to the woman, she should pour a bit of wine over a sapphire three times and each time say, "I pour this wine, in its ardent powers, over you; just as God drew off your splendor, wayward angel, so may you draw away from me the lust of this ardent man." If the woman is unwilling to do this, then another person for whom that love is a problem should do it for her. He should give the wine to the man to drink for three or more days, whether he's eating or not, and whether he knows about it or not. If a woman burns with love for some man, and this is an annoyance to the man, he should do the same thing with the sapphire and the wine, and the burning passion will go away. . . .

Questions: In what ways does demonic affliction overlap with disease? Are there differences? How do these adjurations differ from either baptismal or liturgical exorcisms? Do they have any similarities? How many of these remedies necessitate the involvement of clergy? Are these remedies magical? Why—or why not?

66. BREAKING THE DEVIL'S HOLD

In addition to exorcism, the Church wielded the sacrament of confession as a remedy for demon possession. This is a ritual in which a penitent orally acknowledges sins to an ordained priest. The priest would assess the severity of the faults, command a penance (that is, a form of compensation), and then, with the formal words "ego te absolvo" (I absolve you), grant absolution. Medieval Christians considered confession a powerful tool against evil.

Below you will find stories about the power of the sacrament of confession to frustrate the devil. They are taken from two separate "exempla" collections. Exempla were lively and interesting narratives that were used by medieval preachers to illustrate their sermons. See also docs. 80–83.

The first story comes from Stephen of Bourbon's Treatise on Various Matters for Preaching. *Stephen was a Dominican friar and inquisitor. Trained at the University of Paris, he spent much of his career preaching against the Cathars and Waldensians throughout*

SEVEN: VARIETIES OF POSSESSION AND EXORCISM

southeastern France. In this capacity, he seems also to have been involved in the examination and sentencing of heretics.

The second is taken from an anonymous collection called the Durham Example Book, *written at the end of the thirteenth century by a cleric in the north of England. The Franciscan author claims to have heard this frightening tale from people who were close to the events described.*

Stephen of Bourbon: *Latin, between 1250 and 1261.*
Durham Example Book: *Latin, c. 1277.*

Sources: trans. Richard Raiswell and David R. Winter, from Étienne de Bourbon, *Anecdotes historiques, légendes et apologues tirés du Recueil Inédit d'Étienne de Bourbon* (Paris: Renouard, 1877), pp. 198–99; trans. Richard Raiswell and David R. Winter, from *Liber exemplorum ad usum praedicantium* (*The Durham Example Book*), no. 95, pp. 51–53.

Stephen of Bourbon

[This] section concerns the confession of sins which takes place when the soul—having been enlightened by the gift of wisdom—recognizes the wounds to its heart and the dangerous sickness of its sins, and fearing that these things will lead to eternal death a man hastens to a spiritual physician, revealing these matters to him so that he may be freed through his counsel.

The numerous inconveniences of our enemies and the troubles which follow for them from the confession of our sins ought to remind us of the importance of confessing. Confession erases what has been written by the devil.

Note that when a certain most holy cleric was alive, the devil regarded him enviously, procuring and working for his temptation so that the man might fall into grave sin. The devil wanted to shame the cleric and so, having assumed human form, he accused the cleric before his bishop, and a day was assigned on which the devil was to prove what he had said, bringing before the judge his documents recording the place, time and persons through which the cleric had sinned. The aforesaid cleric, finding himself in a difficult position, confessed everything, weeping and resolving not to return to his sins. When they came before the judge, the devil said that he had many contrary things against the cleric which he could prove through the documents and witnesses he had brought with him. Unrolling his documents, though, he found everything there erased. "Assuredly," he said, "everything which I had against him was written on this earlier today—I don't know who erased all these things." Having said this, he vanished. The cleric had told all these things to the bishop in secret confession.

It is said that when a certain sacristan of a certain abbey awoke in order to ring for Matins he saw a devil carrying a full sack and a book in his hand. When the aforesaid sacristan asked who he was, the devil said that he was the inspector of the offices who made monks stay awake in the dormitory, sleep in the church, and make wicked signs and spew crumbs in the refectory. The sack which he carried, he said, was full of such instances and the book which he bore detailed the neglect of the brothers. But above all things, he said, he hated the chapter house because he often lost everything which he had worked to achieve in the chapter house as a result of confessions, accusations, and penances done there.

Durham Example Book

Concerning confession, there are [several] examples, and they should not be passed over in silence. I place the one that follows first because you will be fully assured by it. . . .

[Once, a bailiff went] alone from one village to another. While he was on the road, he saw in the distance a horrible beast coming toward him. It was so fearsome that he knew immediately that it was the devil in the form of a horrible beast. Thus, he stood there shaking in such great fear so that he was almost taken out of himself. Thinking about what he should do, the light of faith aided him. Acknowledging that he was a sinner, he immediately took the ax that he had in his hand and made a circle around himself in signs of Christ's cross. Despite this, he thought and feared that, on account of his sins, he would be turned over to the power of the devil, and he well knew that, without the help of God, he would not be able to escape the devil.

Understanding, however, that God is merciful, and more ready to show pity than to condemn, he called out to the lord, saying: "Lord, I do not have a priest to whom I can confess my sins. I promise you that I will renounce my sins. Having no other refuge for my faults, I will confess now [directly to you] until I am able to find a priest." He went on, "Lord, I did this and this, such and such." And in this manner he confessed his sins directly to God—as if he were actually in the lord's presence.

And behold, what a marvelous and delightful thing to relate! As soon as he confessed one of his sins, a wall immediately began to grow up on the ground around him. When he confessed another sin, the wall grew a little higher. When he confessed a third sin, it rose up higher still. Thus, little by little, as he continued his confession, the wall grew by divine goodness to the point where, when his confession was complete, the wall was so high all around him that he was able to stand inside it as if it were a very strong tower.

Despite this, he was still so stricken with terror that he did not feel secure in his own heart. No wonder! For in the beginning, when, through the merit of his faith, his penitence, and his confession, he had made the wall begin to rise up, the devil came in that horrible form, and tried with all his might to attack the wall! But as he cried out and continued his [unfinished and imperfect] confession, the devil tried furiously to climb over the unfinished wall; however, on account of God's goodness, he fell backwards. Despite this, the devil tried the same attack again, but, as he attempted to climb over the wall, it grew higher than ever before. The poor fellow inside the wall cried out and almost breathed his last breath at such a terrifying sight! However, just as before, the devil fell down backwards. The devil made repeated charges and attacks on the wall in order to get at the wretch standing within, but the wall continued to grow and each time he attacked, God's goodness repelled the devil and pushed him away.

The wretched man stood there, in his anguish, until the break of day. But after the wall reached its full height, the devil, who could do nothing else, jumped to the top of the wall and raised up his extraordinarily hideous head, so that, in this way, he could confound the man with terror. The poor man was in such fear and terror throughout the whole night that he made so many vows and promises to God that it would be almost impossible for anyone to fulfil them. This is because he would have had to live his life in the most abject poverty, toil, and anguish that it is possible to imagine, that is, if he even managed to have a life, rather than enduring another night such as this one.

Therefore, Christian, see now how much power a true confession made to a priest, according to the order of the church, has against the devil, if this confession, made to God in the middle of a field, was so very powerful against him. Indeed, that confession had no value apart from the fact that the man had good will and the correct intention of confessing his sins in the proper way and amending his life according to the will of God. . . .

[These events] occurred near Dublin, and the man to whom these things happened was at that time the bailiff of Turvey.

Questions: What is sin? What is confession? Does it differ from other adjurations, charms, devices, and rituals intended to protect people again the devil's incursions? To what extent is the devil as he is reflected in these stories a product of the more mercantile orientation of society by this time? Why might the author have chosen to present his arguments in the form of anecdotes?

67. DIVINE POSSESSION, GENDER, AND POLITICS

Birgitta (Bridget) of Sweden (c. 1303–73) was the daughter of wealthy landowners. After the death of her husband when she was in her early forties, Birgitta began to receive a series of "revelations" during which Christ and the Virgin Mary spoke to her, summoning her to be Christ's bride and intermediary. According to Birgitta, she wrote down these revelations in her own hand in her native Swedish shortly after they came to her. They were subsequently translated into Latin by her confessors and read back to her to ensure that they had been accurately recorded.

Against the backdrop of turmoil engulfing Sweden and other nations at this time, many of these revelations had a decidedly political edge to them. Many were critical of the state of the Church and demanded ecclesiastical reform, political change, and the return of the papacy to its traditional home. By itself, this content would have made her revelations controversial to those invested in the status quo. But her gender, the way in which her revelations were given to her, and the fact that they were often couched in imagery lifted from feminine experience further complicated their reception for a fourteenth-century audience. Even Birgitta seems to have worried about them, for perhaps tellingly, the revelatory spirits that seized her heart repeatedly explained why they could not be demonic.

Birgitta received more than 700 revelations during her lifetime. These were collected as The Book of Heavenly Things *after her death and used during the canonization process. The following selections come from that work. Dates for individual revelations are given.*

Latin, c. 1377.

Source: trans. Denis Searby, *The Revelations of Saint Birgitta of Sweden*, vols. 1 and 3 (Oxford: University Press, 2006–15), vol. 1.145–46, 149–51; 3.126–27, 155–56, 264–65.

1340s

Then the lord spoke to the bride [Birgitta]: "Tell your friend that he should take care to set forth these words in writing to his own father [Master Mathias of Linköping], whose heart is according to my heart, and he will convey them to the archbishop [of Uppsala] and later to another bishop. When these have been thoroughly informed, he should send them to a third bishop. . . . Make the words of my mouth publicly known and bring them personally to the head of the church! I shall give you my spirit so that, wherever there be dissension between two persons, you will be able to unite them in my name and through the power given to you, if they but believe. As further evidence of my words, you shall present to the pontiff the testimonies of those people who taste delight in my words. For my words are like lard that melts more quickly the warmer one is inside. Where there is no warmth, it is rejected and does not reach the inmost parts.

1340s

An angel spoke to the bride saying: "There are two spirits, one uncreated, one created. The uncreated has three characteristics. In the first place, he is hot, in the second, sweet, in the third, clean. First, he gives off heat not from created things but from himself, since, together with the father and the son, he is creator of all things and almighty. He gives off heat whenever the whole soul burns for the love of God. Second, he is sweet, whenever nothing pleases the soul or delights it but God and the recollection of his works. Third, he is clean and in him can be found no sin, no deformity, no corruption, or mutability. He does not give off heat like material fire or like the visible sun making things melt. His heat is rather the internal love and desire of the soul that fills her and engrosses her in God. He is sweet to the soul, not in the way that choice wine or sensual pleasure or anything in the world is sweet. Rather, the sweetness of the spirit is incomparable to every temporal sweetness and unimaginable to those who have not tasted it. Third, the spirit is as clean as the rays of the sun in which no blemish can be found.

The second, created spirit likewise has three characteristics. He is burning, bitter, and unclean. First, he burns and consumes like fire, inasmuch as he enkindles the soul he possesses with the fire of lust and depraved desire, so that the soul can neither think nor desire anything other than satisfying this desire, to such an extent that her temporal life is sometimes lost along with all honor and consolation as a result. Second, he is as bitter as bile, inasmuch as he so inflames the soul with his lust that future joys seem like nothing to her and eternal goods but foolishness. Everything that has to do with God and which the soul is bound to do for him turns bitter and is as abominable to her as vomit and bile. Third, he is unclean, since he renders the soul so vile and prone to sin that she does not blush for any sin, and she would not desist from any sin, if she did not have fear being shamed before other people more than before God.

That is why this spirit burns like fire, because he burns for iniquity and enkindles others along with itself. That is why this spirit is bitter indeed, because every good is bitter to him and he wants to make the good bitter for others as well as for himself. That is why, again, he is unclean, because he delights in filth and seeks to make others like himself.

How you might ask me and say: 'Are you not also a created spirit such as that one? Why are you not like that?' I answer you: Of course I am created, by that same God who also created the other spirit, since there is only one God. . . . Both of us were well made and created for the good, since God has created nothing but good. But I am like a star, since I have stood fast in the goodness and love of God in which I was created. . . . The devil is like ugly coal and is uglier than any other creature, because, just as he was more beautiful than the others, he had to be made uglier than others, because he opposed the creator. Just as God's angel shines with God's light and burns incessantly in his love, so the devil is ever burning in the anguish of his malice. His malice is insatiable, just as the grace and goodness of the holy spirit is ineffable. For there is no one in the world so rooted in the devil that the good spirit does not at times visit and move his heart. Likewise, there is no one so good that the devil does not try to touch with temptation. Many good and just people are tempted by the devil with God's permission. This is not because of wickedness on their part but for their greater glory . . . many good people sometimes fall into sin, and their conscience darkened through the devil's falsehood. . . . However, there is nobody who does not realize this in his conscience, whether the suggestion of the devil leads to the deformity of sin or to the good, if he would only think about and examine it carefully.

And so, bride of my lord, you do not have to be in doubt as to whether the spirit of your thoughts is good or bad. For your conscience tells you which things to ignore and which to choose."

1348

The son speaks to the bride: "Write the following words on my part to Pope Clement [VI]: I exalted you and let you ascend through all the ranks of honor. Rise up and establish peace between the kings of France and England, who are like dangerous beasts, betrayers of souls. Then come to Italy and preach the word there and proclaim a year of salvation and divine love [a jubilee year]! Look on the streets paved with the blood of my saints, and I shall give you an everlasting reward. Think of times past when you had the audacity to provoke my anger, and I kept silent, when you did what you wanted and what you should not have done, and I was patient, as though I did not hear. Indeed, my time approaches, and I shall require an account of you for the negligence and audacity of your time. In the same way as I let you ascend through the ranks, you will descend through other ranks that you will truly experience in soul and body, unless you obey my words. Your grandiloquent tongue will be silent. The name by which you are called on earth will be held in oblivion and reproach before me and my saints. I shall require an account of you as to how unworthily you rose through the ranks, though it was with my permission, which I, God, know better than your negligent conscience can recall. I shall seek an account from you with regard to your lukewarmness in re-establishing peace between the kings [of England and France] and your preferential treatment of one of the two parties [the French]. Moreover, it shall not be forgotten how greed and ambition flourished and increased in the church during your time, or that you could have reformed and set many things right but that you, lover of the flesh, were unwilling. Get up, therefore, before your fast approaching final hour arrives, and extinguish the negligence of your past by being zealous in your nearly final hour!

If you are in doubt about to which spirits these words belong, that kingdom and that person are well known in which amazement and wonders have been wrought. The justice and mercy of which I speak are drawing near everywhere on earth. Your own conscience tells you that my exhortation is rational and my proposal charitable. Had you not been saved by my patience, you should have descended lower than all your predecessors. Examine, then, the book of your conscience and see if I am telling the truth!

1340s

On Christmas night such a great and wonderful feeling of exultation came to the bride of Christ in her heart that she could scarcely contain herself in joy. At that very moment she felt a wonderful sensible movement in her heart like that of a living child turning and turning around. When this movement lasted, she disclosed it to her spiritual father and certain spiritual friends in case it might be an illusion. By sight and touch they marveled at the truth of it. At high mass on the same day, God's mother appeared to the bride and said, "Daughter, you are marveling at the movement you feel in your heart. Be assured that it is no illusion but shows a similarity to my own delight and to the mercy done to me. Just as you do not know how this feeling of exultation came so suddenly to your heart, so too my son's coming to me was wonderful and swift. As soon as I gave my consent to the angel who announced to me the conception of God's son, I immediately felt something wonderful and alive in me. When he was born from me, he came forth from my untouched virginal womb with an indescribable feeling of exultation and a wonderful swiftness. Therefore, my daughter, do not fear that it is an illusion. Instead be thankful that this movement that you feel is a sign of the coming of my son into your heart. As my son has called you his new bride, so I call you now my daughter-in-law who belongs to my son. When a father and mother grow old and inactive, they give their daughter-in-law work to do and tell her what has to be done in the house. Similarly, now that God and I have grown old in human hearts and their charity is cold toward us, we want to indicate our intentions to our friends and to the world through you. The movement in your heart will continue in you and grow according to the capacity of her heart.

Questions: What symptoms does she manifest in her visions? Do these differ from those of possession? Are her revelations intended to be private? Why is it necessary for her to assert the orthodoxy of her visions? How might the reception of her revelations have been affected by their content?

CHAPTER EIGHT

DEMONIZATIONS

Figure 8.1 Olaus Magnus, "On Nocturnal Dance of Elves—that is, Specters," from *Historia de gentibus septentrionalibus* (1555), p. 112. This illustration is part of the third section of *Description of the Northern Peoples* by the Swede Olaus Magnus (1490–1557), which deals with what he calls their "superstitious worship of demons." While the work was one of the most detailed and influential accounts of Scandinavia and beyond of its day, as archbishop of Uppsala, Olaus showed little interest in understanding the traditional beliefs of northerners on their own terms.

EIGHT: DEMONIZATIONS

The process of demonization, particularly of Jews and non-Christians, was an integral dynamic of early Christian self-definition (Chapter 3). By defining the faithful in moral rather than in ethnic, national, or cultural terms, Christianity quickly came to construe itself as a community of the good juxtaposed against a hostile world dominated by people in the service of the devil. Tolerance toward difference (either outside or inside the community of the faithful) was morally unacceptable. To negotiate with the devil, after all, was to recognize the authority of another lord beyond that of God.

But while Christianity was firmly established as the dominant religion of western Europe by the High Middle Ages, this dynamic of demonization made the reinvigorated, increasingly more centralized Church that emerged from the reforms of the eleventh century acutely sensitive to deviation and diversity. As a result, Europe's demonized "others"—Jews, idolaters, heretics, and those whose actions otherwise challenged accepted standards of order and conduct—could sometimes find themselves the focus of what modern sociologists have dubbed "moral panics," intimate enemies, secretly subverting society in the service of the devil from the inside through their secret, nefarious rites and rituals. When social tension escalated into violence against such groups, as it periodically did, demonization justified appalling acts of brutality—particularly when reinforced by rumor, popular preaching, or the activities of inquisitors. Such acts were part of a pious purification by the righteous, a process necessary to protect the community of the faithful from contamination. The process was analogous to exorcism—a casting out of society's demons.

Outside the bounds of Christendom, demonization also helped Christians make sense of the rise and military success of Islam, and later the Mongols, turning them into harbingers of the apocalypse and tying them to the lost tribes of Gog and Magog described in Revelation 20.7 (doc. 11) as part of Satan's forces during the end times.

These demonizations of the High Middle Ages expanded the devil's perceived field of action once more, causing him to be found not only underlying the activities of those who had been demonized from the Church's earliest period but also lurking behind new social movements critiquing or seeking to modify existing structures within Christendom. Many of the new powers detected in this period would come to condition the thinking of the demonologists of the fifteenth and sixteenth centuries as they strove to root out women and men they believed acted in a vast Satanic conspiracy to destroy the Christian world.

68. THE ORIGINS OF ISLAM

The anonymous Tultu sceptrum *survives only in a single manuscript, dating from either the late tenth or eleventh century, although the story is likely older. In its construction, it draws heavily on Ezekiel 2, which sees the eponymous Hebrew prophet charged by God with spreading his word to the Israelites, who are described as having become a "rebellious nation." However, whoever wrote the text seems to have had more than a passing familiarity with Islam: the name "Ozim" is likely a variant of "Hashim," the name of Muhammad's clan; the appearance of the wicked angel echoes the description of the appearance of Gabriel in Muhammad's second revelation; and the invocation that Ozim is tricked into teaching the Arabs might be a transliteration of the* takbīr *(Allahu akbar—God is the greatest) and the* shahada *(muhammadun rasūlu llāh—Muhammad is the messenger of God). Latin, tenth century?*

Source: trans. Richard Raiswell and David R. Winter, from *Tultu sceptrum de libro domini Metobii*, from *Corpus scriptorum Muzarabicorum*, vol. 2 (Madrid: Instituto Antonio de Nebrija, 1973), pp. 709–10.

Father Bishop Osius saw an angel of the lord, speaking to him, and the angel said to him, "Go and speak to my governors who remain in Erribon [Medina]. Those to whom I am sending you are a rebellious people who have been given over to the north-west wind; they have a hard face and obstinate heart like those living in the desert. Their fathers have revolted from me. They have broken my covenant. Their sons sully my name in impurity and false dealing. But go and say to them, 'He who hears, let him hear, and he who rests, let him rest, for the house of the lord has been angered.' And say to them, 'Do not be unbelievers—be believers, instead.'["]

But while the bishop was leaving to preach the words of the lord to this people, he was struck ill and called by the lord. But before he died, he instructed one of his monks whose name was Ozim to proceed to Erribon so that he might speak the words the angel of the lord had taught father Bishop Osius to speak to them. When he had heard the words of his teacher which the angel of the lord had taught the bishop, the boy—whose name was Ozim—set out so that he might teach the governors of the people to whom he had been appointed.

As he was coming to Erribon, he found an angel of temptation resembling the other [earlier] angel resting in an oak tree. This evil angel who stood before him said to him, "What are you called?" He replied, "I am called Ozim. I was sent by my teacher, Father Osius, so that I might teach the words which he spoke to me, which the angel of the lord instructed him to speak to this people. However, the angel found him [Osius] on the day of his calling and now his spirit has been called to the heavenly kingdom."

After he had said that, the evil angel said to him, "I am the angel who was sent to Father Bishop Osius. I will tell you the words which you should preach to those governors to whom you were sent." Then he said to him, "You are not called Ozim—rather, you are Muhammad." And the angel who revealed himself to the boy and assigned this name to him taught him to say "Alla occuber Alla occuber + situleilacitus est + Mahamet razulille" [the Muslim call to prayer beginning *Allahu akbar*?] so that they might believe.

But the monk did not know that this phrase invoked demons. Because every "Alla occuber" is an invocation of demons, his heart had already been turned by an evil spirit, and the words which the lord had told him through his teacher were lost to oblivion. And what was a vessel of Christ was made into a vessel of the world and the damnation of his soul. And all those converted by this error and those who were seduced through his persuasion are named among the ranks of hell.

Questions: Where does Islam come from? What is the role of the second angel here? How is this angel different from that in the story of Balaam and the ass (doc. 3)? Does the monk know what he is doing? What does this anecdote suggest about how the author sees the relationship of Christianity to Islam?

69. A SCHOLAR EXPLAINS ISLAM

Peter the Venerable (c. 1092–1156) rose to become abbot of the renowned Benedictine abbey at Cluny in France in 1122. As abbot, Peter oversaw the discipline of many of Cluny's dependent houses, and it was while he was on his way to inspect Spanish Cluniac monasteries and to meet with Alfonso VII, king of Castile and León (r. 1126–57) in 1142 that he developed his interest in Islam. At that time, Alfonso was engaged in a siege of the Muslim city of Coria—part of the movement now often described as the reconquista. But while Cluny had initially embraced Pope Urban II's call to holy war in 1095, Peter found the notion problematic. He resolved instead to develop a new, rationalist attack on Islam through the translation and study of the Qur'an and other Muslim texts. The selection below sought to supply a Christian readership with accurate information about the history and tenets of Islam, its difference from Christianity, and its place within divine history.
    Latin, 1143.

Source: trans. Irven M. Resnick, from Peter the Venerable, *A Summary of the Entire Heresy of the Saracens*, in *Writings Against the Saracens* (Washington, DC: Catholic University of America Press, 2016), pp. 34–50.

This is a summary of the entire heresy and of the diabolical teaching of the Saracens, that is, the Ishmaelites. First and foremost, their first and greatest error that ought to be cursed is that they deny the trinity in the unity of the deity....

Furthermore, these blind ones deny that God the creator is the father, because, according to them, no one becomes a father without sexual intercourse. And although they accept that Christ was conceived from a divine spirit, they do not believe that he is the son of God nor, moreover, that he is God, but that he is a good, most truthful prophet, free from all deceit and sin, the son of Mary, begotten without a father; he never died, because he did not deserve death—instead, although the Jews wanted to slay him, he slipped through their hands, ascended to the stars, and lives there now in the flesh in the presence of the creator, until the advent of the Antichrist. When the Antichrist comes, this same Christ will slay him himself with the sword of his virtue, and he will convert the remaining Jews to his law. Moreover, he will teach his law perfectly to the Christians, who a long time ago lost his law and Gospel owing, on the one hand, to his departure, and on the other hand owing to the death of the apostles and disciples, by which [law] all Christians at that time will be saved, just like his first disciples. Even Christ himself will die with them and with all creatures at one and the same time, when Seraphim—who they say is one archangel—sounds the trumpet; and afterward he will rise with the rest, and he will lead his disciples to judgment, and he will assist them and pray for them, but he will not himself judge them. Indeed, God alone will judge. . . . Thus, to be sure, the most wretched and impious Muhammad has taught them, he who, denying all the sacraments of Christian piety by which men are especially saved, has condemned already nearly a third of the human race to the devil and to eternal death with the unheard of foolishness of fables—by what judgment of God, we do not know.

It seems that one must speak about who he [Muhammad] was, and what he taught, for the sake of those who will read that book, so that they might better understand what they read, and come to know how detestable both his life and teaching were. . . .

This one [Muhammad] . . . lived during the age of the Emperor Heraclius, a little after the time of the great Roman pope, Gregory I, almost 550 years ago; he was one who was of the Arab nation, of low birth, at first a worshipper of the old idolatry—just as the other Arabs still were at that time—unlearned, nearly illiterate, active in business affairs, and, being very shrewd, he advanced from low birth and from poverty to riches and fame. And here, increasing little by little, and by frequently attacking neighbors and especially those related to him by blood with ambushes, robberies, and incursions—killing by stealth those whom he could, and killing publicly those whom he could—he increased fear of him, and because he often came out on top in these encounters, he began to aspire to kingship over his race.

And when, with everyone equally resisting [him] and condemning his low birth, he saw that he could not pursue this path for himself as he had hoped, he attempted to become king under the cloak of religion and under the name of a divine prophet, because he was unable to do so by the power of the sword. And since he lived as a barbarian among barbarians, and as an idolater among idolaters, and among those who, more than all races, were unacquainted with and ignorant of law both human and divine, he knew that they were easy to seduce, and he began to undertake the iniquitous task he had conceived. And since he had heard that God's prophets were great men, and saying that he is his prophet so as to pretend to be something good, he attempted to lead them partly away from idolatry, yet not to the true God but rather to his own false heresy, which he had already begun to bring forth.

Meanwhile, with the judgment of him [God] . . . Satan bestowed success upon error, and he sent the monk Sergius, a sectarian follower of the heretical Nestorius, who had been expelled from the Church, to those parts of Arabia, and united the monk heretic with the false prophet. Accordingly Sergius joined with Muhammad, supplied what he lacked and, explicating for him the sacred scriptures—of both the Old and the New Testament—in accord with the understanding of his master, Nestorius, who denied that our savior is God, [and] partly in accord with his own conception, and at the same time completely filling him up with fables from apocryphal books, he made him into a Nestorian Christian.

And, in order that the complete fullness of iniquity should coalesce in Muhammad, and so that nothing should be lacking for his damnation or for that of others, Jews were joined to the heretic, and lest he become a true Christian, the Jews whispered to Muhammad, shrewdly providing to the man who was eager for novelties not the truth of the scriptures but their fables, which still today they have in abundance. And in this way, taught by the best Jewish and heretical teachers, Muhammad created his Qur'an, and having confected it from both Jewish fables and the foolish nonsense of heretics, he wove together that wicked scripture in his own barbarous fashion. Having created the lie that gradually this was conveyed to him in a book by Gabriel, whose name he knew already from sacred scripture, he poisoned a people that was ignorant of God. . . .

He describes the torments of hell such as it pleased him to do, and such as it was fitting for the great false prophet to invent. He painted a paradise that is not of the company of angels, nor of a vision of the divine, nor of that highest good that . . . but painted one such as truly flesh and blood desired, or rather the dregs of flesh and blood, and one which he desired to have prepared for himself. There, he promises to his followers a meal of meats and of every kind of fruit, rivers of milk and honey, and of sparkling waters; there he promises the embrace and sexual satisfaction of the most beautiful women and virgins, in which the whole of his paradise is defined. Vomiting up again among these nearly all of the dregs of the ancient heresies, which he had absorbed from the devil's instruction, he denies the trinity with Sabellius, rejects the deity of Christ with his own Nestorius, [and] repudiates the death of the lord along with Manichaeus. . . .

Instructing the people in these and similar teachings not for improvement but for damnation . . . he relaxed the reins on gluttony and libidinal pleasure; and, having himself eighteen wives at one and the same time, and the wives of many others, committing adultery as if in response to divine command, he joined a larger number of the damned to himself just as if by prophetic example. And lest he appear completely disgraceful, he commended a zeal for almsgiving and certain acts of mercy, he praised prayer . . . Seeing that, at the persuasion of the monk already mentioned and the aforementioned Jews, he [Muhammad] completely abandoned idolatry, and persuaded those whom he could that it ought to be abandoned, and proclaimed that there is one God that ought to be worshipped, having abandoned a multiplicity of gods, he seemed to say what had not been heard before by those that are rude and unschooled. And because, in the first place, this preaching was in harmony with their reason, they believed him to be God's prophet.

From then, in the progress of time and of error, he was raised up by them to the kingship that he had desired. Thus, mixing good things with evil, confusing true things with false, he sowed the seeds of error, and, partly during his time and partly and especially in the time after him, he produced a nefarious harvest that should be burned up by an everlasting fire. . . .

Although I would name them heretics because they believe some things with us, in most things they depart from us; perhaps more correctly I should name them pagans or heathens, which is worse. For although they say some things about the lord that are true, nonetheless they proclaim many others that are false. . . .

The highest aspiration of this heresy is to have Christ the lord believed to be neither God, nor the son of God, but, although a great man and beloved by God, nonetheless a mere man, and certainly a wise man and a very great prophet. What once, indeed, were conceived by the devil's device, first disseminated by Arius and then advanced by that Satan, namely Muhammad, will be fulfilled completely according to diabolical design through the Antichrist. In fact, since the blessed Hilary said that the origin of the Antichrist was in Arius, then what he began, by denying that Christ is the true son of God and by calling him a creature, the Antichrist will at last consummate by asserting that in no way was he God or the son of God, but also that he was not a good man; this most impious Muhammad seems properly to be provided for and prepared by the devil as the mean between both of them, as one who became in a certain sense both an extension of Arius and the greatest support for the Antichrist who will say worse things before the minds of the unbelievers. . . .

In no way, in fact, could any mortal have invented such fables as the written ones that are singled out here, unless by the assistance of the devil's presence, through which [fables], after many ridiculous and insane absurdities, Satan planned particularly and in every way to bring it to pass that Christ would not be believed to be lord, the son of God and true God, the creator and redeemer of the human race. And in reality this is what he wanted to introduce persuasively [in the early days of the faith but] at length, [he] used that most wretched man Muhammad (and as it is reported by many, one who is possessed by an evil spirit and by epilepsy) as an instrument and implement, as it were, most suited to him; alas, he plunged into eternal damnation, along with himself, a very large race and one which at present can be reckoned as nearly a half part of the world. Why this was permitted to him he alone knows to whom no one can say, "Why do you do this?" and who said, "Even from among the many that are called, few are chosen" [Matt. 20.16 and 22.14].

For this reason I, choosing to tremble all over rather than debate, have briefly noted down these things so that the one who reads them will understand, and if there is such a one as wishes to and can write against this entire heresy, he will know with what kind of enemy he will do battle.

Questions: According to Peter, is Islam a new religion? Why does it matter? What are the Qur'an's sources? Why did Muhammad turn to religion? How is the devil involved? Why is Islam so pernicious? How does Peter see its place and function in sacred history? How can Islam be heretical if it is not a Christian sect?

70. CLERICAL SODOMY

Genesis 19 describes the destruction of the cities of Sodom and Gomorrah. According to the account, the patriarch Lot offered hospitality to two angels disguised as humans. When the men of Sodom heard about these guests, they surrounded Lot's house, demanding that he bring them out so that "we might know them." That the mob then declined Lot's offer to allow them instead to rape his two virgin daughters has generally been interpreted as a sign of Sodom's iniquity and a warning against homosexuality. However, before Peter Damian's vitriolic attack on homosexual practice among the clergy, this reading of the text appeared only sporadically. Most pre-1000 penitentials did devote space to the subject, but aside from the Council of Ancyra (314) which prescribed 15 to 20 years of penance for such encounters, condemnations by ecclesiastical councils were rare. Damian's treatise, then, is the first sustained treatment of homosexuality. However, it is important to see the text as part of the larger clerical reform program initiated by Pope Leo IX (r. 1049–1054). Indeed, Peter's text is dedicated to Leo. However, in his reply to the work, the pope counseled a more humane response than that offered by the monk.

Latin, between 1049 and 1056.

Source: trans. Pierre J. Payer, from Peter Damian, *Book of Gomorrah: An Eleventh-Century Treatise against Clerical Homosexual Practices* (Waterloo: Wilfrid Laurier Press, 1982), pp. 27, 29, 41–43, 59, 63–65, 68, 79, 83.

A certain abominable and terribly shameful vice has grown up in our region. Unless the hand of severe punishment resists as soon as possible, there is certainly a danger that the sword of divine anger will be used savagely against it to the ruin of many. Alas! it is shameful to speak of, shameful to suggest such foul disgrace to sacred ears. But if the doctor shrinks in horror from infected wounds, who will take the trouble to apply the cauter? If the one who is to heal becomes nauseated, who will lead sick hearts back to health? Vice against nature creeps in like a cancer and even touches the order of consecrated men. Sometimes it rages like a bloodthirsty beast in the midst of the sheepfold of Christ with such bold freedom that it would have been much healthier for many to have been oppressed under the yoke of a secular army than to be freely delivered over to the iron rule of diabolical tyranny under the cover of religion, particularly when this is accompanied by scandal to others. . . .

Four types of this form of criminal wickedness can be distinguished in an effort to show you the totality of the whole matter in an orderly way: some sin with themselves alone; some commit mutual masturbation; some commit femoral fornication; and finally, others commit the complete act against nature. The ascending gradation among these is such that the last mentioned are judged to be more serious than the preceding. Indeed, a greater penance is imposed on those who fall with others than those who defile only themselves; and those who complete the act are to be judged more severely than those who are defiled through femoral fornication. The devil's artful fraud devises these degrees of falling into ruin such that the higher the level the unfortunate soul reaches in them, the deeper it sinks in the depths of hell's pit. . . .

O unheard of crime! O outrage to be mourned with a whole fountain of tears! . . . The same sentence is justly inflicted both on one who has ruined a natural daughter and on one who has corrupted a spiritual daughter through a sacrilegious union, unless perhaps in this matter the quality of each crime is distinguished, since although sinning incestuously, nevertheless, they each sinned naturally because they sinned with a woman. However, anyone who commits a sacrilege with his sin is guilty of the crime of incest with a male and breaks the laws of nature. And it seems to me to be more tolerable to fall into shameful lust with an animal than a male. That is, one who perishes alone is judged much more lightly than one who also draws another along with himself to disastrous ruin. . . .

However, that the arguments of diabolical fraud might not lie hidden, I will bring into the light what was fashioned secretly in the workshops of ancient wickedness. I do not accept that this hidden thing should go on, namely, that certain ones who are filled with the poison of this crime, as if taking heart, should confess to one another to keep the knowledge of their guilt from becoming known to others. While they shame the face of men, the authors of this guilt themselves become the judges. The indiscreet indulgence which each desires to be applied to himself, he rejoices to bestow on the other through a delegated change of roles. So it happens that although they ought to be penitents for their great crimes, nonetheless their faces do not pale with fasting, nor do their bodies waste away with thinness. While the belly is in no way restrained from the immoderate reception of food, the spirit is shamefully inflamed to the ardor of habitual lust, with the result that the one who had shed no tears for what was committed continues to commit more seriously what should be mourned. . . .

"The holy synod [that is, the Council of Ancyra of 314] commands that those who have lived irrationally and who have polluted others with the leprosy of this unjust crime are to pray among those who are struck with an unclean spirit." Clearly, while it does not say, "who corrupt others with the leprosy of this unjust crime," but "pollute" which, however, corresponds to the title where it begins with those polluted but not corrupted, it is clear that in whatever way a male is polluted with a male through lustful ardor, he is commanded to pray among the demoniacs and not among Christian Catholics. And so if carnal men do not know how to realize what they are from one another, at least they can be instructed by those with whom they are relegated in the common penitentiary of prayer.

It is just enough that those who commit their flesh to the demons through such filthy intercourse against the law of nature and the order of human reason be allotted the common nook of prayer along with demoniacs. For inasmuch as human nature itself completely rejects these evils and stands opposed to there being any incompatibility between the sexes, it is clearer than day that these men would never presume to do such strange things to which they were disinclined unless evil spirits possessed them fully as if they were "vessels fit for wrath, ready to be destroyed" [Rom. 9.22]. But when they begin to take possession of them, the evil spirits pour the infernal poison of their evil throughout the whole possessed heart which they fill so that the possessed eagerly desire not what the natural motion of the flesh urgently demands, but what diabolical precipitation offers. When a male rushes to a male to commit impurity, this is not the natural impulse of the flesh, but only the goad of diabolical impulse. . . .

Truly, this vice is never to be compared with any other vice because it surpasses the enormity of all vices. Indeed, this vice is the death of bodies, the destruction of souls. It pollutes the flesh; it extinguishes the light of the mind. It evicts the holy spirit from the temple of the human heart; it introduces the devil who incites lust. It casts into error; it completely removes the truth from the mind that has been deceived. It prepares snares for those entering; it shuts up those who fall into the pit so they cannot get out. It opens hell; it closes the door of heaven. It makes a citizen of Jerusalem into an heir of infernal Babylon. It makes the star of heaven the stubble of eternal fire; it cuts off a member of the Church and casts it into the consuming fire of boiling Gehenna. This vice tries to overturn the walls of the heavenly homeland and is busy repairing the renewed bulwarks of Sodom. For it is this which violates sobriety, kills modesty, strangles chastity, and butchers irreparable virginity with the danger of unclean contagion. It defiles everything, stains everything, pollutes everything. And as for itself, it permits nothing pure, nothing clean, nothing other than filth. . . .

This vice casts men from the choir of the ecclesiastical community and compels them to pray with the possessed and with those who work for the devil. It separates the soul from God to join it with devils. This most pestilential queen of the sodomites makes the followers of her tyrannical laws filthy to me and hateful to God. She commands to join in evil wars against God, to carry the military burden of a most evil spirit. She separates from the companionship of angels and captures the unhappy soul under the yoke of her domination away from its nobility. She deprives her soldiers of the arms of the virtues and exposes them to the piercing spears of all the vices. She humiliates the church, condemns in law, defiles in secret, shames in public, gnaws the conscience as though with worms, sears the flesh as though with fire.

She pants to satisfy her desire for pleasure, but on the other hand she fears lest she become exposed and come out in public and become known to me. Should he not fear her, he who dreads with anxious suspicion the very participant in their common ruin? A person who himself participates in a sinful act ought not to be a judge of the crime in confession as long as he hesitates in any way to confess that he has sinned himself by joining in the sin of another. The fact is that the one partner could not die in sin without the other dying also; nor can one provide an opportunity for the other to rise without rising himself. The miserable flesh burns with the heat of lust; the cold mind trembles with the rancor of suspicion; and in the heart of the miserable man chaos burns like Tartarus, while as often as he is pierced with mental stings he is tormented with a certain measure with painful punishment. In fact, after the most poisonous serpent once sinks its fangs into the unhappy soul, sense is snatched away, memory is borne off, the sharpness of the mind of obscured. . . .

Indeed, whomever this most atrocious beast once seizes upon with bloodthirsty jaws, it restrains with its bonds from every form of good work and immediately unleashes him down the steep descent of the most evil depravity. In fact, when one has fallen into the abyss of extreme ruin he becomes an exile from the heavenly homeland, separated from the body of Christ, confounded by the authority of the whole Church, condemned by the judgment of all the holy fathers. He is despised among men on earth and rejected from the community of heavenly citizens. Heaven becomes like iron for him and the earth like bronze. Burdened with the weight of the crime, he cannot arise nor conceal his evil for long in the hiding-place of ignorance. He cannot rejoice here while he lives nor can he hope there when he dies, since he is compelled to bear the disgrace of human derision now and afterwards the torment of eternal damnation. . . .

Unmanned man, speak! Respond, effeminate man! What do you seek in a male which you cannot find in yourself? What sexual difference? What different physical lineaments? What softness? What tender, carnal attraction? What pleasant, smooth face? Let the vigor of the male appearance terrify you, I beseech you; your mind should abhor virile strength. In fact, it is the rule of natural appetite that each seek beyond himself what he cannot find within the cloister of his own faculty. Therefore, if contact with male flesh delights you, turn your hand to yourself. Know that whatever you do not find in yourself, you seek vainly in another [male] body. Woe to you, unfortunate soul, at whose ruin angels are saddened and whom the enemy insults with applause. You are made the prey of demons, the rape of the cruel, the spoils of wicked men. . . .

Nor should those who are placed in sacred orders boast if they live in a detestable way, since the higher they stand in eminence, the deeper they are cast down when they fall. Just as they ought now to precede others in a holy way of life, so afterwards they will be compelled to undergo more atrocious sufferings, since, according to the voice of Peter, "God did not spare the angels who sinned. He held them captive in Tartarus—consigned them to pits of darkness, to be guarded until judgment. And he condemned the cities of Sodom and Gomorrah to destruction, reducing them to ashes, making them an example to those who in the future should live impiously" [2 Pet. 2.4-6]

Why is it that he immediately turns to the destruction of Sodom and Gomorrah after recounting the fall into diabolical damnation unless, as he clearly shows, because those who now are given over to the vice of impurity are to be damned together with the impure spirits in eternal punishment? Those who are troubled by the ardor of sodomite lust afterwards will also burn along with the author of all iniquity in the flames of perpetual burning. . . .

Consider, then, what a dangerous transformation follows because of the fleeting pleasure caused by the momentary emission of semen—a transformation which does not end throughout the course of thousands of years. Think how miserable it is that because of the present satisfaction of one organ's pleasure, afterwards the whole body together with the soul will be tortured forever by the most atrocious, flaming fires.

Questions: To whom are these sections addressed? Why demonize sexual behaviors in this way? Why is homosexuality worse for this group of people than other types of sexual misconduct? What does it do to the partners involved? How do demons use homosexual sex? What does it do to such sinners?

71. THE BLOOD LIBEL

The earliest report of the so-called "blood libel"—the accusation that Jews murdered Christian children for ritual purposes out of hatred for Christ—seems to have come from an English monk, Thomas of Monmouth (fl. 1150s). Thomas's Life and Passion of Saint William of Norwich *describes how a young leatherworker had been kidnapped by members of the town's Jewish community and subjected to all of the torments endured by Christ before finally being murdered. The idea of the blood libel became central to medieval constructions of anti-Semitism, and charges were leveled in most European countries throughout the period and beyond. It also features in literature, most famously in "The Prioress's Tale," part of Geoffrey Chaucer's* Canterbury Tales *(1387–1400).*

The account below is taken from the Greater Chronicle *of the Benedictine Matthew of Paris (1200–59). It centers on the apparent murder of a boy named Hugh. It is one of the few incidents which was subjected to formal investigation by secular authorities. Significantly, though, after the lynching of eighteen wealthy members of Lincoln's Jewish community, those who were transported to London and sentenced to death were eventually released.*

Latin, 1250s.

Source: trans. Richard Raiswell and David R. Winter, from Matthew Paris, *Chronica Maiora*, vol. 5 (London, 1880), pp. 516–19.

In this same year [1255] around the feast of the apostles Peter and Paul [29 June], the Jews of Lincoln stole a boy named Hugh who was around eight years of age. Having shut him up in a most secret room, feeding him on milk and other childish foods, they sent to almost every English city in which Jews lived, summoning some Jews from each city to be present for the boy's sacrifice in Lincoln—for the insult and disgrace of Jesus Christ. They had—as they said—a certain boy hidden away who was to be crucified.

Many of them came to Lincoln. Once together, they appointed a Jew of Lincoln as judge in place of [Pontius] Pilate. In his judgment and with everyone in agreement, the boy was subjected to various tortures. They beat him to the point at which he was bloody and bruised. They crowned him with thorns, spat on him, and mocked him with derisive laughter. In addition, the boy was stabbed by each of them with daggers called *anelacii*, [made to] drink bitter poison, mocked with many disgraces and blasphemies—and with all of the Jews present crowding in upon him, their teeth gnashing, he was called Jesus, the false prophet. After they had ridiculed him in these various ways, they crucified the boy, and stabbed him in the heart with a lance. When the boy had died, they took him down from the cross and eviscerated his tiny body—for what reason it is not known, but it is said that it was for the practicing of magical arts.

EIGHT: DEMONIZATIONS

For several days, the boy's mother diligently sought her absent son. She was told by her neighbors that they had last seen the boy playing with some Jewish boys who were about the same age as him, and that he had gone into the house of one of them. Accordingly, the woman entered that house unannounced, and saw the boy's body in the well into which it had been thrown. With the city bailiffs prudently having been called, the body was found and removed. The sight was astonishing to the people. Through her crying and wailing, the woman—the boy's mother—stirred all the townspeople who were gathering there to sighs and tears.

Lord John of Lexington—a prudent and discreet man, someone who was truly learned—was there, and he said, "We have learned that the Jews are never afraid to attempt such deeds for the disgrace of our crucified lord, Jesus Christ." And, having grabbed the Jew in whose house the boys had been playing, and who was more suspect than the others, he said to him, "Wretch, do you not know that an untimely death awaits you? All the gold of England will not be enough for your rescue or redemption. Nevertheless, I will tell you—despite being unworthy—how you can save yourself, life and limb, and avoid mutilation. I will save you from both if you are not afraid to make clear to me everything that was done in this matter—without any lies."

Therefore, the Jew—whose name was Copin—believing he had found a way of escape, replied, saying, "O lord John, if you make good on what you have said, I will tell you some wonderful things." The relentlessness of lord John inspired and urged him in this. And the Jew said, "The things the Christians say are true. Almost every year, the Jews crucify a boy to offend and insult Jesus—although one is not found every year. They do this in secret, and in concealed and remote places. Our Jews crucified this boy whom they call Hugh mercilessly, and when he died and they wanted to hide his corpse, [they found that] it could not be buried in the earth or hidden. The body of an innocent was considered unfit to be used as an augury—which was why it had been eviscerated. And so in the morning, when it was thought the body was hidden, the earth rejected and vomited it forth, and it appeared unburied on the earth for some time—causing the Jews to be terrified. After a while, it was thrown into a well—but not even there could it be hidden. By searching into all these wicked deeds, the mother eventually found the body and informed the bailiffs." Despite his promise, the lord John held the Jew in prison.

And when these things became known to the canons of the cathedral church of Lincoln, they asked for the little body to be given to them, and it was granted to them. And after it had been viewed by an enormous number of people, the body was buried with honor in Lincoln church as if it had been that of a great martyr. It should be known that the Jews kept the boy alive for ten days fed on milk for all those days so that he might endure the many kinds of torture [inflicted upon him] while he was still alive.

When the king had returned from the northern parts of England and was informed about what had taken place, he rebuked lord John because he had promised life and limb to such a shameful man—a promise he had been unable to keep. Copin, that blasphemer and murderer, deserved a punishment of death in many forms.

Finally, with an unpardonable sentence hanging over him, the Jew said, "my death is imminent. Nor is Lord John able to save me from being destroyed. Now I will tell all of you the truth. Almost all the Jews of England agreed to the death of this boy of which the Jews are accused. A chosen number were called together from almost every town in which Jews live for the sacrifice of that boy—as if to the Paschal sacrifice."

When Copin had said this along with other similar nonsense, he was bound to a horse's tail and dragged to the gallows, where he was handed over body and soul to the demons of the air. The other Jews who had participated in this crime—some ninety-one of them—were taken to London in carts and cast into prison. And if by chance they were pitied by some Christians, they were lamented with dry tears by their rivals, the Caursins [Christian usurers].

[Matthew goes on to report that eighteen of the richer Jews of Lincoln were lynched by a mob on 23 November. Those who were taken to London were convicted and sentenced to death, but later released.]

Questions: According to the logic of the text, why did Lincoln's Jews kidnap Hugh? Why are they unable to bury the body? How does the text present England's Jewish community? Why is Jewish ritual dangerous to other Lincolnians? How does this account draw upon that of Luke's account of Christ's death (doc. 24)? Reading between the lines, what most likely happened to Hugh? Can this incident be said to constitute a moral panic?

72. DIABOLIZED HISTORY

Joachim of Fiore (c. 1135–99) was a highly complicated thinker who believed that he could discern the nature of the final era of world history from a close analysis of scripture. He understood history to be divided into three overlapping periods, each associated with a different person of the trinity. The first period, associated with God the father, was that of the Old Testament. The second period, that of God the son, began with the coming of Christ and aligned with the New Testament. He saw himself living at the very end of this period. A third age, that of the holy spirit, was yet to come. Joachim also argued that the nature of this imminent third age could be discerned by comparing the two testaments of scripture and looking for points of similarity—or "concordances"—between people, events, figures, and tropes in the text.

EIGHT: DEMONIZATIONS

The following selection comes from his Book of Figures *in which Joachim tried to understand the figure of the seven-headed and ten-horned beast described in Revelation 13.1 (doc. 11) as coming out of the sea and then in Revelation 17.3 being ridden by the whore of Babylon. This selection is a translation of the illustration's captions and text. Latin, 1190s.*

Source: trans. Bernard McGinn, Joachim of Fiore, from the *Book of Figures*, in *Apocalyptic Spirituality* (New York: Paulist Press, 1979), pp. 136–41.

Book of Figures, The Fourteenth Table, The Seven-Headed Dragon

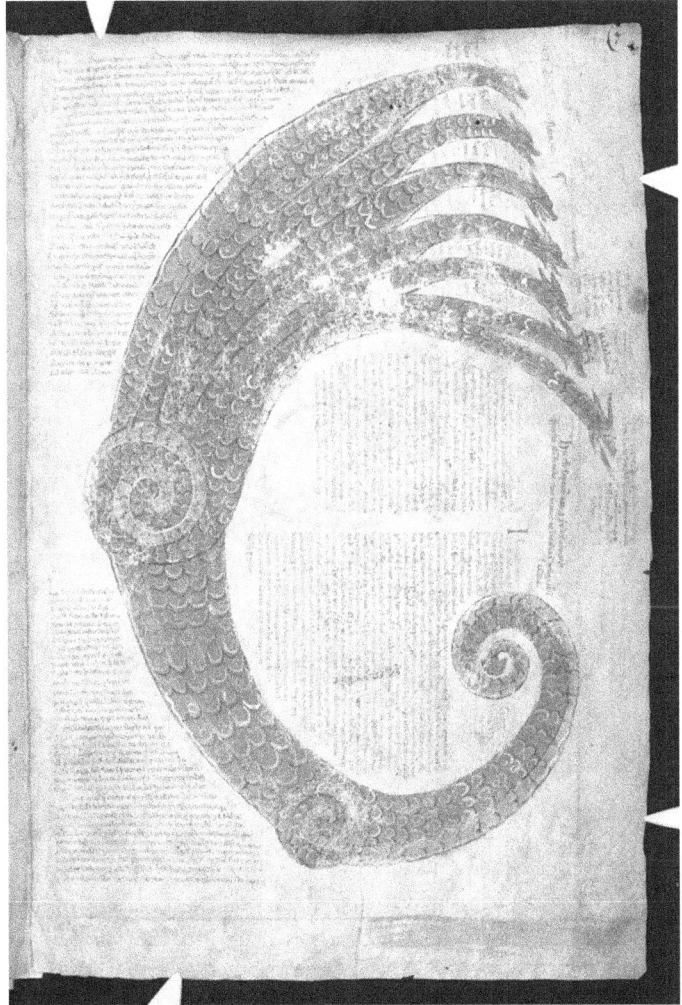

Figure 8.2 The Seven-Headed Dragon.

Captions on the Heads and Tail of the Beast

"There are seven kings. Five have fallen, one is present, and one has not yet come. When he comes, he must remain for a short time" [Rev. 17.9–10].

Herod. The First Persecution, that of the Jews. The Time of the Apostles.

Nero. The Second Persecution, that of the Pagans. The Time of the Martyrs.

[The Arian Roman Emperor] Constantius [II, 337–361]. The Third Persecution, that of the Heretics. The Time of the Doctors.

Muhammad. The Fourth Persecution, that of the Saracens. The Time of the Virgins.

Mesemoth [a North African Muslim ruler?]. The Fifth Persecution, that of the sons of Babylon in the spirit and not in the letter. The Time of the Conventuals. "These five have fallen" [Rev. 17.10]. The fifth persecution belongs to the King of Babylon. You will know later why you can write down Mesemoth for that king.

Saladin. The Sixth Persecution has Begun. The Seventh will Follow. "Another will arise after them and he will be more powerful than the previous ones" [Dan. 7.24]. There are ten kings.

This is the Seventh King, who is properly called Antichrist, although there will be another like him, no less evil, symbolized by the tail. This is that king of whom Daniel says: "There will arise a king of shameless face who will understand dark designs. His power will be strengthened, but not by his own forces. He shall lay waste all things beyond belief." [Dan. 8.23–24]

[Inscribed on the dragon's tail:] "Gog. He is the final Antichrist."

Commentary

A. The Apocalypse: "A great sign appeared in heaven: a vast red dragon having seven heads and ten horns. His tail dragged down a third part of the stars of heaven and cast them to the earth" [Rev. 12.3–4]. The seven heads of the dragon signify seven tyrants by whom the persecutions of the Church were begun. The dragon's sixth head has ten horns because in the time of the sixth king . . . many kings by destiny will be brought together to do battle with Christ and his elect. As it says in the Apocalypse: "The ten horns which you saw are ten kings who have not yet received a kingdom, but will receive kingly power for an hour after the beast. They have one design, and their power and strength they will give to the beast. They will fight with the lamb and the lamb will conquer them. Those who are with him are called elect and faithful. And the ten horns which you saw on the beast will hate the harlot and will make her desolate and naked. They will eat her flesh and burn her with fire" [Rev. 17.12–16].

From all this it can be understood that first of all the sixth king must begin to rule alone, and then later gather many kings to fight with the lamb and to smite the sons of Babylon who say they are Christians and are not, but are the synagogue of Satan. Their intention will be wicked in all things and in every way. Even though they are unwilling and unknowing, they will do God's will in both cases: either by killing the just who are destined to be crowned with martyrdom, or by judging the wicked by whom the earth was corrupted with blood.

After this destruction, which has already in some part begun, the Christians will be victorious. Those who fear the name of the lord will rejoice when that head of the beast over which the sixth king reigns has been brought almost to extermination and ruin. Then, after a few years, its wound will be healed, and the king who will be in charge of it (whether it be Saladin if he is still alive, or another in his place) will gather a much larger army than before and incite universal war against God's elect. Many will be crowned with martyrdom in those days.

In that time also the seventh head of the dragon will arise, namely, that king who is called Antichrist, and a multitude of false prophets with him. We think that he will arise from the West and will come to the aid of that king who will be the head of the pagans. He will perform great signs before him and his army. . . .

I should like to consider more closely why the dragon's two heads are joined together at the same time, and why the Church's tribulations are doubled only in the sixth age so that a twin tribulation arises in this time alone. Just as the old Babylon was struck under the sixth seal, so the new one will be pierced under the present sixth opening. Also under the sixth seal next Holofernes, the leader of the army of the king of Assyria mentioned in the history of Judith, and then Aman from the land of Agag found in the history of Queen Esther hardened their faces to destroy the remnants of the Jewish people everywhere. In the same way, after the imminent tempest and the serenity of the peace that will follow, the eleventh king mentioned in Daniel [Dan. 7.24] will rise up from the Saracen race, though it might not be the one who is present now (because he could fall and rise again after his overthrow, or another could be raised up in his place). There will be another king from a group of heretics who will have an appearance of piety and who will lie hypocritically. I say that he is the king of whom it is said in Daniel: "There will arise a king with a shameless face who will hatch dark designs. His power will be strengthened, but not by his own forces. He shall lay waste all things beyond belief" [Dan. 8.23–24].

These two will make a conspiracy to wipe the name of Christ from the earth. But Christ will conquer them, he who is king of kings and lord of lords [Rev. 19.16]. There are bound to be many who will fight them for the sake of the faith. They will die for Christ's name and will at some time gain a triumph from the tyrants. [God] will permit the two final persecutions to happen in the one sixth time so that at the opening of the seventh seal peace may come and his faithful people can rest from their labors. Therefore, these two last heads are joined together, because both these tribulations of the final week are destined to be fulfilled under the one sixth time.

B. Paul writes about the Antichrist: "He is lifted up and opposed to all that is called God, or that is worshipped, so that he sits in God's temple, showing himself as if he were God" [2 Thess. 2.4; doc. 44]. We should not think, as the holy teachers say, that when he has been judged the end of the world will come soon, just because he is said to come at the end of the world. The end of the world and the last hour are not always to be taken for the final moment, but for the time of the end, as John who wrote over a thousand years ago openly teaches when he says: "Little children, this is the last hour, and as you have heard that Antichrist is coming, so now there are many Antichrists. Hence we know that it is the last hour" [1 John 2.18]. But we must note that John and John's master say many Antichrists will come. Paul, on the other hand, foretells that there will be one. Just as many holy kings, priests, and prophets went before the one Christ who was king, priest, and prophet, so likewise many unholy kings, false prophets, and Antichrists will go before the one Antichrist who will pretend that he is a king, a priest, and a prophet.

After the destruction of this Antichrist there will be justice on earth and an abundance of peace. . . . The Jews and many pagan races will be converted to the lord, and all people will rejoice in the beauty of peace because the great dragon's heads will be crushed and he will be imprisoned in the abyss (that is, in the remaining races who will live at the ends of the earth). God alone knows the number of the years, months, and days of that time. When they have been finished and brought to end, once again Satan will be freed from prison to persecute God's elect, because there is still that other Antichrist who is symbolized in the dragon's tail.

At the end of the times and of the years "Satan will be freed from his prison, and will go forth and seduce the nations that are at the four corners of the earth. He will lead them in battle; their number will be like the sands of the sea. They will surround the camp of the saints and the beloved city" [Rev. 20.7–8]. That will be the final battle, in the last moment at the dragon's tail because the heads will have been already crushed. Then the commander of the army will be Gog, the final Antichrist. God will judge him and his army by fire and brimstone poured down from heaven. The devil who led men astray to do all these evil deeds will be cast into the lake of fire and brimstone where the beast and the false prophet are [Rev. 20.9–10]. The beast and the false prophet (that is, the eleventh king mentioned in Daniel, along with his army) and the seventh king written of above along with his group of false prophets are next thrown into the lake of fire. At the end Gog and his army will be judged; after them the devil and Gog himself will be cast into the lake of fire where the beast and the false prophet already are.

Among all the Antichrists who will appear in the world two are worse than the others: the one who is denoted by the seventh head and the one denoted by the tail. He who is denoted by the seventh head will come in hidden fashion like John the Baptist, who was not known to be Elias. He who is denoted by the tail will come in open fashion like Elias, who will come openly. . . . God's saints have specifically spoken of one Antichrist and nonetheless there will be two, one of whom will be the greatest Antichrist. The devil strives for nothing more than to appear like the most high in every way possible. Because Jesus Christ came in hidden fashion, Satan himself will do his works hiddenly, that is, signs and false wonders will be designed to seduce even the elect if possible. Because at the end of the world Jesus Christ will come to judgment in open fashion, so too the devil himself will go forth at the end of the world and will appear openly in the days of Gog. He will incite the pagan nations and will lead them to war so that he can pretend that he is Christ come to judge with his saints, avenging all who have suffered wrong. Just as Jesus Christ came with true signs, but cloaked and hidden because of the likeness of sinful human nature so that he was hardly recognized as the Christ by even a few, so too the seventh king will come with false signs and will be hidden and cloaked because of his appearance of spiritual justice, so that only a few will be able to recognize that he is the Antichrist. For this reason even the elect may be led into error if possible. And because the same Christ Jesus will come openly in the glory of his majesty surrounded with a heavenly army of angels and men, so too Satan will appear openly with armies of wicked men, so that on the basis of dread of his forces he may pretend to be him who will come to judge the living and the dead and the world by fire.

Questions: How does Joachim understand the structure of history? How does he understand the image of the dragon from Revelation? What is the role of Islam and heresy at the end of time? Why is Saladin given such prominence? Why does he argue that there are multiple antichrists? How does he discern the nature and character of Antichrist?

73. DEVIL-WORSHIPPING HERETICS?

Walter Map (c. 1135–1209), a scholar and courtier, was from a prosperous family of English landowners hailing from the borderlands with Wales. Educated in the schools of Paris, upon his return to England Walter rose quickly through the ranks of the secular clergy, becoming a canon at Lincoln and later Archdeacon of Oxford. In the 1170s, he came to the attention of English king Henry II (r. 1154–89) and entered into his service.

His De nugis curialium *(Courtiers' Trifles) is a curious assortment of material principally intended to entertain. It includes accounts of miracles and marvels, along with satirical material and some historical content. The following selection details the discovery of a new and pernicious sect of heretics. It is based on a story that goes back to Late Antiquity.*
Latin, c. 1182.

Source: trans. F. Tupper and M. Bladen, *Master Walter Map's Book* De nugis curialium *(Courtiers' Trifles)* (London, 1924), pp. 72–75; rev.

There is, too, another old heresy which has recently increased beyond all measure. This traces its origin to those who have forsaken God, when he spoke about eating his flesh and drinking his blood, declaring "This is a hard saying." Going back, they are called Publicans or Patarines. However, they have lurked among Christians everywhere from the days of our lord's passion, and they continue to wander from the truth.

At first, indeed, they occupied single houses in the towns in which they dwelt, and from whatever quarter each man may have come, "he knew his own house in the smoke," so to speak. They do not accept the gospel of John, and they deride our views on the body and blood of Christ, the consecrated bread. Men and women dwell together, but no sons and daughters come from this union. Regaining wisdom, many who have returned to the true faith tell us that, about the first watch of the night, closing all gates and doors and windows, each group sits in expectant silence in their respective synagogues. Then a black cat of marvelous size comes down by means of a rope which hangs in their midst. At the appearance of this creature, they put out all the lights. They sing neither hymns nor even speak articulately, but they gnash with clenched teeth. Then, feeling their way forward, they approach the spot where they have seen their lord, and, when they find him, they kiss him, each with a measure of humility proportioned to the heat of his frenzy, some his feet, many under the tail, and very many his private parts. Then, just as if the license for lust had been received from the place of stench, each seizes the man or woman nearest to them, and they mingle just as far as each one is able to carry this mockery. Moreover, their masters say and teach their novices that perfect charity is to do or suffer whatever brother or sister has sought or desired—that is, to extinguish the fires of their common passions. . . .

Their fellow countrymen also say that they capture their guests with some of their dishes so that those whom they dare not tempt through the hidden meanings of their public sermons thus become like themselves. Hence that incident happened which Lord William, archbishop of Rheims, brother of the queen of France reported to me, corroborating the story by many witnesses.

A noble prince from the neighborhood of Vienne, in constant fear of this detestable seizure always carried exorcised salt with him in his wallet, not knowing into whose house he was going to enter. Fearing everywhere the deceitfulness of the enemy, he was wont even at his own table to sprinkle this on all foods. When it was reported to him that two knights had misled his nephew, who was the lord of many people and towns, he immediately went to his nephew's house. When they were ceremoniously feasting together, the nephew unwittingly had a whole mullet seemingly "pleasant to the eyes and good for food," placed before his uncle. The nobleman sprinkled his salt on it and suddenly the fish disappeared and on the dish was left some substance like pellets of hare dung.

The nobleman was horrified—as were those with him—and after revealing to his nephew the miracle, he devoutly preached repentance to him, and with many tears, taught him the multitude of God's mercies, showing him, moreover, that all the efforts of demons are conquered by faith alone as was the case with the matter he had just seen. The nephew took the speech badly and withdrew to his bedroom. Then the nobleman, indignant at the mockery heaped upon him, led the knights who had seduced his nephew in chains with him, and, in the sight of many people, shut them up in a hut where he bound them fast to a stake. He then burned the whole building with a fire that he kindled beneath. But the fire did not touch them at all, nor indeed was any trace of scorching found on their garments. . . .

[The nobleman then consulted the bishop of Vienne, who imprisoned the offenders in a larger building, binding them to a stake once more.]

Walking around the whole building on the outside, [the nobleman] sprinkled it with holy water to counteract their magic. He then ordered the torch to be applied. But the fire—despite all the fanning and feeding—could neither catch nor consume anything. The city consequently reviled the bishop, and displayed such a loss of faith that many openly taunted him with mad words and, had they not been checked by respect for their prince, they would have cast the bishop himself into the flames and freed the supposedly innocent. Then, beating down the doors, the crowd rushed into the house, and coming to the stake, found charcoal and sparks where flesh and bones had been, and yet they discovered that the chains were unhurt and the stake intact, and that the very righteous flame had only turned against those who had erred. Thus, a kind lord changed the hearts of the erring to penitence and blasphemy to praise.

Questions: What are the features of this sect? Is there anything new here—does Walter think there is anything new? What kind of evidence does he offer? Given the overall nature of De nugis, *can modern historians take this account at face value?*

74. ROOTING OUT HERESY

Conrad of Marburg (1180/90–1233) was one of the most feared inquisitors of the High Middle Ages. Together with Conrad Tors and a man known only as John, he traveled the Germanic lands, charged by Pope Gregory IX (r. 1227–41) with rooting out and prosecuting heresy. The three quickly developed a reputation for uncompromising brutality. Among Conrad's discoveries was that of an apparent sect of Luciferians who worshipped the devil in various forms at secret gatherings. On the basis of this claim, Gregory sent versions of this letter, "Vox in Rama (A voice was heard in Rama)," to the Holy Roman emperor, Frederick II, and a number of senior prelates.

Six weeks after it was written, Conrad was murdered, likely by vassals of some of the nobility who had fallen under his gaze. In the fallout, a number of officials complained that the accused had been interrogated through leading questions, been forced to confess, and then commanded to name accomplices in order to avoid being burned.

Latin, June 1233.

Source: trans. Richard Raiswell and David R. Winter, from *Epistolae saeculi XIII e regestis pontificum Romanorum selectee*, vol. 1, Monumenta Germaniae Historica, no. 537, pp. 432–35.

To the Archbishop of Mainz . . . the bishop of Hildesheim and Master Conrad of Marburg, preacher of the word of God.

A voice was heard in Rama, much weeping and howling [Jer. 3.21; Matt. 2.18]. Rachel—that is, the pious mother church—is weeping for her children whom the devil is slaughtering and destroying. She is receiving no consolation, as it were, because her children are plotting to annihilate her, tearing at the guts of their mother like a viper. Many pressing pains—like those with which a laboring mother is beset—cause her to cry out with the prophet and say, "My bowels are in pain; my bowels are in pain" [Jer. 4.19]. For while—according to the apostle—every creature groans and labors even up until now [Rom. 8.22], the holy womb of the mother church is troubled by a pain in her guts which are being torn to pieces with almost every single bite. Indeed, that twisting snake which—as we read [Job 26.13]—was brought forth from its caverns by the midwifing hand of the lord in the flesh—namely, in the hearts of men—fights outwardly against those of us in whom he does not already rule inwardly, and over whom he has lost internal dominion. He wages wars externally, renewing the persecution of the church as the bride of Christ—more accurately against the bride of Christ herself—through the deeds of his ministers of iniquity. For he—who from the very beginning did not stand in truth but who strives to turn the truth into a lie [Rom. 1.25] so he can pour out the poison of his deceit more widely—goes to great lengths to destroy pregnant souls, lest the fetuses of the faith conceived out of divine love are able to come to term [and be delivered].

On this account, we who are obliged to care for her fecundity are being sliced open as if by a treacherously cutting blade, while we are being assailed in the guts by the poisoned arrows of new error and unheard of confusion of the heretics that are cutting into her womb. All our breath has been shed in anguish. Our liver has been poured out onto the ground. Our soul has been greatly troubled and our stomach filled with pains. Our eyes have failed from weeping and our kidneys tremble on account of such wicked abominations. All our organs have been disturbed and we cannot hold back our tears or contain our sighs [Jer. 31.20; Lam. 2.11].

Since your letters contained a great measure of sadness and immense pain, they were not empty to us. Among the various sorts of heresies which infect Germany—as our sins require—one more loathsome than others and so more common has now broken out among the noble members of the church and very powerful men which is horrible not only in the reporting but in the hearing. This heresy is dissonant to all reason, contrary to all piety, hateful to every heart, hostile to all things celestial and terrestrial, against which not only men using right reason but also those lacking reason—since this plague goes beyond their insanity—even the very elements themselves ought to be armed and rise up.

Initiations such as these are reported of this plague. When any novice is accepted into the heresy and first enters the school of perdition, a certain type of frog appears to him which some people call a toad. Some kissing it on the rear, others on the mouth, they receive the creature's tongue and saliva in their mouth. Sometimes, it appears to be of indeterminate size—sometimes the size of a goose or a duck. Often it takes on the size of an oven. Eventually, the novice having come forward, a man of wondrous paleness, with the darkest eyes, comes to meet him. The man is so thin and emaciated—his flesh having been consumed—that the only remaining skin seems merely to cover his bones. When the novice kisses the man, he feels as cold as ice, and after the kiss his memory of the Catholic faith vanishes completely from his heart.

Afterwards he goes to a banquet with the other guests. When the banquet has finished, a black cat about the size of an average dog descends backwards with its tail raised through a certain type of statue which is usually found in these schools. First the novice then the master then the other members of the order who are worthy and perfect kiss it on its backside in succession. But the imperfect ones, that is those who do not consider themselves worthy, receive a blessing from the master. Then, after everyone has returned to their original place and with certain incantations spoken, they lean their heads toward the cat and the master says, "spare us." The man next to him says this, too. A third man, replying says, "We know, master." A fourth says, "And we must obey."

And after this has been done, the candles are blown out and the gathering turns to the filthiest sort of lechery, with no distinction between women who are family members and those who are not. If perchance those of the virile sex exceed the number of women, the extra men give in to shameful passions with each other. Burning with desire for each other, men perform obscenity with other men. Likewise, women change the use of their anus into that which is contrary to nature damnably performing this obscenity among themselves.

With this most heinous crime completed, and the candles lit again, every person returns to his proper place. Then, from a darkened corner of the school—a place from which the most depraved men are not absent—a certain man advances shining from the waist up, brighter than the sun, as they say. His lower half is hairy like a cat, and his brightness lights up the whole place. Then the master, taking something from the clothes of the novice, says to the shining man, "Master, I am giving you this which was given to me." To this the shining man replies, "You have often served me well, and you will serve me still better. I am entrusting into your care that which you gave me." And with these things said, he immediately vanishes.

They receive the body of the lord every year at Easter from the hand of a priest, and carrying it in their mouths to their houses they spit it into the latrine in contempt of the redeemer. On top of this, these most wicked of all wretches, blaspheming celestial governance with their foul lips, assert in their raving that the lord of heaven violently and deceitfully cast Lucifer down into hell contrary to justice. These wretches believe this and assert that Lucifer is the creator of the heavens and that he will return to his glory with the lord's fall, and they hope they will have eternal bliss with him, not before him. They all confess to not doing things that please God. Rather, they do what he despises.

Oh the pain! Who has ever heard such things? Who could think such wicked things? Who does not loathe such treachery? Who does not get enraged at such wickedness? Who does not become inflamed against the children of such ruin and treachery? Where is the zeal of Moses who, on a single day, killed 23,000 idolaters [Exod. 32.28]? Where is the zeal of Phineas who stabbed a Jew and a Madian with one thrust of a dagger [Num. 25.8]? Where is the zeal of Elias who killed 450 prophets of Baal with his sword at a stream called Cison [3 Kings 18.40]? Where is the zeal of Mathathias whose rage was so inflamed according to the judgment of the law that, coming upon a Jew sacrificing to idols, he killed him on the altar [1 Macc. 2.25]? And where is the authority of Peter who was enraged by Ananias and Sapphira because they were not afraid to lie to the holy spirit [Acts 5.3]?

Surely, were the earth to rise up against such people and the stars of heaven reveal their sins and show their crimes to the whole world so that not only men but the elements themselves were to join together for their ruin and destruction, and wipe them from the face of the earth—sparing neither sex nor age—so that they be cast into eternal damnation with all nations, such a punishment would not be adequate or appropriate enough for them. . . .

EIGHT: DEMONIZATIONS

Questions: What are the features of this sect? Why is this a "school" for heretics? What effect might the fact that this description is contained within a papal letter have on the approach of future inquisitors? Why do Christian writers, preachers, and popes need such heinous enemies, even if the stories about them strain credibility? What might have been the effect of the opening imagery on an audience of listeners?

75. HORDES FROM THE EAST

From the late tenth century, medieval Christianity ceased to be on the defensive. The raids of the Vikings, Magyars, and Muslims had gradually come to an end between c. 950 and 1000. Thus, when the Mongol armies stormed through Russia (Rus) in the late 1230s, leaving in their wake a trail of slaughter and destruction, the shock to Christendom was profound. In December 1240, Kiev and the last principalities of Russia were sacked. In desperation, a combined force of Polish and imperial forces supported by Teutonic knights was assembled to bolster Europe's eastern frontier, but it was almost entirely wiped out at the Battle of Liegnitz on 9 April 1241. Famously, some nine stacks of ears lopped off from the dead were sent back to Mongolia as trophies. Two days later, a Hungarian force to the south was also destroyed, leaving the way open to Vienna. In the following selection, Matthew of Paris (doc. 71) tries to understand the Mongols and their role in history.
Latin, 1240s.

Source: trans. Richard Raiswell and David R. Winter, from Matthew Paris, *Chronica Maiora*, vol. 4: 1240–1247 (London, 1880), pp. 76–78.

So that the joys of human things might not be prolonged and worldly happiness not be celebrated for long without tears, in that year [1240], the detestable people of Satan, namely an infinite swarm of Tartars, broke forth from their mountain-enclosed land. And having smashed through the dense, impenetrable rocks, they came out like demons released from Tartarus—so they are fittingly called *Tartars*, as if from *Tartarus*—and swarming like locusts over the face of the earth, they brought terrible destruction to the eastern parts [of Europe] with pitiable destruction, laying the lands waste through fire and slaughter. Crossing the lands of the Saracens, they razed their cities, cut down their woods, demolished their castles, tore up their vines, destroyed their gardens, and killed all their citizens and farmers. . . .

These men are inhuman and beastly, better called monsters rather than men, thirsting for and drinking blood, ripping and devouring the flesh of people and dogs. They dress in the skins of bulls and are clad in iron plate. They are short and thick in stature, well set in body, vigorous in strength, invincible in battle, and tireless in toil. They are defenseless on the back side of their body—but protected on their other side by their weapons. They drink the blood that flows from their cattle for its exquisite taste, and have huge, strong horses which eat leaves—even trees—and which they mount by means of three steps on account of the shortness of their legs. They lack any human laws, know no mercy, and are more fierce than lions or bears . . . and when they have no blood, they eagerly drink turbid, even muddy, waters. They have swords and daggers sharpened on one side, are wonderful archers, and do not spare sex, age, or merit. They know no other language beyond their own, and about all other peoples they are ignorant. . . .

They came with the speed of lightning up to the bounds of Christendom laying them waste, and committing no small amount of slaughter they struck incomparable fear and dread in everyone. At this, the Saracens desired and entreated to be allied with the Christians so that they might be able to resist these human monsters with an increased number of men. These Tartars—the memory of whom is detestable—are believed to have come from the ten tribes who abandoned the Mosaic law, after the incident of the golden calves. Alexander the Macedonian first tried to enclose them in the precipitous Caspian mountains using large tar-covered blocks [doc. 29]. But when he saw that his task exceeded human effort, he called upon the God of Israel for help, and one after the other, the tops of the mountains came together, making the place inaccessible and impenetrable. On which matter Josephus says, "How much [more] will God do for a faithful man who did so much for an infidel?" From this, it is evident that God did not want the Tartars to be able to escape.

Nevertheless, as it is written in the scholastic history [of Peter Comestor, d. 1178], that they will come out [from the mountains] at the end of the world, causing a great slaughter of men. However, there is some doubt as to whether the Tartars now coming out from the east are these people, for they do not use the Hebrew language, nor do they know the Mosaic law, and they do not use nor are they governed by any established laws. To which it is replied that it is none the less believable that they are from the previously mentioned enclosed region. But just as at the time of Moses's leadership their rebellious hearts were turned in "a reprobate sense" [see Rom. 1.28] to follow foreign gods and strange rites, now, more wondrously, so that it may not be known by every other nation, their heart and language are confused, and their life transformed into that of a cruel and foolish wild beast through the vengeance of God.

They are called Tartars from a certain river which is called the Tartar that flows through their mountains and which they now have crossed.

Questions: What explanations does Matthew provide for the coming of the Mongols? Upon what sources does he draw, and how does he understand them? How might his conception of the role of the Mongols in world history shape popular responses?

EIGHT: DEMONIZATIONS

76. SATAN'S KNIGHTS?

The Knights Templar had been founded after the first crusade as a military-religious order to protect pilgrims traveling to Jerusalem. Quickly, though, they came to assume much of the responsibility for defending European holdings in the holy land. The fall of Acre in 1291 left the order without an overarching purpose. Exceptionally wealthy with extensive property particularly in France, in 1307 the Templars became the targets of King Philip IV of France (r. 1285–1314) in his campaign to bring the Church to heel within his demesne. Across France, Templars were arrested in the name of the Inquisition and charged with heresy. By this time, Pope Clement V (r. 1305–14) was residing at Avignon. Thus he was in no position to offer much opposition to the king's high-handed actions. In August 1308, a detailed list of 127 charges outlining the order's heretical activities was drawn up and individual Templars interrogated and sometimes tortured.

The following is a response to a shorter list of eleven charges that was drawn up at some point. Though these charges no longer survive, the concerns of the inquisitors can be gleaned from the selection below.

Latin, 1308 or 1310.

Source: trans. Richard Raiswell and David R. Winter, from Heinrich Finke, *Papsttum und Untergang des Templerordens* (Münster, 1907), pp. 350–51.

On the Same 11 Articles

On the first day of May in the aforesaid year [either 1308 or 1310].

Brother Hugo Gaysennon of Crest of the diocese of Vaison, serving in the aforesaid order, having been sworn.

While he denied the greater part of the articles, having considered and pondered the questions after an appropriate interval, and asked about the eleven articles, he said that he was received [into the order] by a certain brother Hugo of Monterotundo, then the master of the Temple of Borleta in the aforesaid church about sixteen years ago in the presence of brothers Peter Harteyaut, Estorto de Capella, and many others. Then the same master gave him the very cloak that had been given to the aforesaid master, saying that he should deny the lord Jesus Christ, his mother, and all the holy men and women of God and their works, that Jesus Christ was not the true God, nor the son of God, nor did he suffer or was crucified for the salvation of the human race. That he was rather a false prophet who was crucified for his crimes beyond the sea, and that he ought also not to have any hope in salvation through him, for he could not save him, nor should he believe in him but believe rather in a certain idol or head which was there and had four faces. He ought to adore that. He taught him that he should spit and urinate on the cross placed there on the ground and drag it along the ground and then stretch himself out on it in reproach of Jesus Christ and his cross. But when Brother Hugo utterly refused to do the aforesaid, he was cruelly beaten by the brothers present there so that he did not feel himself better from these lashes for fifteen days. Reluctant but driven by his great fear of them, he denied God, Jesus Christ, the blessed virgin, his mother, the holy men and women of God and their works with his mouth—but not in his heart. He spat and urinated on the aforesaid cross, and dragged it a short distance along the ground and then he stretched himself out on it with his whole robe in reproach of Jesus Christ and his cross, and with his biretta [a square cap worn by clergy] removed, he leaned towards the aforesaid idol and with knees bent, did reverence to it, begging that it do good things for him.

Questioned as to whether he saw any cat there, he said that he did—one, who was next to the aforesaid idol to which, at the command of the aforesaid master, he did reverence and then kissed on the anus.

Questioned as to whether he knows where the aforesaid cat came from, or where it went or what it was, he said that he did not know where it came from or where it went. However, he believes that it was the devil in the form of a cat.

Questioned as to whether at the time of his induction any women appeared there, he said that there were. Questioned as to whether he or any of the brothers sinned with them, he said that they did not as far as he saw.

Questioned as to whether he believes that those women were true women, he said that they were not. Rather, he believes that they were devils in the form of women, for if they were true women they would not have been able to enter the place in which he and the brothers were, for the doors were very strong. But concerning the other brothers who were received into the order, he believes that they were received in the same way as he had been received, and that they did those things which he did—and he saw five men received in like manner doing the same things that he had done.

Questions: Can this confession be taken at face value? Does it tell us more about the actions of Hugh or the concerns of his interrogators? What concerns his interrogators? How do these accusations build upon twelfth- and thirteenth-century fears of demon worship?

77. A PANORAMA OF PAIN

The following selection from Dante's Inferno *(doc. 57) describes the fate of heretics and suicides. Having handed themselves over to the devil through their actions in life, it seemed appropriate to Dante that after life, they should be subjected to punishments that mirrored their crimes.*

Photinus (fl. 344) was a heretic. His writings have not survived, but according to Saint Augustine, he denied the pre-existence of Christ before the incarnation.

Tuscan, 1314.

Source: trans. Henry Longfellow, *The Divine Comedy of Dante Alighieri* (Boston, 1867), pp. 30–31, 34–35, 40–42; rev.

[Having witnessed how the sins of lust, gluttony, avarice, sloth, and wrath are punished, the pilgrims enter the City of Dis, journeying into lower hell.]

Canto IX

As soon as I was within [the city], I cast my eyes around,
And saw on every side an ample plain,
Full of distress and torment terrible.
As at Arles, where the Rhone grows stagnant,
As at Pola near to the Quarnaro,
That shuts in Italy and bathes its borders,
The sepulchers make the whole place uneven;
So likewise did they there on every side,
Saving that there the manner was more bitter;
For flames between the sepulchers were scattered,
By which they so intensely heated were,
That iron more so asks not any art.
All of their lids uplifted were,
And from them issued forth such dire laments,
I was sure they were the wretched and tormented.
And I, "My master, what are all those people
Who, having been buried within these tombs,
Make themselves audible through doleful sighs?"
And he to me, "Here are the arch heretics,
With their disciples of all sects, and many
More than you think are packed within the tombs.
Here like together with like are buried;
And more and less the tombs are heated accordingly."
And when he to the right had turned, we passed
Between the torments and high parapets [of the city]. . . .

Canto XI

[On the edge of a steep bank, the travelers pause to get used to the stench emanating from below. Virgil explains the various circles of the damned they can see.]

"My son, upon the inside of these rocks,"
Began he then to say, "are three small circles,

From grade to grade, like those which you are leaving [those in the part
    of hell through which they have traveled]
They are all full of spirits maledict;
But from this point forth, sight alone should be sufficient for you,
Hear how and why they are in constraint.
Of every malice that wins hate in heaven,
Injury is the end; and all such end
Either by force or fraud afflicts others.
But because fraud is man's peculiar vice,
More it displeases God; and so stand lowest
The fraudulent, and greater dole assails them.
The whole first circle [below] is for the violent;
But since force may be used against three persons,
In three rounds it is divided and constructed.
Against God, ourselves, and our neighbor can we
Use force; I say on them and on their things,
As you shall hear with reason clear.
A death by violence, and painful wounds,
Are to our neighbor given; and in his substance
Ruin, and arson, and injurious levies;
Also homicides, and he who strikes unjustly,
Marauders, and freebooters, the first round
torments all [these] in different groups.
Man may lay violent hands upon himself
And his own goods; and therefore in the second
Round of necessity must repent without avail
Whoever deprives himself of your world,
Who gambles, and dissipates his property,
And weeps [up] there, where he should be joyful.
Violence can be done [against] the deity,
In heart denying and blaspheming him,
And by disdaining nature and her bounty.
And for this reason, the smallest round
Seals with its signet Sodom and Cahors,
And who, disdaining God, speaks from the heart.
Fraud, with which every conscience is stung,
A man may practice upon he who trusts,
And upon he who has no confidence invested.
The latter mode, it would appear, severs
Only the bond of love which nature makes;
Wherefore, within the second circle nestle

Hypocrisy, flattery, and those who deal in magic,
Falsification, theft, and simony,
Panders, and barrators, and the like filth.
By the other mode, forgotten is that love
Which nature makes, and what is after added,
From which there is a special faith engendered.
Hence, [it is] in the smallest circle, where the point is
Of the universe, upon which Dis is situated,
[that] whoever betrays for ever is consumed." . . .

[The travelers ford a river of fire with the help of a centaur named Nessus.]

Canto XIII

Not yet had Nessus reached the other side,
When we had put ourselves within a wood,
That was not marked by any path whatever.
Not foliage green, but of a dusky color,
Not branches smooth, but gnarled and intertangled,
Not apple-trees were there, but thorns with poison . . .
There do the hideous Harpies make their nests . . .
Broad wings have they, and necks and faces human,
And feet with claws, and their great bellies fledged;
They make laments upon the wondrous trees.
And the good master, "Before you enter farther,
Know that you are within the second round,"
Thus he began to say, "and shall be, till
You come out upon the horrible sand;
Therefore, look well around, and you shall see
Things that will give credence to my speech."
I heard on all sides lamentations uttered,
And person none beheld I who might make them,
At which, utterly bewildered, I stood still.
I think he thought that I perhaps might think
So many voices issued through those trunks
From people who concealed themselves from us;
Therefore, the master said, "If you break off
Some little branch from any of those trees,
The thoughts you have will wholly be made vain."
Then stretched I forth my hand a little forward,
And plucked a branchlet off from a great thorn;

> And the trunk cried, "Why do you mangle me?"
> After it had become browned with blood,
> It recommenced its cry, "Why do you rip me?
> Have you no spirit of pity whatsoever?
> Men once we were, and now are changed to trees;
> Indeed, your hand should be more pitiful,
> Even if the souls of serpents we had been."
> As out of a green brand, that is on fire
> At one of the ends, and from the other drips
> And hisses with the wind that is escaping;
> So from that splinter issued forth together
> Both words and blood; at which I let the tip
> Fall, and stood like a man who is afraid.

[The shade turns out to be Pier delle Vigne, who killed himself likely in 1248. After the soul laments his fate, the travelers question him as to how and why he has been imprisoned in a tree.]

> Then blew the trunk heavily, and afterward
> The wind was into such a voice converted,
> "With brevity shall be replied to you.
> When the exasperated soul abandons
> The body from which it ripped itself away,
> Minos consigns it to the seventh abyss.
> It falls into the forest, and no part
> Is chosen for it; but wherever fortune hurls it,
> There like a grain of spelt it germinates.
> It springs like a sapling, and a forest tree;
> The harpies, feeding there upon its leaves,
> Do pain create, and for the pain an outlet.
> Like others for our bodies we shall return;
> But not that any may wear them again,
> For it is not just to have what one casts off.
> Here shall we drag them, and along the dismal
> Forest our bodies shall suspended be,
> Each to the thorn of his molested shade."

Questions: Why are the heretics punished in burning tombs? Why is the punishment of suicides appropriate? Why are they punished more harshly than heretics? Is the economy of hell represented here evil? How do the torments described here differ from those of other accounts of hell?

CHAPTER NINE

THEORIZING THE DEVIL AND SOCIETY IN THE HIGH MIDDLE AGES

Figure 9.1 "Temptation through Pride" (c. 1460). This woodcut is part of a pair that depicts the struggle for a sinner's soul on his deathbed. Here, various demons are tempting the dying man with worldly vanities represented by the crowns one of the demons says he deserves, while Mary, Christ, and God remind him that his faith is strong. Its partner entitled "Consolation through Humility" depicts the demons beaten, with the sinner being attended by various angels.

NINE: THEORIZING THE DEVIL AND SOCIETY IN THE HIGH MIDDLE AGES

The High Middle Ages were a period of sustained growth and stability throughout most of Europe. With the cessation of the raiding activity that had characterized much of the early medieval period, and the development of increasingly durable political structures, the continent began to flourish as it had not done since the days of Rome. Virtually all of its social and cultural institutions showed signs of increasing complexity and sophistication.

Nowhere was this more evident than in Europe's emerging systems of knowledge production, particularly in the universities that developed from the late twelfth century. Although the curriculum was based around the liberal arts and students were trained in the *trivium* and *quadrivium* (an early arts and sciences program), the early universities were shaped by a number of vital historical forces: the recovery of lost classical texts, increased contact with Muslim and Jewish thinkers, an increased need for administrative expertise, and the emergence of the Dominicans and Franciscans with their concern for lay learning and spirituality. As a result, they quickly developed a characteristic approach to learning known as "scholasticism." This was a style of learning that strived to deduce new truths from propositions garnered from scripture and classical texts through the application of Aristotelian logic. Scholastic argumentation used rigorous, closely argued deductive (largely *a priori*) reasoning to arrive at conclusions about philosophical ideas and religious texts. By the late thirteenth and fourteenth centuries, scholars began to use scholastic argumentation in their attempts to explain the operation of nature, psychology, epistemology, politics, and even economics.

In this context, the devil was subjected to far greater (and much more methodical) scrutiny than he had been before. Both the learned and popular writers of the age contended with the meaning and significance of "incarnate evil" as their society increasingly detached itself from the assumptions of the feudal world of the post-Carolingian collapse. During this period, virtually every aspect of Satan's lordship was re-conceptualized or called into question, from his appearance and corporality to the nature and scope of his powers. Moreover, those who sought to address issues of Satan's essence did so using an array of new methods and questions. While these sometimes produced divergent (if not actually contradictory) readings of the devil's fundamental role and essence, students will detect a new emphasis on logic and rational inquiry.

This chapter juxtaposes scholastic, legal, and preaching sources to show how the devil became an increasingly complicated foil for Christianity.

78. THE DEVIL AS NULLITY

Anselm of Canterbury (c. 1035–1109) was one of the most important theologians of the Central Middle Ages. Though he took monastic vows, he rose to become archbishop of Canterbury. As a scholar, Anselm was interested in the radical potential of logic for solving

theological problems. In his most famous work, the Proslogion, *he endeavored to craft a syllogistic argument from exclusively rational premises to prove the existence of God. This is widely known as his "ontological proof." The following selection comes from his* On the Fall of the Devil *and is one of the fullest and most important medieval theological treatments of the devil, particularly of the idea of the devil as a "nullity."*
Latin, 1085–90.

Source: trans. Jasper Hopkins and Herbert Richardson, from Anselm of Canterbury, *The Fall of the Devil*, from *Complete Philosophical and Theological Treatises of Anselm of Canterbury* (Minneapolis: Arthur J. Bannon Press, 2000), pp. 230–35.

Injustice Is Evil Itself and Is Nothing

Student: Then, what shall we say to be the evil, which makes [men and angels] evil, and what shall we say to be the good which makes them good?

Teacher: We ought to believe that justice is the good in virtue of which men and angels are good, or just, and in virtue of which the will is called good, or just. But we ought to believe that injustice is the evil which makes both the will and [men and angels] evil and which we call nothing other than the privation of the good; and so, we maintain that this very injustice is nothing other than a privation of justice. For when a will was first given to rational nature, it was—at the moment of giving—turned by the giver toward what it was supposed to will; or better, it was not *turned* but was *created upright*. As long as the will stood fast in this uprightness (which we call truth or justice) in which it was created, it was just. But when it turned itself away from what it was supposed [to will] and turned toward that which it ought not to have [willed], it did not stand fast in the "original" uprightness, so to speak, in which it was created. When [the will] deserted this original uprightness, it lost something great and received nothing in its place except its privation, which has no being and which we call injustice.

How Evil Seems to Be Something

Student: I concede what you say, viz. [namely], that evil is a privation of good. But nonetheless, I regard good as a privation of evil. And just as I perceive in the case of the deprivation of evil that there results something else which we call good, so I notice in the case of the deprivation of good that there results something else which we call evil.

Now, by means of various arguments evil is proved to be nothing. For example: "Evil is only defect or corruption, which does not at all exist except in some being. And the greater the defect and corruption in this being, the more they reduce it to nothing. Moreover, if this being becomes altogether nothing, defect and corruption are also found to be nothing." Although in this or some other way evil is proved to be nothing, my mind cannot give assent (except by faith alone) unless the [following] counter-argument, which proves to me that evil is only something, is refuted.

For if nothing is signified by the name "evil," then when we hear this name our hearts shudder in vain at what they understand by its signification. Likewise, if the word "evil" is a name, then surely it is significative. However, if it is significative, it signifies. But it signifies only something. Therefore, how is evil nothing if what its name signifies is something?

Finally, while justice is present, there seems to be such great tranquility and peace of mind that in many cases justice (like chastity and patience too) seems to be nothing other than a cessation of evil. But when justice departs, very conflicting and very harsh and very manifold passion besets the mind. Like a cruel master, it compels the wretched and puny man to be afflicted with worry over very many shameful and oppressive tasks and to labor very grievously at them. It would be astonishing if it could be shown that *nothing* accomplishes all these things.

By Means of Their Names, Evil and Nothing Cannot Be Proved to Be Something but [Can Be Proved to Be] As-If-Something

Teacher: I think you are not so mad as to say that nothing is something, even though you cannot deny that "nothing" is a name. Therefore, if by means of the name "nothing" you cannot prove that nothing is something, how do you think that by means of the name "evil" you can prove that evil is something?

Student: An example which resolves one contentious issue by means of another contentious issue accomplishes nothing. For I do not know what this very nothing is. Therefore—since the question at hand is about evil, which you say to be nothing—if you wish to teach me what I may understand evil to be, teach me first what I may understand nothing to be. Then reply to the other arguments (besides [the argument from] the name "evil") by which I said I was troubled about the fact that evil seems to be something.

Teacher: Since to-be-nothing and not-to-be-anything do not at all differ, how can we say what that-which-is not-anything is?

Student: If there is not anything which is signified by the name "nothing," then this name does not signify anything. But if it does not signify anything, it is not a name. But surely it is a name. Therefore, although no one says that nothing is something but we must always admit that nothing is nothing, nevertheless no one can deny that the name "nothing" is significative. But if this name signifies not nothing but, rather, something, then that which is signified seems unable to be nothing and seems rather to be something. Therefore, if that which is signified is not nothing but is something, how will it be true that by means of this name what is nothing is signified? Indeed, if nothing is spoken of truly, then it is truly nothing; and so, it is not anything. Hence, if that which is signified by the name "nothing" is not nothing but is something (as this line of reasoning seems to show), then it is falsely and improperly called by this name.

But on the contrary, if as everyone judges, what is named nothing is truly nothing and is not at all anything, does anything at all seem to follow more logically than that the name "nothing" signifies nothing—that is, does not signify anything?

Thus, why is it that this name, viz., "nothing," does not signify nothing but signifies something, and does not signify something but signifies nothing?

Teacher: Perhaps signifying nothing and signifying something are not opposed.

Student: If they are not opposed then either the word "nothing" signifies (in different respects) both nothing and something or else a thing must be found which is both something and nothing.

Teacher: What if both alternatives can be discovered to be the case—viz., that there is an ambiguity of signification in the name "nothing" and that the same thing is both something and nothing?

Student: I would like to know of both.

Teacher: It is evident that this word, viz., "nothing," does not at all differ, with respect to its signification, from what I term "not-something." Also, nothing is clearer than that the word "not-something" indicates by its signification that absolutely every thing and all that is something should be removed from the understanding, and that no thing whatsoever nor what is at all something should be retained in the understanding. But the removal of a thing cannot at all be signified except together with the signification of that very thing whose removal is signified. (For example, no one understands what "not-man" signifies except by understanding what a man is.) Therefore, it is necessary that the word "not-something" signify something by "destroying" that which is something. But since by removing everything that is something, the word "not-something" signifies no being which it indicates is to be retained in the understanding of the hearer, it signifies no thing nor what is something.

Therefore, by means of these different considerations, the word "not-something" does in some respect signify a thing and something, and does not in any respect signify a thing or something. For it signifies by removing and does not signify by establishing. In this manner, the name "nothing," which destroys everything that is something, signifies something rather than nothing by destroying and signifies nothing rather than something by establishing [by positing]. Therefore, it is not necessary that nothing be something simply because its name somehow or other signifies something. Rather, it is necessary that nothing be nothing, because its name signifies something in the aforementioned way. And so, in this aforementioned way the fact that evil is nothing is not opposed to the fact that the name "evil" is significative—provided that "evil" signifies something by destroying [by negating] it and, thus, is constitutive of no thing.

Student: I cannot deny that in accordance with your reasoning just now the name "nothing" somehow signifies something. But it is well-enough known that the something which in this manner is signified by this name is not named nothing; and when we hear this name ["nothing"], we do not accept it for that thing which it thus signifies. Therefore, I ask about that for which this name stands and about that which we understand when we hear this name. About *that*, I say, I am asking what it is. For this name *properly* signifies that thing; and so, it is a name because it is significative of that thing and not because it signifies something by negating in the aforementioned way. Indeed, it is the name of that thing because of the signifying of which it is reckoned [as a name] among names; and that thing is called nothing. I ask: How is that thing something if it is properly called nothing? Or how is it nothing if the name that is significative of it signifies something? Or how is the same thing both something and nothing? I ask the same questions about the name "evil" and about that which it signifies and about what is named "evil."

Teacher: You are right in asking, because although by the previous consideration "evil" and "nothing" do signify something, nevertheless what is signified is not evil or nothing. But there is another respect in which they signify something and in which what is signified is something—though not really something but only as if something.

Indeed, many things are said according to form which are not the case according to fact. For example, *timere* [to be afraid] is called active according to the form of the word, although it is passive according to fact. So too, blindness is called something according to a form of speaking, although it is not something according to fact. For just as we say of someone that he has sight and that sight is in him, so we say that he has blindness and that blindness is in him, although blindness is not something but rather is not-something. Moreover, to have blindness is not to have something but is rather to be deprived of that which is something. For blindness is nothing other than not-seeing, or the absence of sight where sight ought to be. But not-seeing, or the absence of sight, is not anything more where sight ought to be than where it ought not to be. Therefore, blindness is not anything more in the eye because sight ought to be there than is not-seeing, or the absence of sight, in a stone, where sight ought not to be. Also, many other things which are not something are likewise called something according to a form of speaking, since we speak about them as about existing things.

Therefore, in this way, "evil" and "nothing" signify something; and what is signified is something not according to fact but according to a form of speaking. For "nothing" signifies only not-something, or the absence of things which are something. And evil is only not-good, or the absence of good where good either ought to be or is advantageous to be. But that which is only the absence of what is something is surely not something. Therefore, evil truly is nothing, and nothing is not something. And yet, in a certain sense, evil and nothing are something because we speak about them as if they were something, when we say "Nothing caused it" or "Evil caused it" and "What caused it is nothing" or "Evil is what caused it." [These expressions] resemble our saying "Something caused it" or "Good caused it" and "What caused it is something" or "Good is what caused it." Accordingly, when we flatly deny a statement which someone makes, we say: "That which you are saying is nothing." For "that" and "which" are properly said only of that which is something. And when "that" and "which" are said in the manner I have just mentioned, they are not said about that which is something but about that which is spoken of as if something.

Student: You have satisfied me regarding the argument from the name "evil"—an argument by means of which I used to think I could prove that evil is something.

Questions: What has the application of logic done to reshape the problem of evil? How is the scholastic approach to the devil different from what has come before? What are the theological and social implications of declaring the devil a "nullity"? Outside an academic context, would this definition capture people's experience of evil? How is this a discussion of the devil, unless evil is identical with the devil?

79. A SCHOLASTIC THEOLOGIAN WRESTLES WITH DEMONIC BODIES

Thomas Aquinas (1224/5–74) was one of the most important theologians of the Middle Ages. As a young man, he was educated at the Benedictine Abbey of Monte Cassino, before moving to the new university at Naples in 1239 to study the liberal arts. It was in Naples that Thomas joined the fledgling Dominican order—much to the chagrin of his parents. He was probably attracted to the Dominicans because of their emphasis on education and preaching. From Naples, the young man was sent to the University of Paris, where he studied theology, eventually rising to become a master of theology. Throughout most of the 1260s, Aquinas resided in Rome, where he prepared young Dominican friars for a life of preaching and hearing confession. It was during this period that he began work on his great theological synthesis, his Summa theologiae. *This was a far-reaching scholastic treatment of theology intended for the edification of both those new to the field and more advanced scholars. It was here, too, that he wrote his* Questions on the Power of God, *from which the excerpts below are taken. This relatively short work examines the relationship between God, creation, and nature.*

Latin, 1265–66.

Source: trans. Richard Raiswell and David R. Winter, from Thomas Aquinas, *Quaestiones disputatae de potentia dei*, vol. 2 (London: Burns Oates & Washbourne Ltd., 1933), pp. 183–88, 201–12.

Question 6, Article 5

Whether demons devote themselves to the operation of miracles. It would appear that they do. . . .

[Aquinas sets up the problem by listing a number of biblical examples which seem to suggest that demons can work miracles.]

7. As well, it appears that Job's adversities were brought about through the agency of a demon because the lord gave it power over everything that Job possessed [Job 1.12]. However, these adversities did not occur without a miracle, as can be seen by the fire coming down from heaven and the wind that destroyed Job's house which caused the death of his children. Therefore, demons are able to perform miracles.

8. As well, that Moses changed his staff into serpents [sic] was a miracle. However, when pharaoh's magicians did likewise, this happened through the power of demons [Exod. 7.10–12]. Therefore, it seems that demons are able to perform miracles. . . .

On the contrary. During the time of Antichrist, the demon will be able to do works of the greatest power because, as it says in Revelation 20.3, "he must be loosed for a little time." This refers to the time of Antichrist. However, he will not be able to perform genuine miracles, since it is stated that at the coming of Antichrist, there will be in all things, "power and false signs and wonders" [2 Thess. 2.9]. Therefore, demons cannot perform genuine miracles.

I respond. It can be said that, just as good angels—by means of grace—can do something beyond their natural power, so evil angels can do less than their natural power [allows] because they are restrained by divine providence. Indeed, as Augustine says, because evil angels are able to do certain things only if they are permitted, they are not—accordingly—able to do things that they are not *permitted* to do. On this account, they are said to be "bound" because they are prevented from doing those things to which their natural power extends. But they are said to be "loosed" when they are permitted—by divine justice—to do what they are able to do naturally. But there are certain things that they are not able to do even were they to be permitted . . . because the kind of nature bestowed upon them by God does not permit it.

Nor does God give them power to do things that are beyond their natural capacity. Indeed, because a miraculous work is a divine witness testifying to God's power and truth, were some power to work miracles be given to demons—whose whole will is given over to evil—God would become a witness to something that is false. That would not accord with God's goodness. And so sometimes, when they are permitted by God, demons perform works which are within their natural power but which seem miraculous from the perspective of human beings. . . . [Moreover], by means of their natural power and skill, demons are able to produce only those effects for which there is some natural capacity in the bodies which are subordinate to them. In this way, they are able to manipulate those capacities quickly to produce a particular effect.

Nevertheless, after having made some change to a physical body, they can make things appear in the imagination that are not part of the nature of the thing itself. They do this by manipulating the organ of the imagination according to the disposition of its spirits and humors. When applied in a particular way, some external substances have the effect of causing a thing to appear to have a different form than the one it [actually] has, as is evident in the case of delirium and insanity.

Therefore, demons can work marvelously in us in two ways: the first through a real bodily transformation; the second through a certain delusion of the senses resulting from some manipulation of the imagination. However, neither of these operations is miraculous. Rather, they are the work of the devil's skill. . . . Thus, quite simply, it must be said that true miracles cannot be performed by demons. . . .

Response to the seventh assertion. With God's permission, demons, through some movement of the air, can stir up disasters which we may also see happen naturally with the movement of the wind. The adversities of Job were brought about by demons in this way.

Response to the eighth assertion. Two views about the operation of Pharaoh's magicians are discussed in the Gloss [standard commentary on the Bible]. The first is that there was not a real conversion of their staffs into serpents but that they were only changed in appearance through some deceitful illusion. But Augustine in the same place in the Gloss says that there was a real conversion of the staffs into serpents. He provides a proof of this, for scripture uses the same words for the staff of the magicians and the staff of Moses—the latter of which was really turned into a serpent. Because the [magicians'] staffs were turned into serpents through the work of demons, it was not a miracle. Demons did this by collecting some [serpent] semen which had the power to putrefy the staffs and turn them into serpents. But what Moses did was a miracle because this was done by means of divine power, without the action of any natural power. . . .

Question 6, Article 7

Whether angels or demons can assume bodies. It would seem that they cannot. . . .

1. [If angels as incorporeal substances can be said to have bodies this must be in one of two ways: either in the sense that they are naturally united to them but this Aquinas has earlier shown not to be the case.] Therefore, it follows that they cannot be united with bodies except insofar as they move them. But this does not mean that they assume these bodies. Because the angel and the demon would [accidentally have to] assume every body which moves, which is clearly not the

case. Indeed, the angel moved the tongue of Balaam's donkey but it is not said "he assumed it." Therefore, it cannot be said that an angel or a demon assumes a body.

2. As well, if angels or demons assume bodies, this cannot be out of necessity but either—in the case of good angels—for our instructions, or—in the case of evil ones—for our deception. Regardless, in either case an imaginary vision would be adequate. Therefore, it does seem that they assume bodies. . . .

7. As well, if an angel assumes a body, it must be either a celestial one or one made from the four elements. But it cannot be a celestial body since a celestial body cannot be divided or ripped from its natural place. Similarly, it cannot be a fiery body since it would consume any other bodies to which it adhered. Nor can it be an aerial body because air cannot be shaped. Nor can it be an aqueous body because water does not hold its shape. Nor finally can it be an earthy one because they are quick to disappear—as is clear from Tobias's angel [Tob. 12.21]. Therefore, in no sense can they assume a body. . . .

9. As well, if angels assume bodies, then the bodies assumed by them are either actually as they appear or they are not. Indeed, if they have true forms—since they sometimes appear to have the forms of a real person—the body they assume will be that of a real human body. But that is impossible unless it can be said that an angel becomes a person, which seems unlikely. But if they are not real bodies this also seems unlikely, for such a fiction is not fitting to angels of truth. Therefore in no way does an angel assume a body. . . .

But on the contrary. It is stated in Genesis 18.2 that the angels who appeared to Abraham appeared in assumed bodies—and similarly about the angel who appeared to Tobit.

I respond . . . It must be plainly admitted that angels sometimes assume a body, by fashioning a sensible body perceptible to exterior or corporeal vision, just as by sometimes fashioning images in the imagination, they [can cause themselves to] appear in visions. . . .

Response to the first assertion. An angel does not assume every body that it moves. . . . An angel does not assume a body so that it may join itself to its nature in the same way that a person "assumes" food. Nor does an angel unite a body to its person in the way that the son of God assumed a human nature. Rather, it assumes a body to represent itself in the same way that intelligible things are represented through sensible ones. Thus, an angel is said to assume a body when the body he fashions in this way is suitable for his representation. . . .

Response to the second assertion. Not only is imaginary vision useful for our instruction, so too is corporeal vision. . . .

Response to the seventh assertion. An angel is able to assume a body from any element or from a mixture of many elements. However, it is more fitting that he assumes a body from the air which can easily be condensed and so receive and retain a shape, and become colored from the reflection of other shining bodies as is the case with clouds. Thus, insofar as the matter at hand is concerned, there is no difference between pure air and steam or smoke which extend to the nature of air.

Response to the ninth assertion. The bodies that angels assume have real forms to the extent that the senses are able to perceive them. These forms are sensible in themselves in terms of color and shape, but not in terms of their specific nature which is only accidentally sensible. Nor is it appropriate on this account to say that there is some fiction in this, because angels do not present themselves to our eyes in human forms so that they might be believed to be people. Rather [this happens so that] the powers of angels might be comprehensible to human faculties—just as metaphors, which signify things by means of their likeness to other things, are not false ways of speaking.

Question 6, Article 8

Whether an angel or a demon is able to exercise the functions of a living body through an assumed one. It seems that this is not the case.

1. Whoever is capable of having the power of exercising some function must have the appropriate faculties to do so otherwise he would not be able to perform that function. If that were not the case, such power would be pointless to him. But the functions of living bodies cannot be performed without bodily organs. Therefore, as an angel does not have bodily organs naturally united to itself, it seems that it is not able to perform the aforesaid functions. . . .

6. It could be said that an angel or a demon is able to procreate through an assumed body, not by means of a seed taken from its assumed body, but by means of the [natural] seed of a man carried into a woman—in the same way that a demon causes certain real and natural effects by using other appropriate seeds [as with the putrefying seeds above]. But on the contrary, the seed of an animal used for procreation works chiefly through its natural heat. Were a demon to carry [human] seed some great distance, it would seem impossible for its natural heat not to dissipate. Therefore, the generation of a person cannot be performed in the aforesaid manner.

7. As well, given this, a person could not be generated from such seed except in accordance with the potency of the human seed. Therefore, those who are said to have been generated by demons would not be of any greater stature and strength than others who are generated in the usual way by human seed. However, Genesis 6.4 [doc. 2] states, "when the sons of God had entered into the daughters of men, they brought forth children—giants were born. These are the mighty men of old, men of renown."

8. As well, food is required for the sake of nourishment. Therefore, if angels do not need to be nourished in their assumed bodies, it seems that they also do not eat.

It is said about the angels who appeared to Abraham, "When they had eaten, they said to him, 'Where is your wife, Sarah?'" [Gen. 18.9] Therefore, angels eat and speak in their assumed bodies.

As well, commenting upon that part of Genesis 6.2, "the sons of God, seeing etc." and whether the Hebrew word *Elohim* is plural, Jerome's gloss says, "It denotes both God and gods." On that account, Jerome dared to say that the sons of gods are gods—that is, understanding them as the saints or angels. Therefore, it seems that angels do procreate. . . .

[Aquinas answers that in their assumed bodies angels cannot feel sensation, grow, or require nourishment. However, they can mimic actions such as speech or eating by manipulating the elements through natural actions.]

Response to the first assertion. An angel does not exercise such functions naturally, and so, on that account, it is not necessary that the [appropriate] organs are naturally united to them. . . .

Response to the sixth assertion. Because [human] seed cools, a demon uses a remedy such as moving quickly or other measures to retain the natural heat in the seed.

Response to the seventh assertion. Without a doubt, procreation of this sort happens by virtue of the potency of the human seed. For this reason, a person so generated is not the child of a demon but of the man whose seed it was. Nevertheless, it is possible for stronger and greater people to be generated through such means. This is because demons—wanting to be admired for their works—observe the fixed position of the stars and the complexion of the man [from whom they are extracting the seed] and the woman [being inseminated] to produce this [result]. And this is especially the case if the seeds which they use as their instrument acquire an increase in potency through their use in this way.

Response to the eighth assertion. Eating is attributed to angels in their assumed bodies, but not so much for the [usual] purpose—which is nutrition—but simply for the appearance of eating. It is the same also with Christ after the resurrection, to whose body nothing could then be added. In this, though, there is a difference because Christ's eating really was natural. Namely, in his existence, he had a vegetative soul and so was able to have true growth. But in neither case was the food he consumed turned into flesh and blood. It was rather dissolved into adjacent matter.

Response to the first contrary argument. It has been explained [above] how eating and speaking can be attributed to an angel.

Response to the second contrary argument. By "the sons of God" one understands the sons of Seth who were sons of God through grace, and of the angels by imitation. But the sons of men are understood to be the sons of Cain who abandoned God, living carnally.

Response to the third contrary argument. Angels assume the instruments of sense but not for their use but rather for their signification. On this account, although they do not sense through them, they do not assume them without reason.

Questions: Are angels above nature or part of it? What is the difference between a miracle and the wonders that demons can perform? How are angels and demons said to assume bodies? Why? Can demons procreate with human females? How are they able to create humans who are stronger than most people?

80. THE DEVIL MAKES HIS CASE

Satan's Case against the Divine Virgin before Judge Jesus *is often credited to the eminent fourteenth-century Italian jurist Bartolus of Saxoferrato (1313–57). A doctor of both canon and civil law, Bartolus spent most of his career teaching, first in Pisa and then Perugia. Although he wrote extensively on various legal subjects, Bartolus's approach to law was practical. He was especially concerned with finding rules in ancient legal authorities that might be useful for the modern day. Satan's Case centers upon an imagined legal action brought by the devil against humanity, with Christ acting as judge. The devil argues that humanity became his when Eve sinned. However, after possessing the human race peacefully for several centuries, he claims that he was violently and unjustly dispossessed of his lawful property. Legalistic in tone and at times quite technical, the text narrates the legal wrangling between the two parties as they repeatedly shift their arguments in response to those of their opponent. Scholars believe this document was intended to teach students about various elements of Roman legal procedure and types of pleading.*

Latin, mid-fourteenth century.

Source: trans. Richard Raiswell and David R. Winter, from Bartoli à Saxoferrato, *Processus Satanae Contra D. Virginem coram Iudice Iesu*, from *Processus Iuris Ioco-serius* (Hanover, 1611), pp. 26–31. References to the Codex and Decretals have been removed.

[After arguments as to whether the Virgin Mary's sex precluded her from serving as humanity's advocate at law were resolved in her favor by her son, a demon acting for Satan set out his case.]

"Forgive me," the demon said, "because the time for us to speak of wonderful things is limited, you ought not [to waste it] praising yourself. All praise becomes filthy in one's own mouth.

"But let us turn to other matters. Because God lives in truth and justice, I argue that he ought to punish the great as well as the small. There ought to be no exception of persons with him. That is to say, he ought to punish a friend just as he does a stranger. As this is the case here, I seek the immediate damnation of mankind—and I do so on the basis of this, the strongest of arguments: you know that the Angel Lucifer was thrown out of heaven even though no commandment [against disobedience] had previously been given [to him]. Thus, he cannot be said to have been disobedient. Yet a commandment *was* given to Adam and Eve: they were told that they must not eat the apple [of the forbidden tree] because as soon as they ate it, they would be condemned to death. Despite this, they did not worry about transgressing the commandment that had [explicitly] been given to them. Yet I—to whom no commandment about obedience was given—was thrown from heaven and damned. [Given this], how much more, therefore, ought the human race be damned when it breached the lord's commandment? [Surely] it is a more serious matter to breach a commandment than to act before one has been given. And so I say, the human race ought to be damned—and I ask that the advocate respond."

The advocate replied, "O miserable wretch. What you said about that angel is not the same thing, for the angel who sinned was deservedly punished. Because he had no defect in him that would induce him into sinning—because he had no other infirmity except his conscious malice—he did sin. And as you well know, in no way did he require a commandment [not to sin].

"But when mankind sinned, he had something which induced him to sin— namely a weak body. By contrast, the angel had all wisdom in him without any commandment by virtue of his nature. He knew the truth of good and evil because his nature was perfect. From this perspective, the angel sinned more grievously against the above-said truth because he knowingly preferred himself before God on account of his pride. But man, who was ignorantly deceived, sinned as a result of cunning and wily tricks. For that reason, the angel fell from a higher place. But man did not have such certitude, for his body weighed down his soul [and so impaired its cognition]. What you are saying about the angel, then, is by no means right. Be silent, now, O faithless, damned one, because enough has been said."

"I will not be silent," said the demon. "Open your ears, O advocate of the human race, and you will hear what I have to say to you."

"Let us make an end of this suit," said the advocate. "For you know that you have been defeated in all points—you should not return to what you have previously argued [in order to expound it] more fully. Are you seeking an interlocutory judgment [preliminary verdict] to be given immediately on the basis of what you have argued [before the court] just as you were earlier allowed to seek restitution?"

The demon replied, "O advocate, I am surprised at you, for you wish to place a limit not only on me but on the highest deity. I am concerned with just one point—I press it still: I argue that mankind sinned."

The advocate turned toward her son and said, "my son, you who are the judge of the living and the dead, I know that the cunning one wants to say more. He wants to convince [you] through false sophistry and to show [you] through his arguments that man has sinned, and he wants [the matter] to be concluded as if the things he has claimed originated with a judge. You know, my son, that his proposition and the foundation [of his argument] are false. How can it be believed, therefore, that he is now speaking the truth? This is surely not the case, because once he became evil, he must always be assumed to be evil. The cunning one speaks with so much pride that I do not know now what point of his argument I want to take up. Therefore, I beg you, my son, tell him that he should say in one word what clause he wants to take up and then I will define and gloss it according to the truth."

The demon said, "I hear today about wonderful things in the sun, moon, and stars because the advocate of the world is acting as if she is my advocate although I am reluctant and unwilling [to retain her]. [Her behavior] is against the law because no benefit can be conveyed to the unwilling. She wants to be my tutor and my nurse, and to act for me as she might for boys who do not know how to define or gloss. But I speak my words frankly: I do not need any governing or glossation from the world. Thus, as far as this matter goes, I ask that she not be heard when she wants to play the role of the initiator of the action, [for that] is my role."

By way of reply, the advocate said, "I am a little disturbed. I do not want that cunning one to allege anything false in your presence, for he ought not be heard on the basis of such lying reasoning. If he wants to say something false, let him speak in his own kingdom—but not in yours."

The demon said, "If you do not want to hear me, I will withdraw. So now, frankly, I will see if there is justice in the judging."

Then the almighty father [sic] spoke to his mother, "Let us see whether that crafty one wants to claim justice. For you know that I am justice, and I must give justice to everyone. Therefore, let us see whether the demon supports a just cause."

Replying, the mother then said, "My son, your justice in this is that you do not let him tell a lie in your kingdom."

But the almighty said to his mother, "If that cunning one tells a lie, he will be more sharply punished for that lie. Thus, you should let him speak."

The advocate said, "Therefore, O damned one, you may say what you intended to say."

Then the demon said, "Man sinned. I claim that he deserves to be punished and damned."

The advocate said, "You cannot go beyond this because you have already strayed from the path of justice, for you do not say how he sinned and whether he sinned from his own fault or actually [as a result of] yours. For you know that you were at fault—as was said above—and because of this, you ought to be silent now, because it is time."

Then Jesus spoke, "O mother, let him speak because it is rude not to let him reply or argue to some extent from a legal perspective."

Then the demon said, "man sinned against the infinite good, and I do not care why he sinned—whether it was his own fault or that of someone else. That I induced him to sin has been set forth thousands of times. But it is written in the law that doing and assenting [to a crime] are to be punished equally."

[The demon then proceeds to cite an array of legal passages supporting his position that deciding to break the law should be punished as severely as breaking the law itself.]

["]Thus, it is sufficient for me [to say] that man sinned. Therefore, his punishment ought to correspond with the offence in accordance with the law. Thus, I ask that equality be preserved in this matter: just as I was damned because of my sin, so should man likewise be condemned, for he sinned also.

"Man committed the crime of *lese majesty*, for which he along with his descendants ought to be damned as they deserve, for it is written that sons ought to suffer their father's punishment so that examples of hereditary crimes are feared."

The advocate replied, "Listen my son, you who are always blessed above every creature, in whose name is every heavenly, terrestrial, and infernal knee bent: the cunning one says that man sinned against the infinite good; therefore, he must be punished eternally. To this I respond and argue that you, my son, are God and man, and you are infinite goodness. Therefore, man sinned against you. Therefore, as the injury was inflicted on you, you are able to forgive it—as was said above. Because the cunning one wants to say that either man proceeded into sinning on account of his thoughtlessness and so is not then condemned, or that he proceeded into it through insanity and so then is to be pitied, or out of injustice, in which case then his injustice is to be remedied, he argues, therefore, that man ought not to be punished nor condemned."

The demon replied, "I responded sufficiently above. It is hard for me to have the mother of the judge as advocate against me . . ." and he said to the queen of heaven, "You are acting wickedly because you do not want man to be punished for the sin he committed."

Then Jesus said to the demon, "Be silent now. You well know that I hung on the cross for the redemption of the human race because it was damned for its sin once. For this reason, it is not just that we sentence the human race for the same sin a second time. . . Therefore, await the day of judgment, because then I will destroy the wicked, but I will make the good triumphant in the joy of heaven."

The demon said, "Lord Jesus, king of glory, don't interrupt me, because you well know that man sinned infinitely. Accordingly, his punishment is extended from the time [that the action took place] until the present. Therefore, he ought to be punished even today. . . ."

The advocate replied, "You conclude falsely. You know that this is not true because it rests on something which is absent. If there was guilt in man—which I do not believe—you know that it was annulled through grace and struck out by God's mercy. Therefore, where there is no fault, there is likewise no punishment. . . ."

Then the demon said to Jesus, "Lord, I seek to be shown justice, otherwise there is not any judgment that will support your reputation—if there is no justice in you because you are without justice, you are not a judge."

The advocate replied, "Up to this point, you have spoken evilly. You know that God created man in his image and likeness, and that he intended man to be the heir to eternal life. He promised this to Abraham and his offspring. Therefore, the human race cannot be yours. Rather, he ought to be placed in the joy of celestial glory."

The demon replied, "You know, advocate, that God created man. But I know one thing—that he created him with wisdom. Therefore, man had wisdom and in his wisdom he sinned. Therefore, he sinned knowingly and deceitfully. Accordingly, God ought not to defend his treachery. Therefore, man must be punished—and this is what I seek to be pronounced."

The advocate replied, "Be silent now, son of iniquity. Did I not say to you that man was led into sin because of the weakness of a woman? This is undoubtedly the case. Thus, it is not man that is liable for punishment but you, devil: he who gives the opportunity for damnation is considered to have caused the damnation. It is not necessary to press this matter any further because it has been discussed enough and I said many things which do not need to be restated . . . Therefore, I seek my dearest son—king of glory and savior of the world—that you give an opinion in favor of the human race, and that human race be thoroughly absolved from the legal claim of the procurator of infernal wickedness."

[The arguments concluded, Jesus announced his judgment on Easter Sunday.]

"In the name of the eternal, Amen. We, Jesus, savior of the world, having considered the claim against the human race, and having considered the documents produced by the procurator and the allegations made by the procurator of infernal wickedness, and having considered the allegations made by the Virgin Mary, advocate of the human race, and having considered the charges, responses, exceptions, and rejoinders, and the laws cited by both parties—having considered and deliberated on all the things aforesaid—and about the aforesaid—which needed to be considered and deliberated upon, sitting for judgment on our usual bench of law placed above the thrones of the angels in our heavenly palace where we make our personal residence, by means of this definitive statement we absolve the human race, and we grant absolution from the suit of the procurator of infernal wickedness, for doing so agrees with holy scripture and the truth of justice which we wish to follow in this matter. Also, we order the procurator of infernal wickedness to go immediately to the perpetual damnation of hell where there are tears and gnashing of teeth without end."

Terrified, the accursed devil, ripping his clothes, fled back to hell in indignation. . . .

[Sentence given] A.D. 1311, the 2nd interdiction, 6th day of the month of April.

Then the angels and the heavenly choir seeing these things began talking to the glorious virgin, saying "Hail queen, mother of mercy, our life, sweetness and hope."

Questions: Does the devil have a strong case, morally or legally? Is he treated fairly by the judge? What traditions of the devil does the author draw upon? What use might this story have been to its intended audience?

81. CONTEMPLATING THE DEVIL'S PLACE IN NATURE

"Bestiaries" were catalogues of the natural world compiled by scholars who wanted to give their audiences an idea of how God's creation was organized. Dozens of different bestiary collections survive from the medieval period (in hundreds of handwritten manuscripts). Many of them were ultimately based on the works of classical Greco-Roman naturalists such as Pliny the Elder (c. 23–79 CE). The Physiologus, *mentioned in this reading, was one such early—and anonymous—collection. Typically, medieval bestiaries listed entries for various birds, fish, and animals that would have been familiar to the reader, but they might also include material about more exotic creatures such as elephants, crocodiles, and giraffes. Because medieval authors were uncertain where to draw the line between the natural and preternatural worlds, they often incorporated material about creatures that we would unequivocally characterize as supernatural: unicorns, centaurs, dragons. Of course, the existence of a dragon must have seemed just as likely as the existence of an elephant to an author who had seen neither. While bestiaries were designed to provide empirical information about the creatures listed, they were also intended to show how God's hand worked providentially in nature. Thus, most of the creatures contained in these sorts of collections were "allegorized"; that is, authors attempted to show how an animal's innate characteristics or behavior aligned with the Christian worldview. The way they acted or their appearance provided important information about salvation, God's continuing intervention in human affairs, or enactments of the virtues or vices.*

The reading below comes from a twelfth-century work entitled Concerning Beasts and Other Matters, *variously attributed to the French scholars Hugh of Saint Victor (c. 1096–1140) or Hugh of Fouilloy (c. 1103–72), or sometimes to the English bishop Hugh Foliot (1155–1234). The phrase "The wolf is in the fable" (*lupus est in fabula*) is a medieval Latin form of the modern English aphorism "Speak of the devil and he shall appear." It also seems to mean "Shut up!"*

Latin, mid- to late twelfth century.

Source: trans. Richard Raiswell and David R. Winter, from Hugh Foliot (uncertain), *De bestiis et aliis rebus* (Migne, *PL* 177: 67B–68C).

In Greek, the wolf is called *lukos* or *lycos*, also *luka*, which is "light of morning." This is apt on account of its greed, and it is called this for its rapacity. For this reason, we also call prostitutes "wolves," since they lay waste to the wealth of their lovers. Others say wolves are called "*lu-pos*" because they are "*leo-pedes*" ("lion-feet"), which is to say that, like lions, their strength is in their paws. For this reason, whatever they might capture by foot will not survive. The beast is a predator, desiring blood.

Concerning this creature, rustics claim that if a wolf sees a man before the man sees him, he will lose his voice. For this reason, when someone is suddenly silent, it is said: "The wolf is in the fable!" Certainly, if a wolf senses that it has been seen, it loses the audacity of its fierceness. Wolves copulate not more than twelve days in the whole year. The wolf has its power in its arms or shoulders, or in its jaws, less so in its haunches. The *Physiologus* describes these animals as lethal. It is not able to bend its neck back. It is reported that it lives sometimes on prey, sometimes on earth, and occasionally even on the wind.

It is also said that the she-wolf will only bear her pups in the month of May, when it thunders; she is so cunning that she will not take her prey when she is near her cubs, but at a distance. If it is necessary that she must seek prey at night, she will go like a tame dog to the sheepfold, and lest the sheepdogs accidentally sense the stench of her breath, and they wake the shepherds, she goes upwind; and if a breaking branch or twig should make a noise under her paw, she will bite the paw sharply as punishment.

In the night, the wolf's eyes shine like lanterns. It has such a nature that, if it should see a man first, that man loses the ability to shout, or so it will seem to him. As [the third-century geographer] Julius Solinus reports, who has much to say about the nature of beasts, the wolf has at the end of its tail a tuft of fur that is a charm for lovers. If it greatly fears capture, it will tear out this tuft with its teeth.

The devil, who always envies the human race, bears the form of the wolf, since he hunts at the edges of the churches of the faithful so that he might devour and destroy souls. That it bears its young during the first thunder of the month of May signifies the devil, who was cast down from heaven at the first stirring of his pride. That it carries its power in its forelimbs and not in its hindmost parts also signifies the devil, who before his fall was an angel of light in heaven, but now has made himself an apostate below (but if you should oppose him, he will flee from you). The wolf's eyes shine in the night because the works of the devil seem beautiful and salubrious to blind and foolish men. When the wolf feeds her pups, she does not take her prey unless she is far from them. This is because the devil comforts with worldly goods those whom he is certain will be forced to suffer with him the confinement of eternal Gehenna. But he constantly pursues those who distance themselves from him through good works. As we read concerning the blessed Job, in order to make him abandon the lord, the devil stole Job's entire fortune and assaulted his sons and daughters. That the wolf cannot turn his head without turning his whole body demonstrates that the devil never turns towards the correction of penance. But what can be done for a man when the wolf takes away his power to shout, when he does not have the power of speech? He loses the help of those who stand at a distance. But what is to be done? The man should take off his clothes and stomp upon them underfoot. And taking two stones in his hands, he should bang them together. What happens then? The wolf, losing the boldness that comes with its courage, will flee. The man, saved by his ingenuity, will be free, just as he was in the beginning.

This is to be understood spiritually and may be elevated to a superior allegorical sense. For who does the wolf signify if he is not the devil? And who is the man if not the whole human race? And what are the clothes if not sin? And what are the stones if not the apostles and the other saints and our lord, Jesus Christ? For all of the saints are called by the prophet [Ezekiel] the "living stones of adamantine" [Ezek. 3.9]. Before we were redeemed, we were under the power of the enemy and had lost the ability to call out for help. Even though our sins made this necessary, God could not hear us, nor could the saints offer us their assistance. However, after God in his mercy granted us grace through his son, in the sacrament of baptism, we laid aside, like old clothes, the person we had been beforehand, and we donned, like a new garment, the new person who, according to the apostle, has been made in justice. Then, picking up stones, we beat them against one another, because, with our prayers, we gain the attention of God's saints, who now reign with him in heaven. We bear unto them our prayers, that they may gain for us the ear of our judge, and they might procure for us a pardon, lest we discover that Cerberus will swallow us up, rejoicing in our destruction.

Questions: Is this description intended to be read literally? What does it suggest about how scholars viewed the natural world? Does such an approach shed new light on the devil? What other sources might a scholar draw upon to understand the devil in more detail? How might it have influenced those seeking to represent the devil pictorially?

82. A PREACHER'S STORIES ABOUT THE DEVIL

*Jacques de Vitry (c. 1165–1240) was one of the most famous preachers of the thirteenth century. He also led an eventful life that took him from one end of the Mediterranean to the other. Born in north-central France to parents of middling social standing, he attended classes at the University of Paris, studying under Peter the Chanter (d. 1197) and other famous schoolmen. He was a regular canon at Oignies in modern Belgium before becoming bishop of Acre around 1216. He was an ally of Pope Innocent III (r. 1198–1216) and, between c. 1200 and 1216, preached the fourth, fifth, and Albigensian crusades. For his preaching efforts and services to the papacy, he was named cardinal bishop of Tusculum in about 1229 by Pope Gregory IX (d. 1241). In addition to his pastoral duties, Jacques wrote two important histories (one of western Europe, the other of the holy land) as well as a large body of sermons and other works. His sermons were embellished with a large number of illustrative tales (*exempla*), and these were excerpted by his admirers and issued in* promptuaria *(searchable story collections). The exempla in this reading have been taken from Jacques's* Sermones vulgares vel ad status *(his* Sermons for Common Folk or for Various Stations of Life*).*

Latin, early thirteenth century.

Source: trans. Richard Raiswell and David R. Winter, from Thomas Frederick Crane, *The exempla or illustrative stories from the Sermones vulgares of Jacques de Vitry* (London: The Folklore Society, 1890), pp. 6, 14, 37–38, 50–51, 67, 72, 97, 101–2, 124–25.

The Devil Keeps Dropped Syllables from the Monks' Mass in a Sack

I have heard that a certain holy man, while he was in the choir, saw the devil carrying a sack as if it were greatly loaded. When he adjured the devil to tell him what he was carrying, the fiend responded: "These are omitted syllables, words, and psalm verses, which this morning those clerks stole from God. I have diligently saved them in order to accuse them." Therefore watch that the people are not overcome with anger at Mass.

The Roman Emperor, Nero, Comforts Lawyers in Hell

It is read in a certain tragedy by Seneca that it seemed to a certain man that he saw Nero bathing in a bath of boiling gold with attendants all around him, and when he saw a group of lawyers coming towards him, he said, "Come here you lawyers, you venal race of men! Draw near, my friends, so that you might be with me in this bath! The place that I have reserved for you remains free!" Therefore, lawyers should beware, lest they sell their souls to the devil!

A King's Son Who Has Been Brought Up in a Cave Is Told That Women Are Demons; He Prefers Them over Everything Else in Creation

We read of a certain king who, because he had no male children, was very sad. Then, he had a male child, and this made him overjoyed with great gladness. However, learned doctors told the king that it had been foreordained that, if he saw the sun or any fire within ten years, this boy would go blind. Hearing this, the king enclosed his son in a cave, together with nurses. For ten years, he did not see any light. After this, he led the boy from the cave, and because he had no information about the world, the king commanded that he be shown everything that existed in the world according to its type: men and women separately, horses gathered in another place, gold, silver, precious stones; and everything that his eyes beheld delighted him! He asked the names of everything, and when he came to the women, a certain servant of the king told him playfully, "These creatures are demons, seducers of men!" The heart of the boy lusted after them more than any of the other things (he had seen). And when the king asked the boy of all the things he had seen, which he loved the most, the boy replied, "I love those demons who seduce men more than anything else I have seen!" Behold, how

NINE: THEORIZING THE DEVIL AND SOCIETY IN THE HIGH MIDDLE AGES

human nature is liable to falter in this respect and that is why those who seek to be chaste must flee women!

Demons Fill a Usurer's Mouth with Red-Hot Coins

I have heard that there was a certain man who, when he labored in his final sickness, did not want to relinquish all of his money. He called his wife and children to his side and made them swear that they would fulfil his final wishes. He ordered them to swear that they would divide his money into three parts. His wife would have one part so that she might be able to remarry. His sons and daughters would have the second part. They would tie a third part in a sack around his neck and they were to bury it with him. One night, after he had been buried with the ponderous weight of coins, his heirs wanted to recover the money. However, when they opened his grave, they saw demons placing red-hot coins in the mouth of the usurer, and terrified, they fled!

The Demon, Guinehochet, Publicly Embarrasses a Man Who Thought He Had Two Sons; the Demon Tells Him One Is the Priest's Child

I have heard that there was a certain demon in France, who went by the name of Guinehochet. He would enter the mouth of a demoniac and reveal many hidden things. It was the general opinion that, in doing so, he did not tell lies. When people came to him and asked him many questions, Guinehochet responded honestly to everyone. At length, one man tempted him, saying, "Tell me, how many sons do I have?" To which Guinehochet responded, "You have one single son." The man gathered all the people around and said, "It is claimed that this wretch never lies, but behold, he has openly lied to me! He told that I have but a single son, when, as you all know, I have two sons!" The demon Guinehochet laughed and cackled and responded, "I spoke the truth! You have only one son, for the other boy is the priest's son!" The man was embarrassed and furious and said, "Tell me which of the two boys is the son of the priest, so that I might throw him from my house!" The demon responded, "I will not tell you, for you ought either to feed them both or cast them out!"

A Devil Rides on the Train of a Matron's Dress

I have heard of a certain woman who dragged the train of her dress along the ground, and leaving a trail behind her, she stirred up dust all the way to the altar and the image of the crucifix. When she left the church, however, she lifted her dress to avoid the dirt. A certain holy man saw a devil laughing, and he adjured the fiend to tell him why he was laughing. The devil said, "A certain friend of mine is right now sitting on the train of that woman's dress and uses her as a chariot. When the woman lifts the train, my friend tumbles from the dress and falls into the dirt, and this is why I'm laughing!"

The Devil's Nine Daughters and Their Marriages

It is commonly said that the devil has sired nine daughters with his exceedingly foul and lustful wife, who is black as coal because of the burning of her depraved desire. She is fetid on account of her infamy. She has swollen eyes on account of her pride. She has a long and crooked nose because of the machinations and devices of her sins. She has large and gaping ears because of her curiosity. She freely hears not only vain rumors, but false and evil words. Her hands are stained by her grasping nature and unceasing greed. She has drooping lips and a stinking mouth because of her filthy, evil talk. She has splayed feet, that is, because of her unsteady disposition. She has huge, itching, protuberant, scabrous breasts, one of which serves poison to the whelps of her carnal desire, while the other expresses the wind of worldly vanity! From eight of his daughters, the devil has sired as many types of men: Simony gave him prelates and clerics; Hypocrisy gave him monarchs and false monks; Rapine gave him soldiers; Usury gave him townsmen; Deceit gave him merchants; Sacrilege gave him farmers, who attempt to withhold sacred tithes from ministers of the church; False Service gave him laborers; Pride and Excess gave him women. The ninth daughter is Lust, who did not want to be married. Instead, like a harlot, she prostituted herself wickedly to every sort of man, mingling with all, sparing no type of man! Indeed, men race headlong to the stench of perfumes of her brothel like birds to a net, mice to cheese, or fish to the hook! Once she seizes a man it is difficult to escape her grasp!

A Dicer Defeats the Devil with His Refusal to Deny the Blessed Virgin Mary

I have heard concerning another man that, when he lost all that he had while playing dice, he began to despair and blaspheme god. Then he called upon the devil. And when he approached a certain great Jew, the Jew said to him, "Deny Christ and his mother and the saints, and I will make it so that you have more than you have ever had before!" The dicer replied, "I will deny god and the saints, but there is no way that I will deny his most pious mother." Hearing this, the angry Jew drove him away. When, on a certain day, he came across an image of the holy virgin, the image bowed as if returning the man's friendship. A certain rich man who was in the church saw this. And when he saw the man walk before the image a second time, once again the image bowed to him. Seeing this, the rich man was astonished, and he called the dicer, who was naked. The rascal approached the rich man, who said to him, "What a marvel that the image of the virgin should twice bow her head to you!" He answered, "I don't know why she did it, for I am the worst of sinners. I have lost all my father's goods by living luxuriously and playing dice." The rich man said, "How can this be? Have you ever done any kind of service to Blessed Mary?" He said, "I have served neither god, nor her." Finally, he remembered (what had happened earlier) and said, "A certain Jew wanted to give me riches if I denied Blessed Mary, but I would prefer to remain poor than to deny her!" And greatly inspired, the rich man said, "You have done well!" And he gave the man his daughter and all his riches, and thus, by blessed Mary's intervention, he became far richer than the Jew had promised. Behold how good it is to serve the blessed virgin and to honor her!

Questions: What sorts of concerns does Jacques appear to focus on? In what ways do these stories popularize scholastic ideas of demonology? Where do they differ? Why? What do you think a parish priest or preacher would do with these sparse tales? Are some of the devils "good"? What does this suggest?

83. DEMONS IN MONASTIC TRAINING MANUALS

Though trained by eminent teachers in the cathedral school of Cologne, Caesarius of Heisterbach (c. 1170–1240) spent virtually his entire life cloistered in the Cistercian monastery of St-Peter, Heisterbach, near modern Oberdollendorf, Germany. Considered one of the most pious and gifted of monks in his order, he was entrusted with the important office of Master of Novices. This made him responsible for the spiritual formation of all the young Cistercians who entered the abbey. It was largely for them that he compiled his two most important works: The Dialogue on Miracles *and* Eight Books of Miracles. *These treatises are ponderous storehouses of pious exempla, and with them Caesarius became one of the most celebrated raconteurs of the scholastic age. While they range over a number of subjects, both books were expressly designed to inculcate the values of the order in the young monks. He was, as the titles of his books suggest, particularly interested in miracles, prodigies, and the intrusion of preternatural forces into human affairs. Indeed, book five of his* Dialogue on Miracles, *from which the stories below have largely been extracted, was devoted entirely to the machinations of the devil.*

Latin, c. 1220.

Sources: trans. C. C. Swinton-Bland, Caesarius of Heisterbach, *Dialogue on Miracles* (New York, 1929), vol. 1, pp. 364–65, and vol. 2. pp. 180–82, rev.; "Concerning the Devil," trans. Richard Raiswell and David R. Winter, from Caesarius of Heisterbach, *Libri octo miraculorum*, in *Die Wundergeschichten des Caesarius von Heisterbach* (Bonn, 1933), pp. 101–2.

Of the Knight Thiemon, Whose Bowels Were Torn Out by the Devil, after Playing Dice with Him

In Soest, which is a town in the diocese of Cologne, there lived a knight called Thiemon, who was so thoroughly given up to a game of dice that he could not rest without it night or day. He used to carry a bag of money with him, so that he might be ready if he encountered anyone willing to play. So skilled and lucky was he at dicing that very few people ever played with him without coming away losers. However, in order that posterity might know just how contrary to god's will are all such games—in which anger, envy, quarrels, and losses are quite common, and in which sinful words are bandied back and forth—the devil was allowed to play with this man who had outplayed so many. He was also permitted to disembowel him who had disemboweled so many purses in his time. One night, a demon went into the knight's house in the form of a man who wished to gamble. He carried under his arm a bag stuffed full of coins. He sat down at the table, staked his money boldly, then threw the dice and won. He continued to do so until the knight had no more money left to wager. The knight exclaimed: "Surely you must be the devil himself!" To which, the man replied: "We have had enough now. The dawn is near. We must go." Then he snatched up the knight and dragged him through the roof so roughly that his bowels were torn out by the broken roof-tiles. What became of his body, or where it was thrown, is not known to this day, either by his son or by any of his acquaintances. But in the morning the remains of his entrails were found clinging to the tiles, and were buried in the cemetery. The devil allows his servants to prosper well enough in this world, but always betrays them in the end.

Of a Demon Whom Albert Scothart Drove Out in Amusing Fashion

The abbot of Ahringberg, a wealthy abbey of the Benedictine Order in Saxony, recently passed our way, and told us of a very amusing miracle concerning the healing of a certain demoniac girl. He said, "Among us, there is a pious knight named Albert Scothart. Before taking vows, he was so vigorous a soldier and so famous in war that almost all the nobles of our land rivaled one another in sending him gifts, such as warhorses and costly garments, so as to win his friendship.

One day, a twelve-year-old girl, the daughter of a knight, was sitting in a church being exorcised by the monks. She broke out into a laugh and cried, "Look, here comes my friend, here comes my friend!" When they asked about whom she was speaking, she answered: "You will see him momentarily." For she meant the knight, Albert, who at the moment was still some distance from the church. But the nearer he came, the more she showed her delight. When he entered the church, she rose up to meet him, clapping her hands, and greeting him. "Good day," she said:

"Here is my friend. Go! Go and let him come here." Now, the knight was dressed in slashed scarlet, and approaching the girl, he said to her, "Am I your friend?" To which the devil replied from the mouth of the girl, "Yes, my best friend! For you do everything I want." At these words, the knight was very confused, although he pretended not to be. Instead, he said with a smile, "You are a stupid and silly devil. If you had any sense, you would go with us to tournaments, where men are injured and slain. Indeed, why do you torment this innocent girl without any reason?" At this, the devil said, "If you want me to go with you, let me enter your body." The knight replied, "You shall certainly not enter me." And the devil said, "Let me sit on your saddle." And when the knight refused to allow this, the devil begged for a place on some part of the horse or the bridle, but to every request, he said, "No." Next, the devil said to him, "I am unable to run on my feet. So, if you wish me to go with you, you must give me at least some place near your person." The knight, feeling pity for the girl, said to the devil, "If you promise to leave her, I will allow you to enter the opening of my coat. However, it is only on the condition that you do not harm me in any way, and that you will only stay with me while I am on my way to the tournament. When I give you the order, you will leave me of your own free will and without any argument." The devil took an oath and said, "I will not harm you. In fact, I will help you."

And, leaving the girl, he leapt into the opening of the knight's coat, moving with marvelous speed. From that moment, the knight earned unrivaled glory at all the tournaments: he overthrew whomever he wished with his lance, and he took captives at will. Wherever he went, the devil accompanied him and they talked frequently with one another. When the knight prayed too long in church, the devil would say, "Now you are mumbling too much." Whenever he sprinkled himself with holy water, again the devil would say: "Be careful that you do not touch me!" The knight replied, "I would be sorry if even a single drop touches you."

Once, when the cross was being preached and the knight entered a church to take it up, the devil tried to restrain him, saying, "What are you doing here?" The knight replied, "I propose to serve God and to renounce you. Therefore, flee from me!" When the knight said this, Satan answered, "What have I done to displease you? I have never hurt you, but instead, I have enriched you. Because of me, you have become extraordinarily famous. However, I cannot remain with you without your consent, because I made the promise." Then, the knight said: "Behold, I now take up the cross, and I adjure you in the name of the crucified to leave me and never to return."

So, the devil left him. And, thus signed with the cross, he journeyed across the sea, and fought for Christ in the holy land for two years. Then he returned and built a great and very rich guesthouse for poor travelers. He did so because he had a yearly income of more than three hundred pounds according to the aforesaid abbot. To this day, in that guesthouse, he and his wife wear religious habits and serve the followers of Christ. They are devoted servants of all men of religion and especially of monks of our order. To them he used to say in jest: "You lords abbots and you monks are not holy! We knights who busy ourselves with tournaments are the holy ones, for the devils obey us and we drive them out."

Novice: I did not know that devils could be cast out in such a merry fashion.

Monk: It was not jesting, but rather, the power of mercy that cast out that particular devil.

Concerning the Devil, Who, Appearing to a Recluse in the Form of Saint Mary, Presented His Foot to Be Kissed by Her

Master Wiger, provost of Utrecht, recently converted to the Order of Friars Minor [Franciscans], told me what I am about to relate. A certain female recluse who singularly loved Our Lady, the Virgin and Holy Mother of God, Mary. She frequently showed emotion around sacred images of her, bowing her head before them, adoring them, kissing them and burning incense in front of them. One night, when she was praying in her little cell, and she called upon the mother of mercy, a light of great clarity illuminated the place. The clarity surpassed the brightness of the noonday sun. In this clear light, the form of a woman appeared. She resembled the Virgin, greatly transcending mortals both in her body and in every aspect of her dress. And when the woman was frightened by this unusual light, the shining woman said, "I am the mother of Christ. I have come to you so that you might see me. Approach therefore, my cherished one, and as a sign of love, kiss my foot." Hearing these words, the holy woman began to have doubt in her heart. She thought that this was uncharacteristically haughty, and so responded, "What is this that you are saying, my sweetest lady? Indeed, you are the humble mother of all humility. Why are you asking me to kiss your foot?" Having said this, the holy woman got up and signed herself with the sign of cross. And immediately, the fantastic vision disappeared. The devil is the author of all iniquity: so, leaving a sign of his presence, he filled the little cell with such a stench that the woman was scarcely able to stand it.

The angel of Satan, according to the testimony that we have from divine scriptures, always transforms himself into an angel of light [2 Cor. 11.14]. He instills fear, but there is no consolation for the troubled mind. Conversely, an angelic vision or a vision of another saint relieves and consoles the frightened mind, just as we have the example of the mother of the lord, whose fear was immediately consoled by the angel, saying, "Do not fear, Mary, etc." [Luke 1.30].

Questions: How do these stories differ from those aimed at secular Christians (doc. 82)? Why? How do possession narratives in this section differ from those described in Chapter 7? What might account for these differences? What do these stories suggest about tension between the three orders of society?

84. VARIOUS *EXEMPLA* DEMONS FROM THE BRITISH ISLES

While Jacques de Vitry and Caesarius of Heisterbach are very well-known medieval storytellers, they were by no means the only raconteurs to collect pious tales. The university and state archives of Europe teem with manuscripts containing large collections of exempla *and other kinds of pious narrations. Below is a representative assemblage of preaching stories about the devil taken from manuscripts in the British Library in London. Many of the stories appear in translation for the first time.*

Latin, twelfth to fourteenth centuries.

Source: trans. Richard Raiswell and David R. Winter, from London, British Library MSS Royal 7.D.i, addit 16589, addit. 27909 B.

Concerning Those under Religious Vows

A certain monk and nun were apprehended on the basis of information and incarcerated. As they awaited trial in prison, they called upon the Blessed Virgin whom they had both served, that she might free them. The Blessed Virgin immediately commanded it, and, so, they were restored to their previous honor; these things occurred through the power of the glorious Virgin. When the people gathered to witness the trial, they found demons in the prison in the form and dress [of the former prisoners], and the monk and nun were found in their respective lodgings. At this, the people wondered who had taken the form of the prisoners. When, at length, they asked those who had been incarcerated who they were, and who the others who had been freed were, the demons replied, "You have not incarcerated those whom you intended, but rather, us!" Saying this, they vanished from sight and thus, through the favor of the glorious Virgin, the former prisoners were freed from infamy and prison.

The Devil Appears as the Goddess Diana

Likewise, it is read in the *Life of Saint Nicholas* that when pilgrims went to visit the church of St-Nicholas across the sea, the devil appeared to them in the churning ocean in the form of the great Diana. She said that she wanted to make a pilgrimage and to visit the grave of Saint Nicholas with a certain very noble unguent which she had purchased and brought with her. She asked them whether they wanted to carry this unguent because she was hindered, and it would be difficult for her to make the journey. Saint Nicholas appeared to those who acquired the unguent saying that it was infernal oil. So, they opened the little box and dumped it into the sea. All the waters of the ocean that it touched were set ablaze.

Demons of Avarice

It is read that three demons stood in the way of a certain hermit. When he asked them their names, the first said that he was called "Closed heart." The second, "Closed mouth." The third, "Closed purse."

Concerning a Certain Heretic

It is read concerning a certain heretic that he was thrown twice into the fire but did not burn because Lucifer (in whom he believed) always cast him out. And the Christians wanted to believe his heresy on account of his holiness. So, they attacked the priests with stones until one of the priests advised that he should carry the most holy body of the lord and they would beg God with great, weeping devotion that he show his grace and that the man again be thrown into the fire so that he might be burned immediately. The heretic began to invoke Lucifer, who, not appearing, replied in a cloud, saying, "Do better now that you are able! I am no longer able to reside in you. I cannot resist more forcefully him who is coming for me." And the man was burned.

Demons Carry Away a Boy Who Peed in a Cemetery

The son of a certain widow was accustomed to urinating in the cemetery, and he did not want to amend his ways. Finally, one night, while he was peeing, the souls of the dead came to him and accused him; they demanded that, on a certain day, in that same place, he should respond to them for his crime and that he should tell his mother. Fearing for her son, on the day in question she went, together with the priest, [a vial of] blessed water, and a multitude of people to the place that the souls had stipulated. While he was there, evil spirits spotted the boy and seized him. He was never seen again.

On Slander

While a certain very holy man was celebrating the mass, he saw the devil behind the Altar writing down on parchment all the superfluous words and slanders that were being spoken by those who were in the church; with his teeth he pulled at the parchment so that it might be extended. The mass having been celebrated, the holy man collected it so that he might learn what he had written on the parchment. The devil said to him, "I have written down the lies and the prattle that were pronounced today in this church." The holy man then showed this parchment to the people, and he began to persuade them through preaching not to do such things again, and then they began to weep and repent. Thereafter the holy man saw that everything which the demon had written on the parchment had disappeared.

Lust and Conjuration

Magicians say that when they want to conjure demons, it is necessary that men abstain from sex for three days, otherwise the demons will not obey them. In this it appears that the sin of lust is something that displeases those demons.

On the Devil's Feast Days

There were four feast days observed on the devil's calendar, namely: love of the world, carnal pleasure, pride, and glory in sin.

On the Devil's Mass

While in church, seeing that one person sings the mass while others respond, the devil called his demons to form a choir. A male or female demon sang while others responded. The devil raised his arms or extended them in contempt of the lord's crucifixion and passion. And the demons always pulled to the left because they were hastening to hell.

Questions: Considering how abbreviated some of these narrations are, how much room do you suppose ordinary preachers had for embellishment and improvisation? In what ways do the devils of the preacher seem designed to promote social control? Do these stories present a compelling portrait of evil—or is the devil being used as a metaphor for something else?

85. AN ANONYMOUS PREACHER ALLEGORIZES HELL

This very short exemplum *seems to be the schematic for a preacher to develop a much longer, more in-depth sermon using allegorical images. The ability to turn this very short synopsis into a gripping call to repentance would have depended, to a considerable extent, on a given preacher's literary and oratorical skills.*
   Latin, thirteenth century.

Source: trans. Richard Raiswell and David R. Winter, from British Library MS Addit. 27909 B.

On Death

The unicorn (that is, death) followed a man into a cave (that is, the world) that was great and deep. In the middle of it, there was a tree (that is, life). Where he stood at the root, there was a dragon (that is, the devil), who was expecting him, and two beasts, one white (that is, day), the other black (that is, night) which stood at the root of the tree and gnawed upon it. Below, there was an exceedingly deep abyss (that is, hell) full of fire and sulfur. The man saw honey, and fell from the tree into the pit and perished.

Questions: What would a preacher do with a story like this? How might he make this story resonate with his audience? What does this suggest about the freedom of preachers to craft their own sermons?

CHAPTER TEN

EXPERIENCING THE DEVIL IN WORD AND IMAGE

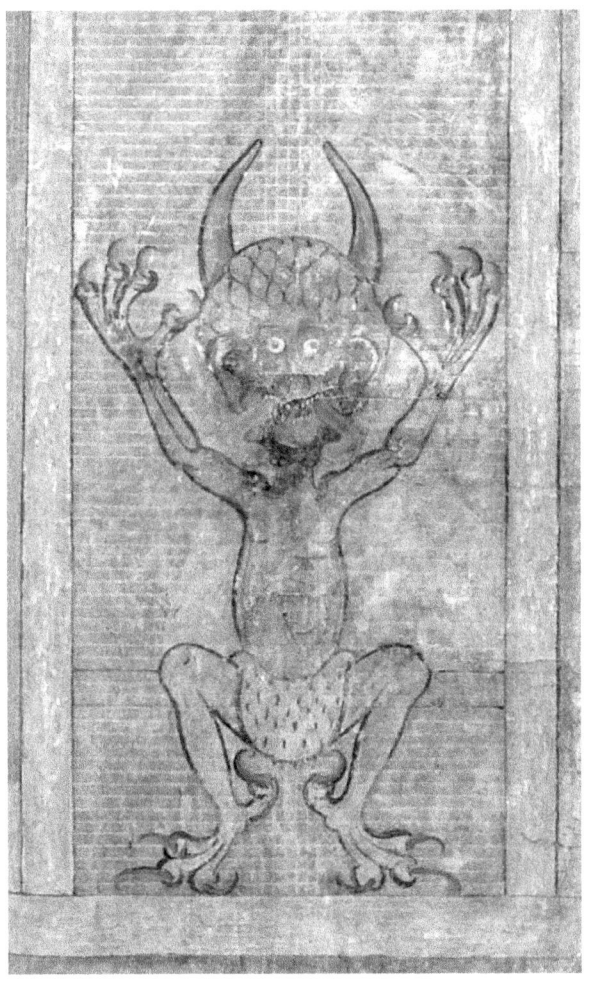

Figure 10.1 *Codex Gigas*, f. 290r (thirteenth century). The *Codex Gigas* or *The Giant Book* is part of a high medieval tradition of large bibles and was likely produced at the small Benedictine monastery of Podlažice in modern Czechia. It comprises both the Old and New Testaments, which are separated by the works of Josephus, Isidore of Seville, and several medical texts. This illustration is 920 x 500 mm and comes immediately at the end of the New Testament. The preceding page contains a similarly large illustration of the heavenly Jerusalem.

TEN: EXPERIENCING THE DEVIL IN WORD AND IMAGE

General literacy levels in Europe trailed off in the period after Rome's political collapse in the fifth century, and they did not begin to rise in any substantial way outside the mercantile communities of the major commercial centers of the Mediterranean until after the appearance of the moveable-type printing press in the fifteenth century. This means that, for most of the period covered by this book, the majority of Europeans were pre- or non-literate. Most of those who continued to read and write were Christian clergy. This makes sense, as the religion was established on the revelations and insights of written scripture, and the Church was the only institution, particularly in the Early Middle Ages, with the capital, access to resources, and know-how to produce books. Taken together, however, clerics probably never represented more than about ten percent of the general population. Thus, for most Europeans, the central beliefs of their religion were imparted using forms of communication that did not necessitate access to a text.

One of the main ways in which people encountered ideas about the devil was through popular stories. Unlike those told by preachers to teach moral lessons (docs. 80–83), these would have been read or performed before an audience in a social environment, serving primarily as a form of entertainment. Thus, while people may not have had access to any given text—and, if they did, they may not have been able to read it—they could still have been familiar with its ideas. That most medieval Europeans were not literate did not mean that they did not have access to ideas that emanated from high culture in some capacity.

The readings in this chapter all come from literary sources that would have circulated and been consumed primarily outside an ecclesiastical context. As you work through this material, think of how people would have encountered these sources—whether they would have been read aloud or performed. Think about the social setting in which they would have been presented—the tavern or the court, or somewhere in between? And what stratum of people would have been there? It is important to keep in mind that people anticipated these entertainments in the same way that modern audiences wait for new seasons of streaming shows or the next installment of a popular movie or videogame franchise.

Another way in which people would have become familiar with ideas about the devil was through images. In the sixth century, Gregory the Great (docs. 42 and 59) actively encouraged the creation of publicly accessible art to instruct the faithful in the basic stories and tenets of the faith. This tradition of Christian art blossomed in the illuminated manuscripts produced in the continent's monasteries and then in the works of the great painters and sculptors of the High Middle Ages and early Renaissance.

86. THE MIRACLE OF THEOPHILUS

The story of Theophilus of Adana, set in the middle of the sixth century, is first recounted in a Greek manuscript attributed to a scribe named Eutychianus, who claimed to have witnessed the events described. It was translated into Latin at the end of the eighth century by a monk named Paul the Deacon—not to be confused with the great historian of the Lombards who wrote a century earlier. The story proved very popular and circulated in various forms through the Middle Ages. Medieval translations can be found in most European vernaculars, including Icelandic and Old Swedish. In the sixteenth century, it served as the inspiration for the Faust legend popular in Protestant countries, although crucially, Faust, unlike Theophilus, was not able to repent.

This version of the story, reworked into a play, was composed in the middle of the thirteenth century by the Parisian trouvère (or troubadour) Rutebeuf (fl. 1245–85). Some scholars have suggested that the work may have been composed for clerics at the University of Paris. Old French, 1261.

Source: trans. Richard Axton and John Stevens, from Rutebeuf, *Le miracle de Théophile*, from *Medieval French Plays* (Oxford: Blackwell, 1971), pp. 165–92.

Théophile enters from his "house."

> Théophile
> O God, almighty, glorious lord!
> I have always kept your word
> In mind; I've given away my goods
> And offered beggars all I could:
> What's left is not worth a sack.
> Like chess, the bishop told me, "Check!"
> He'd cornered me—I was fool's mate.
> He's left me poor and desolate,
> And I'm compelled to starve to death
> Unless I pawn my robe for bread.
> But what will all my household do?
> Will God feed them? I don't know.
> God? Yes, him? What does he care?
> They will have to go elsewhere,
> For in this place God's ears are deaf;
> He thinks my prayers are so much chaff.
> I shall turn him a mocking face:
> Curse all those who enjoy his grace!
> There's nothing one would not undertake
> For the sake of wealth. I scorn God's threats.
> Shall I go drown myself, or hang?
> I can't reproach God for this thing,
> Because one cannot ever reach

Him there. If man could only catch
A hold of him to strike him back—
That would be a good day's work.
But he has placed himself so high
To avoid his many enemies
That one can't pull or hurl him down.
If I could only threaten him,
Struggle with him, fight and slash,
I'd make him tremble in his flesh!
He lives in happiness up there
While I, poor wretch, am caught in the snare
Of poverty and suffering.
My fiddle's broken and unstrung—
They'll say I'm senile and they'll mock;
And make me into a laughing stock.
I shall not dare see anyone
Nor sit in company again
Without someone pointing a finger
At me. I don't know any longer
What to do: God has cheated me.

Here Théophile comes to Salatin, who was able to speak with the devil whenever he liked. Salatin enters from his "house."

Salatin
What's the matter, Théophile?
For God's sake, what misfortune
Has made you so unhappy, man?
You always used to be so happy.

Théophile
They used to call me "Monsignor"
And "Father of the Town"—as you know well.
Now they've not left me anything!
I'm more distressed, Salatin,
Because I've never ceased to pray
Both in Latin and in French
To the God who wants to punish me
And who has had me stripped so bare
I've nothing left to call my own.
There's nothing now so desperate,

No practice so irregular,
I would not gladly undertake
To get my reputation back.
The loss has shamed and wounded me.

Salatin
My dear sir, you're talking common sense.
If a man has learned what wealth can be,
It is a sad and painful thing
When he declines and must depend
On others for his food and drink—
And has to hear so much abuse! . . .

Théophile
To come to the point, Salatin:
If you know any means at all
By which I might regain my post,
My influence and self-respect,
There's nothing that I would not do.

Salatin
Would you be willing to renounce
The God to whom you've always prayed,
His holy things and all his saints?
And, with clasped hands, would you become
The loyal servant of a lord
Who could restore your dignities,
So that you would have greater honors
(If you always worshipped him)
Than otherwise you'd ever have?
Trust me; leave your present master.
Well? Tell me what you wish to do?

Théophile
I should like that very much—
I'll do anything you ask.

Salatin
Then you can go home quite secure;
Whatever they may do to you,

I shall get back your post again.
Return tomorrow in the morning.

Théophile
I will indeed, friend Salatin.
May the god you worship and believe
Bless you, if you achieve this plan.

[Having agreed to renounce God, Théophile immediately has doubts. Nevertheless, he is determined to have revenge on God, for God has wronged him.]

Salatin goes to hell's mouth.
Here Salatin shall speak with the devil and say:

Salatin
A Christian has come to me,
I've waited on him busily,
For you are not my enemy,
Satan, do you hear?
If you'll receive him, he comes at dawn;
I've promised him four times and sworn.
Wait for him then,
For he has been a powerful man,
A priceless gift for us to own;
So lavish your riches upon him.
Give me your ear!
I think that I shall make you come
Running quick.
You shall come now, while it is dark
For your delay destroys my work.
I've longed for this!

Here Salatin shall conjure up the devil.

Bagahi laca bachahé
Lamac cahi achabahé
Karrelyos
Lamac lamec bachalyos
Cabahagi sabalyos
Baryolas

Lagozatha cabyolas
Samahac et famyolas
Harrahya

Now the devil shall come, having been conjured, and he shall say:

The Devil
You spoke the proper formula well—
Your teacher forgot no part of the spell.
You pester me!

Salatin
There's no reason you should fail
To help me, or oppose my will,
When I command.
I can make your hide run with sweat!
You want to hear the latest sport?
We've got a clerk,
A splendid prize, as we've long known—
We've often been distressed by him
In our affairs.
What do you think should be done
With this clerk so willing to be won?

The Devil
What is he called?

Salatin
Théophile's his proper name;
He's been a person of some fame
Throughout this land.

The Devil
Ha! Every day I fought with him
And not one battle could I win.
Since he's decided to give in,
Let him come down,
Without a friend, without a horse;
That will not trouble him, of course,
Since it is close.
Satan will freely give him grace,

So will the devils in this place.
He must not pray
To Jesus, holy Mary's son;
No kindness could we show him then.
I go my way.
Now you must pay me more respect.
Don't bother me for several weeks!
No Hebrew prayers and none in Latin!
Go Salatin!

Salatin returns to his "house."
Now Théophile shall return to Salatin.

> *Théophile*
> Am I too early in the morning?
> What have you done?
>
> *Salatin*
> I've dealt so quickly with your case
> That the bishop, cause of your disgrace,
> Will now restore
> Your office, with a large reward.
> You'll be monsignor and a greater lord
> Than ever before.
> Instead of being poor, despised,
> You shall be happy, rich and praised.
> Don't be afraid.
> You must go down without delay;
> It will not help for you to pray
> Or ask God's aid,
> If you want to help your interests.
> In the love of your God you'd too much trust
> And he has failed.
> You came out of it unhappily:
> He would have hurt you cruelly
> Had I not helped.
> The devils wait and you must pass
> This way at once.
> Stifle all thoughts of repentance.
>
> *Théophile*
> I'll go. God cannot harm me now

> Nor help my need.
> I can no longer pray or plead.

Here Théophile shall go to the devil in great fear, and the devil shall say to him:

> *The Devil*
> Come this way! Get moving there!
> Don't imitate some peasant oaf
> Creeping to the offertory!
> What is it your master has commanded
> And forces you to do? He's a tyrant!
>
> *Théophile*
> He is, my lord. He was the chancellor
> And thinks to drive me out to seek
> For food. And so, I've come to pray
> That you will help my desperate need.
>
> *The Devil*
> You ask me?
>
> *Théophile*
> Yes.
>
> *The Devil*
> Then clasp your hands
> Together, and do me proper homage,
> And I shall help you all I can.

Théophile kneels in feudal submission. The devil takes his offered hands between his own, accepting Théophile into his service.

> *Théophile*
> Witness the homage I make to you.
> If I could just get back my loss,
> Great Master, for the rest of my life.
>
> *The Devil*
> In return, I make this pact with you:
> I'll set you up in such great power—
> They'll not have seen a greater lord

Than you. And now, since we're agreed,
You ought to know that for your part
I must have deeds of covenant,
Sealed and unequivocal.
Many folk have cheated me
Because I did not take their deeds—
That's why I like things cut and dried.

Théophile makes his deed, writing in his own blood and sealing the document with his ring.

Théophile
Here they are—signed, sealed, and delivered.

Théophile hands his deed to the devil, and the devil orders him to behave like this:

The Devil
Théophile, my dearest friend,
Now that you've made yourself my man,
I'll tell you what you have to do:
You mustn't have pity on the poor.
If a poor, decrepit man should beg,
Turn a deaf ear and go your way.
If anyone bows reverently,
Treat him with pride and cruelty.
If a beggar comes knocking at your door,
Make sure he goes away with nothing.
Gentleness, humility,
Pity, love and charity,
Keeping fasts and penitence,
Strike a pain into my guts.
Giving alms and prayers to God—
These things grieve and anger me.
Loving God and living chastely
Make me feel a snake or viper
Tears at my heart inside my chest.
When anyone goes to the hospital
To visit a sick person there,
My heart feels dead and beats so feebly
I scarcely know that I am alive.
Doing good is pain to me.
Go back; you shall be seneschal.

Leave doing good; do wickedness.
Be sure you never give fair judgment,
For that would be great foolishness
And contrary to my command.

Théophile
I'll carry out what I must do.
It's only right to try and please,
Since that's the way to regain favor.

The Devil goes into Hell's Mouth . . .

[The bishop has a sudden change of heart and realizes that he has treated Théophile poorly and reinvests him. However, true to his bargain, Théophile has become a thoroughly unpleasant man, and is belligerent and anti-social toward anyone he meets.]

Seven years pass.
Now Théophile repents and shall come to a chapel of Our Lady and say:

Théophile
Pathetic wretch! What will become of me?
How can the earth support my sinful weight,
When I've renounced my God and venerate
A fiend as lord, who causes sin and misery?
God I denied—the secret can't be kept.
I've lost the balm of life; I'm caught
Upon the Judas tree. The devil bought
My title deeds: my soul must pay the debt.
What will you do with this unhappy fool,
O God, whose spirit will go to the boiling heat
Of hell, there to be trampled by devils' feet?
Break open, earth, and swallow up my soul!
Lord God, what will this desperate outcast do?
Despised by God, exposed to ridicule
By men, betrayed and trapped by fiends in hell—
Shall I be hounded by all creation too?
I was puffed up with ignorance and pride,
When I rejected God for that small gain.
The worldly wealth I wanted to obtain
Has drowned me here; I can't escape the tide.
Satan, I walked your way for seven years;

Your evil music tempted me to spill
My store of life; the price I pay is cruel—
My flesh sliced through by fiendish slaughterers!
A man's soul must be loved, but mine was not.
Our Lady might save it—I dare not ask. Bad seeds
Were sown at seeding time; and choked with weeds
My soul sprang up, to droop in hell and rot.
A fiendish master—oh, what slavery!
Tormented in my soul and in my body!
If I dared to trust the sweet grace of Our Lady,
My soul might now be saved from purgatory.
Filthy I am; I must go to filth beneath.
In filthiness I've lived; God must know—
He lives for ever. My dying will be slow,
Poisoned by the bite of devils' teeth.
No refuge on the earth nor in the skies—
What place could shelter me? I loathe the thought
Of offering myself in hell. I fought
My lord and cannot claim his paradise.
I dare not call God's saints, nor beg again
For grace. I served the fiend; hands clasped, I kneeled.
The devil has the bond my ring has sealed.
I curse the riches that will cause me pain!
I dare not call on saints, nor say God's name,
Nor hers, whom all should love, our sweet,
Our Lady. But since no harshness or deceit
Is in her, in begging grace I cannot be to blame.

[Théophile offers a long prayer to the Virgin and she comes to him.]

Here Our Lady shall speak to Théophile and say:

> *Our Lady*
> Who are you, walking in this place?
>
> *Théophile*
> Have mercy, mother, full of grace!
> It is the wretched
> Théophile, who is shunned
> By men, by devils caught and bound.
> I come to pray

To you, Lady, and to ask your power
That I may never see the hour
Of torment come
With him who has thrust me in such pain.
Once you embraced me as your son,
O lovely queen!

Our Lady
I will not hear your hypocrite's babble.
Go! Go! Get out of my chapel!

Théophile
I dare not go.
Rose, eglantine, lily flower,
Whom God's own son has made his bower,
What shall I do?
I feel myself cruelly pledged
To serve a fiend that is enraged
I do not know.
I shall never cease to cry
To you, Virgin, meek and holy,
Highly favored.
I know my soul will be devoured
Completely, if it is immured
With pagan gods.

Our Lady
Théophile, I once knew you,
When you served me—long ago.
Now, in your need,
Trust me to reclaim the deed
That ignorance made you concede.
I'll fetch it back.

Now Our Lady shall go for Théophile's covenant.

Our Lady
Satan, where are you concealed?

The Devil enters from Hell's Mouth.

TEN: EXPERIENCING THE DEVIL IN WORD AND IMAGE

Our Lady
If you've come to the battlefield
Hoping to make my servant yield,
That thought's a curse!
Give me the deed you took from the clerk;
You have gone too far in your hellish work.

The Devil
I—give it back?
I'd rather they would hang me first
Once I gave him back his post,
And in return he sacrificed
Quite readily
All his substance, soul and body.

Our Lady
Then I shall trample on your belly.

Our Lady raises her cross, the Devil falls and she treads him underfoot. She takes the covenant. The Devil crawls back into Hell's Mouth.
Now Our Lady shall carry the covenant back to Théophile.

My friend, I bring the charter back.
Your soul's ship was almost wrecked
Without hope of better luck.
Now hear my words:
Go to the bishop, do not wait;
Give him the charter that you made,
To read aloud
Inside the church, before a crowd,
So that good men are not seduced
By such deceit—
The man who sells his soul for greed
Shall be downtrodden and abused.

Théophile
I will! Body and soul
Should have withered to the root:
The seeds of evil bear no fruit—
I see that now.

Enter the bishop, his court and congregation.
Now Théophile shall go to the bishop and give him his covenant and say:

> Théophile
> My lord, for God's mercy, listen:
> Despite my sins, I kneel here chastened.
> Soon you shall know
> By what I have been so oppressed;
> I was poor and naked, cold, diseased
> Through poverty.
> The devil, who assaults good men,
> Made my soul commit a sin
> For which I should die;
> But Our Lady, who directs her own,
> Turned me from the path of wrong,
> Where I had strayed
> And lost my way. Without her aid
> I would by now have been conveyed
> By the devil to hell.
> The devil made me turn from God,
> The father of hope; all works of good
> He made me leave.
> What he dictated formed my deed;
> Whatever he required, I sealed.
> The dreadful pain
> Almost split my heart and brain.
> Then the Virgin brought my deed again—
> God's own mother,
> Whose goodness shines bright and clear.
> I beg you as my reverend father
> That this be read
> So others may not be deceived,
> If they have not yet perceived
> The devil's treachery.

Now the bishop shall read the charter and say:

> The Bishop
> For Jesus' sake, Mary's son,

TEN: EXPERIENCING THE DEVIL IN WORD AND IMAGE

Good people, listen; you shall learn
Of Théophile,
Whom the devil cheated by his guile.
This miracle is as true a tale
As the gospel.
It ought to be told to you in full.
Now listen carefully to what I shall tell:
"To all who shall see this charter publicly
Satan makes known that Fortune turned her wheel:
The bishop was abhorred by Théophile
Because he'd left him no authority.
When thus insulted, Théophile despaired;
He came to Salatin, in a passionate rage,
And said that he would willingly do homage
To Satan, if his wealth and honor were repaired.
Throughout his saintly life I battled hard,
But I was never victor of the field.
When he came to beg, I longed to make him yield;
He worshipped me and his power was restored.
This deed was sealed with the ring upon his hand.
There was no ink—he wrote it in his blood
And signed before I promised that I would
Restore him to his dignities and land."
And that is what this good man did.
The blessed maid has freed his soul
From chains of sin.
Our Lady Mary, holy Virgin,
Snatched the devil's reckoning.
To celebrate this miracle
Arise and sing
Te Deum laudamus!

Thus ends the miracle of Théophile.

Questions: How does the nature of Théophile's faith compare to that of Job (doc. 6)? What is the nature of the relationship between Théophile and Satan after the pact? Which characters have been wronged here and who has committed these sins? Why does Mary help Théophile? How does this story compare to those of Cyprian (doc. 42) and Gerbert (doc. 43)? How would this play likely resonate with a medieval audience?

87. AN ALTERNATIVE CREATION STORY

Fabliaux *(sing.* fabliau*) were short comic tales in verse that seem to have originated with the* jongleurs *of the north and northeast of what is now France, although many were likely based on older tales that circulated orally. Popular throughout the High Middle Ages, they were recited and likely performed in the markets and fairs of the growing towns of the region. Frequently obscene, scatological, and often permeated by a deep misogyny, they stand in stark contrast to the literature of the aristocratic courts of the period (though there is evidence that the nobles also enjoyed these crude tales). Populated by stock characters including adulterous spouses, cheating merchants and artisans, dispossessed knights, cunning peasants, and hypocritical clergy, through their satire of contemporary morality and sensibilities,* fabliaux *reflect the values, tensions, and shifting social relations of the urban society in which their audiences resided.*

Old French, thirteenth century?

Source: trans. Nathaniel Dubin, *The Cunt Made with a Spade*, from *The Fabliaux: A New Verse Translation* (New York: Liveright, 2013), pp. 5–9.

The Cunt Made with a Spade

Adam, created by our lord,
who afterward defied his word
turning against him as a rebel
by taking a bite of apple,
if we can trust what scriptures say. . .
God formed man from a lump of clay,
and then he took one of the ribs
he'd placed in his side, and with this,
nor more nor less, with his own two
hands he created women, too.
To suffer blows is woman fated
because from bone she was created
Get your wife used to thrashings, say
two or three or four times a day
on the first of the week, or ten
or twelve times every fortnight; then
whether she's fasting or not,
she'll grow in value quite a lot.
The woman had a lovely neck
and face, but God forgot to make
a cunt, so little care he took.

TEN: EXPERIENCING THE DEVIL IN WORD AND IMAGE

The devil came and had a look,
leaned down a bit on an incline
and at the third bump on her spine
saw there was only just one hole.
He went to speak to God and told
Him, "Sire, you made an awful gaffe:
The woman's incomplete by half!
So get to work! Make haste, go back to 'er
and install in her hinder sector
the thing that is most necessary,
because a woman isn't very
valuable when there's no burrow
placed close by her posterior furrow."
"Eh, what?" said God. "I can't see to it.
You'll have to go yourself and do it."
The devil answered, "I? And how?"
"I'm telling you to do it now,
and I mean what I say. Eschew
putting in something made by you
and remove nothing that I've made."
"I'll do just that," the devil said.
The devil gathered hammers, adzes,
chisels, mattocks, sharpened axes,
cutting tools with double blades,
pruning hooks and trenchant spades,
and gave the tools a close inspection
in order to make his selection
to the job he undertook,
saying that no one will rebuke
him if he makes a spacious trough.
(An ample suit from other's cloth.)
He looked at every implement
one by one, not much time he spent,
and when he'd taken time to view
them all, he was convinced he knew
that with the sharp edge of the spade
a great, deep crevice could be made
in scarcely any time at all.
He said that there's no better tool
on earth, and takes the spade and pushes
it all in till the handle touches.

Thus with a spade he made the cunt.
He squatted down a bit in front
of her and farted on her tongue.
That's why all women, old and young,
must chatter on and talk such drivel.
Faced with the fart laid by the devil,
she tried to push it from her mouth,
but still today their bodies house
the fart the devil left inside
when he crouched by the woman's side.
It's something we have to accept:
She won't give up talking except
to be nice or to wheedle gifts.
I pray that God never forgives
whoever seeks to vilify
them or their cunts, no matter why,
for there's fine workmanship in them,
but they've destroyed many good men,
who've come to grief and been disgraced
and lost what wealth they once possessed.

Questions: How does this "creation story" both supplement and parody the biblical account of the creation of humanity? Why is the devil granted the role that he is? What does this demonization imply about female sexuality? Female speech? What sort of audience would have heard this story recounted or acted?

88. DEMONIC HORSEPLAY

Along with fellow Florentines Dante Alighieri and Francesco Petrarch, Giovanni Boccaccio (1313–75) was one of the most influential authors of the later Middle Ages. After a period in Naples working for the Bardi bank and studying law, Boccaccio returned to Florence in 1341, where he became a writer. The Decameron, *from which the selection below comes, is a collection of 100 short tales told in the Tuscan (Florentine) vernacular by ten characters over the space of ten days as they took refuge from the plague through the summer of 1348. While a good number of these tales center on the stock themes of medieval romances and concern knightly prowess and courtly love,* The Decameron *also reflects the values of urban, commercial Florence, where money could matter more than blood, where men could make a fortune through their wits, and where the socially ambitious sought to rise above what should have been their natural station. The excerpt below comes from the ninth story told on the eighth day.*

Tuscan, 1348–53.

TEN: EXPERIENCING THE DEVIL IN WORD AND IMAGE

Source: trans. J. M. Rigg, from Giovanni Boccaccio, *The Decameron of Giovanni Boccaccio*, vol. 2. (London, 1921), pp. 235–49; rev.

Every day, we see our citizens come back to us from Bologna—this man a judge, that one a physician, the other a notary—flaunting their status in ample flowing robes, adorned with scarlet and fur, and with an array of other very fine things. How far their actions correspond with this fair appearance, though, is also a matter of daily experience.

Among these was a certain Master Simone da Villa—one whose patrimony was richer than his learning. He came back wearing the scarlet with a broad stripe on his shoulder—calling himself a doctor, taking a house in the street that we now call Via del Cocomoro. Now, this Master Simone—being thus, as we have said, newly returned—had among his other singular habits, that he could never see a soul pass along the street without asking who he was. He was as observant of the doings of all men and as diligent in remembering such matters as if they were details necessary to help him compound the drugs appropriate for his patients.

Now, of all those that he saw, those that he watched most closely were two painters—Bruno and Buffalmacco—who were always together and were his neighbors. It struck him that these two men were more carefree and lived more lightheartedly than any others that he knew—as indeed they did—so he asked not a few people as to their status. Being told by all of them that they were both poor men and painters, he could not understand how they could live so contentedly in poverty. Informed, as he was, that they were clever men, he convinced himself that they must have some secret source from which they drew immense gains. For this reason, he decided to get on friendly terms with one or both of them, and eventually he succeeded in befriending Bruno.

Bruno did not need much time to see that this physician was an idiot and enjoyed palming off strange stories on him. The physician, for his part, was always wonderfully delighted by Bruno. Having invited him to breakfast, and thinking that because he had done so he might talk freely with him, he expressed his amazement at the fact that both he and Buffalmacco, being but poor men, could live so lightheartedly, and asked Bruno to tell him how they managed. At this fresh proof of the doctor's simplicity and fatuity, Bruno was inclined to laugh, but he resolved instead that it would be better to answer him in the spirit the question demanded.

"Master, there are not many people to whom I would disclose our manner of life, but, as you are my friend, and I know you will not let it go further, I do not mind telling you. It is true that my friend and I live not only as lightheartedly and jovially as you see, but much more so. Yet neither our art nor any property that we possess provides us enough to keep us in water—not that I would have you think that we go thieving: no! Rather, we stay the course, and by so doing we get all that we need—nay, all that we desire—without the least harm to a soul. And this is how we live as lightheartedly as you see."

The doctor would have been quite ready to believe this explanation had he known what it meant. Lost in wonder, he immediately burned with a most vehement desire to know what "staying the course" could mean, and immediately pressed Bruno to explain it, assuring him that he would never tell a soul.

"Alas, Master Doctor," said Bruno, "what is this you ask of me? It is a great secret you would have me impart to you. It would be enough to ruin me, to send me packing out of this world—nay, even into the very jaws of the Lucifer of San Gallo if it became known. But such is the respect I have for your quid[d]itative pumpionship [essential magniloquence] of Legnaia, and the trust I place in you, that I cannot deny you anything you ask of me; and so I will tell you, on condition that you swear by the cross at Montesone that you will keep your promise, and never repeat it to a soul." The master gave the required assurance.

"You should know, my sweet master," said Bruno, "that not long ago in this city there was a great master of necromancy called Michael Scot, for he was from Scotland. He was held in great esteem by not a few gentlemen—most of whom are now dead. But when it came time for him to depart from Florence, at their request he left behind two of his pupils—adepts both—whom he told should always be ready to serve those gentlemen who had done him honor. And they served these gentlemen very well in certain of their love affairs and other trifling matters. Finding the city and the manners of its citizens agreeable to them, they made up their minds to stay here always. They grew friendly and very intimate with some of the citizens, making no distinction between gentle and simple, rich or poor, as long as they were conducive to their ways. And to please these friends, they formed a company of perhaps 25 men who would meet together at least twice a month at a place chosen by them. At these meetings, everyone present was to declare his desire, and immediately—that very night—the two men supplied it. Now, Buffalmacco and I, being extraordinarily great and close friends with these two adepts, were admitted into this company by them, and are still members of it. And I assure you that, whenever we are assembled together, the adornments of the room in which we eat are a marvel to see. The tables are laid as if for kings, and there are multitudes of stately and handsome servants—women as well as men—at the beck and call of every member of the company. And the basins and the jugs, the flasks and the cups and everything else that is used for eating and drinking are all made of nothing but gold and silver. Moreover, the abundance and variety of the dishes that are set before us, one after another, each suited to the tastes of the diner, are marvelous, too. . . .

But among all the delights of the place none may compare with the fair ladies who, as soon as one might wish, are brought there from every part of the world.

Why, you may find there the great lady of the Barbanichs, the queen of the Basques, the consort of the sultan, the empress of Osbech, the ciancianfera of Norrieca, the semistante of Berlinzone, and the Scalpedra of Narsia. But why try to list them all? They include all the queens of the world, even the schinchimurra of Prester John, who has the horns sprouting out of her backside—so that's a sight. Now when these ladies have finished eating and drinking, they dance a measure or two with the man at whose behest they have been brought. And afterwards each retires to her chamber with her man. . . .

Among the luckiest of all the company I reckon Buffalmacco and myself, for Buffalmacco generally has the queen of France fetched for him, and I really like the queen of England, for they are the finest women in the world, and we have been known to carry on with them so that we are the very eyes of their heads. So I'll leave it to your judgment to determine whether or not we have good reason to live and carry ourselves with lighter hearts than others, for we are loved by two such great queens—to say nothing of the thousand or two thousand florins that we have from them whenever we want. This is—in the vulgar—what we call "staying the course," because, as the corsairs prey upon the world, so do we. The difference, though, is that whereas corsairs never return their spoils, we do just as soon as we have done it. So now, my worthy master, you understand what we mean by "staying the course." And you can see for yourself how important it is for you to keep this secret—so I will spare you any further exhortations.

The master, whose skill did not reach, perhaps, much beyond the treatment of children for dry skin, took everything that Bruno said as gospel, and burned with so vehement a desire to be admitted into this company, that he could not have yearned for the highest good itself with more ardor. So, after telling Bruno that it was hardly surprising that they bore themselves lightheartedly, he could barely refrain from asking him there and then to have him enrolled. However, he deemed it more prudent to defer his request until, after lavishing honors upon Bruno, he had won the right to press his case with more confidence.

[For some time, Master Simone wined and dined Bruno assiduously, showing him every affection. Alone with Bruno one night, the master finally thought he was in a position to beg for entry to the company.]

"God knows, Bruno, there is not a man for whom I would do as much as for you. Why, if you ask me to go all the way from here to Peretola [a suburb of Florence], I almost think I would do so! Therefore, I trust you will not think it strange if I talk to you as an intimate friend and in confidence. You know that not long ago you told me about that merry company and its doings. This has stirred in me such a desire as never there was to know more about it. I have good reason to become a member of this company, as you will hear. You can laugh at me if I do not then immediately have fetched for me the fairest maid you have ever seen. I saw her last year at Cacavincigli and I am entirely besotted by her.

By the body of Christ, I offered her 10 Bolognese groats to pleasure me, but she wouldn't do it. Accordingly, I most earnestly entreat you to tell me what I must do to make myself fit for membership in the company. Never doubt that you will have a true and loyal friend in me—one who will do you honor. But above all, you will see what a fine person I am, how well furnished I am with legs, and with a face as fresh as a rose. And on top of that, I am a doctor of medicine—I hardly think you have such a person in your ranks. Besides, I have a few excellent stories to tell, and know many a good song by heart. I'll sing one to you." And immediately he began to sing. Bruno wanted to laugh so hard he could barely contain himself, but he kept a grave countenance.

When the master finished his song, he asked, "How do you like it?"

"Truly," replied Bruno, "no straw lyre could compete with you, so artargutically [a nonsense word] you refine your strain."

"I'm sure," replied the master, "you would not have believed it had you not heard me yourself."

"Indeed," said Bruno, "what you say is true."

"I have other songs as well," said the master, "but enough of that for now. You must know that I—as you see me—am the son of a gentleman, even though my father lived in the contado. On my mother's side, I come from the Vallecchio family. As you may have observed, I have quite the finest library and wardrobe of all the physicians in Florence. God's faith! I have a robe that cost, all told, close to a hundred pounds in bagattini [a small-value Venetian coin] more than ten years ago. Accordingly, I must ask you immediately to get me enrolled. If you do so—God's faith—however ill you might become, you shall never have to pay a penny for me to tend you."

At this, Bruno muttered to himself—as he had done many times before—that the doctor was a numbskull.

[Bruno convinces the master that as incoming captain of the company it would be wise for him to cultivate Buffalmacco in much the same way that he had cultivated him. After enjoying the master's hospitality for some time, Buffalmacco and Bruno bring him word of his election to the company, promising that he would have the Countess di Civillari—Countess of the Cesspool—as his mistress.]

On the day of the next nocturnal gathering, the doctor had the two men to breakfast, after which he asked them how he was to meet up with the company.

"See here, master," replied Buffalmacco. "You will need to be stout of heart, otherwise you may meet with some difficulty and, in so doing, cause us much embarrassment. Now, let us tell you why you will need a stout heart. Tonight, at the first hour after dark, you must contrive to be on one of those raised tombs that have recently been placed outside Santa Maria Novella. Make sure that you wear one of your best gowns, for your first appearance will give the company the proper impression of your dignity. But we have also been told—for we were not present at the time it was discussed—that because you are a gentleman, the countess intends to make you a knight of the Bath at her own expense. So you wait there until one whom we shall send comes for you. But so that you know exactly what to expect, the one who will come for you will be a horned, black beast. Although he is not very great in size, he will go snorting and bounding about the piazza in front of you trying to terrify you. But when he thinks that you are not afraid, he will draw near to you quietly, and when he is close to you, fear nothing and get down from the tomb. Forgetting both God and the saints, mount him, and when you are well set on his back, fold your arms on your breast, as if in submission, and do not touch him again. Then he will carry you to us, going gently. But I warn you: should you invoke God or the saints, or give in to fear, he might drop you, or smash you against something that you would not find pleasant. So, if your heart is weak, it would be better for you not to come, for you would assuredly do yourself harm, and our reputations would be hurt in the process."

"You clearly don't know me yet," said the doctor. "Is it because I wear gloves and a long robe that causes you to doubt me? Ah. But were you to know about some of the feats I did years ago in Bologna, when I used to chase women with my friends, you would be lost in amazement. God's faith! On one of those nights, there was a girl, a poor sickly creature she was too, who stood not a cubit in height, who would not come with us. So first I treated her to many a good slap, and then I picked her up with force and carried her almost as far as a crossbow will send a bolt, until I eventually made her to come with us. And on another occasion I recall, having no one else with me but my servant, a little after the hour of Ave Maria, I passed by the Franciscan cemetery, and though a woman had been interred there that very day, I was not afraid at all. So on this score, you can rest easy, for indeed I am a man of exceeding courage and prowess. And to make sure I appear before you with the appropriate dignity, I will don my scarlet gown—the one I wore when I took my doctor's degree—and we will see if the company does not give me a hearty welcome, and make me a captain on the spot. As soon as I am there, you'll see how things go. How else is it that this countess—who has not even seen me yet—is already so enamored of me that she intends to make me a Knight of the Bath? And whether I will find knighthood agreeable or know how to support the dignity well and proper, leave that to me."

"Well said, excellently well said," exclaimed Buffalmacco. "But do not disappoint us, either by not coming or by not being found when we send for you. I say this because the weather is cold and you medical gentlemen take great care of your health."

"God forbid," replied the doctor, "I am not one of those cold-blooded men. I do not fear the cold. It is rare indeed when I leave my bed at night to answer the call of nature—as one must do at times—that I do more than throw a fur coat over my nightgown. So rest assured: I will be there." So they parted.

Toward nightfall, the master found a pretext to leave his wife. Secretly, he got out his fine gown, which he put on, and headed down to the tombs. Having perched himself on top of one of them, he curled up—it was a very cold night—and awaited the coming of the beast.

Meanwhile, Buffalmacco, who was a tall man and strong, procured for himself one of those masks that used to be worn at certain festivals that have now gone out of fashion, and, having put on a black fur coat which he had turned inside out, he looked like a bear, except for the fact that the mask had the face of a devil, and was furnished with horns. With Bruno following close behind, keen to see the fun, Buffalmacco hurried to the piazza of Santa Maria Novella. And, as soon as he saw that the master was on the tomb, he began to career about in a most wild and furious manner, to and fro across the piazza, snorting, bellowing and ranting like someone demented. When the master saw this, every single hair on his head stood on end. He began to tremble in every limb. Being in truth more timid than a woman, he wished that he was safely at home. But as he was there, he resolved to keep his spirits up, so overwhelming was his desire to see the marvels of which Bruno and Buffalmacco had told him.

After a while, Buffalmacco allowed his fury to abate, and came up quietly to the tomb where the master was and stood still. Still trembling with fear, the master could not at first make up his mind as to whether to get on the beast's back or not. At length, though, fearing that it might be worse for him if he did not mount the beast, he overcame the one dread by means of the other and getting down from the tomb, he muttered under his breath, "God help me!" He seated himself very comfortably on the beast's back, and then, still quaking in every limb, he folded his arms as he had been told to do.

Buffalmacco now started, going on all-fours, at a very slow pace, in the direction of Santa Maria della Scala, and in this way brought the master within a short distance of the Convent of the Ladies of Ripoli. Now, in that quarter of the city there were various trenches, into which the farmers of those parts were wont to discharge the Countess di Civillari, so that she might afterwards manure their land. Buffalmacco skirted the edge of one of these trenches as he passed by, and, seizing his opportunity, raised a hand. Grabbing the doctor by one of his feet, he threw him headfirst off his back right into the trench, and then, making a terrific noise and frantic gestures as he had before, went bounding off towards Santa Maria della Scala and the field of Ognissanti, where he found Bruno, who had taken himself there so he could laugh at his leisure. And there the two men remained laughing uproariously watching from a distance how the filth-covered doctor would behave.

Finding himself in so loathsome a place, the master struggled with all his might to raise himself and climb out. Again and again, though, he slipped back in, swallowing some mouthfuls of the excrement. Eventually, bemired from head to foot, sorrowful and crestfallen, he did at last get out, leaving his hood behind him. Then, removing as much of the filth as he could with his hands, not knowing what else to do, he went home, where, after much knocking, he was at last allowed in. Scarcely had the door closed behind the malodorous master than Bruno and Buffalmacco were at it, keen to hear how he would be received by his wife. And they were rewarded by hearing her give him the soundest scolding that ever a bad husband received. . . .

The next morning, Bruno and Buffalmacco, having painted their bodies all over with bruises to give themselves the appearance of having been thrashed, came to the doctor's house. Finding that he had already risen, they went in, being saluted from all sides by a foul smell, for time had not yet served thoroughly to cleanse the house. Being informed that they had come to see him, the doctor advanced to meet them, and bade then good morning. Having prepared their answer in advance, Bruno and Buffalmacco replied, "You will have no good morning from us! Rather, we pray God to give enough bad years to make an end of you, for there lives a no more notorious and faithless traitor. We, who did our best to honor and entertain you, have almost been slaughtered like dogs. Your faithlessness has cost us this night as many sound blows as would more than suffice to keep an ass trotting all the way from here to Rome. Besides that, we're in danger of being expelled from the company in which we arranged your enrolment. If you doubt our words, just look at our bodies—what a state they are in." And so, baring their breasts they gave him a glimpse of the patches they had painted there, and then covered them up again.

The doctor would have made excuses to them, and recounted his misfortunes, explaining how he had been thrown into the trench, but Buffalmacco broke in: "Would that he had thrown you from the bridge into the Arno! Why did you invoke God and the saints? Did we not warn you?"

"God's faith," replied the doctor, "I did not do that."

"What?" asked Buffalmacco, "You did not? You did more than that, for he that we sent for you told us that you trembled like an aspen, and that you knew not where you were. You have played a sorry trick on us. But you shall never do another. And as for you, we will give you such reward as you deserve."

The doctor now began to beg their pardon, and to implore them, for God's sake, not to expose him to shame. He used all the eloquence at his command to make his peace with them. And if he had honorably entertained them before, from this point forth, for fear that they should make public his disgrace, he did so even more abundantly, and courted them both by entertaining them at his table, and in other ways.

And so now you have heard how wisdom is imparted to those who do not acquire it at Bologna.

Questions: *What is the role of the devil in the story? How would Boccaccio's readers have understood the secret company to which the two painters claim to belong? What is the role of the devil as a literary device here? What does this suggest about popular attitudes toward necromancy?*

89. ANTICHRIST TAKES THE STAGE

"Antichrist," an edited and modernized version of which appears below, is part of the cycle of "mystery plays" performed in the English city of Chester from the late fourteenth century. The Chester cycle—like similar productions elsewhere—enacted the whole drama of creation from the story of Adam and Eve up to the crucifixion and last judgment through a series of discrete but connected plays. These were typically performed in the vernacular for a diverse audience of townsmen and townswomen. Plays would be staged on large, decorated "pageant wagons" that would progress in a circuit around the city. At designated stations, the wagons would halt and the play would be acted out. Each play, then, would be performed multiple times through the course of the day. Although it is likely that the early shape of these dramas had been sketched by ecclesiastics, by the early fifteenth century, the financing and organizing of these individual plays had passed into the hands of the town's various craft and trade guilds. They often reworked the material to reflect the community's concerns in any given year. As a result, there are no definitive "scripts" for any of these dramas. Five versions of the Chester cycle survive, but all date from the late sixteenth and early seventeenth centuries, after their performance had been suppressed by Protestant authorities.

Each guild would traditionally sponsor a particular play. In Chester, "Antichrist" was produced by the cloth dyers.

English, fifteenth century.

Source: *Antichrist*, from *The Chester Plays: A Collection of Mysteries Founded Upon Scriptural Subjects*, vol. 2 (London, 1867), pp. 150–77, 224–25; rev.

> *Antichrist*
> All peoples in the land now be joyful,
> Who will be ruled throughout by right.
> Your savior now is in your sight
> Here you may assuredly see.
> Messiah, Christ, and he most in might,
> Who in the law was promised you,
> All mankind for joy prepared,
> Has come—for I am he.
> Of me was spoken in prophecy,
> By Moses, David and Isaiah,

TEN: EXPERIENCING THE DEVIL IN WORD AND IMAGE

> I am he they call "Messiah,"
> Redeemer of Israel.
> Those that believe in me steadfastly
> I shall save from torment—
> And joy just as I have
> With them I will think to share.

It is said concerning me in Ezekiel 36[.24]: I will take you from among the gentiles and I will gather you out of all the countries and I will lead you back into your own land. And he says:

> But one has belied me here in this land,
> Jesus is his name, I understand,
> To further falsehood he has tried
> And fired with fantasy.
> His wickedness he would not stop,
> Till he was taken and put in bond,
> And slain through the power of my mission,
> This is truth, with certainty.
> My people the Jews he did disperse,
> So that into their land they never came,
> On them I must have in mind now,
> and restore them again.
> To build the temple I will not delay,
> As God will be honored therein,
> And endless profit I shall win for them,
> And all those that be obedient to me.

It is said in Psalm [5.8] about me: "I will worship towards your holy temples in your fear." And let him say . . .

> Also he [the prophet, Daniel] told them, believe you me,
> That I with gifts should bestow freely—
> Which prophecy shall be done,
> When I my realm have won.
> And that I should grant mercy,
> Abundant riches, land and fee,
> It shall be done, that you shall see,
> When I have come hither.

"He will give them power and will divide the land into many parts for nothing," Daniel 13 [actually 11.39]. And he says:

What say you, kings, that here reside?
Are not my words to your approval,
That I am Christ omnipotent?
Do each of you not believe this?

1st King
We believe, lord, without a doubt,
That Christ has not yet come.
If you are he, you shall be set
In the temple as God above.

2nd King
If you are Christ, called Messiah,
That from our woe shall us acquire,
Do before us a miracle—
A sign that we may see.

3rd King
Then will I believe that it is so,
If you do wonders before you go.
So that you save us from our woe,
Then honored you shall be.

4th King
Sinfully have we believed many a year,
And of our expectation we had much doubt.
If you be Christ now come here,
Then may you stop all strife.

Antichrist
That I am Christ and Christ will be,
By true signs you shall see,
For dead men through my power,
Shall rise from death to life.
Now will I overturn all through my thought:
Trees down, the roots up right,
That is a marvel to your sight—
And fruit growing upon it!
So shall they grow and multiply,
Through my might and my power,

I will take you out of heresy
If you believe upon me.
And bodies that are dead and slain,
If I can raise them up again,
Honor me with might and strength,
And then shall you grieve for no man.
In truth, after that I will die,
And rise again through my power.
If I can do this marvelously,
I advise you to believe in me.
Men buried in graves, as you may see,
What marvel is it now, ask you,
To raise them up through my power,
And all through my own accord?
Whether I am in my godhead,
By true signs you shall see:
"Rise up, dead men, and honor me,
And know me for your lord."

Then the dead arise from sepulchers.

   1st Dead Man
   O lord, from you I ask mercy.
   I was dead, but now I live.
   Now I know well and truly,
   That Christ has hither come.

   2nd Dead Man
   We and all men honor him,
   Devoutly kneeling on our knee:
   "You are worshipped here, amen."
   In our name, Christ has come!

   Antichrist
   That I shall fulfil holy writ,
   You shall know and know it well,
   For I am the font of all profit and wit,
   And lord of every land.
   And as the prophet Sophony [Zephaniah]
   Speaks of me right truly,

> I shall readily repeat here
> So that clerks shall understand:

[Antichrist quotes Zeph. 3.8 in Latin, "Expect me on the day of my resurrection that is to come, for my judgment is that I assemble the gentiles and gather the kingdoms."]

> Now I will die—that you shall soon see—
> And rise again through my power,
> I would that you put me in the grave
> And worship me alone.
> For in this temple a tomb is made,
> Therein my body shall be laid.
> Take notice of me each one.
> And after my resurrection,
> I will I sit in great renown,
> And send down my ghost to you,
> In the form of fire, full soon.
> I die, I die! Now I am dead.

1st King
> Now since this worthy lord is dead,
> And his grace to us is led,
> To take his body is my advice,
> And bury it in a grave.

2nd King
> Assuredly. And as he said to us,
> In a tomb he would be laid.
> Now let us all go forth immediately,
> So he may us save from distress.

Then they cross over to Antichrist.

3rd King
> We take the body of this sweet,
> And bury it low under the ground.
> Now, lord, comfort us, we beseech you,
> And send to us your grace.

4th King
> And if he rises soon through his might,

TEN: EXPERIENCING THE DEVIL IN WORD AND IMAGE

> From death to life as he promised,
> I will honor him, day and night,
> As God in every place.

They withdraw from the tomb up to the ground.

> *1st King*
> Now know I well that he is dead,
> For now in a grave we have him laid.
> If he rise, as he has said,
> He is full of great might. . . .

> *4th King*
> I will mourn, with all my strength,
> Till Christ is risen up again,
> That miracle will make us glad.
> "Rise up, lord, so that we may see."

Then Antichrist lifts up his body, rising from the dead.

> *Antichrist*
> I rise, now! Do reverence to me,
> God glorified, created by decree.
> If I be Christ, now believe in me.
> And work according to my will . . .

[The kings make sacrifices to Antichrist. He ascends to his throne and gives them his blessing.]

> You kings, I shall advance you all,
> And because your regions are but small,
> Cities and castles shall to you befall,
> With towns and towers most excellent.
> I am the true God of might,
> All things I made through my might,
> Sun and moon, day and night,
> And to bliss I may bring you.
> And the gifts that I promise,
> You shall have—as is good and right.
> Hence before I go out of your sight,
> Each one shall know his share:

To you I give Lombardy,
And to you Denmark and Hungary,
And you take Ponthous [Pontus?] and Italy,
And Rome shall be yours.

2nd King
Many thanks, lord, for your gifts today!
We will honor you always.
For truly we were never so rich,
Nor any of our kin.

Antichrist
Therefore, be true and steadfast always,
And truly believe in my law.
For I will listen to you today,
If resolute I find you.

Then Antichrist will withdraw and Enoch and Elias will come.

Enoch
Almighty God in majesty,
Who made the heaven and earth to be,
Fire, water, stone and tree,
And man, through your might,
The workings of your mystery
For any earthly man to see
Are impossible, as I think,
For any worldly creature.
Gracious lord, who art so good,
For those who so long in flesh and blood
Has granted life and heavenly food,
Let our thoughts never be defiled.
But give us, lord, might and strength
Before we be slain by this rogue,
To convert your people again,
Who he has thus beguiled.
Since the world's beginning,
I have lived in great joy,
Through the help of the high heavenly king,
In paradise without torment,
Till we heard a portent

Of this thief's coming,
Who is now on earth reigning,
And destroys God's folks.
To Paradise I was taken at that time,
To await this thief's coming,
And Elijah, my brother, here beside,
Was after sent to me.
With this champion we must dispute,
Who now walks across the world,
To disprove his pomp and pride,
And impair all his power.

Elijah
Oh, lord, that made all things,
And who gave us life so long ago,
Never let the devil's power spring,
Which this man has within.
God give you grace, both old and young,
To know the deceit that he is doing,
So that you may come to that joy
Of bliss that never shall end.
I warn you, all men, truly,
This is Enoch, I am Ely,
Who have come to destroy his errors,
That he now shows to you.
He calls himself "Christ" and "Messiah,"
He lies, indeed, openly.
He is the devil, to torment you,
For nothing else does he know . . .

And thus, Enoch and Elijah will cross towards Antichrist.

Enoch
Say, you true devil's limb,
Who sits so grisly and so grim,
From him you came and shall return,
For all the souls you deceive.
You have deceived men for many a day,
And moved the people into your pay,
And bewitched them onto a wrong way,
Wickedly through your wiles.

Antichrist
Ah, false deceivers, flee from me!
Am not I most in majesty?
What men dare address me thus,
Or make such trouble?

Elijah
Fie on thee, deceiver! Fie on thee,
The devil's own nursling!
Through him you preach and have power
For a while through sufferance.

Antichrist
Oh, you hypocrites that do so cry!
Wretches, clowns, so loudly you lie!
To overthrow my law you try,
That speech is good to spare.
You who defy my true faith,
And trouble my folk divine,
Get from hence hastily—but if you do not go,
To you comes sorrow and care.

Enoch
Your sorrow and care come on your head,
For falsely—through your wicked counsel—
The people are put to pain.
I would your body were from your head,
Twenty miles from it led,
Till I brought it back again.

Antichrist
Out with you, hypocrite, with your wiles,
For falsely my people you beguile,
I shall hang you hastily!
And that clown that stands by you,
He puts my folk in great torment
With his false flattering tongue.
But I shall teach you courtesy,
Your savior to know at once on high;
False thieves, with your heresy,
And if you dare, abide . . .

Enoch
We are no thieves, we tell you,
You false fiend, coming from hell . . .
And thereto we are well prepared
As all men may now hear.

Antichrist
My might is most, I tell you.
I died and rose through my power,
As all these kings saw with their eyes—
And every man and wife.
And miracles and marvels I did also.
I counsel both of you, therefore,
To worship me and no other,
And let us now strive no more.

Elijah
They were not miracles, but marvelous things,
That you showed to these kings,
Into falsehood you bring them,
Through the fiend's craft!
And as the flower now springs,
Falls, fades and hangs,
So your joy now reigns,
Which soon shall be ripped from you. . . .

Antichrist
Out with you, thieves! Why do you act like this?
Would you rather have pain or bliss?
I may save you from all that is amiss.
I made the day and also the night,
And all that on earth is growing,
Flowers fresh and fair did spring,
And the stars that are so bright.

Elijah
You lie! Vengeance on you befall!
Out with you, wretch! Wrath on you I shall make.
You call yourself king and lord of all,
But a fiend you are within.

Antichrist
You lie falsely, I tell you.
You will be damned into hell.
I made you man from flesh and skin,
And all that is living.
For other gods you have none,
Therefore, worship me alone—
Who made the water and stone
And all to my liking.

Enoch
Truly, you lie falsely.
You are a fiend come to torment
God's people that stand by us.
In hell I wish you were. . . .

Antichrist
Wretches, fools, you are blind,
God's son I am, and from him sent.
How dare you maintain your intent,
Since he and I are one?
Have I not, since I came from him,
Made the dead rise and go? . . .

Enoch
Now of your miracles I would like to see . . .
Bring forth these men here into our sight,
That you have raised against the right.
If you be of such great might,
Make them eat and drink.
For the true God we will know you to be,
Through such a sign if you will show,
And we will do you reverence in a row.
All at your pleasure. . . .

Antichrist
You dead men, rise through my power,
Come, eat and drink that men may see,
And prove me worthy of deity,
And thereby end all this strife.

1st Dead Man
Lord, thy bidding I will always do,
And I will try to eat.

2nd Dead Man
And I also, all that I may,
Will do your bidding here.

Elijah
I have here bread for both of you.
But I must bless it before I go
So that the fiend, mankind's foe,
Will have no power on it.
This bread I bless with my hand,
In Jesus's name, I understand,
Who is lord of sea and land,
And king in heaven so high.
[in Latin] "In the name of the father" through whom everything is
    wrought,
"And the virgin's son" who dear us bought,
"And the holy spirit" is all my thought.
One God and persons three.

1st Dead Man
Alas! Put that bread out of my sight.
To look upon it I am not able.
That print that is upon it fixed,
It fills me with great fear!

2nd Dead Man
To look on it, I am not able.
That bread is so bright to me,
And is my foe, both day and night,
And fills me with great dread!

Enoch
Now, you men that have done amiss,
You see well what his power is.
Convert to him I counsel, indeed,
That on the cross has bought you.

3rd King
And now we know clearly,
We have been brought into heresy.
With you to death we will go, therefore,
And never turn our thought again.

4th King
Now, Enoch and Eli, it is undeniable,
You have attainted the tyrant this same day.
Blessed be Jesus, born of a maid,
In him I believe upon.

1st King
You deceiver, full of fantasy!
With sorcery, witchcraft and necromancy,
You have us led into heresy.
Fie on thy works every one! . . .

Antichrist
Ah, false traitors, do you turn away now?
You shall be slain—I make a vow.
And those traitors that so turned you,
I shall make them much troubled.
That all others, by true sight,
Shall know that I am most in might,
Because with this sword I think to fight,
For all you shall be slain.

Then Antichrist kills Enoch and Elijah and all the converted kings with his sword. Then he will return to his throne while Michael with a sword in his right hand should say:

Archangel Michael
Antichrist, now this day has come,
Reign no longer now you may.
He that has led you always,
Now to him you must go.
No more men shall be slain by you.
My lord wills that you be dead.
He that has given you his power
Your soul shall receive.

TEN: EXPERIENCING THE DEVIL IN WORD AND IMAGE

In sin you first were engendered,
In sin have you led your life.
In sin an end you now make,
Who has marred many a one.
Three year and half of one truly,
You have had leave to destroy
God's people wickedly,
Through your foul counsel.
Now you shall know and understand on high,
That God's power is more
Than even the devil's and yours thereby,
Now that you shall be dead.
You have always served Satanas,
And had his power in every place,
Therefore you get no more grace.
With him you must be gone.

Then Michael kills Antichrist and as he is being killed Antichrist shouts [in English], "Help! Help! Help! Help!"

Antichrist
Help, Satanas and Lucifer,
Beelzebub, bold youth,
Ragnel! Ragnel! You who are so dear.
Now fare I wondrously evil!
Alas! Alas! Where is my power?
Alas! My wits are all in doubt.
Now body and soul are both in fear,
And all goes to the devil.

Then Antichrist will die and two demons will come and say as follows:

1st Demon
Anon, master, anon! Anon!
From the grounds of hell I heard you groan.
I thought not to come myself alone,
Out of esteem for your estate.
With us to hell you shall be gone.
For his death, a great moan we make,
To win more souls into our care,
It is now too late.

2nd Demon

With me you shall go. From me you came,
From me shall come your final doom.
For this, you have well deserved.
Through my might and my strength,
You have lived in dignity,
And many a soul deceived.

1st Demon

This body was begotten by my assent,
In pure whoredom, truthfully,
In his mother's womb before he went,
I was him within.
And always taught him my intent—
Sin—by which he shall be ruined.
Because he followed my commandment,
His soul shall never rest.

2nd Demon

Now, fellow, in faith, a great moan we may make,
For this lord of estate who stands in this place.
Many a fat morsel we had for his sake
On souls that should be hanging in hell by the head.

Then the body of Antichrist is carried off by the demons.

1st Demon

I have taken his soul with sorrow in my hand.
Yea, penance and pain soon shall he feel!
To Lucifer, that lord, it shall be present,
And shall burn like a brand. His sorrow we shall not feel.

2nd Demon

This proctor of prophecy has procured many a one
To believe in his laws and lose for his sake.
Their souls now are in sorrow, and his shall be soon,
Such accomplishments through my might, many a one do I make.

After the demons have spoken, Enoch and Elijah cut down by Antichrist will rise up again and will point out their condition to the audience.

TEN: EXPERIENCING THE DEVIL IN WORD AND IMAGE

1st Demon
With Lucifer that lord long shall he linger.
In a seat full of sorrow with him shall he sit.

2nd Demon
Yea, by the heels in hell shall he hang,
In a dungeon deep, right in hell pit.

1st Demon
To hell I will hurry, without any fail,
With this present of value, thither to bring.

2nd Demon
You take him by the top and I by the tail.
A sorrowful song in faith he shall sing.

1st Demon
Ah, fellow, a doleful look that you now deal
To all this fair company, before you go there.

2nd Demon
Yea, sorrow and care always shall they feel.
All sinful shall dwell in hell at their last end.

Questions: How does Antichrist convince his would-be followers of his divinity? Does this differ from how Christ established his status? What is the relationship between Antichrist and the demons? Is there any way a pious Christian might be able to tell the difference between the demonic and the divine? How is the portrait of Antichrist here different from that provided by doc. 47? What does the play suggest about how popular notions of Antichrist have developed since that point?

90. IMAGES OF THE DEVIL

Most artistic representations in the Middle Ages were intended to impart a moral or spiritual lesson. Because the devil was such a powerful emblem of evil, he and his minions were frequently depicted visually. Some of these images were created to be viewed publicly, while others were used to decorate texts that would be experienced in a more private context.

Most of the images that introduce the chapters of this book come from the later Middle Ages. Some come from early printed books, which become increasingly accessible to those prepared to pay for them beginning in the 1460s and 1470s. Considering these images, think first about which were intended for a wide public reception and which were intended to be viewed by individuals alone. Why does this make a difference?

Questions: What stories are the illuminators attempting to depict? Are these demons terrifying? What problems do illustrators seem to have in depicting the devil? To what extent do these artists seem to be aware of contemporary theological developments? How might these images have been used? What might their effect have been on the viewer?

CHAPTER ELEVEN

TOWARD THE EARLY MODERN AGE

Figure 11.1 Anonymous, "Hell with Satan" (1460–80). This late-fifteenth-century Italian engraving depicts Satan with a sinner in each of his three mouths, as described by Dante (doc. 57). Around him are various sinners being tormented by demons, arranged in tiers according to their transgressions. At the top right, the gaping mouth of hell is visible.

ELEVEN: TOWARD THE EARLY MODERN AGE

The fourteenth and fifteenth centuries were marked by a succession of profound existential crises across Europe. The Great Famine (1315–22), which probably killed a tenth of the continent's population, was followed a generation later by the first outbreak of the Black Death (1347–50), which killed at least a third and returned—albeit with progressively lessening severity—almost every decade into the seventeenth century. This was an age of renewed violence, too. The rebalancing of relations between landlords and tenants engendered by the plague led to sporadic rebellions of peasants and workers across the continent. The Hundred Years' War (1327–53) between France and England compounded this chaos, adding to the death toll while making much of France impassable for merchants. In a common motif of the period, King Death ruled the earth.

In the face of this mass mortality, the Church was unable adequately to meet the increased demand for transformative spiritual services. It was also wracked with its own problems. From 1309 to 1376, the papacy was based in the city of Avignon. Although the city was just outside the territories of the French crown, all the popes who ruled during this so-called "Babylonian Captivity of the Church" were French and tended to avoid antagonizing the king. As scandalous as it seemed to have Saint Peter's descendants resident outside his city, squandering large sums building a new and grand papal infrastructure in Avignon, attempts to return the papacy to its traditional home resulted in the Great Schism (1378–1415). This saw first two popes (one in Rome, the other in Avignon) and then briefly three (the third based in Pisa). Against this backdrop, the Church had to deal with rising anti-clericalism, popular mystics claiming access to direct knowledge of God, and two new and pernicious heresies: Lollardy in England and Hussitism in Bohemia. Disaster, disorder, and disobedience seemed endemic—and they were all watchwords of the devil.

In this turbulent age, a number of threads of demonism were woven together to create what would become the figure of the demonic witch—an image that came to preoccupy the attentions of many secular and ecclesiastical judges and inquisitors from the middle of the fifteenth century. This process brought together a fear of demonically worked magic—necromancy—and occult conspiracy, with a desire for moral reform in both the growing cities of Europe and the countryside. This involved rooting out traditional folk-medicine and divinatory practices that were increasingly demonized. Yet this process was not straightforward: medieval witches did not seem to operate in the way that fifteenth-century men asserted concerning the sorceresses they claimed to have found. The canon *Episcopi* made it clear that the crimes that "sorceresses" confessed to could not be real, for they were attributing powers to the devil that had never before been ascribed to him.

The result was a new devil—a creature no longer *of* nature but who could sometimes be *beyond* nature.

91. WORKING WITH DEMONS

The Sworn Book of Honorius *was one of the most influential texts of ritual magic to circulate in the Latin west during the High Middle Ages. According to its prologue, a council of eighty-nine masters assembling at Naples designated a certain Honorius of Thebes to record the secrets of their art in order to preserve them from their enemies. While the text's thematic and methodological consistency suggests that it was composed by a single author, the attribution to Honorius is undoubtedly spurious.*

The Sworn Book *provides instructions for the conjuration of spirits, both good and bad, who can be compelled to grant the magical operator what he desires. The process is complicated, involving specially prepared objects and intricate rituals, many of which mimic those of the Church. The central ritual involves contriving the "beatific vision" through the composition and application of what is called "the seal of the true and living God." The ritual below seeks more worldly ends.*

The word "daemones" in the translation has been corrected to "demons."

Latin, early thirteenth century?

Source: trans. Joseph Peterson, from Honorius of Thebes, *Sworn Book of Honorius* (Lake Worth, FL: Ibis Press, 2016), pp. 151, 223–29, 239–43, 265, 273–77.

Here Begins the Topics of the Third Treatise of This Work, Which Is about the Spirits of the Air

Concerning the constraint of spirits through words . . . Calling forth lightning and thunder. Concerning the required burnings. Concerning the purification of the air. Concerning the corruption of the air. To make snow and frost. To make dew and rain. To call forth flowers and fruit. Concerning invisibility. Concerning a horse, which will carry you anywhere you wish in a single night. To bring an absent person back safely in an hour. To transport something wherever you wish, in a moment. To have something removed. To recall something. To transfigure anything. To cause a river on dry land. To incite a kingdom against its ruler. To destroy a kingdom or state. To have power over anyone. To have a thousand armed soldiers. To form an indestructible fortress. How to make a mirror of destruction. How to destroy a place or an enemy using the mirror of destruction. The apparition of the world in a mirror. To return anything which a thief has stolen. To open locks. To cause discord. To cause agreement. To have the good will and favor of all persons. To have the desire of women. To have wealth. To cure any sickness. To make anyone sick, whenever you wish. To kill anyone. To hold back storms and dangers of the earth and sea. To hold back a ship at sea using the adamant stone, or otherwise to bring it back again. To avoid all danger. To flock birds together, and collect them. To cause fish to gather and be caught. To cause woodland and domestic animals to gather and be caught. To make burning appear. To make appear jesters and girls babbling. To make griffins and dragons appear. To make all wild beasts appear. To make hunters appear with dogs. To make someone appear as if they were somewhere other than where they actually are. To make all pleasures appear.

End of the Topics, and Beginning of the Preface on the Aerial Spirits

. . . The air is a corruptible element, fluid, and subtle, capable of receiving qualities from the other [elements], and is plainly invisible, but it is seen to be composed of parts of itself. In which are spirits, which the holy mother church calls damned, but they themselves assert the opposite to be true, and therefore we prefer to call then neither good nor evil. And those spirits that are governed by air act according to the nature of air itself, and therefore we can understand their nature. . . .

Beginning of the Manner of Working with [Angels and Spirits]

If therefore anybody wishes to operate with those spirits [of the air], we must first warn him strictly that he must be thoroughly purified. . . . Then when the mass of the holy spirit is being said or celebrated, when the operator is receiving the body of Christ, he should say prayers 19 and 20. . . .

[Prayer 19: Ioht. omaza, behea. Theon. megal. menehon. exhehal. tirigel. herapheiocon. semenoyn. sehmneny. hechmathan. hiemarayn. gemehehon. lucharanochyn. exnotheyn. themelihen. segyhon. hihoueuyr. hacrisentheon.]

[Prayer 20: Hofob. O God, infinitely great father, from whom proceeds all good, the greatness of [your mercy] is incomprehensible. Hear my prayers today, which I offer in your sight, and grant me the gift which I beg from you. . . .]

When the priest is holding up the body of Christ, to reveal it to the congregation, he should pray on behalf of the operator, saying thus:

Prayer

"O Lord Jesus Christ . . . I beg you in this critical moment, by the power of your sacraments, in order that such N[ame], by your gift and by your will, without condemnation of body and soul that the spirit N[ame] may make himself subject in all things, that he may constrain them to appear, to complete, to guard, to answer to all orders that he hopes and desires. Amen."

. . . With this done, he should draw a circle of nine feet across . . . in which he should draw two circles, where the first is one foot away from the other, between which you should write the names of the angels of the day and hour, of the month, of the time . . . saying:

"O you holy and powerful angels, may you be my assistants in this work."

Then draw within those two circles a regular heptagon, suitable for all invocations . . .

Note: you must be very careful while working . . . because it is hard for a person not knowing the powers of the spirits and their malice, without the greatest fortification to abide with them somehow. . . . It is well therefore to be cautious, because the nature of the strengths prevail, and therefore it is necessary to be very shrewd when making the circle, because therein lies the defense of the operator.

First you must prepare the place thus, for the earth should be flat and level, and free from stones or vegetation, and when it has been drawn, mark the air above yourself to two diameters every way, saying, "I put the Seal of Solomon over me for salvation and defense, in order that it protect me in the face of the enemy. In the name of the father and the son, and the holy spirit. Amen." Thus with your circle complete, exit and write outside in the earth or on small pieces of paper, the seven names of the creator, which are L[a]ialy, Lialg, Veham, Yalgal, Narath, Libarre, Libares, and nothing more is accomplished this night. . . .

Beginning of the Invocation

Strengthened by the name and in the name of the almighty God, the living and true Sabaoth, to whom all things stand open and to whom nothing is hidden, under whose will all creatures are subject, I, N[ame], the son of N[ame], although a sinner, yet I receive the gift of divine majesty, and in him I call you forth, O Barthan, Thaadas, Caudas, Yalchal, Formione, Guth, Muguth, Guth[r]yn, Iammax . . . and all other spirits, souls, demons, and winds which serve, obey, and are placed under you, I call forth, conjure, call upon you and bind you through these his holy names . . . and God himself calls you forth, causing you to tremble, to feel dread and fear, so that you come and are constrained to appear, obedient, cheerful, beautiful, and subdued, and truthful, next to this circle . . . in the form of N[ame], not harming any creatures, nor striking, roaring, raging, nor frightening me or my associates or any creatures, nor shocking anyone, but prepared to obey my decrees at once. And I order you and exorcise you to thoroughly fulfil all my commands without any deceit, through his power . . . Amen.

Here Begins the Placating of the Spirits

"Geneolia, Chide, ministers of the Tartarean seat of Primachia, mighty princes of the seat of Apologia, powers of Maonamiria. I invoke you and by invoking you I conjure and protected by the strength of the heavenly majesty, I potently command you and through him who spoke, and it was done, whom all creatures obey, and through this ineffable name 'Tetragrammaton': IOHT, HE, VAU, DALETH, . . . that you cease all pretexts and come quickly and without delay, from all parts of the world, responding rationally to everything which I will ask, not harming me nor my associates, not speaking deceptively, but rather truthfully and may you come peacefully, revealing what we wish, being conjured with the eternal name of the living and true God."

With that done, immediately infinite visions and illusions will appear, such as choirs, organs, lutes, and all the sorts of the sweetest instruments, in order to provoke the associates to flee, because they are able to exert no such influence over the master. After this armies of soldiers and bailiffs will come, in order to frighten them to flee from the circle. After these archers with all types of wild beasts will come, and act as if they intended to devour them. But he should speak with caring to the associates saying, "Have no fear. Behold the sign of the lord, our creator. Turn back to him, because he has the power to snatch you away from the jaws of the wicked."

Then the master, with closed hands, says as follows to the spirits: "Flee hence with your iniquities, by virtue of the banner of God." And then he should uncover [the Seal of God], to compel them to obey . . . then, in the middle of the circle, he should hold his right hand in the air, saying, "Behold the most sacred work. . . . Behold the [sign] of Solomon with its letters, characters, and figures, which I have brought before your presence. Behold the person of the exorcist in the midst of the exorcism, who has been well fortified by God, undaunted, prepared with powers, who has powerfully called you, and calls you with exorcising. Come therefore with all haste. . . ."

Here he should whistle once on each side, and immediately he will see movements and relevant signs, but they will not harm anything. And then he should speak like one bearing the command of divine majesty, and as if they are humbly satisfying your needs, "Why are you not yet here? . . . Hurry and obey the commands of your master, Bachac rushing upon Abrac, Abeor over Aberor." And they will come immediately in their proper forms, and while they are gathering around the circle, the master showing to them the seal, should say: "Behold your conjuration, if you become disobedient." And immediately he will see them in a most beautiful form, and peaceful, saying, "Ask what you wish; we are now prepared to fulfil whatever you order, because the lord has subjugated us." Then ask what you wish, and it will be done for you, or for others, on behalf of whom you wished to work.

Questions: What is the nature of the demons described here? Is anything different about them? Upon what traditions of the demonic does the conjuration draw? How does the magician seek to control the demons he calls upon? Is it possible to deduce anything about the magician's gender, age, and background?

92. MAGIC, DEMONS, AND HERESY

Pope John XXII (r. 1316–34) was the second of the Avignon popes. From early in his pontificate, John seems to have been concerned about the rise of demonic magic among the upper ranks of the Church. This uneasiness did not originate with John, but it assumed new proportions with the discovery of Arabic magical texts alongside those of Aristotle in the twelfth century. Scholarly interest in such works caused the bishop of Paris, Stephen Tempier, to preface his 1277 Condemnation of Errors *with an injunction against any works dealing with necromancy or the invocation of demons.*

In April 1317, John authorized an investigation into the bishop of Cahors, Hugues Géraud, who, he alleged, had sought to kill him and other cardinals with the assistance of a Jewish magician and certain magical images. After having the bishop executed, the pope ordered a wide-ranging investigation of members of the papal court. Concerned about his cardinals' use of necromancy, he issued the bull Super illius specula *(Upon his Watchtower), reproduced below. The authenticity of the bull has been questioned by some modern scholars, for it is not included in any of the papal registers. The earliest copies are found in the work of a mid-fourteenth-century Catalan inquisitor.*

Latin, 1326.

Source: trans. James J. Walsh, *The Popes and Science: The History of the Papal Relations to Science during the Middle Ages Down to our Own Time* (New York, 1913), pp. 147–48, compared with the Latin at 415–16 and rev.

Against Those Who Sacrifice to Demons or Seek Answers and Aid from Them or Who Own Books Dealing with Such Errors

Contemplating how the sons of men know and serve God through the practice of the Christian religion, we look down from the watchtower upon which—though undeservedly—we have been placed by the favoring mercy of he who made the first man in his own image and likeness. . . . With grief we discover—and the very thought of it wrings our soul with anguish—that there are many who are Christians only in name, who have turned away from the light of truth which was once theirs, and their minds have become so clouded by the darkness of error that they have entered into a league with death and a pact with hell: they sacrifice to demons and adore them; they make or have made for them images, rings, mirrors, phials, or such things in which demons can be enclosed by the art of magic. From them they seek and receive replies, and ask aid so they can satisfy their depraved desires. For a foul purpose they submit to the foulest slavery. Alas! This deadly malady is increasing more than usual in the world and inflicting ever greater ravages upon the flock of Christ.

Since, therefore, we are bound by the duty of our pastoral office to bring back wandering sheep who have strayed from the path to Christ's sheepfold and to exclude from the lord's flock those who are diseased, lest they infect the others, by this edict—which is to remain in perpetual effect—in accordance with the counsel of our brother bishops, we warn each and every person reborn in the font of baptism through the virtue of holy obedience and under pain of anathema that they may not teach or study any of the aforesaid perverse teachings, or—what is even worse—practice them in any manner on anyone.

And because it is fitting that those who spurn the most high through their perverse works should be punished for their sins by means of appropriate penalties, we pronounce the sentence of excommunication on each and every person who presumes to act contrary to our most salutary warnings and commandments—which we wish them to incur for that very reason. We firmly decree that in addition to the aforesaid penalties, a process will be begun before competent judges for the infliction of each and every penalty to which heretics are subject according to the law—except the confiscation of goods—if they have not amended their lives in the aforesaid matters within eight days from the time this admonition was given.

Indeed, since it is necessary that no opportunity should be given for such wicked practices to spread, we . . . ordain and command that no one may presume to have or possess booklets or writing of any kind containing the aforesaid condemned errors, or to make a study of them. On the contrary, we greatly desire and order by the virtue of holy obedience that anyone who may have any of the aforesaid writings or booklets shall—within the space of eight days from their knowledge of our edict on this matter—destroy and burn them and every part of them absolutely and completely. Otherwise, we decree that they incur the sentence of excommunication for that very reason—when the evidence is clear, that other greater penalties be inflicted upon such culprits.

Questions: Why does John deem such people heretics? Does John's approach have precedent? How does John's view of magic differ from that in the canon Episcopi *(doc. 32) or that in* The Sworn Book of Honorius *(doc. 91)? How does a society protect itself against the spread of falsities?*

93. THE CHURCH OF ANTICHRIST

The Lantern of Light *is an anonymous vernacular text associated with the Lollard heresy in England. Lollardy grew from the preaching and writing of Oxford theologian John Wyclif (c. 1325–78). Concerned by the wealth and power of the Church, Wyclif contrasted the vast, worldly, multinational institution of his day with the simple community of the faithful begun by Christ and described in the New Testament. Arguing that the Church's pursuit of wealth was the source of most of its problems, Wyclif attacked the venality of the pope and* the ecclesiastical hierarchy, going so far as to argue that Church property should be seized by secular governments. Finding authority in scripture alone, Wyclif translated the Bible into English and left it unglossed.

The Lantern *seems to have been written shortly after the promulgation of the archbishop of Canterbury Thomas Arundel's 1409* Constitutions, *which endeavored to stamp out Lollard preaching by requiring that all preachers be examined for orthodoxy. Those who attempted to preach without an official license did so under pain of excommunication. Those who read Lollard tracts—including the Lollard Bible—were likewise to be deemed heretics.*

The unusual spelling of "Caym" in the document is both a reference to Cain, the biblical son of Adam who murdered his brother [Gen. 4.18], and a Lollard acronym for the four orders of friars: the Carmelites, Augustinians, Jacobites (Dominicans), and Minorites (Franciscans).

Middle English, c. 1409–15.

Source: *The Lanterne of Lizt*, Early English Text Society, original series 151 (London, 1917), pp. 2–21; rev.

This Is the Prologue

God . . . have mercy upon us now and forever, and give us grace to hold to the way of truth in these days of great tribulation. For now, many people who seemed to have been constant in virtue have fallen from their holy purpose, fearing the loss of worldly goods and bodily pain. . . . For now the devil has bewildered this world through his lieutenant—Antichrist—so that men are tossed about in doubts, like the waves of the sea, wretchedly divided, holding extraordinary ideas, each different to that of his neighbor. But Saint Paul made an agreement for all Christendom, saying in Eph. 4, "There is but one lord who all men should fear and love, one faith that all men should believe without wavering, one baptism or Christendom that all men should maintain without defiling." Alas, how this oneness and unity has been broken—so that unruly men pursue their own lusts as if they were beasts in the grain. Assuredly, the wicked man about whom Christ speaks has done this deed, as Matt. 13 says, "The enemy of God has sown weeds upon the seed" of Jesus Christ. This wicked man is Antichrist who patches his laws like filthy rags to the clean cloth of Christ's gospel, and has awakened Judas's child in malice while Simon [Peter] sleeps and pays no attention. O you wicked man. Is there anyone other than Jesus Christ who can save souls? . . .

Are you not, then, a wicked man, a false shepherd, a cruel beast, the son of perdition and Antichrist himself—you who claim for yourself and your followers the power to bind and loose, to bless and curse, separate from the name of Jesus? People without number, following you and your divided laws, have been separated from Christ Jesus [and] go with you like blind men to hell for eternity. And this is greatly to be lamented to such an extent that Christ grieves about the matter.

... And this is Antichrist.... For whoever does not receive Christ on pain of sin is compelled and bound to receive Antichrist. Therefore, in this time of hideous darkness, some seek the lantern of light about which the prophet speaks in Ps. 118, "Lord, your word is a lantern at my feet." For as far as the light of the lantern shines, that far the darkness of sin and the clouds of the fiend's temptations vanish away and may not remain. . . .

What Antichrist Is in General with Six Conditions

To speak in general . . . Antichrist is every man who lives contrary to Christ, as Saint John says [1 John 2] "In truth, now there are many antichrists." And therefore Saint Augustine says, "Whoever lives contrary to Christ, he is an antichrist, either inwardly or overtly." And if you live contrary to Christ, you are but chaff, and of this chaff Christ says, "Truly, the chaff will burn in a fire that cannot be quenched" [Matt. 3.12], for it will burn and never be quenched, and the soul that is the chaff shall forever suffer and never die. As the prophet says [Isa. 9], "Every proud soul that rises and swells against its God and every body that is defiled in gluttony and in lechery shall burn and be food for the fire.". . . There are six sins against the holy ghost that turn the wretched soul into this chaff.

[There follows an extensive discussion of the sins of presumption, despair, hardness of heart, unrepentance, envy, and fighting against the truth.]

What Antichrist Is, and, in Particular, His Three Parts

But of the great chief Antichrist who surpassingly and in a particular manner brings forth false laws against Jesus Christ and feigns himself most holy, the Lord God teaches this through his prophet Isaiah, book 9, "A man of great age and revered by the world, he is the head and chief Antichrist; a prophet or a preacher teaching lies, he is the tail of this Antichrist." Of this tail, Saint Peter speaks more plainly, saying [2 Pet. 2], "These are merchants of spiritual matters who will bargain with the people using fraudulent words," and with their seemingly sweet speech, they beguile the hearts of innocents. For Jude 2 says, "They shall worship the persons of men for material gain." This tail of Antichrist shall not preach freely. . . . And Saint John the evangelist says [Rev. 13], "In that time, no man shall buy or sell—whether he be a slave or a freeman—unless he has the mark of the beast," either on his forehead or on his right hand or else his number. That is to say, no man shall preach God's word in those days, or hear it, unless he has a special letter of license that is called the mark of this beast Antichrist, or else that they maintain by word or by deed—or by both—that his law and his commandments are good and true and worthy to be upheld by the people. But what follows afterwards is frightening. Saint John says [Rev. 14], "whoever worships this beast Antichrist, and takes this foresaid mark will drink a draft of the wine of God's wrath, and will be tormented in fire and brimstone in the sight of the holy angels and in the sight of the lamb. And the smoke from there torments will rise up into the world of worlds—that is, [the world] without end."

Of this Antichrist, God says this to the prophet Zacharias, in book 11, "Take the vessels of a false shepherd to yourself. For lo, I will let Antichrist to be exalted across the land. He will not visit those that have been forsaken, nor will he seek those who have been scattered, nor shall he heal those who are in pain." O you false shepherd, Antichrist! God says that you are an idol in a bishop's habit—but you have neither the virtue nor the spirit, the way of life nor the behavior that belong to a bishop. For Paul says in Romans 8, "He who does not have the spirit of Christ, he is not his servant," even if he has the outward trappings. Therefore, Saint John says in Revelation 16, "The fifth angel poured his vial upon the seat of the beast, and his realm is made dark, and they eat their tongues together out of sorrow, and they blasphemed the God of heaven for their sorrows and their wounds, and they did no penance for their deeds." That means that archbishops and bishops are the seat of the beast Antichrist, for through them he sits and reigns over other people in the darkness of his heresy. And in this, they take delight, glorifying with their tongues their false commandments, which is painful to men of true understanding, and thus they spurn God's holy law because of the preaching of Christ's gospel—which is sorrowful for them—engendering sins in their souls that wound them to death. And thus wounded, they should never do worthwhile penitential deeds, and for this they shall be damned. [Robert Grosseteste, the thirteenth-century bishop of] Lincoln says, "I quake, I dread and I am terribly afraid. . . . The spring, the beginning, and the cause of all ruin and mischief is the court of Rome." By the authority of God and with the complete agreement of his holy saints, an obvious conclusion now follows—one unfortunately grounded in true belief: that in the court of Rome is the head of Antichrist, and in the archbishops and bishops are Antichrist's body. And in the patchwork of sects—monks, canons and friars—is the venomous tail of Antichrist. The apostle Jude warned of these three factions, saying in Chapter 1, this way, "Woe to those who walk in the way of Caym [Cain]; these are false possessors. Woe to those who have been separated out for reward after the error of Balaam. These are the mighty, pointless mendicants. And woe to those who have perished in the gainsaying of Core. These are proud, sturdy defenders."

How this Antichrist is to be destroyed God himself teaches through his prophet Daniel, book 8, saying "This Antichrist will be destroyed not by hand," that is, not by the power of man. For Paul says in 2 Thess. 2, "Christ will slay Antichrist by means of the spirit of his mouth," [doc. 44] that is, by means of the holy word of his law. And "the lord will destroy him by the glory of his coming," that is, by turning men's hearts by his grace to his law just before his judgment. But God taught this lesson more fully to Job and said in Job 40, "Lo," God says, "the trust that Antichrist has in riches and in worldly favor will bring him to naught. And in the sight of all men, he will be thrown headlong downwards, so that all people will mourn for him with great lamentation, cursing him and damning him for all his false commandments."

What Antichrist Is, in Particular, with His Five Strategies

Now at last we should recall and consider holy King David who had given to him the full spirit of prophecy, and he, predicting the coming of Antichrist with his lying and falsity, notes five hideous attacks, which he will use against the servants of God. . . .

The first assault of Antichrist is constitutional, as the prophet [David] says, "Lord, put in place a lawmaker over the people" on account of their sin, for they would not consent to the truth. That is to say, Antichrist uses false, profitable, or grasping laws—such as absolutions, indulgences, pardons, privileges, and every other heavenly reward that can be sold—to despoil the people of their worldly goods. Chiefly, he uses these new constitutions [of Arundel] by whose power Antichrist places churches under interdict, indicts preachers, suspends those who receives them, depriving them of their benefices, damns listeners, and takes away the goods of those that facilitate the preaching of a priest . . . unless that priest shows the mark of the beast which has been given a new name and called a "special letter of license" for the further blinding of the ignorant people.

The second assault of Antichrist is affliction, as the prophet says, "Antichrist greatly vexes the people, tempting them with idolatry and the worship of idols." But Antichrist often makes them hope that they might go on pilgrimage, and for this he is cursed of God, who says, through the prophet Isaiah 5, "Woe to you who see good as evil and evil as good, turning light into darkness and darkness into light, turning sweet into bitter and bitter into sweet." And this is what Antichrist does when he turns virtues into vices and vices into virtues, as he does when he turns pilgrimage into outrage and outrage into pilgrimage. And because of this subversive intent, God despises Antichrist and all of his deluded people, and loathes all the goods misspent for the sake of these afflictions.

The third assault of Antichrist is investigation. As the prophet says, Antichrist inquires, searches and listens for where he may find a man or a woman leading their life pleasingly, according to the will of God, writing, reading, learning, or studying God's law in their mother tongue. Eventually, he catches them in these censured activities, and when he does, he smites them as is his wont, hurting them most grievously. . . .

The fourth assault of Antichrist is persecution. As the prophet says, Antichrist sits with rich men in their lairs, besotted with the disputes of this world. But the poor, meek, simple, and lowly, these are the people he hunts and pursues; these are the people he overruns and pounces upon, grasping hold of them both in body and spirit. . . . "I saw," said Saint John in Revelation 16, "out of the mouth of the dragon (that is, the head of Antichrist) and out of the mouth of the beast (that is, the body of Antichrist), and out of the mouth of the pseudo-prophet or false preacher (that is, the tail of Antichrist) three unclean spirits come out in the form of frogs." Frogs sitting in holes by the water's edge control the ground above them and on either side of them, but that which is underneath them they want neither to lose nor to cede any part. So these three spirits croaking in covetousness, gluttony, and lechery betoken Antichrist in his three parts. For they acquire from lords that are above them a great part of their goods through flattering speech and lying hypocrisy; and from the commoners around them they wheedle into their hands the greater part of their possessions. But that which they have won they hold tightly against the authority of both of God's laws. And with these riches they feed wild, sturdy, and lawless knaves who pursue those who would speak out against this accursed sin. . . .

The fifth assault of Antichrist is execution, as the prophet says, when Antichrist says that he does not benefit from these aforesaid torments, then he carries out his malice against Christ's chosen people. About this, Saint John in his Apocalypse 13 says, the beast of the earth will give power to the beast of the sea, for in this time of action the pernicious part of the laity—from the highest to the lowest—will agree to carry out the wickedness of the pernicious part of the clergy. Then this prophecy [of Ps. 78] will be fulfilled[:] "They will shed innocent blood and no man will dare bury their bodies, for they will cast their flesh to the fowls of the air and their bodies to the beasts of the earth." To this, the prophet says—as Saint Augustine declares—when Antichrist thinks that he has lordship over all the servants of God, raising against them various engines of torment, then he will fall into open disgrace for evermore.

The full reign of Antichrist will last for three and a half years. . . .

Questions: What is the current state of the world? What is the difference between the general and the particular Antichrist? How is Antichrist constructed as an agent for social and political reform? Would any of this be problematic for Church authorities?

94. THE PROBLEM OF SATAN AS AN "ANGEL OF LIGHT"

Jean Gerson (1363–1429) was chancellor of the University of Paris and one of the leading theologians of the period as well as a successful pamphleteer. As such, he was deeply engaged in the struggle to end the great schism. Gerson led the French delegation at the Council of Constance (1414–18), the ecclesiastical assembly that orchestrated the removal of all three rival popes and the election of Martin V. As a scholar, Gerson was troubled by the growing influence of charismatic visionaries and mystics and by the potential that Christians might misconstrue demonism for godly religion. Mindful that Satan could take the form of "an angel of light," Gerson wrote three treatises on the problem of discernment. The excerpt below comes from On the Testing of Spirits, *written in 1415 as the council was considering the revelations of Birgitta of Sweden (doc. 67).*

Jean de Varennes (1340/45–96?) was known for his preaching against clerical abuses and wealthy lords. Jan Hus (c. 1372–1415) was a Bohemian reformer influenced by Wyclif's writings. He was declared a heretic at Constance and burned. The reference to a so-called "Pythoness" is to the priestesses of the Temple of Apollo at Delphi. In Saint Jerome's fourth-century translation of the Bible, the term is used to denote any soothsayer or person claiming to be able to predict the future while possessed by a spirit.

Latin, 1415.

Source: trans. Richard Raiswell and David R. Winter, from Jean Gerson, "*De probatione spirituum*," in *Opera omnia* (Antwerp, 1706), vol. 1, pp. 37–43.

First Consideration

The disciple whom Jesus loved orders "test spirits to see if they are from God" [1 John 4.1]. Nor was that disciple unaware of the pronouncement of his fellow apostle who said, "the angel of Satan transforms himself into an angel of light" [2 Cor. 11.14] so that he can become the noonday demon [Ps. 90.6] while being permitted to hide the darkness of his error for a while as he pretends to bring forth the clear light of truth. . . .

Second Consideration

Testing "spirits to see whether they are from God" is not something given to everyone but only to some people by the holy spirit. . . . Therefore, just as not everyone is able to prophesy, or able to preach the gospel, or interpret words [gifts of the holy spirit as described by 1 Cor. 12.8–10]—since that is a role given to particular people up to the end of days—so not everyone is able to test spirits to see if they are from God. It is a gift given to them. Such people are spiritual men whose anointing [by the holy spirit] instructs them in all things so they can judge all things—even from one day to another.

Third Consideration

Testing "spirits to see whether they are from God" can be done in many ways. Indeed, one way is by using knowledge and general learning acquired through diligent and pious study of the lessons of holy scripture. Without a doubt, there are [parts of scripture] which we accept through faith and which contain the way to discern false prophets from real ones, and illusions from legitimate revelations. The other way is found through secret inspiration or internal wisdom—whether through a certain sweet experience or illumination from the eternal mountains [Ps. 120.1?]—which scatters the darkness of all doubt. . . .

Fourth Consideration

Testing "spirits to see whether they are from God" by means of a general and infallible rule in any particular case is either impossible or barely possible by human means. Rather, the gift of the holy spirit is required which the apostle called "the discernment of spirits" [1 Cor. 12.10]. By means of this gift, the mind comes to know not only how to test the spirits in itself to see if they are from God, but also how to test the spirits in or affecting others. . . . And so, just as no one knows what things are of the spirit unless he himself is a spiritual man, so no one knows with infallible certainty that which is happening in the soul of another person unless it is known through experience alone or through some inner sense or feeling. Therefore, just as no one can easily state a general rule which infallibly distinguishes between a dream vision and one which occurs when awake—on account of the various similarities between these two sorts of visions—so it is more difficult when it comes to the matter of spirits. . . .

Fifth Consideration

We have found not one but many tracts composed on this matter by various authors which it would be good now to have at hand to study diligently while this holy council [of Constance] is discussing the canonization of saints and examining their teachings. In this capacity, a woman named Brigitta [of Sweden] claims that she had received heavenly visions not only from angels but from Christ and Mary, and from Agnes and other saints, talking with them intimately like a husband to his wife. But there is a danger both in accepting and in rejecting such claims. For what would be more unworthy or more foreign to this holy council than approving false, illusory or frivolous visions, treating them as true and genuine revelations? However, rejecting these things which are said to have been proven by various peoples in many ways would cause no small anxiety within the Christian religion and to people's devotion. . . .

Sixth Consideration

Anyone who has not experienced internal spiritual battles—who has not at one moment ascended into the heavens and then at the next plummeted into the abyss, and seen there the wonders of God—can test spirits through their skill and learning derived from their knowledge of holy scripture alone. Only those who sail on this mystical sea full of varied and profound signs—which are tossed like waves crashing against themselves—can describe its wonders. What do those who have never experienced such things know about them? . . .

Indeed, when we seek to test spirits systematically in this way in people we do not know, whose hearts can neither be seen nor assessed closely, it is fitting that we collect signs [of their nature] from their works, for as Christ said, "you will know them from their fruits" [Matt. 7.16]. However, one sign or even a few can deceive if we find they are not consistent. Cicero, Boethius, and Aristotle say the same thing about making a conclusion from a conjecture.

But since the confusion in assessing the significance of these signs is infinite, we can reduce the issues to a few points. . . . *Who* is it to whom the revelation was made? *What* does the revelation say and what does it mean? *Why* is it said to have occurred? *To whom* was it revealed as advice? *What sort of* life does that person live and from *where* does he come?

Seventh Consideration

When a testing of spirits is begun, it must first be determined whether the person who claims to be receiving the visions is of good and sound judgement, and of normal reasoning because the judgement of the rational faculty can be impaired by an injured brain. If an injured person suffers from delusions, then great effort need not be spent determining from which spirit such melancholic and illusory visions come. As is evident in cases of madness and various other [mental] sicknesses, while they are awake, such people think they see, hear, taste etc. things that others do while they are dreaming. . . . Moreover, any profound passion leaves its own wound, its own intoxication, its own demon, as Origen argues. This is clear in those seized by love, as well as in those who are jealous, angry, envious, or greedy. . . .

It should be determined whether the visionary is a novice in his zeal for God because the fervor of a novice quickly cools if he is without guidance. This is particularly the case in adolescents and women—the ardor of whom is too great, greedy, changeable, unrestrained, and for that reason, suspect.

Moreover, it is very important to consider what kind of person he is and was, the nature of his learning, his habits and delights, and the people with whom he associates. It is also important to ask if he is wealthy or destitute, for in the first instance we may suspect pride or some secret lust, whereas in the other we may suspect deception.

Eighth Consideration

The testing of spirits involves not only considering the character of the visionary but also an assessment of the visions themselves to determine if they are true in every detail—even up to the smallest proposition—for there can be nothing untrue in the spirit of truth. By contrast, while there may be a thousand plain truths in [visions given by a] lying spirit, it may hide a single falsehood among them. For this reason, Christ prohibited demoniacs from testifying about the truth as they confessed—as Paul did with the pythoness [Acts 16.16]. It must also be considered whether there is wisdom coming from above in these visions . . . and whether these visions go beyond the usual way of understanding—either that grounded in sacred scripture or that based on natural reason or morality. If they are not, they should be attributed to false revelation. . . . Disregarding the study of divine scripture, the greater part of Christians have turned their eyes and ears tingling in anticipation to these visions, such things being more interesting as they are more recent. And so they would prefer to remain ignorant of necessary things. . . .

Ninth Consideration

Beware, therefore, if you listen to or consult such a visionary, that you do not applaud such a person or praise her on that account, or marvel as if she were a saint and deserving of adoration on the basis of her revelations and miracles. Better, oppose her. Rebuke her harshly. Spurn her of whom it is said "and her heart was exalted, and her eyes were lofty so that she walked in great matters and in wonderful things above her" [see Ps. 130.1]. Were you not to do so, she might think herself worthy to effect her own salvation not as in the way of other people but through her own learning—namely of the scriptures and the saints, and with the principles of natural reason—unless one assumes she has some counsel, not only from angels but from God himself, and not only once out of necessity but almost constantly or in daily communication. . . .

Tenth Consideration

The testing of spirits investigates the reason why these visions are said to have occurred, not only their immediate or obvious purpose but their hidden and final one, too. And so, the first purpose can appear to be good, healthy, and beneficial, and for the enlightenment of others. But, nevertheless, it can eventually slip into many types of scandal, either because the final goal does not correspond to the original one, or because something false and erroneous was discovered in the person which had originally been taken as a sign of sanctity and devoutness. Our age has taught us this from the preaching of masters Jean de Varennes and Jan Hus, and other similar men.

Eleventh Consideration

The testing of spirits investigates how and in what way the person who claims to have visions has conducted himself. . . .

If the person is a woman, it is particularly necessary to investigate how she has conducted herself with her confessors and instructors—whether she holds continuous conversations with them under the pretext of making numerous confessions, sometimes recounting her visions at length, and at other times engaging in other types of discussion. Believe those who are experienced in such matters—particularly Augustine and [the thirteenth-century theologian] Master Bonaventure. There is hardly any other plague or more harmful or more incurable condition than this. Even if nothing else detrimental occurred beyond this extensive waste of precious time, this would be more than enough for the devil. . . .

Twelfth Consideration

The testing of spirits investigates where a spirit comes from and where it goes. . . . But what else? Much similarity can be found in various spirits in terms of their emanation: there is the spirit of God, the spirit of the good angel, the spirit of the evil angel, the human spirit—both the rational and the animal. A similar vision can be inspired by any of these spirits in their own way—the latter of these in various ways—but it is easy to perceive the difference. But this similarity means that those without experience in these matters cannot know how to distinguish such things—neither those who have learned through their own natural talents, nor those who have acquired it through the study of theology or nature, nor even those who have been taught by others. . . .

I wonder whether those who fear God and who flee from sin and who always keep watch against temptations, find their perception of sin is merely imaginary or reasonable? It is not easy to distinguish perception from reality. How much more difficult it is, then, particularly when one is influenced by a passion or strong inspiration, to distinguish the four types of spirits named above: those from God, from a good angel, from an evil angel, or from one's own nature?

Questions: What attitude should people adopt toward those who claim direct revelation from God? How can the actions of divine spirits be distinguished from demonic? Do any earlier readings betray a similar anxiety about discerning the nature of spirits? What does this suggest about the context in which Gerson operated? What would he have thought about Brigitta's revelations?

95. INTERROGATORS' VIEW OF JOAN OF ARC

Joan of Arc (1412–31) grew up in France during the Hundred Years' War. From age 13, she claimed to be guided by divine voices that eventually told her that she was destined to drive the English from France. With the support of King Charles VII (r. 1422–61), she was able to break the English siege at Orléans and win a string of military victories that led to Charles's formal coronation at Rheims a few months later. But unable to wrest Paris from English hands, she was captured by Burgundian forces and handed over to the English at Rouen in May 1430, where she was put on trial for heresy.

Joan's trial lasted from late February to 24 May 1431, at which point she recanted and abjured her errors, confessing before a large public gathering that she had lied about her visions, had practiced divination, and had worshipped evil spirits. For this, she was sentenced to perpetual imprisonment. Once in jail, though, she reverted to wearing men's clothing and admitted to hearing divine voices again. As a relapsed heretic, she was handed over to the secular authorities and burned on 30 May.

The trial was exceptionally well documented. But these records are not without problems, for they are reworkings of the notes made in French by the two notaries, which were then translated into Latin and reproduced along with other documents in a text intended to justify proceedings to a wider and likely hostile audience.

The selection below comes from a series of seventy "articles of accusation" addressed to various officials, which were presented to Joan by her prosecutor on 27 and 28 March.

Latin, 1431.

Source: trans. Daniel Hobbins, *The Trial of Joan of Arc* (Cambridge, MA: Harvard, 2007), pp. 123–55, 221–22.

Tuesday 27 March 1431

I come before you for this this reason: a certain woman named Joan, called *la Pucelle* in the vernacular, was recently found, captured, and detained within your territory and the diocese of Beauvais, reverend father. . . . She was greatly suspect, slandered, and grievously and notoriously denounced by upright and eminent persons for the things that follow. Let her be pronounced and declared, O judges, a sorceress, diviner, false prophetess, conjurer of evil spirits, superstitious, entangled in and practicing the magic arts, evil thinking in the catholic faith, schismatic, doubting and misled in the article "One holy Church," etc., and other articles of the faith, sacrilegious, idolatrous, apostate from the faith, evil speaking and maleficent, blaspheming God and his saints, scandalous, seditious, a disturber of peace and an obstacle to it, inciting wars, cruelly thirsting for human blood and encouraging its shedding, wholly forsaking the decency and reserve of her sex, utterly without modesty and shamelessly having taken the disgraceful clothing and state of armed men; for these and for other reasons an abomination to God and man, a transgressor of divine and natural laws and ecclesiastical discipline, seductress of princes and peoples; permitting and allowing herself to be worshipped and adored in injury and contempt of God, giving her hands and garments to be kissed, usurping divine honor and adoration; a heretic, or at least greatly suspect of heresy. For these crimes let her be canonically and legitimately punished and corrected according to divine and canonical decrees, and all other due and appropriate ends. . . .

Article 1

First, both by divine and by canon and civil law, it belongs to you—one as ordinary judge, the other as inquisitor of the faith—to expel, destroy, and utterly eradicate from your diocese and from all the kingdom of France the heresies, sorceries, superstitions, and other crimes declared above. . . .

Article 2

The accused has performed, composed, participated in, and enacted numerous sorceries and superstitions not only this year, but from childhood, and not only in your diocese and jurisdiction, but far and wide throughout this kingdom. She prophesied the future and let herself be worshipped and adored. She invoked demons and evil spirits, took counsel with and visited them, concluded pacts and had discussions and assemblies with them, and was familiar with them. She also bestowed counsel, aid, and favor upon others so doing and seduced them to do so, by saying, believing, affirming, and maintaining that to do so and to believe in and perform such sorceries, prophecies, and superstitious acts was not sinful . . . thus leading numerous persons of various estates and of both sexes into those errors and evil acts, and imprinting such things on their hearts. . . .

To this second article Joan said that she denies the sorceries, the superstitious works, and the prophecies; as to the adoration, if some people kissed her hands or garments, it was not by her request or wish; she has guarded against this and resisted it as best she could. She denies the rest. . . .

Article 4

In childhood this Joan was not taught or instructed in the faith or its basic principles. Instead, she learned through custom and the training of certain old women to practice sorcery, divination, and other superstitions or magic arts. Many inhabitants of these towns have long been known to practice these evil spells. Joan herself said that from many of them, and especially from her godmother, she had heard much about visions and appearances of fairies or fairy spirits, *fées* in French; and still others taught her and initiated her into evil and wicked errors about these spirits, such that she confessed to you at trial that even then she did not know whether fairies were evil spirits.

With regard to this article, Joan said she acknowledges the first part . . . as to the fairies, she does not understand. But regarding her instruction, she learned her faith and was well and duly taught to behave as a good child should. . . .

Article 5

Near the town of Domrémy stands a large, thick, ancient tree, which common people call *l'arbre charmine fée de Bourlémont* [the charmed fairy-tree of Bourlémont], and near this tree is a spring. Evil spirits called fairies, *fées* in French, are said to gather there, and those who cast spells are accustomed to dance with them at night around the tree and spring.

With regard to this article on the tree and the spring, she refers to the answer she made about them; she denies the rest.

[During interrogation on 24 February, Joan had described what she called the "tree of the fairies" in her home village where old folk claimed fairies gathered. Young girls decorated the tree with wreaths and sometimes danced there. Joan could not remember dancing herself but admitted singing by the tree. On 1 March, she asserted that her voices never spoke to her by the tree, but that they had spoken to her at a nearby spring that was reputed to have healing properties.]

Article 6

Joan used to visit the spring and tree, mostly at night but sometimes during the day, especially when the divine office was being celebrated in church, in order to be alone. Then, while dancing around the spring and tree, she would hang garlands she had made from herbs and flowers on the branches. Beforehand and afterward, she would utter certain incantations and sing songs with invocations, sorcery, and other evil spells. The next morning, these garlands would no longer be there.

With regard to this article . . . she said that she refers to the answer she made elsewhere, and she denies the rest. . . .

Article 13

Joan attributes to God, to his angels, and to his saints orders that are injurious to the honor of women, prohibited by divine law, abominable to God and man, and forbidden by ecclesiastical ordinances under pain of anathema—such as wearing short, tight, and immodest clothing, undergarments, and hose as well as other articles. Following their orders, she often wore extravagant and magnificent clothing made of precious fabrics and cloth of gold, with fur lining. She wore not only short tunics, but sleeveless coats and robes slit on the sides. And her crimes were notorious, for she was captured wearing a cape of gold cloth, completely open, a cap, and her haircut round like a man's. In general, casting aside all feminine modesty, flouting not only womanly decency but even the conduct of virtuous men, she enjoyed all the ornamentation and attire of the most dissipated men, and even carried weapons of attack. To attribute this to the command of God, holy angels, and even holy virgins, is to blaspheme God and his saints, to overturn God's law, to violate canons, to offend the female sex and its honor, to pervert all decency of outward attire, and to approve and encourage utterly depraved behavior.

With regard to this article, Joan says she did not blaspheme God or his saints. . . .

Article 17

When Joan came thus clothed and armed before Charles, she promised him three things, among others: first, she would lift the siege of Orléans; second, that she would have him crowned at Rheims; and third, that she would avenge him against his enemies and would either kill them or drive them from the kingdom by her art, all the English and Burgundians. Joan frequently and publicly boasted of these promises in many places. And to inspire greater confidence in her words and deeds, from that time forward she practiced frequent divination, uncovering the behavior, manners, and secret actions of those who came to her, whom she had never seen or heard of before. And she boasted that she knew these things by revelation.

With regard to this article, Joan says she bore news to her king from God, that our lord would restore his kingdom, have him crowned at Rheims, and drive out his enemies. And she was God's messenger in this, to tell him to set her boldly to the task and she would raise the siege at Orléans. . . .

Wednesday 28 March

Article 31

From her childhood onward, Joan boasted, and she boasts daily, that she had and has many revelations and visions. And though she was charitably warned and duly and legally asked about them under oath, she would not and will not swear, or explain them clearly by word or by sign; but she did and does delay, deny, and refuse. And formerly denying her oath, she stated and affirmed many times in court and elsewhere that she would not make known her revelations and visions to you even if her head were cut off or her body dismembered, and that no one could drag from her the sign that God showed her, and which proved that she came from God.

With regard to this article, she says that as for revealing the sign and the other contents of the article, she may well have said she would not reveal it. . . .

Article 32

In these matters, you absolutely can and should conclude that the revelations and visions, if Joan had them, proceeded from lying, evil spirits rather than from good; and everyone should treat them as such, especially considering her cruelty, pride, haughtiness, actions, lies, and contradictions apparent here and in many other articles; such things in fact are and should be considered indisputable presumption.

With regard to this article . . . she says she denies it. She acted by revelation from Saint Catherine and Saint Margaret and will maintain this until death. . . .

Article 49

Trusting solely to her imagination, Joan adored these spirits, kissing the ground she said they passed over, kneeling to them, embracing and kissing them and paying them other reverence, thanking them with her hands clasped, encouraging their familiarity, even though she did not know whether they were good spirits; when instead, considering the circumstances, she should have judged them as they seemed to be, as evil spirits rather than good. These devotions and observances seem to tend towards idolatry and towards a pact with demons.

To this article . . . she replied, as to the beginning "I've already answered"; and as to the end: "I trust to our lord." . . .

Article 62

Joan strives to shock the people, persuading them to put absolute trust in all she says and will say. So she takes upon herself the authority of God and the angels, and raises herself above all ecclesiastical power to lead people into error, as the false prophets used to do when they founded sects of error and damnation and set themselves apart from the one body of the church. This is destructive of the Christian religion and, if prelates of the church took no action, could overturn all ecclesiastical authority. Men and women will rise up on every hand, pretend to have revelations from God and the angels, and sow lies and errors, as we have seen now these many times after this woman lifted herself up and began scandalizing Christian people and spreading her deceits abroad.

With regard to this article . . . she said she would answer it Saturday.

Questions: What do Joan's interrogators suspect? What issues seem to pique their attention? Why do they consider it significant that she wore masculine attire? How do her revelations differ from those of Birgitta of Sweden (doc. 67)? Would trying Joan for demon-inspired offences be an easy way for the English to deal with an inspirational military leader in the 1430s?

96. THE SYNAGOGUE OF SATAN

From the 1380s, inquisitors were active in Savoy in the western Alps, and it is from this region that the first trials linking heresy to demonic sorcery occurred. Among the various charges to which they confessed, the Savoy heretics admitted to gathering regularly at a meeting the inquisitors called "a synagogue." This was an allusion to Revelation 2.9, where John of Patmos, writing to the church in Smyrna, says, "you are blasphemed by those who call themselves Jews and are not. They are the synagogue of Satan." To John, the phrase was intended to cast such critics of the church as hypocrites—people who had accepted aspects of the new faith, but had not gone as far as him.

The Errors of the Heretics is an anonymous tract produced in the 1430s. It describes the events of the synagogue as the inquisitors discovered them.

Latin, between 1430 and 1437.

Source: trans. Richard Raiswell and David R. Winter, from *Errores Gazariorum, seu illorum qui scopam vel baculum equitare probantur*, in *L'imaginaire du sabbat: édition critique des textes les plus anciens (1430 c.–1440 c.)* (Lausanne: Université de Lausanne, 1999), pp. 277–99.

The Errors of the Gazarii or of Those Who Have Been Proven to Ride a Stave or Broom

First, when a person of one sex or the other is seduced by someone at the persuasion of the enemy of human nature, the seducer—casting the seduced person into the pit of evil doers—makes him swear that every time it is required of him, he will hurry with him to the synagogue, dropping all other matters, mindful of the fact that the aforesaid seducer will furnish him with appropriate ointments for this together with a broom—which he does.

Concerning the same, when they reach the site of the synagogue, the seducer hurries to present the seduced person to the devil, the enemy of the rational creature. The enemy sometimes appears in the form of a black cat, sometimes in the form of a man—though not a perfect man—or in the likeness of some other animal, but most often in the likeness of a black cat. After the seduced person has been asked by the devil whether he wants to remain and continue in the fellowship, he replies in response to a nod of the seducer that he does. Having heard this, the devil exacts an oath of fidelity from the seduced in the following manner. First, he swears that he will be faithful to the master who presides over the whole fellowship. Second, that he will recruit everyone he can into the fellowship in so far as he is able. Third, that he will not reveal the secrets of the aforesaid sect even up to his death. Fourth, that he will kill and bring to the synagogue all the children he can strangle and kill—by "children" it is understood to mean those three years old or younger. Fifth, that every time he is called to the synagogue, he will set everything else aside and hurry there immediately. Sixth, that he will impede every marriage he can through magic and other sorcery insofar as he can. Seventh, that he will avenge injuries done to the sect or its members collectively or separately.

When these things sworn and promised, the poor seduced person adores the presiding [master] and does homage to him. As a sign of homage, he kisses the devil, whether he is appearing in human form or—as aforementioned—in some other likeness, on the buttocks or anus, pledging to him a limb of his body after death by way of tribute. When these things have been done, all members of this pestilential sect rejoice at the coming of a new heretic, eating whatever is near them—particularly dead children who have been roasted and boiled. When this most wicked banquet has been completed, and after they have danced as much as they want, the light is extinguished and the presiding devil shouts, "Mestlet, mestlet" [perhaps from the French "mêlez" meaning "mingle"]. As soon as they hear his voice, the people join together carnally—man with woman, or man with another man. Sometimes a father [couples] with his daughter, a son with his mother, a brother with his sister, little observing the proper order of nature. When these wicked, heinous, and unnatural deeds—as aforementioned—have been completed, and the light is relit, they eat and drink again. And should they have to withdraw, they urinate into [wine] barrels, mixing it together with excrement. Asked why they do this, they say that they do it equally in contempt of the sacrament of the eucharist and in disdain for what is consecrated out of the wine [Christ's blood]. After these things have been done, each person returns home.

Concerning the same, after the seduced person does homage to the presiding devil, the devil gives him a container full of ointment, a stave, and all the other things which the seduced person needs to go to the synagogue, and he teaches the man how and in what way he ought to anoint the stave. The ointment is made out of the fat of roasted and boiled children and other ingredients by means of diabolical malice, as will become clear.

Concerning the same, another ointment is made from the aforesaid fat of children mixed with the most poisonous animals, such as serpents, toads, lizards, and spiders—all of which are mixed together with the help of the aforesaid [demonic] agency. If anyone is touched once with this ointment, he will immediately and fatally succumb to a bad death, sometimes languishing in sickness for a long time, sometimes dying quickly.

Notes from the Magistrate of Vevey and Many Others

Concerning the same, they make powders to kill men. These powders are made from the guts of children mixed with the aforesaid poisonous animals, which, having been thoroughly pulverized, are sprinkled as a mist through the air at an agreed upon time by one of the fellowship. Those touched by that powder will either die or suffer a long and serious illness. And this is the reason why there is [great] mortality in some towns and villages of a certain region, while in other places nearby there is very intemperate weather.

Concerning the same, these aforesaid noxious people, when they capture a red-headed man who is not part of the sect but rather a faithful catholic, strip him naked, tying him to a bench in such a way that he cannot move either his hands or his other limbs. Once bound, poisonous animals are brought out and placed around him. These are brought there by some especially cruel and merciless men from the sect so that they might bite the poor man so that he, suffering through these torments, is overcome by the poison and dies. After he has died, they hang him by his feet, placing some earthen or glass vessel under his mouth to capture the waste and poison dripping from the man's mouth and other orifices. Once this has been collected, with diabolical agency they make another ointment from the fat of the man suspended from the gallows, the guts of children, and the aforesaid poisonous animals which had poisoned him. Contact alone with this ointment kills all men.

Concerning the same, with the aforesaid [demonic] agency, they take the skin of a cat and fill it with barley, grain, wild oats, and grapes. They place the said filled skin in a living spring, leaving it there for three days. Retrieving and drying it, they then pulverize the contents. Climbing up a mountain during a windy period, they sprinkle the powder above and around the most fertile regions and properties. They say that this causes sterility, and because of this sacrifice, the devil destroys the fruits of the earth over which the aforesaid powders are sprinkled.

Concerning the same, some from that sect who have already been burned have confessed that at the command of the devil many of them congregate in the mountains to break the ice during stormy periods—and often great piles of ice have been found on the mountains. They say that some—not all because not all of them have the power or the audacity to do this—carry the ice through the air during storms, with diabolical agency, and use their stave to destroy the fertile lands of their enemies and those of other neighbors.

Concerning the same, according to the depositions of some—even all members of the sect—those who enter this damned fellowship generally do so for [one of] three reasons. First, because there are some who, unable to live peacefully, make many enemies for themselves, "their hands [raised] against everyone and everyone against them, living like the sons of Ishmael" [Gen. 16.12]. Seeing that they are not able to exact vengeance against their enemies by human means, they ask for vindication from the devil. The devil—because he is accustomed to exploiting the credulity of simpletons—promptly introduces the aforesaid error [of wanting vengeance] into the minds of such people through their dreams, and to compound their seduction and deception, he urges some members of the sect to approach him as neighbors, thereby making the deception more effective. Approaching him feigning consolation—as they say—they ask him the reason for his unhappiness. And given the variety of reasons, they condemn him into the pit of sin in various ways. Promising him vengeance, they induce and persuade him to join their fellowship, promising him a free and splendid life beyond his wishes. And to whatever [reasons for unhappiness] they hear [from the man], they agree immediately [to exact vengeance].

Concerning the same, there are some who are accustomed to living lavishly but who through such [a manner of living] consume all their goods. There are others who want to eat exquisite food continuously. Having noted these things, the devil persuades some of the sect to bring such a person or those with him to the synagogue, having first informed them about the sect's ceremonies concerning their desire. After these things have been explained, at a set time the devil leads them to the houses of powerful prelates, nobles, townsfolk, and others, in whose houses he knows there is bread and wine agreeable to their wishes and desires. At the third hour of the night, the storerooms of these potentates are opened to them and they are led in. They stay there until the middle of the night or thereabout, but no more, "because this is their hour and the powers of darkness" [Luke 22.53]. After they have eaten and drunk their fill, each one is returned to his business.

Concerning the same, the third reason people enter that damned fellowship is because there are some who long wantonly to be able to take pleasure in the carnal act, and because there [at the synagogue] they can wantonly exercise their desires at will, etc.

Concerning the same, it should be noted that the devil forbids anyone from the sect stealing gold, silver, or precious objects, lest the sect be exposed because of the quantity and value of these aforesaid goods.

Concerning the same, it is confessed that when someone breaks the rules of the sect, he is brutally whipped by some of the fellowship at the command of the master at night, and because of this, they are remarkably afraid to offend the master or his allies in the sect.

Concerning the same, according to the confession of John Stipulis and others who have been burned, when one enters this sect for the first time, after swearing fidelity and doing homage—as aforesaid—the devil draws blood from the left hand of the seduced person by means of a certain instrument, and with this blood he writes certain words on a leaf of parchment which he keeps to himself. Many from the sect have seen this, as they have testified.

Concerning the same, when they want to strangle children while their father and mother are asleep, with the devil's help, they enter the house of their parents in the silence of the dead of night. Grasping the child by its throat or sides, they suffocate it until it is dead. And in the morning, when the child is conveyed to the tomb, the man or woman or people who strangled and killed the child join the procession, lamenting the child's death with its parents and their friends. But on the following night, they open the grave and take the child, sometimes leaving the child's head, hands, and the feet in the grave, because unless they plan to work some sorcery with the child's hand, they never take these parts with them. With the body removed and the grave filled in again, they carry the child to the synagogue, where it is roasted and eaten, as was said before.

And note that there are some who kill their own sons and daughters and eat them at the synagogue, such as Joanna Vacanda who was burned at a place called Chavannes on Saint Lawrence's day [10 August]. Before everyone, she admitted that she had killed and eaten her daughter's son with another woman who was named at her trial.

Concerning the same, from the confession of those who have been burned, it is clear that members of the sect appear to be better than other members of the faith [true Christians]. They usually attend mass and confess often throughout the year. They often take the holy eucharist just like Judas who [received it?] from the hand of the lord. They do this because were they to withdraw from receiving the sacraments, they might be discovered and their error be exposed.

Questions: What sort of person likely wrote this text, and what sources does he seem to have used? Might this color what is described? What is the sect's purpose? How is this different to earlier apparent sects of devil-worshippers? Why does the author stress the importance of ritual to this sect? Does this document contradict any earlier ideas about the devil and his power?

97. MERGING TRADITIONS

Roughly contemporary with The Errors of the Heretics, *Johannes Nider's* The Ant Hill *is perhaps the most important early-fifteenth-century text that clearly shows the emerging conflation of sorcery, necromancy, and demonism—a conflation that would culminate in the witch hunts of the end of the century. Nider (c. 1385–1438) was a Dominican theologian and reformer, and it was in those capacities that he attended the opening sessions of the Council of Basel (1431–49). Although proceedings quickly became bogged down over the issue of papal power and the pope's relationship to ecumenical councils, the council served as an important point for the dissemination of information about the trials for demonic sorcery that had been occurring throughout the western Alps over the previous fifteen years. At least nine of the officials who had been involved in the trial of Joan of Arc were present, too. Although* The Ant Hill, *composed shortly after Nider had became a professor of theology at the University of Vienna, is concerned primarily with the issue of spiritual reform (particularly of the laity), the fifth chapter deals with demonic sorcery. The text circulated quite widely and at the end of the century was an important source for the authors of the* Malleus maleficarum *(doc. 98).*

Latin, 1438.

Source: trans. Richard Raiswell and David R. Winter, from Johannes Nider, *Formicarius*, in *L'imaginaire du sabbat: édition critique des textes les plus anciens (1430 c.–1440 c.)* (Lausanne: Université de Lausanne, 1999), pp. 122–99.

On Those Who Have Been Deceived by Dreams and Visions

Theologian: I heard it reported by my master that a certain father [priest] from our order entered a village where he found a woman who had been driven mad in such a way that she believed she was carried through the air in the night with [the goddess] Diana and other women. When the father tried to expel this faithlessness by means of healthy words, this obstinate woman asserted that she believed her own experience more. To this, the father said, "Allow me to be present the next time you go off." She replied, "It is agreed—you will see me leave in the presence of suitable witnesses, if you wish."

So that this zealot of souls might convince the deluded woman, when the day which the old woman had set for her departure arrived, the father was in attendance along with various other worthy men of the faith. The woman took a small bowl in which dough was usually made that had been placed on a bench and, sitting there, began. After she had applied an ointment and uttered some magical words, she fell asleep with her head leaning back. Immediately—through the work of a demon—she had dreams about Lady Venus along with some other superstitious things that were so powerful that she cried out with a low shout. Clapping her hands during her disturbances, she moved the bowl in which she was sitting enough that she fell headlong from the high bench, narrowly missing the head of an old woman below. The father cried out to the woman—now awake but lying motionless on the ground—saying, "Where are you, I ask you? Were you with Diana, for according to the testimony of those here present, you never left the bowl?" And so, through these events and the mediation of health-giving words, the father was able to move her mind to detest her error. . . .

The reason and cause for this is given in the canon Episcopi [doc. 32]. . . .

Lazy Man: I know from the blessed Isidore [of Seville, d. 636] that there are many types of superstition. But as you mentioned sorcerers, now explain how they are able to harm their neighbors.

Theologian: Seven means occur to me by which sorcerers can harm human affairs—but they can never do so without God permitting it. But when they are said to harm, they do not cause the effect or passion directly themselves—rather, they are said to harm through words, rites, and deeds, as if through pacts entered into with demons. For it is rather the demons that directly cause these damaging effects. . . .

Lazy Man: I ask to be fully informed about all these practices because there are people who deny them completely or ascribe them only to natural causes or who concede them only in part.

Theologian: . . . I will provide you with examples and some teachings in response to your request which I have taken partly from the doctors of our faculty and partly from the experience of a certain honest and trustworthy secular judge, a man who has learned many things through questions and confessions, and through public and private experiences—and with whom I have often had wide ranging and deep discussions of such matters. This is Master Peter, a citizen of Bern in the diocese of Lausanne who has burned many sorcerers of both sexes and expelled others from the lordship of Bern. Likewise, I have discussed these things with Dom Benedict, a monk of the order of Saint Benedict, who—although he is now a very religious man and living in a reformed monastery in Vienne—nevertheless, ten years ago when he was living in the secular world, was a necromancer, a very great juggler and trickster, famous among the secular nobility and considered expert at such things. Likewise, I heard certain parts of the following from an inquisitor of Autun, a devout reformer from our order in the community at Lyons. He investigated many accused of sorcery in the diocese of Autun.

Therefore, as that inquisitor and Master Peter have related to me and common knowledge has it, there are around the district of the lordship of Bern—or at least there have been recently—certain sorcerers of both sexes who, against the inclination of human nature—indeed against the disposition of every sort of beast, except only the she-wolf—are accustomed to eating and devouring the infants of their own species.

For in the town of Boltingen in the diocese of Lausanne, a certain powerful sorcerer called Stadlin captured by the aforesaid Peter (the judge for that region), confessed that in a nearby house where a man and wife lived together, he had killed around seven infants successively while they were in the wife's womb through his harmful magic, so for many years the woman always miscarried. In the same house, he did a similar thing to all the pregnant cattle, none of which delivered a live birth during those years, as events proved. When the aforesaid wicked man was asked whether he was guilty of these things and how he accomplished them, he admitted his crime. He said that he himself had placed a lizard under the lintel of the doorway of the house, and predicted that were it to be removed, fertility would be restored to the inhabitants. But when they looked for the snake under the lintel, it was not found—perhaps because it had been reduced to dust. They removed the dust and earth from under that place and in that same year fertility was restored to the wife and all the beasts belonging to the house. He confessed all these things under torture—not freely—and afterwards was handed over to the fires by the aforesaid judge.

Next, I learned from the foresaid inquisitor—who reported it to me this year—that in the dutchy of Lausanne certain sorcerers cooked and ate their own newborn infants. The way they learned to do such a thing, as he said, was that the sorcerers came to a certain gathering and, as a result of what they worked there, they visibly saw a demon that had assumed the form of a man. The disciple had to give his word to the demon that he would deny Christianity, never adore the eucharist, and trample on the cross whenever he was able to do so secretly.

In addition, as the aforesaid Judge Peter reported to me, it was common knowledge that in the territory of Bern, thirteen infants had been devoured by sorcerers in a short space of time which is why public justice burned harshly for such parricides. But when Peter asked a certain captured sorceress about the way in which they ate infants, she replied, "The way is this. We lie in ambush for infants who have not yet been baptized and even for those who have been baptized—particularly if they are not yet protected by the sign of the cross and prayers. We kill them through our ceremonies while they are in their cradles or lying by the side of their parents so that they are deemed to have been crushed or to have died from some other cause. Afterwards, we secretly remove them from their tombs. We cook them in a cauldron until the bones have come loose and nearly all the flesh has become liquid and drinkable. From the more solid parts of this material we make an ointment suitable for our purposes, rites, and transmutations. From the more liquid humor, we fill a flask or skin. After having performed a few other ceremonies, he who drinks from it is immediately made a partner and the master of our sect."

Another young sorcerer who was captured and burned—although I believe that he was truly penitent—revealed the same method more clearly. . . . The aforesaid young man was arrested with his wife in the jurisdiction of Bern and placed in a different tower to her. He said, "If I could obtain pardon for my crimes, I would freely admit everything I know about sorcery, for I see that it is necessary for me to die." When he heard from some learned men that if he were truly penitent he would be able to obtain a complete pardon for himself, he joyously offered himself up to death, and revealed the ways he had first been corrupted. "The ritual by which I was seduced is as follows," he said. "On the first Sunday before the holy water is consecrated, a prospective disciple is to enter the church with the masters. There, in front of all of them, he denies Christ, his faith, baptism, and the whole church. Then he does homage to the *magisterulus*, that is, to 'the little master.' This is what they call the demon—they have no other name for it. After that, he drinks from the skin described above. And after this is done, he immediately perceives inside himself imprints of our art and the fundamental rites of our sect which he understands and remembers. I was seduced in this manner along with my wife. But as for her, I believe she is so stubborn that she would rather endure the fire than confess even the smallest truth of the matter. But we are both guilty."

What the young man said was entirely true. After he had confessed, the young man was seen to die in great contrition. His wife, though convicted by witnesses, was prepared to admit nothing of the truth—not even under torture, not even in death. Instead, when the fire had been prepared by the executioner, she cursed him in the vilest words and thus she was burned.

Lazy Man: Because you made mention of necromancers, I ask whether there is any difference between them and sorcerers and if there is, what are the things they do?

Theologian: Properly speaking they are called necromancers who declare that they are able to raise the dead from the earth by means of superstitious rites so that they might speak about occult things. . . . Nevertheless, in ordinary usage, they are called necromancers who—by means of a pact with demons and through a belief in rituals—predict future things, or reveal some hidden things through the revelation of demons, or who harm their neighbors by means of sorcery and are themselves often harmed by demons. . . .

In addition, I heard from the above mentioned judge Peter how, in the territory of Bern and in neighboring places, for about sixty years, the above described sorcery was practiced by many people—the originator of which was a certain man called Scavius. He publicly dared to boast that whenever he wanted he had the power to make himself into a mouse in the sight of his rivals and so slip from the hands of his mortal enemies. And in this way, as he said, he was often able to escape from the hands of his deadly enemies. But when divine justice wanted to put an end to his wickedness, he was watched cautiously by his enemies as he sat in a certain room by a window. While he had not suspected assassins in that place, he was unexpectedly stabbed by swords and spears through the window and wretchedly died there on account of his crimes.

However, Scavius left behind the techniques of his deceit to his disciple called Hoppo—and he made the above mentioned Stadlin into the master of sorcery. These two men knew how—whenever it pleased them—to carry off a third part of the manure, hay, or grain or anything else from their neighbor's field to their own without anyone seeing; to cause devastating hailstorms and harmful winds with lightning bolts; to throw infants walking along beside the water under the gaze of their parents into it without anyone noticing; to cause sterility in men and beasts; to harm neighbors in property and body; to make horses frantic under their riders, as if they were holding the stirrup for the one mounting the animal; to travel—as they believe—through the air from place to place; to emit terrible smells from themselves when they were likely to be captured; to cause a great trembling in the hands and minds of those seizing them; to reveal hidden things to others and to predict certain future things; to make absent things seem present;

to kill whoever they want with a stroke of lightning; and to cause many other destructive things when the justice of God allows.

Questions: Does Nider accept the conclusions of Episcopi *(doc. 32)? Is there a difference here between sorcery and necromancy? What sort of things do both of these types of magician do? How are they able to accomplish these feats? What evidence does he use for these assertions?*

98. TOWARD THE WITCH HUNTS

The Malleus maleficarum *(usually translated as* The Hammer of Witches*), attributed to two Dominican inquisitors, Henrich Kramer (c. 1430–1505)—sometimes known by the Latinized form of his name "Institoris"—and Jacob Sprenger (1436/8–92), is one of the most infamous texts from the Late Middle Ages. Printed—rather than circulating in manuscript form—the text helped disseminate the conception of diabolic sorcery that would prove so deadly during the witch hunts of the early modern period.*

The text is divided into three parts. The first, from which the selections below come, is structured as an abstract scholastic argument, similar in form to that made by theologians like Thomas Aquinas (doc. 79) in the universities. The second section covers similar territory but is grounded upon the evidence of witch testimony and that of supposed witnesses. The final part outlines the legal procedures to be followed to ensure a safe and effective prosecution.

Pseudo-Dionysius (his real identity is unknown) was a theologian of the fifth or sixth century whose mystical treatises were enormously influential. Raymond of Peñafort (d. 1275) was a Dominican friar responsible for a compilation of papal decretals that came to be incorporated into canon law. On "Pythons," see "Pythonesses" in doc. 94.

Latin, 1487.

Source: trans. Christopher S. Mackay, *The Hammer of Witches: A Complete Translation of the* Malleus Maleficarum (Cambridge: Cambridge University Press, 2006), 7A, 7B–8C, 10B–10D, 13D, 20B–20D, 21B–22B, 22D–23B, 24B, 74C–75B.

Part I: Question 1

Whether claiming that sorcerers exist is such a Catholic proposition that to defend the opposite view steadfastly is altogether heretical. . . .

Response. Here three heretical errors must be attacked, and once they have been refuted, the truth will be clear. According to the teaching of Saint Thomas [Aquinas] . . . where he treats the impediment caused by sorcery, certain people have tried to claim that there is no sorcery in the world except in the opinion of humans, who ascribe to sorcerers natural effects whose causes are unknown. There are others who grant the existence of sorcerers but claim that it is only in their imagination and fantasy that they co-operate in bringing about effects of sorcery. The third of those who say that the effects of sorcery are purely fantastical and imaginary, though a demon does in fact co-operate with the sorceress. The errors of these groups are explained and refuted as follows.

The first are censured completely for heresy by the Doctors . . . especially by Saint Thomas . . . He says that this opinion is completely contrary to the authorities of the Saints and is rooted in lack of faith. His reasoning is that since the authority of the holy scripture says that demons have power over bodily objects and over the imagination of humans when they are allowed to by God, as is known from many passages of holy scripture, those who say that there is no sorcery in the world except in the opinion of humans likewise believe that demons exist only in the opinion of the common people. Consequently, a person attributes to the demon the terrors that he creates for himself, the sorts of figures that the human imagines appear in the perception from the vividness of the imagination, and in that case he believes that he sees demons (let us say that this applies to sorcerers too). Since these ideas are rejected by the true faith, by which we believe that angels fell from heaven and that demons exist, we also avow that as a result of the subtlety of their nature, they have many powers that we do not. Those who induce them to do such things are called sorcerers. Thus Aquinas. Because lack of faith in someone who has been baptized is called heresy, such people are censured for heresy.

The two other errors do not deny the existence of demons and their power but contradict each other regarding the effectiveness of sorcery and the sorceress herself. While one grants that sorceresses really do work together with the demon to achieve the result, though this result is not real but fantastic, the author grants the real effect in the person harmed but thinks that the sorceress only imagines that she works with the demon. They derive the basis of this error from two passages of the Canon . . . *Episcopi* [doc. 32]. First, women who believe that they ride on horseback with Diana or Herodias during the night-time hours are censured . . . and adherents of that error think that because it is stated that such things happen only fantastically in the imagination, this is the case with all other effects. Second, it is stated in the Canon that whoever believes or claims that some creature can be made or changed for the better or worse or turned into a different form or appearance in any way other than by God, the creator of all things, is an infidel and worse than a pagan, and on the basis of the phrase ". . . changed for the worse . . . ," they say that this effect is not real in terms of the person affected by sorcery and is only imaginary.

That these errors smack of heresy and contradict the healthy understanding of the Canon is shown both by divine and by ecclesiastical and civil law, first in general terms and then specifically through citation of the words of the Canon . . . [for] in many passages, divine law prescribes that sorceresses should be not only shunned but killed. It would not impose penalties of this kind, if they did not actually co-operate with devils in bringing about real effects and injuries. For the death of the body is inflicted only in the case of serious bodily sin, though the case is different with the death of the soul, which can result from an illusion of the fantasy or from temptation. . . .

[The authors proceed to cite the arguments of various theologians and the views of lawyers of both kinds defending this position.]

The conclusion reached on the basis of all the foregoing is that it is a very true and Catholic proposition to claim the existence of sorcerers who, with the assistance of demons on account of an agreement entered into with them, can cause real effects of sorcery with the permission of God. . . . Because the foundation for two errors in particular is based on the words of the Canon . . . it is necessary to proceed to a healthy understanding of the Canon. . . . Here it is to be noted that while there are fourteen main varieties within the category of superstition, for the sake of brevity it would not be appropriate to list them . . . because they are clearly listed by Isidore [of Seville] and by Saint Thomas. . . . While the variety [category] in which such women are placed is called the variety of "pythons" (these are people in whom a demon either speaks or performs wondrous works . . .), the variety in which sorcerers are categorized is called the variety of sorcerers. Because they greatly differ from one another, and it is not appropriate that someone who functions under one variety should be encompassed under the others too, therefore since the Canon mentions those women and not the sorceresses, it is a false interpretation of the Canon when they wish to ascribe such imaginary transportations of bodies to the entire category of superstition and to all its varieties, so that all sorceresses are transported only in the imagination in the way that those women are. The Canon is further falsified by anyone who would wish to argue on the basis of it that it is only in the imagination that a sorceress co-operates [with a demon] in using sorcery to bring about an effect consisting of sickness or disease. . . .

Question 2

Whether it is a Catholic proposition to claim that in order to achieve an effect of sorcery the demon always has to co-operate with a sorcerer or that one without the other (the demon without a sorcerer or the other way around) can produce such an effect . . .

Here it should be noted that since three elements must co-operate to bring about such an effect, namely the demon, the sorceress, and God's permission, Augustine says that this superstitious vanity was discovered as a result of a baneful alliance of humans and demons. Therefore, the origin and increase of this heresy is derived from this pestilential alliance. This fact can be deduced from other information.

First, let it be noted that this Heresy of Sorcerers differs from other heresies, not only in that, whereas the difficult nature of the things that must be believed in all the other, straightforward heresies means that assent is given to the errors without any implicit or explicit agreement being entered into with demons (though not without the instigation of the sower of all lack of faith), the heresy of sorceresses uses agreements that are not merely expressed but ratified as treaties, and for this reason it is crazed with the desire to insult the creator and harm his creations in every way. It also differs from every harmful and superstitious art in that, in a way that surpasses all the other varieties of divination, this heresy of sorcerers reaches the highest level of evil, since it takes its designation from evil-doing [*maleficere*] or having an evil opinion [*male sentire*] about the faith. . . . Let it also be noted that among other actions they must follow four practices that serve to increase that breach of faith: they renounce the Catholic faith in whole or part with a sacrilegious speech, solemnly devote themselves in body and soul, offer babies not yet reborn [in baptism] to the evil one, and persistently engage in the devil's filthy deeds through carnal acts with incubus and succubus demons. If only it were true that all these things were devoid of any truth and that they should be called figments . . . ! Unfortunately, this wish is precluded both by what the Apostolic See has established through its bull and by experience, the teacher of reality, which has, on the basis of the women's own confessions and the crimes committed by them, made us so certain that we cannot now cease to conduct inquisitions into these people without the loss of our own salvation. . . .

Question 3

[Whether] it is a Catholic proposition to claim that humans can be begotten by incubus and succubus demons. . . .

[Argument 1] The begetting of humans was instituted by God before the introduction of sin, in that he shaped woman as an aid for man from his rib. To them he said, "Grow and increase in number" [Gen. 1.28]. . . . Therefore, other methods of begetting humans should not be posited. . . .

[Argument 2] Also, to beget a human is the act of a living body, but demons cannot give life when they have assumed bodies, because life flows in a formal sense only from the soul, and this is the act of a physical, organic body that has the power of life. Therefore, they cannot perform the works characteristic of life through such assumed bodies. . . .

But to the contrary. Augustine says, "Demons gather seeds which they use for bodily effects," and this cannot happen without a movement in location. Therefore, the demons can receive seeds from some people and pour them into others. . . .

[The authors note that readers who wish to know about the effects the devil can produce through sorcery—including the transformation and transvection of bodies, and his ability to manipulate people's intellect and will—should refer to the works of various theologians.]

Response . . . for the understanding of the question about incubus and succubus demons, it should be said that to claim that humans are sometimes begotten through incubus and succubus demons is such a Catholic proposition that to claim the opposite is contrary not simply to the sayings of the Saints but also to the tradition of holy scripture. . . .

The reason why demons make themselves into incubi or succubi is not for the sake of pleasure, since a spirit does not have flesh and bones, but the strongest reason is that through the fault of debauchery they may harm the nature of both aspects of man (the body and the soul), so that humans will in this way become more inclined to all [other] faults. . . .

[Response to Argument 1] . . . just as with God's permission the sacrament of marriage can be vitiated by the work of the devil through acts of a sorceress . . . the same can happen in connection with any other sexual act between male and female. . . .

[Response to Argument 2] . . . it is true that to beget a human is the act of a living body. When it is said that demons cannot give life because it flows in a formal sense from the soul, this again is true, but it is emitted as matter from the seed and the demon incubus can send it in with God's permission through sexual union, doing so not as if the seed were emitted by him but with another human's seed that he has taken for this purpose, as the Saintly Doctor [Aquinas] says. . . . For the same demon who is a succubus in terms of a man becomes an incubus in terms of the woman. . . . Hence, if it is asked whose child one born in this way is, it is clear that it is not the child of the demon but of the man whose seed was taken. . . .

When it is concluded that the demon can both receive and pour in seed invisibly, this is true, but he instead does this work visibly as a succubus and incubus, so that in this way he may use a foul act like this to taint the body and soul in each person (both the man's and woman's). . . .

It could happen that in place of one succubus demon another one receives the seed from him and makes himself an incubus in his place. There would be three reasons for this. Perhaps the demon delegated to the woman received the seed from another demon delegated to the man, so that in this way each would be able to practice an act of sorcery in connection with the person entrusted to him by the prince of the demons. . . . Another reason is the foulness of the act, which one demon balks at committing, since . . . the nobility of their nature causes certain demons to balk at committing certain actions and filthy deeds. The third reason is that the demon invisibly interposes himself next to the woman and introduces into her his own seed (the seed that the incubus took) in place of her husband's. . . .

Question 14

... That sorceresses deserve the most serious punishments compared to all the criminals of the world.

That the crimes of these people surpass all the sins of others in terms of deserving penalty is explained, first, in regard to the penalty imposed on heretics, and, second, in regard to the penalty to be inflicted on apostates.

Heretics are punished in four ways according to Raymund [of Peñafort]: excommunication, dismissal from office, confiscation of property, and physical death. . . . [But] it does not seem to be sufficient to punish sorceresses in these ways, since they are not straightforward heretics but also apostates, and furthermore in this kind of apostasy they do not renounce the faith to humans on account of fear or the pleasures of the flesh . . . they also do homage to the demons by offering them their bodies and souls. From these facts it seems probable enough that however much they repent and return to the faith, they should not be imprisoned for life like other heretics but should be punished with the ultimate penalty. . . . How much more [severely must] sorcerers [be punished], when the laws say that the punishment of [mere] fortune-tellers is the confiscation of their goods and decapitation!

Questions: Why would the authors begin the work by asserting the centrality of demonic sorcerers to Catholic belief? How is the conception of sorcery different here to that underlying the witch of Berkeley, the Sworn Book of Honorius, or that described by Nider (docs. 33, 91, and 97)? What are its features? Why do they argue that this form of sorcery is so heinous? How and why do the authors endeavor to get round the canon Episcopi *(doc. 32)? How does their conception of demonic procreation differ from that of Aquinas (doc. 79)?*

SELECT BIBLIOGRAPHY OF MODERN WORKS ON THE DEVIL

While the literature on the early modern witch hunts has grown exponentially over the last forty years, that on the biblical and medieval devil that fed directly into witchcraft discourse has not entirely kept pace. The following is a list of general studies, available in English, dealing with the construction and role of the devil through the period covered by this collection. The emphasis is on providing students with useful starting points for research. We have made no effort to include any of the many important article-length studies dealing with aspects of the medieval devil or demonism.

Almond, Philip. *The Devil: A New Biography.* Ithaca, NY: Cornell University Press, 2014.

Bernstein, Alan E. *The Formation of Hell: Death and Retribution in the Ancient and Early Christian Worlds.* Ithaca, NY: Cornell University Press, 1993.

Boureau, Alain. *Satan the Heretic: The Birth of Demonology in the Medieval West.* Translated by Teresa Lavender Fagan. Chicago: University of Chicago Press, 2006.

Camporesi, Piero. *The Fear of Hell: Images of Damnation and Salvation in Early Modern Europe.* Translated by Lucinda Byatt. University Park, PA: The Pennsylvania State University Press, 1991.

Clark, Stuart. *Thinking with Demons: The Idea of Witchcraft in Early Modern Europe.* Oxford: Oxford University Press, 1997.

Dendle, Peter. *Demon Possession in Anglo-Saxon England.* Kalamazoo: Medieval Institute Publications, Western Michigan University, 2014.

———. *Satan Unbound: The Devil in Old English Narrative Literature.* Toronto: University of Toronto Press, 2001.

Elliott, Dyan. *Fallen Bodies: Pollution, Sexuality, and Demonology in the Middle Ages.* Philadelphia: University of Pennsylvania Press, 1999.

Forsyth, Neil. *The Old Enemy: Satan and the Combat Myth.* Princeton, NJ: Princeton University Press, 1987.

Kelly, Henry Ansgar. *The Devil at Baptism: Ritual, Theology and Drama.* Eugene, OR: Wipf and Stock Publishers, 1985.

———. *The Devil, Demonology and Witchcraft: The Development of Christian Belief in Evil Spirits.* Rev. ed. Eugene, OR: Wipf and Stock Publishers, 1974.

———. *Satan: A Biography.* Cambridge: Cambridge University Press, 2006.

Link, Luther. *The Devil: A Mask Without a Face.* London: Reaktion Books, 1995.

Muchembled, Robert. *A History of the Devil: From the Middle Ages to the Present.* Translated by Jean Birrell. Cambridge: Polity, 2003.

Pagels, Elaine. *The Origin of Satan: How Christians Demonized Jews, Pagans, and Heretics.* New York: Vintage Books, 1995.

Raiswell, Richard, and Peter Dendle. *The Devil in Society in Premodern Europe.* Toronto: Centre for Reformation and Renaissance Studies, 2012.

Russell, Jeffrey Burton. *The Devil: Perceptions of Evil from Antiquity to Primitive Christianity.* Ithaca, NY: Cornell University Press, 1977.

———. *Lucifer: The Devil in the Middle Ages.* Ithaca, NY: Cornell University Press, 1984.

———. *Satan: The Early Christian Tradition.* Ithaca, NY: Cornell University Press, 1981.

Stokes, Ryan E. *The Satan: How God's Executioner Became the Enemy.* Grand Rapids, MI: William B. Eerdmans, 2019.

Trachtenberg, Joshua. *The Devil and the Jews: The Medieval Conception of the Jew and Its Relation to Modern Antisemitism.* New Haven, CT: Yale University Press, 1943.

Walton, John H., and J. Harvey Walton. *Demons and Spirits in Biblical Theology: Reading the Biblical Text in Its Cultural and Literary Context.* Eugene, OR: Cascade Books, 2019.

SOURCES

Adso of Montier-en-Der. "Letter on the Origin and Time of the Antichrist," in *Apocalyptic Spirituality: Treatises and Letters of Lactantius, Adso of Montier-en-Der, Joachim of Fiore, The Franciscan Spirituals, Savonarola.* Trans. Bernard McGinn. New York: Paulist Press, 1979.

Anselm of Canterbury. *The Fall of the Devil from Complete Philosophical and Theological Treatises of Anselm of Canterbury.* Trans. Jasper Hopkins and Herbert Richardson. Minneapolis: Arthur J. Bannon Press, 2000.

"Antichrist," from *The Chester Plays: A Collection of Mysteries Founded Upon Scriptural Subjects,* vol. 2. London: 1867.

Thomas Aquinas. *Quaestiones disputatae de potentia dei,* vol. 2. Trans. Richard Raiswell and David R. Winter. London: Burns Oates & Washbourne Ltd., 1933.

Athanasius. *Life of Antony from Nicene and Post-Nicene Fathers,* 2nd ser. vol. 4. Trans. H. Ellershaw. New York: 1892.

Augustine of Hippo. *De divinatione daemonum liber unus* (Migne, *Patrologia Latina* 40: 0354–0430).

Augustine of Hippo. "The Divination of Demons," in *Treatises on Marriage and Other Subjects.* New York: 1955.

Notker Balbulus. *Gesta Karoli Magni,* in MGH *Scriptores rerum Germanicarum,* vol. 12. Trans Richard Raiswell and David R. Winter. Berlin: 1959.

Bartoli à Saxoferrato. "Processus Satanae Contra D. Virginem coram Iudice Iesu," in *Processus Iuris Ioco-serius.* Trans. Richard Raiswell and David R. Winter. Hanover: 1611.

Bernard of Clairvaux. *In dedicatione ecclesiae* (Migne, *Patrologia Latina* 183: 0523D–526B). Trans. Richard Raiswell and David R. Winter.

Giovanni Boccaccio. *The Decameron of Giovanni Boccaccio,* vol. 2. Trans. J. M. Rigg. London: 1921.

The boke of Iohn Maunduyle. London: 1496.

Boniface. "Letter XIII," in *The English Correspondence of Saint Boniface.* Trans. Edward Kylie. London: 1911.

E. A. Budge, trans. "A Discourse Composed by Jacob of Sērûgh upon Alexander," in *The History of Alexander the Great.* Cambridge: University Press, 1889.

Caesarius of Heisterbach. "Concerning the Devil," *Libri octo miraculorum,* in *Die Wundergeschichten des Caesarius von Heisterbach.* Trans. Richard Raiswell and David R. Winter. Bonn: 1933.

Caesarius of Heisterbach. *Dialogue on Miracles,* vol. 1 and vol. 2. Trans. C. C. Swinton-Bland. New York: 1929.

H. R. Charles, trans. "Apocalypse of Moses," in *The Apocrypha and Pseudepigrapha of the Old Testament,* vol. 2. Oxford: The Clarendon Press, 1913.

H. R. Charles, trans. "Book of Enoch," in *The Apocrypha and Pseudepigrapha of the Old Testament*, vol. 2. Oxford: The Clarendon Press, 1913.

H. R. Charles, trans. "Book of Jubilees," in *The Apocrypha and Pseudepigrapha of the Old Testament*, vol. 2. Oxford: The Clarendon Press, 1913.

John Chrysostom. "Baptismal Homily 2," in *Early Christian Baptism and Catechumenate*, vol. 1. Trans. Thomas M. Finn. Collegeville, PA: Liturgical Press, 1992.

T. O. Cockayne. *Leechdoms, Wortcunning, and Starcraft of Early England*, vol. 3. London: 1864.

F. C. Conybeare, trans. "The Testament of Solomon," in *Jewish Quarterly Review*, vol. 11.1. 1898.

Thomas Frederick Crane. *The Exempla or Illustrative Stories from the Sermones Vulgares of Jacques de Vitry.* Trans. Richard Raiswell and David R. Winter. London: The Folklore Society, 1890.

Peter Damian. *Book of Gomorrah: An Eleventh-Century Treatise against Clerical Homosexual Practices.* Trans. Pierre J. Payer. Waterloo, ON: Wilfrid Laurier Press, 1982.

Marie-Françoise Damongeot-Bourdat. "Un nouveau manuscript de l'Apocalypse de Paul (Paris, BnF, nouv. Acq. lat. 2676)." Trans. Richard Raiswell and David R. Winter. Bulletin du Cange 67, 2009.

Nathaniel Dubin, trans. "The Cunt Made with a Spade," in *The Fabliaux: A New Verse Translation.* New York: Liveright, 2013.

Einhard and the Monk of Saint Gall. *Early Lives of Charlemagne.* Trans. Arthur James Grant. London: 1905.

Étienne de Bourbon. *Anecdotes historiques, légendes et apologues tirés du Recueil Inédit d'Étienne de Bourbon.* Trans. Richard Raiswell and David R. Winter. Paris: Renouard, 1877.

Eusebius of Caesarea. *Praeparatio Evangelica (Preparation for the Gospel).* Trans. E. H. Gifford. Oxford: 1903.

Heinrich Finke. *Papsttum und Untergang des Templerordens.* Trans. Richard Raiswell and David R. Winter. Münster: 1907.

Flavius Josephus. *History of the Antiquities of the Jews in The Works of Flavius Josephus.* Trans. John Court. London: Penny and Janeway, 1733.

Hugh Foliot (uncertain). *De bestiis et aliis rebus* (Migne, *Patrologia Latina* 177: 67B–68C). Trans. Richard Raiswell and David R. Winter.

Jean Gerson. "De probatione spirituum," in *Opera omnia*, vol. 1. Trans. Richard Raiswell and David R. Winter. Antwerp: 1706.

Giacomino of Verona. "De Babylonia infernali," in *The De Jerusalem Celesti and the De Babylonia Infernali.* Trans. Robert Buranello. London: Oxford, 1930.

R. K. Gordon, trans. "Genesis B," in *Anglo-Saxon Poetry.* London: J. M. Dent & Sons, 1922.

SOURCES

Gregory I. "Moralium Libri, sive Expositio," in *Librum Job* XXV.16.34 and XXIX.7.15 (Migne, *Patrologia Latina* 76: 0343B–0344A and 0484A–0487C). Trans. Richard Raiswell and David R. Winter.

Gregory I. *Sancti Gregorii papae dialogorum libri IV.* (Migne, *Patrologia Latina* 77: 0168D–0169A, 0177A–0177B, 0196b–0197A, 0200B–0205A, and 0272B–0273A). Trans Richard Raiswell and David R. Winter.

Gregory of Nazianzus. "Oration 24," in Selected Orations, Fathers of the Church, vol. 107. Trans. Martha Pollard Vinson. Baltimore: Catholic University of America, 2004.

Gregory of Nyssa. "Great Catechism," in *Nicene and Post-Nicene Fathers,* second series, vol. 5. Trans. William Moore and Henry Austin Wilson. Grand Rapids, MI: Wm. B. Eerdmans Publishing Company, 1892.

Gregory of Nyssa. "Great Catechism," in *Nicene and Post-Nicene Fathers,* second series, vol. 5. New York: Charles Scribner's Sons, 1917.

Gregory of Tours. "De passione et virtutibus sancti Iuliani martyris," in MGH: SS rev. Merov. 1.2. Trans. Richard Raiswell and David R. Winter. Hannover: Impensis Bibliopolii Hahniani, 1969.

Johannes Herolt. *Sermones discipuli in Quadragesima.* Trans. Richard Raiswell and David R. Winter. Venice: Haeredes Melchioris Sessae, 1599.

Honorius of Thebes. *Sworn Book of Honorius.* Trans. Joseph Peterson. Lake Worth, FL: Ibis Press, 2016.

Irenaeus. *Against Heresies from Ante-Nicene Fathers,* vol. 1. Trans. Alexander Roberts and James Donaldson. Buffalo, NY: Christian Literature Publishing Co., 1885.

Ivo of Chartres. "Council of Arles," in *Decretum* (Migne, *Patrologia Latina* 161: 0758B–0759A). Trans. Richard Raiswell and David R. Winter.

Joachim of Fiore. *Book of Figures in Apocalyptic Spirituality.* Trans. Bernard McGinn. New York: Paulist Press, 1979.

Lactantius. "Divine Institutes," in *Ante-Nicene Fathers,* vol. 7. Trans. William Fletcher. Buffalo, NY: Christian Literature Publishing Co., 1886.

The Lanterne of Lizt, original series 151. London: Early English Text Society, 1917.

Latin Vulgate, The Holy Bible (Douay-Rheims version). Trans. Gregory Martin et al.; rev. Richard Challoner (1749–1752). Douay: The English College, 1609–10.

Henry C. Lea, trans. *Materials Toward a History of Witchcraft,* vol. 1. Philadelphia: University of Pennsylvania Press, 1939.

Henry Longfellow, trans. *The Divine Comedy of Dante Alighieri.* Boston: 1867.

E. A. Lowe. "Vatican MS of the Gelasian Sacramentary and its Supplement at Paris," in *Journal of Theological Studies,* vol. 27.108. Trans. Richard Raiswell and David R. Winter. 1926.

Christopher S. Mackay, trans. *The Hammer of Witches: A Complete Translation of the Malleus Maleficarum.* Cambridge: University Press, 2006.

Walter Map. *De nugis curialium (Courtiers' Trifles).* Trans. F. Tupper and M. Bladen. London: 1924.

Martin of Braga. "Reforming the Rustics," in *Iberian Fathers*, vol. 1. Trans. Claude W. Barlow. Washington, DC: Catholic University of America, 1969.

John T. McNeill, trans. "The Penitential of Columban," "The Penitential of Theodore," "Burgundian Penitential," and "The Corrector and Physician," in *Medieval Handbooks of Penance: A Translation of the Principal libri poenitentiales and Selections from Related Documents*. New York: Octagon, 1965.

Johannes Nider. *Formicarius*, from *L'imaginaire du sabbat: édition critique des textes les plus anciens (1430 c.–1440 c.)*. Trans Richard Raiswell and David R. Winter. Lausanne: Université de Lausanne, 1999.

Origen. *Contra Celsum*, in *Ante-Nicene Fathers*, vol. 4. Trans. Frederick Crombie. Buffalo, NY: Christian Literature Publishing Co., 1885.

Origen. "De principiis," in *Ante-Nicene Fathers*, vol. 4. Trans. Frederick Crombie and Kevin Knight. Buffalo, NY: Christian Literature Publishing Co., 1885.

Matthew Paris. *Chronica Maiora*, vol. 4: 1240–1247. Trans. Richard Raiswell and David R. Winter. London: 1880.

Matthew Paris. *Chronica Maiora*, vol. 5. Trans. Richard Raiswell and David R. Winter. London: 1880.

Peter the Venerable. "A Summary of the Entire Heresy of the Saracens," in *Writings Against the Saracens*. Trans. Irven M. Resnick. Washington, DC: Catholic University of America Press, 2016.

Philo Judaeus. "On the Giants," in *The Works of Philo Judaeus: The Contemporary of Josephus*, vol. 1. Trans. Charles Yonge. London: 1854.

Philo Judaeus. *Questions and Solutions to those Questions which Arise in Genesis*, vol. 4. Trans. Charles Yonge. London: 1855.

Plato. "The Symposium and The Laws," in *The Dialogues of Plato*, vol. 1 and vol. 4. Trans. Benjamin Jowett. Oxford: University Press, 1892.

Quodvultdeus. "Liber promissionum ac praedictorum dei in Opera omnia," in *Corpus Christianorum Series Latina*, vol. 60. Trans. Richard Raiswell and David R. Winter. Turnholt: Brepols, 1976.

Richard Raiswell and David R. Winter, trans. *Acta Apostolorum Apocrypha*. Ed. Richard Lipsius and Maximilian Bonnet. Leipzig: 1891.

Richard Raiswell and David R. Winter, trans. "Akten der römischen Synode vom Jahre 745," in *Die Briefe des heiligen Bonifatius und Lullus*, MGH Epistolae selectae I. Berlin: 1916.

Richard Raiswell and David R. Winter, trans. "[Anon], Errores Gazariorum, seu illorum qui scopam vel baculum equitare probantur" in *L'imaginaire du sabbat: Edition critique des textes les plus anciens (1430 c.–1440 c.)*. Lausanne: Université de Lausanne, 1999.

Richard Raiswell and David R. Winter, trans. *Conversio et Passio S. Afrae*, in MGH *Scriptores rerum Merovingicarum*, vol. 3. Hanover: 1896.

Richard Raiswell and David R. Winter, trans. *Epistolae saeculi XIII e regestis pontificum Romanorum selectee,* vol. 1, *Monumenta Germaniae Historica,* no. 537.

Richard Raiswell and David R. Winter, trans. *Liber exemplorum ad usum praedicantium* (The Durham Example Book), no. 95.

Richard Raiswell and David R. Winter, trans. *Manuale ambrosianum,* vol. 2. Milan: 1904–1905.

Richard Raiswell and David R. Winter, trans. MS Addit. 27909 B. London: British Library.

Richard Raiswell and David R. Winter, trans. MSS Royal 7.D.i, addit 16589, addit. 27909 B. London: British Library.

Richard Raiswell and David R. Winter, trans. "Navigatio Sancti Brendani Abbatis," in *Early Latin Manuscripts*. Notre Dame, IN: University Press, 1959.

Richard Raiswell and David R. Winter, trans. "Tultu sceptrum de libro domini Metobii," in *Corpus scriptorum Muzarabicorum,* vol. 2. Madrid: Instituto Antonio de Nebrija, 1973.

Robert E. Raymo. "A Middle English Edition of the Epistola Luciferi ad Cleros," in *Medieval Literature and Civilization: Studies in Memory of G. N. Garmonsway*. London: Athlone Press, 1969.

Regino of Prüm. *De ecclesiasticis disciplinis* (Migne, *Patrologia Latina* 132:0352–3053).

Rutebeuf. *Le miracle de Théophile from Medieval French Plays*. Trans. Richard Axton and John Stevens. Oxford: Blackwell, 1971.

Denis Searby, trans. *The Revelations of Saint Birgitta of Sweden,* vols. 1 and 3. Oxford: University Press, 2006–15.

Sulpicius Severus. "Life of Saint Martin," in *Nicene and Post-Nicene Fathers,* vol. 11. Trans. Alexander Roberts. New York: 1894.

Henrietta Szold, trans. *The Legends of the Jews,* vol. 1. Philadelphia: The Jewish Publication Society of America, 1913.

Tertullian. *Adversus Marcionem*. Ed. Ernest Evans. Trans. Richard Raiswell and David R. Winter. Oxford: Clarendon, 1972.

Tertullien. *La toilette des femmes (De cultu feminarum)*. Trans. Richard Raiswell and David R. Winter. Paris: Les Éditions du Cerf, 1971. http://www.tertullian.org/latin/de_cultu_feminarum_1.htm.

The Trial of Joan of Arc by Daniel Hobbins, Cambridge, Mass.: Harvard University Press, Copyright © 2005 by the President and Fellows of Harvard College. Used by permission. All rights reserved.

Hildegard von Bingen. *Physica: Complete English Trans of her Classic Work on Health and Healing*. Trans. Priscilla Throop. Rochester, NY: Healing Arts Press, 1998.

Richalm von Schöntal. *Liber revelationum*. Trans. Richard Raiswell and David R. Winter. Hannover: Hahnsche Buchhandlung, 2009.

James J. Walsh, trans. *The Popes and Science: The History of the Papal Relations to Science during the Middle Ages Down to our Own Time.* New York: 1913.
John Wickstrom, trans. *The Life and Miracles of St. Maurus, Disciple of Benedict, Apostle of France.* Collegeville, PA: Cistercian Publications, 2008.
William of Malmesbury. *Gesta Regum Anglorum atque historia novella,* vol. 1. Trans. Richard Raiswell and David R. Winter. London, 1840.
R. McL. Wilson, trans. "The Gospel of Nicodemus," in *New Testament Apocrypha,* vol. 1. 1922.

FIGURES

Figure 1.1: School of Albrecht Dürer, *Job on the Dunghill.* Amsterdam: Rijksmuseum, 1509.
Figure 2.1: School of Albrecht Dürer, *Archangel Michael Fighting the Dragon.* Amsterdam: Rijksmuseum, 1450–1470.
Figure 3.1: Michael Wolgemut, "Witch of Berkeley" in *Nuremberg Chronicle.* Wikipedia Commons, c. 1493, f. 189v.
Figure 4.1: *Antony attacked by Demons.* Amsterdam: Rijksmuseum, c. 1474.
Figure 5.1: Albrecht Dürer, *Knight, Death, and the Devil.* Amsterdam: Rijksmuseum, 1513.
Figure 6.1: Antonio Manetti, "Overview of Hell," from *Dialogo di Antonio Manetti, Cittadino fiorentino, circa al sito, forma, & misure dello inferno di Dante Alighieri.* Wikipedia Commons, 1506, sig. G.2r.
Figure 7.1: Basilica of Sant'Apollinare Nuovo, *Exorcism of the Gerasene Demoniac.* Ravenna, Italy: Wikipedia Commons, early sixth century.
Figure 8.1: Olaus Magnus, "On Nocturnal Dance of Elves—that is, Specters," in *Historia de gentibus septentrionalibus.* Wikipedia Commons, 1555, p. 112.
Figure 8.2: Both sets of fragments rebound in 1949. Bequeathed to the College by Brian Twyne (CCC 1594, d.1644). © Corpus Christi College, Oxford. MS 255A.
Figure 9.1: *Temptation through Pride.* Wikimedia Commons, c. 1460.
Figure 10.1: *Codex Gigas.* Wikimedia Commons, thirteenth century, f. 290r.
Figure 11.1: Anonymous, *Hell with Satan.* Amsterdam: Rijksmuseum, 1460–1480.

INDEX OF TOPICS

Topics are listed according to document number. The index is intended to be used in conjunction with the table of contents. The topics "devil," "demon/demons," "God," "angels," and "Bible" are common to almost all readings and are not listed below.

Abraham 10, 50, 64
Adam 1, 8, 15, 17, 19, 42, 46, 51
adultery/fornication 10, 12, 23, 25, 28, 30, 48, 52, 64, 69, 70
Alexander (conqueror) 29, 75
Alexandria 16, 18
Alighieri, Dante 57, fig. 6.1, fig. 11.1
Angel of Death 8
Angel of Light 10, 94
angels/archangels (by name)
    Abaddon 50
    Apollyon (*see* Abaddon)
    Asteraoth 22
    Balthial 22
    Bartchiachel 22
    Exterminans (*see* Abaddon)
    Gabriel 12, 30, 69
    Joel 22
    Lanzechalal 22
    Marmarath 22
    Michael 8, 11, 12, 15, 22, 30, 47, 51, fig. 2.1
    Raphael 12, 22, 30
    Uriel 12, 22
angels, watcher 12, 13, 29
angels, wicked (by name)
    Ananel 12
    Araklba 12
    Armaros 12
    Asael 12
    Azazel 12
    Baraqijal 12
    Batarel 12
    Danel 12
    Ezeqeel 12
    Jomjael 12
    Kokablel 12
    Ramlel 12
    Samlazaz 12
    Samsapeel 12
    Sariel 12
    Satarel 12
    Semjaza 12
    Tamlel 12
    Turel 12
    Zaqiel 12
Angels of Satan 3, 27, 83, 94
animals
    basilisk 56, 64
    beast (multi-headed) 11
    bull (animal) 34, 75
    cats 73, 74, 76, 96
    caterpillars 61
    dragon(s) 11, 29, 34, 37, 52, 56
    glanos (fish) 22
    lion 34, 50
    lizards 56
    locusts 50
    scorpions 50
    serpent/snakes/viper 1, 8, 10, 11, 14, 15, 19, 27, 29, 34, 55, 56, 59, 64, 65, 70, 74, 77, 79, 86, 96
    toads 56, 74, 96
    wolves 30, 34, 56, 81, 97
    worms 52, 55
Antichrist 29, 30, 35, 45, 47, 48, 69, 79, 89, 93
Arab people 43, 62, 68, 69
astrology 25, 43
auguries 28, 33, 71

Babylon 4, 47, 48, 49, 56, 70, 72
Balaam 3, 79, 93
Benedict, Benedictines 41, 83, 97
black/blackness 33, 34, 37, 56, 73, 74, 82,
    85, 88, 96

Christ 3, 9, 10, 11, 16, 18, 24, 25, 27, 28,
    29, 30, 34, 35, 37, 40, 42, 43, 44, 45,
    47, 48, 51, 52, 54, 55, 56, 58, 59, 60,
    61, 62, 64, 67, 68, 69, 70, 72, 74, 76,
    79, 80, 82, 83, 86, 89, 91, 93, 94
conjuration 59, 84, 86, 91, 95
creed 28, 65
cross
    sign of 28, 34, 39, 41, 49, 53, 61, 62, 65
    stamping upon 28

Daniel (prophet) 64, 89, 93
David (patriarch) 11, 22, 40, 42, 43, 64
deadly sins
    anger/wrath 14, 22, 29, 48, 67, 70, 82,
        83, 86
    covetousness/envy 8, 17, 21, 22, 23, 25,
        28, 34, 36, 45, 48, 52, 65, 83, 93
    gluttony 31, 33, 48, 69, 77, 93
    greed 25, 36, 43, 45, 49, 56, 67, 81, 82,
        86, 94
    lust 12, 15, 25, 34, 41, 42, 43, 55, 65,
        67, 70, 73, 77, 82, 84, 93, 94
    pride 4, 8, 28, 30, 34, 42, 45, 46, 47, 48,
        64, 80, 81, 82, 84, 86, 89, 94, 95
    sloth 48, 77
demoniacs 58, 61, 62, fig. 7.1
demons (by name)
    Adinus (?) 30
    Asmodeus 22
    Barachin 56
    Beelzeboul 22
    Beelzebub 56
    Guinehochet 82

    Klothod 22
    Macometo 56
    Onoskelis 22
    Ornias 22
    Raguel (?) 30
    Sabaoc (?) 30
    Serapis 36
    Simiel 30
    Trifon 56
    Tubuel (?) 30
    Uriel (?) 30
desert/wilderness 4, 6, 9, 11, 12, 34, 48,
    58, 64, 68
devil
    daughters of 82
    physical description 8, 35, 39, 66, 67
    wife of 82
devil, names of
    Belial 22, 25, 62, 64
    Lucifer 4, 18, 48, 56, 80, 84, 88, 89
    Mastêmâ 13
    Satan 3, 6, 8, 10, 11, 13, 15, 16, 17, 18,
        19, 24, 27, 28, 32, 37, 38, 44, 47, 48,
        51, 56, 59, 63, 64, 69, 72, 75, 80, 83,
        86, 88, 94
disease 20, 21, 26, 33, 36, 59, 60, 86,
    92, 98
    divination/diviners 28, 31, 36, 43, 47,
        59, 95, 98

Easter 39, 54, 61, 74, 80
Eden (*see* paradise)
Egypt/Egyptians 26, 31, 37, 60
elements 20, 22, 31, 36, 41, 47
Elias/Elijah 35, 47, 74, 89
elves/fairies/fairy tree 95, fig. 8.1
enchanters/enchantment 31, 47
Enoch 12, 13, 47
Episcopi (canon) 92, 97, 98
Eve 15, 17, 25, 46

INDEX OF TOPICS

exorcism/adjuration/exorcists 22, 51, 59, 60, 61, 63, 64, 73, 82, 83, 91
   Eleazar (exorcist) 60
   Sceva (sons of) 59
Ezekiel 17, 18, 32, 81

flight 11, 22, 27, 32, 46, 50, 56, 96, 97, 98
Franciscans 48, 49
Franks 30, 47
fraud 19, 21, 39, 48, 56, 70, 77, 93
fruit 1, 8, 52

Gaul/Gauls 30, 43
gentiles 3, 23, 26, 36, 52, 59, 89
giants 2, 12, 14, 57
Gog/Agog 11, 29
Gomorrah 52, 64, 70

hell 4, 11, 21, 28, 41, 43, 46, 48, 49, 50, 51, 52, 53, 54, 55, 56, 57, 64, 68, 69, 70, 74, 77, 80, 84, 85, 86, 92, 93, fig. 11.1
   abyss 22, 37, 50, 52, 53, 55, 58
   cocytus 57
   Gehenna 48, 64, 70, 81
   Hades 51
   Sheol 13, 50
   Tartarus 22, 26, 51, 52
heresy/heretics 16, 30, 32, 48, 69, 72, 73, 74, 77, 84, 89, 92, 93, 95, 96, 98
   Aldebert (heretical cleric) 30
   Clemens (Irish heretic) 30
   Marcion (heretic) 17
homage 8, 28, 43, 46, 86, 96, 97, 98

idols/idolatry 23, 28, 76, 93
illusions 32, 36, 39, 41, 44, 98
incantations 7, 25, 28, 31, 43, 60, 65, 74, 95
incest 28, 70
inquisition/inquisitors 67, 76, 96, 67, 90, 95, 97, 98

invocation 21, 28, 30, 39, 42, 54, 59, 60, 63, 64, 65, 68, 84, 88, 91, 95, 65
Isaiah 18, 41, 89, 93
Islam 68, 69

Jerusalem 9, 22, 43, 47, 53, 70
Jesus (see Christ)
Jews/Jewish 3, 10, 16, 22, 24, 27, 47, 51, 59, 60, 69, 71, 72, 82, 89
   Hyrcanus (Jewish high priest) 43
Joan of Arc 95
Job 6, 18, 42, 45, 64, 79, 81, 93
John (apostle) 32
John (evangelist) 56
John the Baptist 35, 48, 51
Judas 24, 37, 45, 54, 57, 64, 93, 96

knots 31

law, lawyers 23, 25, 30, 37, 47, 48, 53, 69, 74, 75, 80, 82, 89, 92, 93, 95, 96, 98
Lazarus 50, 51, 64
Legion (possessing demons) 58
lent 39
lettuce 61
Lollards, Lollardy 93
Lombards, Lombardy 49, 61
lord's prayer 28, 65
Lucifer (see devil, names of)

magic/magicians 10, 21, 27, 28, 32, 42, 45, 47, 48, 52, 60, 62, 64, 65, 71, 73, 77, 79, 84, 92, 95, 96, 97
   Elymas (magician) 10, 64
   Salatin (sorcerer?) 86
   Simon Magus 27, 45, 48
Magog 11, 29
maleficium (see magic)
Martin of Braga 28
martyrs 30, 47, 62, 64, 71, 72

Mary (mother of Jesus) 42, 52, 55, 69, 80, 82, 86, 94
Mass 43, 49, 54, 62, 67, 82, 91, 96
Matthew (evangelist) 56
monasteries 35, 40, 43, 62
monks 34, 35, 47, 54, 61, 83, 84
Moses 14, 15, 27, 45, 50, 64
Mount of Olives 24, 47
Muhammad 68, 69
murder/murderer 10, 22, 23, 24, 28, 64, 71, 77

necromancy 43, 91, 92
nephilim (*see* giants)
Noah 12, 13, 28
Noah's ark 64
nuns 33, 61, 84

oracles 26, 60

pact 42, 43, 63, 86, 91, 92, 95
pagan deities/paganism
   Apollo 47, 60
   Diana 32, 84, 97, 98
   Hercules 47
   Juno 28
   Jupiter 28, 35, 47
   Lamias 28
   Mars 28
   Mercury 28, 35, 47
   Minera 28, 35
   Neptune 28
   Pan 26
   Saturn 28
   Venus 28, 37, 62
paradise 1, 4, 8, 15, 14, 17, 18, 25, 28, 42, 51, 54, 65, 69, 86, 89
paternoster (*see* lord's prayer)
patience 11, 40, 52, 67, 78
perjury 23, 28, 48
Persians/Persian empire 29, 47

pharaoh 45, 64, 79
Pilate, Pontius 24, 54
poison 15, 21, 28, 36, 56, 65, 69, 70, 71, 74, 77, 82, 86, 96
popes/papacy 92, 93
   Clement VI 67
   Gregory VI 33
   John XXII 92
   Martin V 94
   Sylvester 43
   Zacharias 30
prodigies 30, 47
prostitutes/prostitution 28, 37, 81, 82
Psalms 14, 33, 37, 62, 82, 89
pythons, pythonesses (seers) 59, 60, 64, 94, 98

Qur'an 69

relics 30, 38, 62
Richalm (abbot of Schöntal) 41
Roman empire/emperor 47, 48
   Diocletian 26, 21
   Domitian 47
   Nero 27, 47, 82
   Tiberius 26
   Vespasian 60
Rome 26, 43, 56

sacraments 63, 64, 69, 81, 91, 96
   baptism, baptizing 25, 28, 35, 51, 56, 64, 81, 92, 93, 97, 98
   confession/penance 25, 28, 30, 31, 43, 50, 52, 59, 63, 66, 70, 81, 89, 93, 94, 96, 97, 98
   eucharist 52, 62, 96
sacrifices (human) 23
saints
   Afra 37
   Antony 34, fig. 4.1
   Birgitta 67

INDEX OF TOPICS

Boniface 30, 53
Brendan 54
Columban 31
Cyprian 42
Julian 62
Martin of Tours 35, 62
Maurus 38
Paul/Saul 9, 3, 10, 18, 27, 30, 32, 45,
    47, 52, 59, 64
Peter 27, 30, 48, 64
Stephen 31, 62
Saracens (*see* Arab people)
Satan (*see* devil, names of)
Saul (king) 42, 64
scholasticism 78, 79
Seth (son of Adam) 51
sex 96
simony 48
Sodom 52, 64
Solomon 22, 28, 43, 45, 47, 60, 91
soothsayers 28, 31
sorcery 32, 33, 42, 60, 89, 95, 96, 97, 98
Synagogue of Satan 48, 72, 96

transmutation 31, 34
transvection (*see* flight)
Tree of the knowledge of Good and Evil
    1, 8
Tyre 4, 17, 18

usury 56, 82

watchers (*see* angels)
weather
    hail 50, 65, 97
    lightning 11, 17, 18, 50, 59, 64, 65, 75,
        91, 97
    storms 31, 36, 49
    thunder 26, 41, 49, 50, 51, 65, 81, 91
Wiger of Utrecht (friar) 83
witches/witchcraft 98
    Berkeley 33
    Hulda 31
wizard 31, 47
woman/womankind 14, 25, 82

Zion 29, 40

READINGS IN MEDIEVAL CIVILIZATIONS AND CULTURES
Series Editor: Paul Edward Dutton

"Readings in Medieval Civilizations and Cultures is in my opinion
the most useful series being published today."
—William C. Jordan, Princeton University

I—Carolingian Civilization: A Reader, Second Edition
edited by Paul Edward Dutton

II—Medieval Popular Religion, 1000–1500: A Reader, Second Edition
edited by John Shinners

III—Charlemagne's Courtier: The Complete Einhard
translated & edited by Paul Edward Dutton

IV—Medieval Saints: A Reader
edited by Mary-Ann Stouck

V—From Roman to Merovingian Gaul: A Reader
translated & edited by Alexander Callander Murray

VI—Medieval England, 500–1500: A Reader, Second Edition
edited by Emilie Amt & Katherine Allen Smith

VII—Love, Marriage, and Family in the Middle Ages: A Reader
edited by Jacqueline Murray

VIII—The Crusades: A Reader, Second Edition
edited by S.J. Allen & Emilie Amt

IX—The Annals of Flodoard of Reims, 919–966
translated & edited by Bernard S. Bachrach & Steven Fanning

X—Gregory of Tours: The Merovingians
translated & edited by Alexander Callander Murray

XI—Medieval Towns: A Reader
edited by Maryanne Kowaleski

XII—A Short Reader of Medieval Saints
edited by Mary-Ann Stouck

XIII—Vengeance in Medieval Europe: A Reader
edited by Daniel Lord Smail & Kelly Gibson

XIV—The Viking Age: A Reader, Third Edition
edited by Angus A. Somerville & R. Andrew McDonald

XV—Medieval Medicine: A Reader
edited by Faith Wallis

XVI—Pilgrimage in the Middle Ages: A Reader
edited by Brett Edward Whalen

XVII—Prologues to Ancient and Medieval History: A Reader
edited by Justin Lake

XVIII—Muslim and Christian Contact in the Middle Ages: A Reader
edited by Jarbel Rodriguez

XIX—The Twelfth-Century Renaissance: A Reader
edited by Alex J. Novikoff

XX—European Magic and Witchcraft: A Reader
edited by Martha Rampton

XXI—Medieval Warfare: A Reader
edited by Kelly DeVries & Michael Livingston

XXII—Medieval Travel and Travelers: A Reader
edited by John F. Romano

XXIII—The Intolerant Middle Ages: A Reader
edited by Eugene Smelyansky

XXIV—The Medieval Devil: A Reader
edited by Richard Raiswell and David R. Winter

www.ingramcontent.com/pod-product-compliance
Lightning Source LLC
Chambersburg PA
CBHW052007070526
44584CB00016B/1659